PENGUIN BOOKS

RED SKY AT SUNRISE

PRAISE FOR *CIDER WITH ROSIE*

'Remains as fresh and full of joy and gratitude for youth and its sensations as when it first appeared. It sings in the memory' *Sunday Times*

'One of the great writers of the twentieth century' *Independent*

'An enchanting book, an exquisite farewell, not only to childhood, and boyhood, but also to an England that has vanished' J. B. Priestly

'He had a nightingale inside him, a capacity for sensuous, lyrical precision' *Guardian*

PRAISE FOR *AS I WALKED OUT ONE MIDSUMMER MORNING*

'A beautiful piece of writing' *Observer*

'He writes like an angel and conveys the pride and vitality of the humblest Spanish life with unfailing sharpness, zest and humour' *Sunday Times*

'There's a formidable, instant charm in the writing that genuinely makes it difficult to put the book down' *New Statesman*

PRAISE FOR *A MOMENT OF WAR*

'A work of lyrical intensity. Read it and salute one of Britain's finest writers' *Daily Mail*

'This story aches with unforgotten cold and trembles with unforgotten terror' *Guardian*

Laurie Lee was born in Stroud, Gloucestershire, in 1914, and was educated at Slad village school and Stroud Central School. At the age of nineteen he walked to London and then travelled on foot through Spain, where he was trapped by the outbreak of the Civil War. He later returned by crossing the Pyrenees, as described in his book *As I Walked Out One Midsummer Morning*. In 1950 he married Catherine Polge and they had one daughter.

Laurie Lee published four collections of poems: *The Sun My Monument* (1944), *The Bloom of Candles* (1947), *My Many-Coated Man* (1955) and *Pocket Poems* (1960). His other works include *The Voyage of Magellan* (1948), a verse play for radio; *A Rose for Winter* (1955), which records his travels in Andalusia; *The Firstborn* (1964); *I Can't Stay Long* (1975), a collection of his occasional writing; and *Two Women* (1983). He also wrote three bestselling volumes of autobiography: *Cider with Rosie* (1959), which has sold over six million copies worldwide; *As I Walked Out One Midsummer Morning* (1969); and *A Moment of War* (1991), which are published together in this volume.

Laurie Lee died in May 1997. In its obituary the *Guardian* wrote, 'He had a nightingale inside him, a capacity for sensuous, lyrical precision', and the *Independent* praised him as 'one of the great writers of this century whose work conjured up a world of earthly warmth and beauty'.

LAURIE LEE

RED SKY AT SUNRISE

CIDER WITH ROSIE

AS I WALKED OUT ONE MIDSUMMER MORNING

A MOMENT OF WAR

PENGUIN BOOKS

PENGUIN BOOKS

Published by the Penguin Group
Penguin Books Ltd, 80 Strand, London WC2R 0RL, England
Penguin Group (USA) Inc., 375 Hudson Street, New York, New York 10014, USA
Penguin Group (Canada), 90 Eglinton Avenue East, Suite 700, Toronto, Ontario, Canada M4P 2Y3
(a division of Pearson Penguin Canada Inc.)
Penguin Ireland, 25 St Stephen's Green, Dublin 2, Ireland (a division of Penguin Books Ltd)
Penguin Group (Australia), 707 Collins Street, Melbourne, Victoria 3008, Australia
(a division of Pearson Australia Group Pty Ltd)
Penguin Books India Pvt Ltd, 11 Community Centre, Panchsheel Park, New Delhi – 110 017, India
Penguin Group (NZ), 67 Apollo Drive, Rosedale, Auckland 0632, New Zealand
(a division of Pearson New Zealand Ltd)
Penguin Books (South Africa) (Pty) Ltd, Block D, Rosebank Office Park,
181 Jan Smuts Avenue, Parktown North, Gauteng 2193, South Africa

Penguin Books Ltd, Registered Offices: 80 Strand, London WC2R 0RL, England

www.penguin.com

Cider with Rosie first published by The Hogarth Press 1959
Published in Penguin Books 1962
Copyright © the Partners of the Literary Estate of Laurie Lee, 1959
As I Walked Out One Midsummer Morning first published by André Deutsch 1969
Published in Penguin Books 1971
Copyright © the Partners of the Literary Estate of Laurie Lee, 1969
A Moment of War first published by Viking 1991
Published in Penguin Books 1992
Copyright © the Partners of the Literary Estate of Laurie Lee, 1991
This omnibus edition first published by Viking 1992
Reissued in this edition by Penguin Books 2014

006

ISBN: 978-0-241-95327-3

www.greenpenguin.co.uk

Contents

A Preface

This trilogy is a sequence of early recollections, beginning with the dazzling lights and sounds of my first footings on earth in a steep Cotswold valley some three miles long. For nineteen years this was the limit of my world, then one midsummer morning I left home and walked to London and down the blazing length of Spain during the innocent days of the early thirties. Never had I felt so fat with time, so free to go where I would. Then such indulgence was suddenly broken by the savage outbreak of the Civil War.

The last volume tells of my winter return to Spain to join the International Brigade. Naïve and idealistic as I was, I felt it was a debt I owed to my beleaguered friends. Writing this book also taught me the full extent of that indebtedness.

These autobiographies, written with slow and miserly care, span the first twenty-three years of my life. They cover both the light and the dark, as do most remembrances, but I still feel I have much left to confess and celebrate.

Laurie Lee
Slad, August 1992

Cider with Rosie

Illustrated by John Ward

To My Brothers and Sisters
– The Half and the Whole

Contents

Contents

1

First Light

I was set down from the carrier's cart at the age of three; and there with a sense of bewilderment and terror my life in the village began.

The June grass, amongst which I stood, was taller than I was, and I wept. I had never been so close to grass before. It towered above me and all around me, each blade tattooed with tiger-skins of sunlight. It was knife-edged, dark, and a wicked green, thick as a forest and alive with grasshoppers that chirped and chattered and leapt through the air like monkeys.

I was lost and didn't know where to move. A tropic heat oozed up from the ground, rank with sharp odours of roots and nettles. Snow-clouds of elder-blossom banked in the sky, showering upon me the fumes and flakes of their sweet and giddy suffocation. High overhead ran frenzied larks, screaming, as though the sky were tearing apart.

For the first time in my life I was out of the sight of humans. For the first time in my life I was alone in a world whose behaviour I could neither predict nor fathom: a world of birds that squealed, of plants that stank, of insects that sprang about without warning. I was lost and I did not expect to be found again. I put back my head and howled, and the sun hit me smartly on the face, like a bully.

From this daylight nightmare I was awakened, as from many another, by the appearance of my sisters. They came scrambling and calling up the steep rough bank, and parting the long grass

7

found me. Faces of rose, familiar, living; huge shining faces hung up like shields between me and the sky; faces with grins and white teeth (some broken) to be conjured up like genii with a howl, brushing off terror with their broad scoldings and affection. They leaned over me – one, two, three – their mouths smeared with red currants and their hands dripping with juice.

'There, there, it's all right, don't you wail any more. Come down 'ome and we'll stuff you with currants.'

And Marjorie, the eldest, lifted me into her long brown hair, and ran me jogging down the path and through the steep rose-filled garden, and set me down on the cottage doorstep, which was our home, though I couldn't believe it.

That was the day we came to the village, in the summer of the last year of the First World War. To a cottage that stood in a half-acre of garden on a steep bank above a lake; a cottage with three floors and a cellar and a treasure in the walls, with a pump and apple trees, syringa and strawberries, rooks in the chimneys, frogs in the cellar, mushrooms on the ceiling, and all for three and sixpence a week.

I don't know where I lived before then. My life began on the carrier's cart which brought me up the long slow hills to the village, and dumped me in the high grass, and lost me. I had ridden wrapped up in a Union Jack to protect me from the sun, and when I rolled out of it, and stood piping loud among the buzzing jungle of that summer bank, then, I feel, was I born. And to all the rest of us, the whole family of eight, it was the beginning of a life.

But on that first day we were all lost. Chaos was come in cartloads of furniture, and I crawled the kitchen floor through forests of upturned chair-legs and crystal fields of glass. We were washed up in a new land, and began to spread out searching its springs and treasures. The sisters spent the light of that first day stripping the fruit bushes in the garden. The currants were at their prime, clusters of red, black, and yellow berries all tangled up with wild roses. Here was bounty the girls had never known before, and they darted squawking from bush to bush, clawing the fruit like sparrows.

Our Mother too was distracted from duty, seduced by the rich wilderness of the garden so long abandoned. All day she trotted to and fro, flushed and garrulous, pouring flowers into every pot and jug she could find on the kitchen floor. Flowers from the garden, daisies from the bank, cow-parsley, grasses, ferns, and leaves – they flowed in armfuls through the cottage door until its dim interior seemed entirely possessed by the world outside – a still green pool flooding with honeyed tides of summer.

I sat on the floor on a raft of muddles and gazed through the green window which was full of the rising garden. I saw the long black stockings of the girls, gaping with white flesh, kicking among the currant bushes. Every so often one of them would dart into the kitchen, cram my great mouth with handfuls of squashed berries, and run out again. And the more I got, the more I called for more. It was like feeding a fat young cuckoo.

The long day crowed and chirped and rang. Nobody did any work, and there was nothing to eat save berries and bread. I crawled about among the ornaments on the unfamiliar floor – the glass fishes, china dogs, shepherds and shepherdesses, bronze horsemen, stopped clocks, barometers, and photographs of bearded men. I called on them each in turn, for they were the shrines and faces of a half-remembered landscape. But as I watched the sun move around the walls, drawing rainbows from the cut-glass jars in the corner, I longed for a return of order.

Then, suddenly, the day was at an end, and the house was furnished. Each stick and cup and picture was nailed immovably in place; the beds were sheeted, the windows curtained, the straw mats laid, and the house was home. I don't remember seeing it happen, but suddenly the inexorable tradition of the house, with its smell, chaos, and complete logic, occurred as though it had never been otherwise. The furnishing and founding of the house came like the nightfall of that first day. From that uneasy loneliness of objects strewn on the kitchen floor, everything flew to its place and was never again questioned.

And from that day we grew up. The domestic arrangement of the house was shaken many times, like a snow-storm toy, so that beds and chairs and ornaments swirled from room to room, pursued by the gusty energies of Mother and the girls. But always these things resettled within the pattern of the walls, nothing escaped or changed, and so it remained for twenty years.

Now I measured that first growing year by the widening fields that became visible to me, the new tricks of dressing and getting about with which I became gradually endowed. I could open the kitchen door by screwing myself into a ball and leaping and banging the latch with my fist. I could climb into the high bed by using the ironwork as a ladder. I could whistle, but I couldn't lace my shoes. Life became a series of experiments which brought grief or the rewards of accomplishment: a pondering of patterns and mysteries in the house, while time hung golden and suspended, and one's body, from leaping and climbing, took on the rigid insanity of an insect, petrified as it were for hours together, breathing and watching. Watching the grains of dust fall in the sunny room, following an ant from its cradle to the grave, going over the knots in the bedroom ceiling – knots that ran like Negroes in the dusk of dawn, or moved stealthily from board to board, but which settled again in the wax light of day no more monstrous than fossils in coal.

These knots on the bedroom ceiling were the whole range of a world, and over them my eyes went endlessly voyaging in that long primeval light of waking to which a child is condemned. They were archipelagos in a sea of blood-coloured varnish, they were armies grouped and united against me, they were the alphabet of a macabre tongue, the first book I ever learned to read.

Radiating from that house, with its crumbling walls, its thumps and shadows, its fancied foxes under the floor, I moved along paths that lengthened inch by inch with my mounting strength of days. From stone to stone in the trackless yard I sent forth my acorn shell of senses, moving through unfathomable oceans like a South Sea savage island-hopping across the Pacific. Antennae of eyes and nose and grubbing fingers captured a new tuft of grass, a fern, a slug, the skull of a bird, a grotto of bright snails. Through the long summer ages of those first few days I enlarged my world and mapped it in my mind, its secure havens, its dust-deserts and puddles, its peaks of dirt and flag-flying bushes. Returning too, dry-throated, over and over again, to its several well-prodded horrors: the bird's gaping bones in its cage of old sticks; the black flies in the corner, slimy dead; dry rags of snakes; and the crowded, rotting, silent-roaring city of a cat's grub-captured carcass.

Once seen, these relics passed within the frontiers of the known lands, to be remembered with a buzzing in the ears, to be revisited when the stomach was strong. They were the first tangible victims of that destroying force whose job I knew went on both night and day, though I could never catch him at it. Nevertheless I was grateful for them. Though they haunted my eyes and stuck in my dreams, they reduced for me the first infinite possibilities of horror. They chastened the imagination with the proof of a limited frightfulness.

From the harbour mouth of the scullery door I learned the rocks and reefs and the channels where safety lay. I discovered the physical pyramid of the cottage, its stores and labyrinths, its centres of magic, and of the green, spouting island-garden upon which it stood. My Mother and sisters sailed past me like galleons in their busy dresses, and I learned the smells and sounds which followed in their wakes, the surge of breath, air of carbolic, song and grumble, and smashing of crockery.

How magnificent they appeared, full-rigged, those towering girls, with their flying hair and billowing blouses, their white-mast arms stripped for work or washing. At any moment one was boarded by them, bussed and buttoned, or swung up high like a wriggling fish to be hooked and held in their lacy linen.

The scullery was a mine of all the minerals of living. Here I discovered water – a very different element from the green crawling scum that stank in the garden tub. You could pump it in pure blue gulps out of the ground, you could swing on the pump handle and it came out sparkling like liquid sky. And it broke and ran and shone on the tiled floor, or quivered in a jug, or weighted your clothes with cold. You could drink it, draw with it, froth it with soap, swim beetles across it, or fly it in bubbles in the air. You could put your head in it, and open your eyes, and see the sides of the bucket buckle, and hear your caught breath roar, and work your mouth like a fish, and smell the lime from the ground. Substance of magic – which you could tear or wear, confine or scatter, or send down holes, but never burn or break or destroy.

The scullery was water, where the old pump stood. And it had everything else that was related to water: thick steam of Mondays edgy with starch; soapsuds boiling, bellying and popping, creaking and whispering, rainbowed with light and winking with a million windows. Bubble bubble, toil and grumble, rinsing and slapping of sheets and shirts, and panting Mother rowing her red arms like oars in the steaming waves. Then the linen came up on a stick out of the pot, like pastry, or woven suds, or sheets of moulded snow.

Here, too, was the scrubbing of floors and boots, of arms and necks, of red and white vegetables. Walk into the morning disorder of this room and all the garden was laid out dripping on the table. Chopped carrots like copper pennies, radishes and chives, potatoes dipped and stripped clean from their coats of mud, the snapping of tight pea-pods, long shells of green pearls, and the tearing of glutinous beans from their nests of wool.

Grown stealthy, marauding among these preparations, one nibbled one's way like a rat through roots and leaves. Peas rolled under the tongue, fresh cold, like solid water; teeth chewed green peel of apples, acid sharp, and the sweet white starch of swedes. Beaten away by wet hands gloved with flour, one returned in a morose and speechless lust. Slivers of raw pastry, moulded, warm, went down in the shapes of men and women – heads and arms of unsalted flesh seasoned with nothing but a dream of cannibalism.

Large meals were prepared in this room, cauldrons of stew for the insatiate hunger of eight. Stews of all that grew on these rich banks, flavoured with sage, coloured with Oxo, and laced with a few bones of lamb. There was, it is true, little meat at those times; sometimes a pound of bare ribs for boiling, or an occasional rabbit dumped at the door by a neighbour. But there was green food of great weight in season, and lentils and bread for ballast. Eight to ten loaves came to the house every day, and they never grew dry. We tore them to pieces with their crusts still warm, and their monotony was brightened by the objects we found in them – string, nails, paper, and once a mouse; for those were days of happy-go-lucky baking. The lentils were cooked in a great pot which also heated the water for the Saturday-night baths. Our small wood-fire could heat sufficient water to fill one bath only, and this we shared in turn. Being the youngest but one, my water was always the dirtiest but one, and the implications of this privilege remain with me to this day.

Waking one morning in the white-washed bedroom, I opened my eyes and found them blind. Though I stretched them and stared where the room should be, nothing was visible but a glare of gold, flat on my throbbing eyelids. I groped for my body and found it there. I heard the singing of birds. Yet there was nothing at all to be seen of the world save this quivering yellow light. Was I dead, I wondered? Was I in heaven? Whatever it was I hated it. I had wakened too soon from a dream of crocodiles and I was not ready for this further outrage. Then I heard the girls' steps on the stairs.

'Our Marge!' I shouted, 'I can't see nothing!' And I began to give out my howl.

A slap of bare feet slithered across the floor, and I heard sister Marjorie's giggle.

'Just look at him,' she said. 'Pop and fetch a flannel, Doth – 'is eyes've got stuck down again.'

The cold edge of the flannel passed over my face showered me with water, and I was back in the world. Bed and beams, and the sun-square window, and the girls bending over me grinning.

''Oo did it?' I yelled.

'Nobody, silly. Your eyes got bunged up, that's all.'

The sweet glue of sleep; it had happened before, but somehow I always forgot. So I threatened the girls I'd bung theirs up too: I was awake, I could see, I was happy. I lay looking out of the small green window. The world outside was crimson and on fire. I had never seen it looking like that before.

'Doth?' I said, 'what's happening to them trees?'

Dorothy was dressing. She leaned out of the window, slow and sleepy, and the light came through her nightdress like sand through a sieve.

'Nothing's happening,' she said.

'Yes it is then,' I said. 'They're falling to bits.'

Dorothy scratched her dark head, yawning wide, and white feathers floated out of her hair.

'It's only the leaves droppin'. We're in autumn now. The leaves always drop in autumn.'

Autumn? In autumn. Was that where we were? Where the leaves always dropped and there was always this smell. I imagined it continuing, with no change, for ever, these wet flames of woods burning on and on like the bush of Moses, as natural a part of this new found land as the eternal snows of the poles. Why had we come to such a place?

Marjorie, who had gone down to help with the breakfast, suddenly came tumbling back up the stairs.

'Doth,' she whispered; she seemed excited and frightened; 'Doth . . . 'e's turned up again. 'Elp on Loll with 'is clothes and come on down, quick.'

We went down and found him sitting by the fireside, smiling, wet, and cold. I climbed up to the breakfast table and stared at him, the stranger. To me he did not so much appear to be a man as a conglomeration of woody things. His face was red and crinkled, brilliant like fungus. There were leaves in his mud-matted hair, and leaves and twigs on his crumbling clothes, and all over him. His boots were like the black pulp you find when you dig under a tree. Mother gave him porridge and bread, and he smiled palely at us all.

'It must have been cruel in the wood,' said our Mother.

'I've got some sacks, mam,' he said, spooning his porridge. 'They keep out the wet.'

They wouldn't; they'd suck it up like a wick and wrap him in it.

'You oughtn't to live like that,' said Mother. 'You ought to get back to your home.'

'No,' smiled the man. 'That wouldn't do. They'd jump on me before you could say knife.'

Mother shook her head sadly, and sighed, and gave him more porridge. We boys adored the look of the man; the girls, fastidious, were more uncertain of him. But he was no tramp or he wouldn't be in the kitchen. He had four bright medals in his pocket, which he would produce and polish and lay on the table like money. He spoke like nobody else we knew; in fact, we couldn't understand many of his words. But Mother seemed to understand him, and would ask him questions, and look at the photographs he carried in his shirt and sigh and shake her head. He talked something of battles and of flying in the air, and it was all wonderful to us.

He was no man from these parts. He had appeared on the doorstep one early morning, asking for a cup of tea. Our Mother had brought him in and given him a whole breakfast. There had been blood on his face and he had seemed very weak. Now he was in a kitchen with a woman and a lot of children, and his eyes shone brightly, and his whiskers smiled. He told us he was sleeping in the wood, which seemed to me a good idea. And he was a soldier, because Mother had said so.

I knew about war; all my uncles were in it; my ears from birth had been full of the talk of it. Sometimes I used to climb into the basket chair by the fire and close my eyes and see brown men moving over a field in battle. I was three, but I saw them grope and die and felt myself older than they.

This man did not look like a soldier. He was not brassoed,

leather-belted, and wax-whiskered like my uncles. He had a beard and his khaki was torn. But the girls insisted he was a soldier, and said it in whispers, like a secret. And when he came down to our house for breakfast, and sat hunched by the fire, steaming with damp and coated with leaves and dirt, I thought of him sleeping up there in the wood. I imagined him sleeping, then having a go at the battle, then coming down to us for a cup of tea. He was the war, and the war was up there; I wanted to ask, 'How's the war in that wood?'

But he never told us. He sat drinking his tea, gulping and gasping, the fire drawing the damp out of his clothes as if ghosts were rising from him. When he caught our eyes he smiled from his beard. And when brother Jack shot at him with a spoon, saying, 'I'm a sodger,' he replied softly, 'Aye, and you'd make a better one than me, son, any day.'

When he said that, I wondered what had happened to the war. Was he in those rags because he was such a bad soldier? Had he lost the war in the wood?

When he didn't come any more, I knew he had. The girls said some policemen had taken him away in a cart. And Mother sighed and was sad over the poor man.

In weather that was new to me, and cold, and loud with bullying winds, my Mother disappeared to visit my father. This was a long way off, out of sight, and I don't remember her going. But suddenly there were only the girls in the house, tumbling about with brooms and dishcloths, arguing, quarrelling, and putting us to bed at random. House and food had a new smell, and meals appeared like dismal conjuring tricks, cold, raw, or black with too much fire. Marjorie was breathless and everywhere; she was fourteen, with all the family in her care. My socks slipped down, and stayed down. I went unwashed for long periods of time. Black leaves swept into the house and piled up in the corners; it rained, and the floors sweated, and washing filled all the lines in the kitchen and dripped sadly on one and all.

But we ate; and the girls moved about in a giggling flurry, exhausted at their losing game. As the days went by, such a tide of muddles mounted in the house that I didn't know which room was which. I lived free, grubbing outside in the mud till I was black as a badger. And my nose ran free, as unchecked as my feet. I sailed my boots down the drain, I cut up sheets for puttees, and marched like a soldier through the swamps of leaves. Sensing my chance, I wandered far, eating all manner of raw objects, coloured berries, twigs, and grubs, sick every day, but with a sickness of which I was proud.

All this time the sisters went through the house, darting upstairs and down, beset on all sides by the rain coming in, boys growing filthier, sheets scorching, saucepans burning, and kettles boiling over. The doll's-house became a mad house, and the girls frail birds flying in a wind of chaos. Doth giggled helplessly, Phyl wept among the vegetables, and Marjorie would say, when the day was over, 'I'd lie down and die, if there was a place to lie down in.'

I was not at all surprised when I heard of the end of the world. Everything pointed to it. The sky was low and whirling with black clouds; the wood roared night and day, stirring great seas of sound. One night we sat round the kitchen table, cracking walnuts with the best brass candlestick, when Marjorie came in from the town. She was shining with rain and loaded with bread and buns. She was also very white.

'The war's over,' she said. 'It's ended.'

'Never,' said Dorothy.

'They told me at the Stores,' said Marjorie. 'And they were giving away prunes.' She gave us a bagful, and we ate them raw.

The girls got tea and talked about it. And I was sure it was the end of the world. All my life was the war, and the war was the world. Now the war was over. So the end of the world was come. It made no other sense to me.

'Let's go out and see what's happening,' said Doth.

'You know we can't leave the kids,' Marge said.

So we went too. It was dark, and the gleaming roofs of the village echoed with the buzz of singing. We went hand in hand through the rain, up the bank and down the street. A bonfire crackled in one of the gardens, and a woman jumped up and down in the light of it, red as a devil, a jug in her hand, uttering cries that were not singing. All down the other gardens there were other bonfires too. And a man came up and kissed the girls and hopped in the road and twisted on one toe. Then he fell down in the mud and lay there, working his legs like a frog and croaking a loud song.

I wanted to stop. I had never seen a man like this, in such a wild good humour. But we hurried on. We got to the pub and stared through the windows. The bar seemed on fire with its many lamps. Rose-coloured men, through the rain-wet windows, seemed to bulge and break into flame. They breathed out smoke, drank fire from golden jars, and I heard their great din with awe. Now anything might happen. And it did. A man rose up and crushed a glass like a nut between his hands, then held them out laughing for all to see his wounds. But the blood was lost in the general light of blood. Two other men came waltzing out of the door, locked in each other's arms. Fighting and cursing, they fell over the wall and rolled down the bank in the dark.

There was a screaming woman we could not see. 'Jimmy! Jimmy!' she wailed. 'Oh, Jimmy! Thees'll kill' im! I'll fetch the vicar, I will! Oh, Jimmy!'

'Just 'ark at 'em,' said Dorothy, shocked and delighted.

'The kids ought to be in bed,' said Marjorie.

'Stop a minute longer. Only a minute. It wouldn't do no 'arm.'

Then the schoolhouse chimney caught on fire. A fountain of sparks shot high into the night, writhing and sweeping on the wind, falling and dancing along the road. The chimney hissed like a firework, great rockets of flame came gushing forth, emptying the tiny house, so that I expected to see chairs and tables, knives and forks, radiant and burning, follow. The moss-tiles smouldered with sulphurous soot, yellow jets of smoke belched from cracks in the chimney. We stood in the rain and watched it entranced, as if the sight had been saved for this day. As if the house had been saved, together with the year's bad litter, to be sent up in flames and rejoicing.

How everyone bellowed and scuffled and sang, drunk with their beer and the sight of the fire. But what would happen now that the war was over? What would happen to my uncles who lived in it? – those huge remote men who appeared suddenly at our house, reeking of leather and horses. What would happen to our father, who was khakied like every other man, yet special, not like other men? His picture hung over the piano, trim, haughty, with a badged cap and a spiked moustache. I confused him with the Kaiser. Would he die now the war was over?

As we gazed at the flaming schoolhouse chimney, and smelt the burning throughout the valley, I knew something momentous was occurring. At any moment I looked for a spectacular end to my already long life. Oh, the end of the war and the world! There was rain in my shoes, and Mother had disappeared. I never expected to see another day.

2

First Names

Peace was here; but I could tell no difference. Our Mother returned from far away with excited tales of its madness, of how strangers had stopped and kissed each other in the streets and climbed statues shouting its name. But what was peace anyway? Food tasted the same, pump water was as cold, the house neither fell nor grew larger. Winter came in with a dark, hungry sadness, and the village filled up with unknown men who stood around in their braces and khaki pants, smoking short pipes, scratching their arms, and gazing in silence at the gardens.

I could not believe in this peace at all. It brought no angels or explanations; it had not altered the nature of my days and nights, nor gilded the mud in the yard. So I soon forgot it and went back to my burrowing among the mysteries of indoors and out. The garden still offered its corners of weed, blackened cabbages, its stones and flower-stalks. And the house its areas of hot and cold, dark holes and talking boards, its districts of terror and blessed sanctuary; together with an infinite range of objects and ornaments that folded, fastened, creaked and sighed, opened and shut, tinkled and sang, pinched, scratched, cut, burned, spun, toppled, or fell to pieces. There was also a pepper-smelling cupboard, a ringing cellar, and a humming piano, dry bunches of spiders, colliding brothers, and the eternal comfort of the women.

I was still young enough then to be sleeping with my Mother, which to me seemed life's whole purpose. We slept together in the first-floor bedroom on a flock-filled mattress in a bed of brass rods and curtains. Alone, at that time, of all the family, I was her chosen dream companion, chosen from all for her extra love; my right, so it seemed to me.

So in the ample night and the thickness of her hair I consumed my fattened sleep, drowsed and nuzzling to her warmth of flesh, blessed by her bed and safety. From the width of the house and the separation of the day, we two then lay joined alone. That darkness to me was like the fruit of sloes, heavy and ripe to the touch. It was a darkness of bliss and simple languor, when all edges seemed rounded, apt and fitting; and the presence for whom one had moaned and hungered was found not to have fled after all.

My Mother, freed from her noisy day, would sleep like a happy child, humped in her nightdress, breathing innocently and making soft drinking sounds in the pillow. In her flights of dream she held me close, like a parachute to her back; or rolled and enclosed me with her great tired body so that I was snug as a mouse in a hayrick.

They were deep and jealous, those wordless nights, as we curled and muttered together, like a secret I held through the waking day which set me above all others. It was for me alone that the night came down, for me the prince of her darkness, when only I would know the huge helplessness of her sleep, her dead face, and her blind bare arms. At dawn, when she rose and stumbled back to the kitchen, even then I was not wholly deserted, but rolled into the valley her sleep had left, lay deep in its smell of lavender, deep on my face to sleep again in the nest she had made my own.

The sharing of her bed at that three-year-old time I expected to last for ever. I had never known, or could not recall, any night spent away from her. But I was growing fast; I was no longer the baby; brother Tony lay in wait in his cot. When I heard the first whispers of moving me to the boys' room, I simply couldn't believe it. Surely my Mother would never agree? How could she face night without me?

My sisters began by soothing and flattering; they said, 'You're a grown big man.' 'You'll be sleeping with Harold and Jack,' they said. 'Now what d'you think of that?' What was I supposed to think? – to me it seemed outrageous. I affected a brainstorm and won a few extra nights, my last nights in that downy bed. Then the girls changed their tune: 'It'll only be for a bit. You can come back to Mum later on.' I didn't quite believe them, but Mother was silent, so I gave up the struggle and went.

I was never recalled to my Mother's bed again. It was my first betrayal, my first dose of ageing hardness, my first lesson in the gentle, merciless rejection of women. Nothing more was said, and I accepted it. I grew a little tougher, a little colder, and turned my attention more towards the outside world, which by now was emerging visibly through the mist . . .

The yard and the village manifested themselves at first through magic and fear. Projections of their spirits and of my hallucinations sketched in the first blanks with demons. The thumping of heart-beats which I heard in my head was no longer the unique ticking of a private clock but the marching of monsters coming in from outside. They were creatures of the 'world' and they were coming for me, advancing up the valley with their heads stuck in bread-baskets, grunting to the thump of my blood. I suppose they were a result of early headaches, but I spent anxious days awaiting them. Indefatigable marchers though they were, they never got nearer than the edge of the village.

This was a daylight uneasiness which I shared with no one; but night, of course, held various others about which I was far more complaining – dying candles, doors closed on darkness, faces seen upside down, night holes in the ground where imagination seethed and sent one shrieking one's chattering head off. There were the Old Men too, who lived in the walls, in floors, and down the lavatory; who watched and judged us and were pitilessly spiteful, and were obviously gods gone mouldy. These Old Men never failed to control us boys, and our sisters conjured them shamelessly, and indeed in a house where no father ruled they were the perfect surrogates.

But there was one real old pagan of flesh and blood who ruled us all for a while. His visits to the village were rare yet deliberate; and when he appeared it was something both sovereign and evil that walked among us, though it was the women who were most clearly affected.

The first time I actually saw him myself had a salt-taste I still remember. It was a frost-bright, moon-cold night of winter, and we were sitting in the kitchen as usual. The fire boiled softly, the candles quivered, the girls were drowsily gossiping. I had fallen half-asleep across the table, when Marjorie suddenly said, 'Ssssh! . . .'

She had heard something of course, somebody was always hearing something, so I woke up and listened vaguely. The others were in attitudes of painful attention; they would listen at the drop of a feather. I heard nothing at first. An owl cried in the yew trees and was answered from another wood. Then Dorothy said 'Hark!' and Mother said 'Hush!' and the alarm had us all in its grip.

Like a stagless herd of hinds and young our heads all went up together. We heard it then, far away down the lane, still faint and unmistakable – the drag of metal on frosty ground and an intermittent rattle of chains.

The girls exchanged looks of awful knowledge, their bright eyes large with doom. 'It's him!' they whispered in shaky voices. 'He's broke out again! It's him!'

It was him all right. Mother bolted the door and blew out the lamps and candles. Then we huddled together in the fire-flushed darkness to await his ominous coming.

The drag of the chains grew louder and nearer, rattling along the night, sliding towards us up the distant lane to his remorseless, moonlit tread. The girls squirmed in their chairs and began giggling horribly; they appeared to have gone off their heads.

'Hush,' warned our Mother. 'Keep quiet. Don't move . . .' Her face was screwed in alarm.

The girls hung their heads and waited, shivering. The chains rattled nearer and nearer. Up the lane, round the corner, along the top of the bank – then with a drumming of feet, he was here . . . Frantic, the girls could hold out no longer, they leapt up with curious cries, stumbled their way across the firelit kitchen, and clawed the dark curtains back . . .

Proud in the night the beast passed by, head crowned by royal horns, his milky eyes split by strokes of moonlight, his great frame shaggy with hair. He moved with stiff and stilted strides, swinging his silvered beard, and from the tangled strength of his thighs and shoulders trailed the heavy chains he'd broken.

'Jones's goat! –' our Dorothy whispered; two words that were almost worship. For this was not just a straying animal but a beast of ancient dream, the moonlight-walker of the village roads, half captive, half rutting king. He was huge and hairy as a Shetland horse and all men were afraid of him; Squire Jones in fact kept him chained to a spike driven five feet into the ground. Yet when nights were bright with moon or summer neither spike nor chains could hold him. Then he snorted and reared, tore his chains from the ground, and came trailing his lust through the village.

I had heard of him often; now I saw him at last, striding jerkily down the street. Old as a god, wearing his chains like a robe, he exuded a sharp whiff of salt, and every few steps he sniffed at the air as though seeking some friend or victim. But he walked alone; he encountered no one, he passed through an empty village. Daughters and wives peeped from darkened bedrooms, men waited in the shadows with axes. Meanwhile, reeking with power and white in the moon, he went his awesome way . . .

'Did you ever see a goat so big?' asked Dorothy with a sigh.

'They knocks you down and tramples you. I heard he knocked down Miss Cohen.'

'Just think of meeting him coming home alone . . .'

'Whatever would you do?'

'I'd have a fit. What would you do, Phyl?'

Phyl didn't answer: she had run away, and was having hysterics in the pantry.

Jones's terrorist goat seemed to me a natural phenomenon of that time, part of a village which cast up beasts and spirits as casually as human beings. All seemed part of the same community, though their properties varied widely – some were benevolent, some strictly to be avoided; there were those that appeared at different shapes of the moon, or at daylight or midnight hours, that could warn or bless or drive one mad according to their different natures. There was the Death Bird, the Coach, Miss Barraclough's Goose, Hangman's House, and the Two-Headed Sheep.

There is little remarkable about a two-headed sheep, except that this one was old and talked English. It lived alone among the Catswood Larches, and was only visible during flashes of lightning. It could sing harmoniously in a double voice and cross-question itself for hours; many travellers had heard it when passing that wood, but few, naturally enough, had seen it. Should a thunderstorm ever have confronted you with it, and had you had the presence of mind to inquire, it would have told you the date and nature of your death – at least so people said. But no one quite relished the powers of this beast. And when the sheet-lightning flickered over the Catswood trees it was thought best to keep away from the place.

The Bulls Cross Coach was another ill omen, and a regular midnight visitor. Bulls Cross was a saddle of heathland set high at the end of the valley, once a crossing of stage-roads and cattle-tracks which joined Berkeley to Birdlip, and Bisley to Gloucester Market. Relics of the old stage-roads still imprinted the grass as well as the memories of the older villagers. And up here, any midnight, but particularly New Year's Eve, one could see a silver-grey coach drawn by flaring horses thundering out of control, could hear the pistol crack of snapping harness, the screams of the passengers, the splintering of wood, and the coachman's desperate cries. The vision recalled some ancient disaster, and was rehearsed every night, at midnight.

Those who hadn't seen it boasted they had, but those who had seen it, never. For the sight laid a curse upon talkative witnesses, a curse we all believed in – you went white in the night, and your teeth fell out, and later you died by trampling. So news of the phantom usually came second-hand. 'They sin that coach agen last night. 'Arry Lazbury sin it, they says. He was comin' from Painswick a-pushin' 'is bike. 'E dropped it, an' run 'ome crazy.' We committed poor Harry to his horrible end, while the coach ran again through our minds, gliding white on its rocking wheels, as regular as the Post.

As for the tiny tragedy behind the phantom, it had been jealously remembered to haunt us. The tilted coach, the splintered shafts, the wheels crooked against the moon, the sobbing horses kicking out each other's brains, the passengers dying on the moor – the image of that small but local disaster still possessed qualities to appal which the more grandiose carnage of recent times has never quite overshadowed.

As for Bulls Cross – that ragged wildness of wind-bent turves – I still wouldn't walk there at midnight. It was a curious tundra, a sort of island of nothing set high above the crowded valleys. Yet its hollows and silences, bare of all habitations, seemed stained by the encounters of strangers. At this no-man's crossing, in the days of foot-pads and horses, travellers would meet in suspicion, or lie in wait to do violence on each other, to rob or rape or murder. To the villages around, it was a patch of bare skyline, a baldness among the woods, a wind-scarred platform which caught everybody's eye, and was therefore just the place for a gibbet. A gibbet, consequently, had stood there for years, which the old folk could still remember.

Below Bulls Cross stood a dank yellow wood which we knew as Deadcombe Bottom. My brothers and I discovered a cottage down there, roof-fallen, in a garden run wild. We played there often among its rotting rooms, running up the littered stairs, picking and gorging on the small sharp apples which hung round the shattered windows. It was a damp dark ruin in the damp depth of the wood; its rooms reeked of old beds and fungus.

And behind the door, blood-red with rust, hung a naked iron hook.

To this silent, birdless, sunless shambles we returned again and again. We could do what we liked here, wreak what damage we wished, and strangely enough no one disturbed us. Only later did we learn the history of the place: that it had been the home of the Bulls Cross hangman, that he had lived there with his son, and worked at his trade, and had later killed himself here.

The cottage in the wood had been specially chosen, close to his work, yet hidden. The times were hungry, his days were busy; he was a discreet and skilful man. Night after night he strolled up the hill to load the gallows with local felons. After a routine summons one storm-black evening, he was handed a shivering boy. Used to working in darkness, he dispatched the lad quickly, then paused to light up his pipe. He was turning to go when a cloud moved from the moon and lit up the gallows clearly, and in the rain-washed face that stared crookedly down at him the hangman saw his son. To the men who stood by he said nothing at all. He just walked back to his cottage, drove a hook into the wall, fixed up a noose, and hanged himself.

Since when no one had lived in Hangman's House, which crumbled in Deadcombe Bottom, where we played, and chewed apples, and swung from that hook, and kicked the damp walls to pieces . . .

From the age of five or so I began to grow acquainted with several neighbours – outlaws most of them in dress and behaviour – whom I remembered both by name and deed. There was Cabbage-Stump Charlie, Albert the Devil, and Percy-from-Painswick, to begin with.

Cabbage-Stump Charlie was our local bruiser – a violent, gaitered, gaunt-faced pigman, who lived only for his sows and for fighting. He was a nourisher of quarrels, as some men are of plants, growing them from nothing by the heat of belligerence and watering them daily with blood. He would set out each evening, armed with his cabbage-stalk, ready to strike down the first man he saw. 'What's up then, Charlie? Got no quarrel with thee.' 'Wham!' said Charlie, and hit him. Men fell from their bicycles or back-pedalled violently when they saw old Charlie coming. With his hawk-brown nose and whiskered arms he looked like a land-locked Viking; and he would take up his stand outside the pub, swing his great stump round his head, and say 'Wham! Bash!' like a boy in a comic, and challenge all comers to battle. Often bloodied himself, he left many a man bleeding before crawling back home to his pigs. Cabbage-Stump Charlie, like Jones's Goat, set the village to bolting its doors.

Albert the Devil was another alarmer – a deaf-mute beggar with a black beetle's body, short legs, and a mouth like a puppet's. He had soft-boiled eyes of unusual power which filled every soul with disquiet. It was said he could ruin a girl with a glance and take the manhood away from a man, or scramble your brains, turn bacon green, and affect other domestic disorders. So when he came to the village on a begging trip, and we heard his musical gurgle approaching, money and food was put on the tops of the walls and then people shut themselves up in their privies.

Percy-from-Painswick, on the other hand, was a clown and a ragged dandy, who used to come over the hill, dressed in frock-coat and leggings, looking for local girls. Harmless, half-witted, he wooed only with his tongue; but his words were sufficient to befuddle the girls and set them shrieking with pleasure and shock. He had a sharp pink face and a dancer's light body and the girls used to follow him everywhere, teasing him on into cheekier fancies and pinning ribbons to his swallow-tail coat. Then he'd spin on his toes, and say something quick and elaborate, uttered smoothly from smiling teeth – and the girls would run screaming down over the bank, red-faced, excited, incredulous, hiding in bushes to exclaim to each other was it possible what Percy just said? He was a gentle, sharp, sweet-moving man, but he died of his brain soon after.

Then there was Willy the Fish, who came round on Fridays, mongering from door to door, with baskets of mackerel of such antiquity that not even my family could eat them. Willy was a loose-lipped, sad-eyed man who had lost his girl to his trade. He would lean by our door, and blow and scratch, and lament how it was he'd lost her. But transport was bad, and the sea far away; and the truth was poor Willy stank.

Among others I remember was Tusker Tom, who sold sacks of tree-roots for burning. And Harelip Harry, Davis the Drag, Fisty Fill, and the Prospect Smiler. The first-named three were orbiting tramps, but the last was a manic farmer. Few men I think can have been as unfortunate as he; for on the one hand he was a melancholic with a loathing for mankind, on the other, some paralysis had twisted his mouth into a permanent and radiant smile. So everyone he met, being warmed by his smile, would shout him a happy greeting. And beaming upon them with his sunny face he would curse them all to hell.

Bulls Cross itself had two daylight familiars: John-Jack and Emmanuel Twinning. John-Jack spent his time by the Bulls Cross signpost staring gloomily into Wales. Silent, savage, with a Russian look, he lived with his sister Nancy, who had borne him over the course of years five children of remarkable beauty. Emmanuel Twinning, on the other hand, was gentle and very old, and made his own suits out of hospital blankets, and lived near by with a horse.

Emmanuel and the skewbald had much in common, including the use of the kitchen, and one saw their grey heads, almost any evening, poking together out of the window. The old man himself, when seen alone, seemed to inhabit unearthly regions, so blue and remote that the girls used to sing:

O come, O come, E-mah-ah-ah-new-el!
An' ransom captive Is-rah-ah-ah-el! . . .

At this he would nod and smile gently upon us, moving his lips to the hymn. He was so very old, so far and strange, I never doubted that the hymn was his. He wore sky-blue blankets, and his name was Emmanuel; it was easy to think he was God.

In the long hot summer of 1921 a serious drought hit the country. Springs dried up, the wells filled with frogs, and the usually sweet water from our scullery pump turned brown and tasted of nails. Although this drought was a relief to my family, it was a scourge to the rest of the village. For weeks the sky hung hot and blue, trees shrivelled, crops burned in the fields, and the old folk said the sun had slipped in its course and that we should all of us very soon die. There were prayers for rain; but my family didn't go, because it was rain we feared most of all.

As the drought continued, prayer was abandoned and more devilish steps adopted. Finally soldiers with rifles marched to the tops of the hills and began shooting at passing clouds. When I heard their dry volleys, breaking like sticks in the stillness, I knew our long armistice was over. And sure enough – whether from prayers or the shooting, or by a simple return of nature – the drought broke soon after and it began to rain as it had never rained before.

I remember waking in the night to the screams of our Mother, and to rousing alarms of a howling darkness and the storm-battered trees outside. Terror, the old terror, had come again, and as always in the middle of the night.

'Get up!' cried Mother. 'It's coming in! Get up or we'll all be drowned!'

I heard her banging about and beating the walls in accents of final doom. When Mother gave her alarms one didn't lie back and think, one didn't use reason at all; one just erected one's hair and leapt out of bed and scrambled downstairs with the others.

Our predicament was such that we lived at nature's mercy; for the cottage, stuck on its steep bank, stood directly in the path of the floods. All the spouts of the heavens seemed to lead to our door, and there was only one small drain to swallow them. When this drain blocked up, as it did in an instant, the floods poured into our kitchen – and as there was no back door to let them out again I felt it natural at the time we should drown.

'Hell in Heaven!' wailed Mother. 'Damn it and cuss! Jesus have mercy on us!'

We grizzled and darted about for brooms, then ran out to tackle the storm. We found the drain blocked already and the yard full of water. The noise of the rain drowned our cries and whimpers, and there was nothing to do but sweep.

What panic those middle-night rousings were, those trumpet-calls murdering sleep; with darkness, whirlwind, and invisible rain, trees roaring, clouds bursting, thunder crashing, lightning crackling, floods rising, and our Mother demented. The girls in their nightdresses held spitting candles while we boys swept away at the drain. Hot rods of rain struck straight through our shirts; we shivered with panic and cold.

'More brooms!' shouted Mother, jumping up and down. 'Run, someone, in the name of goodness! Sweep harder, boys! Sweet saints above, it's up to the doorstep already!'

The flood-water gurgled and moved thickly around us, breeding fat yellow bubbles like scum, skipping and frothing where the bullet rain hit it, and inching slowly towards the door. The drain was now hidden beneath the water and we swept at it for our lives, the wet candles hissed and went out one by one, Mother lit torches of newspapers, while we fought knee-deep in cries and thunder, splashing about, wet-through, half-weeping, over-whelmed by gigantic fears.

Sometimes, in fact, the water did get in; two or three inches of it. It slid down the steps like a thick cream custard and spread all over the floor. When that happened, Mother's lamentations reached elegiac proportions, and all the world was subpoenaed to witness. Dramatic apostrophes rang through the night; the Gods were arraigned, the Saints called to order, and the Fates severely ticked off.

There would be a horrible mess in the kitchen next morning, mud and slime all over the matting, followed by the long depressed drudgery of scraping it up and carrying it away in buckets. Mother, on her knees, would wring her hands and roll her eyes about.

'I can't *think* what I've done to be so troubled and tried. And just when I got the house straight. Neither saints nor angels would keep their patience if they had such things to put up with ... My poor, poor children, my precious darlings – you could die in this filthy hole. No one would care – not a bell-essed soul. Look out with that damn-and-cuss bucket!' ...

Apart from the noise and the tears and the dirt, these inundations were really not much. But I can't pretend they didn't scare me stiff. The thought that the flood-waters should actually break into our house seemed to me something worse than a fire. At the mid-hour of night, when the storms really blew, I used to lie aghast in my bed, hearing the rain claw the window and the wind slap the walls, and imagining the family, the house, and all the furniture, being sucked down the eternal drain.

It was not till much later that I reasoned things out: that our position on the hillside made it unlikely we should drown, that Mother's frenzies and scares belonged to something else altogether, and that it was possible after all to sleep through rain in peace. Even so, to this day, when the skies suddenly darken, and a storm builds up in the west, and I smell rain on the wind and hear the first growl of thunder, I grow uneasy, and start looking for brooms.

3

Village School

The village to which our family had come was a scattering of some twenty to thirty houses down the south-east slope of a valley. The valley was narrow, steep, and almost entirely cut off; it was also a funnel for winds, a channel for the floods and a jungly, bird-crammed, insect-hopping sun-trap whenever there happened to be any sun. It was not high and open like the Windrush country, but had secret origins, having been gouged from the escarpment by the melting ice-caps some time before we got there. The old flood-terraces still showed on the slopes, along which the cows walked sideways. Like an island, it was possessed of curious survivals – rare orchids and Roman snails; and there were chemical qualities in the limestone-springs which gave the women pre-Raphaelite goitres. The sides of the valley were rich in pasture and the crests heavily covered in beechwoods.

Living down there was like living in a bean-pod; one could see nothing but the bed one lay in. Our horizon of woods was the limit of our world. For weeks on end the trees moved in the wind with a dry roaring that seemed a natural utterance of the landscape. In winter they ringed us with frozen spikes, and in summer they oozed over the lips of the hills like layers of thick green lava. Mornings, they steamed with mist or sunshine, and almost every evening threw streamers above us, reflecting sunsets we were too hidden to see.

Water was the most active thing in the valley, arriving in the long rains from Wales. It would drip all day from clouds and trees, from roofs and eaves and noses. It broke open roads, carved its way through gardens, and filled the ditches with sucking noises. Men and horses walked about in wet sacking, birds shook rainbows from sodden branches, and streams ran from holes, and back into holes, like noisy underground trains.

I remember, too, the light on the slopes, long shadows in tufts and hollows, with cattle, brilliant as painted china, treading their echoing shapes. Bees blew like cake-crumbs through the golden air, white butterflies like sugared wafers, and when it wasn't raining a diamond dust took over which veiled and yet magnified all things.

Most of the cottages were built of Cotswold stone and were roofed by split-stone tiles. The tiles grew a kind of golden moss which sparkled like crystallized honey. Behind the cottages were long steep gardens full of cabbages, fruit-bushes, roses, rabbit-hutches, earth-closets, bicycles, and pigeon-lofts. In the very sump of the valley wallowed the Squire's Big House – once a fine, though modest sixteenth-century manor, to which a Georgian façade had been added.

The villagers themselves had three ways of living: working for the Squire, or on the farms, or down in the cloth-mills at Stroud. Apart from the Manor, and the ample cottage gardens – which were an insurance against hard times – all other needs were supplied by a church, a chapel, a vicarage, a manse, a wooden hut, a pub – and the village school.

The village school at that time provided all the instruction we were likely to ask for. It was a small stone barn divided by a wooden partition into two rooms – The Infants and The Big Ones. There was one dame teacher, and perhaps a young girl assistant. Every child in the valley crowding there remained till he was fourteen years old, then was presented to the working field or factory with nothing in his head more burdensome than a few mnemonics, a jumbled list of wars, and a dreamy image of the world's geography. It seemed enough to get by with, in any case; and was one up on our poor old grandparents.

This school, when I came to it, was at its peak. Universal

education and unusual fertility had packed it to the walls with pupils. Wild boys and girls from miles around – from the outlying farms and half-hidden hovels way up at the ends of the valley – swept down each day to add to our numbers, bringing with them strange oaths and odours, quaint garments and curious pies. They were my first amazed vision of any world outside the womanly warmth of my family; I didn't expect to survive it for long, and I was confronted with it at the age of four.

The morning came, without any warning, when my sisters surrounded me, wrapped me in scarves, tied up my bootlaces, thrust a cap on my head, and stuffed a baked potato in my pocket.

'What's this?' I said.

'You're starting school today.'

'I ain't. I'm stopping 'ome.'

'Now, come on, Loll. You're a big boy now.'

'I ain't.'

'You are.'

'Boo-hoo.'

They picked me up bodily, kicking and bawling, and carried me up to the road.

'Boys who don't go to school get put into boxes, and turn into rabbits, and get chopped up Sundays.'

I felt this was overdoing it rather, but I said no more after that. I arrived at the school just three feet tall and fatly wrapped in my scarves. The playground roared like a rodeo, and the potato burned through my thigh. Old boots, ragged stockings, torn trousers and skirts, went skating and skidding around me. The rabble closed in; I was encircled; grit flew in my face like shrapnel. Tall girls with frizzled hair, and huge boys with sharp elbows, began to prod me with hideous interest. They plucked at my scarves, spun me round like a top, screwed my nose, and stole my potato.

I was rescued at last by a gracious lady – the sixteen-year-old junior-teacher – who boxed a few ears and dried my face and led me off to The Infants. I spent that first day picking holes in paper, then went home in a smouldering temper.

'What's the matter, Loll? Didn't he like it at school, then?'

'They never gave me the present!'

'Present? What present?'

'They said they'd give me a present.'

'Well, now, I'm sure they didn't.'

'They did! They said: "You're Laurie Lee, ain't you? Well, just you sit there for the present." I sat there all day but I never got it. I ain't going back there again!'

But after a week I felt like a veteran and grew as ruthless as anyone else. Somebody had stolen my baked potato, so I swiped somebody else's apple. The Infant Room was packed with toys such as I'd never seen before – coloured shapes and rolls of clay, stuffed birds and men to paint. Also a frame of counting beads which our young teacher played like a harp, leaning her bosom against our faces and guiding our wandering fingers . . .

The beautiful assistant left us at last, and was replaced by an opulent widow. She was tall, and smelt like a cart-load of lavender; and wore a hair net, which I thought was a wig. I remember going close up and having a good look – it was clearly too square to be hair.

'What are you staring at?' the widow inquired.

I was much too soft-hearted to answer.

'Go on. Do tell. You needn't be shy.'

'You're wearing a wig,' I said.

'I can assure you I'm not!' She went very red.

'You are. I seen it,' I said.

The new teacher grew flustered and curiously cross. She took me upon her knee.

'Now look very close. Is that really a wig?'

I looked hard, saw the net, and said, 'Yes.'

'Well, really!' she said, while the Infants gaped. 'I can assure you it's *not* a wig! And if you only could watch me getting dressed in the morning you'd know it wasn't one either.'

She shook me from her knee like a sodden cat, but she'd stirred my imagination. To suggest I might watch her getting dressed in the morning seemed to me both outrageous and wonderful.

This tiny, white-washed Infants' room was a brief but cosy anarchy. In that short time allowed us we played and wept, broke things, fell asleep, cheeked the teacher, discovered the things we could do to each other, and exhaled our last guiltless days.

My desk companions were those two blonde girls, already puppy-ishly pretty, whose names and bodies were to distract and haunt me for the next fifteen years of my life. Poppy and Jo were limpet chums; they sat holding hands all day; and there was a female self-possession about their pink sticky faces that made me shout angrily at them.

Vera was another I studied and liked; she was lonely, fuzzy, and short. I felt a curious compassion for stumpy Vera; and it was through her, and no beauty, that I got into trouble and received the first public shock of my life. How it happened was simple, and I was innocent, so it seemed. She came up to me in the play-ground one morning and held her face close to mine. I had a stick in my hand, so I hit her on the head with it. Her hair was springy, so I hit her again and watched her mouth open up with a yell.

To my surprise a commotion broke out around me, cries of scandal from the older girls, exclamations of horror and heavy censure mixed with Vera's sobbing wails. I was intrigued, not alarmed, that by wielding a beech stick I was able to cause such a stir. So I hit her again, without spite or passion, then walked off to try something else.

The experiment might have ended there, and having ended would have been forgotten. But no; angry faces surrounded me, very red, all spitting and scolding.

'Horrid boy! Poor Vera! Little monster! Urgh! We're going to tell teacher about you!'

Something was wrong, the world seemed upset, I began to feel vaguely uneasy. I had only hit Vera on her wiry black hair, and now everybody was shouting at me. I ran and hid, feeling sure it

would pass, but they hunted me down in the end. Two big righteous girls hauled me out by the ears.

'You're wanted in the Big Room, for 'itting Vera. You're 'alf going to cop it!' they said.

So I was dragged to that Room, where I'd never been before, and under the savage eyes of the elder children teacher gave me a scalding lecture. I was confused by now and shaking with guilt. At last I smirked and ran out of the room. I had learned my first lesson, that I could not hit Vera, no matter how fuzzy her hair. And something else too; that the summons to the Big Room, the policeman's hand on the shoulder, comes almost always as a complete surprise, and for the crime that one has forgotten.

My brother Jack, who was with me in the Infants, was too clever to stay there long. Indeed he was so bright he made us uncomfortable, and we were all of us glad to get rid of him. Sitting pale in his pinafore, gravely studying, commanding the teacher to bring him fresh books, or to sharpen his pencils, or to make less noise, he was an Infant Freak from the start. So he was promoted to the Big Room with unprecedented promptness, given a desk and a dozen atlases to sit on, from which he continued to bully the teachers in that cold clear voice of his.

But I, myself, was a natural Infant, content to serve out my time, to slop around and whine and idle: and no one suggested I shouldn't. So I remained long after bright Jack had moved on, the fat lord of my nursery life, skilled at cutting out men from paper, chalking suns on the walls, making snakes from clay, idling voluptuously through the milky days with a new young teacher to feed on. But my time was slowly running out; my Big Room bumps were growing. Suddenly, almost to my dismay, I found that I could count up to a hundred, could write my name in both large and small letters, and subtract certain numbers from each other. I had even just succeeded in subtracting Poppy from Jo, when the call came down from on high. Infant no longer, I was being moved up – the Big Room was ready for me.

I found there a world both adult and tough, with long desks and inkwells, strange maps on the walls, huge boys, heavy boots, scratching pens, groans of labour, and sharp and sudden persecutions. Gone for ever were the infant excuses, the sanctuary of lisping charms. Now I was alone and unprotected, faced by a struggle which required new techniques, where one made pacts and split them, made friends and betrayed them, and fought for one's place near the stove.

The stove was a symbol of caste among us, the tub of warmth to which we cleaved during the long seven months of winter. It was made of cast-iron and had a noisy mouth which rattled coke and breathed out fumes. It was decorated by a tortoise labelled 'Slow But Sure', and in winter it turned red hot. If you pressed a pencil against it, the wood burst into flames; and if you spat on the top, the spit hopped and gambolled like tiny ping-pong balls.

My first days in the Big Room were spent in regret for the young teacher I'd left in the Infants, for her braided breasts and unbuttoning hands and her voice of sleepy love. Quite clearly the Big Room boasted no such comforts; Miss B, the Head Teacher, to whom I was now delivered, being about as physically soothing as a rake.

She was a bunched and punitive little body and the school had christened her Crabby; she had a sour yellow look, lank hair coiled in earphones, and the skin and voice of a turkey. We were all afraid of the gobbling Miss B; she spied, she pried, she crouched, she crept, she pounced – she was a terror.

Each morning was war without declaration; no one knew who would catch it next. We stood to attention, half-crippled in our desks, till Miss B walked in, whacked the walls with a ruler, and fixed us with her squinting eye. 'Good a-morning, children!' 'Good morning, Teacher!' The greeting was like a rattling of swords. Then she would scowl at the floor and begin to growl 'Ar Farther . . .'; at which we said the Lord's Prayer, praised all good things, and thanked God for the health of our King. But scarcely had we bellowed the last Amen than Crabby coiled, uncoiled, and sprang, and knocked some poor boy sideways.

One seldom knew why; one was always off guard, for the

punishment preceded the charge. The charge, however, followed hard upon it, to a light shower of angry spitting.

'Shuffling your feet! Playing with the desk! A-smirking at that miserable Betty! I will not have it. I'll not, I say. I repeat – I will not have it!'

Many a punch-drunk boy in a playground battle, out-numbered and beaten to his knees, would be heard to cry: 'I will not have it! I'll not, I say! I repeats I will not have it!' It was an appeal to the code of our common suffering, and called for immediate mercy.

So we did not much approve of Crabby – though she was responsible for our excellent reflexes. Apart from this, her teaching was not memorable. She appears in my recollection as merely a militant figure, a hunched-up little creature all spring-coils and slaps – not a monster by any means, but a natural manifestation of what we expected of school.

For school in my day, that day, Crabby's day, seemed to be designed simply to keep us out of the air and from following the normal pursuits of the fields. Crabby's science of dates and sums and writing seemed a typical invention of her own, a sour form of fiddling or prison-labour like picking oakum or sewing sacks.

So while the bright times passed, we sat locked in our stocks, our bent backs turned on the valley. The June air infected us with primitive hungers, grass-seed and thistle-down idled through the windows, we smelt the fields and were tormented by cuckoos, while every out-of-door sound that came drifting in was a sharp nudge in the solar plexus. The creaking of wagons going past the school, harness-jingle, and the cries of the carters, the calling of cows from the 17-Acre, Fletcher's chattering mower, gunshot from the warrens – all tugged and pulled at our active wishes till we could have done Miss B a murder.

And indeed there came the inevitable day when rebellion raised its standard, when the tension was broken and a hero emerged whom we would willingly have named streets after. At least, from that day his name was honoured, though we gave him little support at the time . . .

Spadge Hopkins it was, and I must say we were surprised. He was one of those heavy, full-grown boys, thick-legged, red-fisted, bursting with flesh, designed for the great outdoors. He was nearly fourteen by then, and physically out of scale – at least so far as our school was concerned. The sight of him squeezed into his tiny desk was worse than a bullock in ballet-shoes. He wasn't much of a scholar; he groaned as he worked, or hacked at his desk with a jack-knife. Miss B took her pleasure in goading him, in forcing him to read out loud; or asking him sudden unintelligible questions which made him flush and stumble.

The great day came; a day of shimmering summer, with the valley outside in a state of leafy levitation. Crabby B was at her sourest, and Spadge Hopkins had had enough. He began to writhe in his desk, and roll his eyes, and kick with his boots, and mutter; 'She'd better look out. 'Er, – Crabby B. She'd better, that's all. I can tell you . . .'

We didn't quite know what the matter was, in spite of his meaning looks. Then he threw down his pen, said; 'Sod it all,' got up, and walked to the door.

'And where are you going, young man, may I ask?' said Crabby with her awful leer.

Spadge paused and looked her straight in the eye.

'If it's any business of yourn.'

We shivered with pleasure at this defiance. Spadge leisurely made for the door.

'Sit down this instant!' Crabby suddenly screamed. 'I won't have it!'

'Ta-ta,' said Spadge.

Then Crabby sprang like a yellow cat, spitting and clawing with rage. She caught Spadge in the doorway and fell upon him. There was a shameful moment of heavy breathing and scuffling, while the teacher tore at his clothes. Spadge caught her hands in his great red fists and held her at arm's length, struggling.

'Come and help me, someone!' wailed Crabby, demented. But nobody moved; we just watched. We saw Spadge lift her up and place her on the top of the cupboard, then walk out of the door and away. There was a moment of silence, then we all laid down our pens and began to stamp on the floor in unison. Crabby stayed where she was, on top of the cupboard, drumming her heels and weeping.

We expected some terrible retribution to follow, but nothing happened at all. Not even the trouble-spark, Spadge, was called to account – he was simply left alone. From that day Crabby never spoke to him, or crossed his path, or denied him anything at all. He perched idly in his desk, his knees up to his chin, whistling in a world of his own. Sometimes Miss B would consider him narrowly and if he caught her glance he just winked. Otherwise he was free to come and go, and to take time off as he pleased.

But we never rebelled again; things changed. Crabby B was replaced by a new Head Teacher – a certain Miss Wardley from Birmingham. This lady was something quite new in our lives. She wore sharp glass jewellery which winked as she walked, and she sounded her 'gees' like gongs. But she was fond of singing and she was fond of birds, and she encouraged us in the study of both. She was more sober than Crabby, her reins looser but stronger; and after the first hilarity of her arrival and strangeness, we accepted her proper authority.

Not that she approved very much of me. 'Fat-and-Lazy' was the name she called me. After my midday dinner of baked cabbage and bread I would often nod off in my desk. 'Wake up!' she would cry, cracking my head with a ruler, 'you and your little red eyes!' She also took exception to my steady sniff, which to me came as natural as breathing. 'Go out into the road and have a good blow, and don't come back till you're clear.' But I wouldn't blow, not for anyone on earth, especially if ordered to do so: so I'd sit out on the wall, indignant and thunderous, and sniff away louder than ever. I wouldn't budge either, or come back in, till a boy was sent to fetch me. Miss Wardley would greet me with freezing brightness. 'A little less beastly now? How about bringing a hanky tomorrow? I'm sure we'd all be grateful.' I'd sit and scowl, then forget to scowl, and would soon be asleep again . . .

My brothers, by this time, were all with me at school. Jack, already the accepted genius, was long past our scope or help. It was agreed that his brains were of such distinction that they absolved him from mortal contacts. So he was left in a corner where his flashes of brilliance kept him twinkling away like a pin-table. Young Tony came last, but he again was different, being impervious either to learning or authority, importing moreover a kind of outrageous cheekiness so inspired that it remained unanswerable. He would sit all day picking holes in blotting paper, his large eyes deep and knowing, his quick tongue scandalous, his wit defiant, his will set against all instruction. There was nothing anyone could do about him, except to yelp at the things he said.

I alone, the drowsy middleman of these two, found it hard to win Miss Wardley's approval. I achieved this in the end by writing long faked essays on the lives and habits of otters. I'd never seen an otter, or even gone to look for one, but the essays took her in. They were read out aloud, and even earned me medals, but that's nothing to boast about.

Our village school was poor and crowded, but in the end I relished it. It had a lively reek of steaming life: boys' boots, girls hair, stoves and sweat, blue ink, white chalk, and shavings. We learned nothing abstract or tenuous there – just simple patterns of facts and letters, portable tricks of calculation, no more than was needed to measure a shed, write out a bill, read a swine-disease warning. Through the dead hours of the morning, through the long afternoons, we chanted away at our tables. Passers-by could hear our rising voices in our bottled-up room on the bank; 'Twelve-inches-one-foot. Three-feet-make-a-yard. Fourteen-pounds-make-a-stone. Eight-stone-a-hundred-weight.' We absorbed these figures as primal truths declared by some ultimate power. Unhearing, unquestioning, we rocked to our chanting, hammering the gold nails home. 'Twice-two-are-four. One-God-is-Love. One-Lord-is-King. One-King-is-George. One-George-is-Fifth ...' So it was always; had been, would be for ever; we asked no questions; we didn't hear what we said; yet neither did we ever forget it.

So do I now, through the reiterations of those days, recall that schoolroom which I scarcely noticed – Miss Wardley in glory on her high desk throne, her long throat tinkling with glass. The bubbling stove with its chink of red fire; the old world map as dark as tea; dead field-flowers in jars on the windowsills; the cupboard yawning with dog-eared books. Then the boys and the girls, the dwarfs and the cripples; the slow fat ones and the quick boney ones; giants and louts, angels and squinters – Walt Kerry, Bill Timbrell, Spadge Hopkins, Clergy Green, the Ballingers and Browns, Betty Gleed, Clarry Hogg, Sam and Sixpence, Poppy and Jo – we were ugly and beautiful, scrofulous, warted, ringwormed, and scabbed at the knees, we were noisy, crude, intolerant, cruel, stupid, and superstitious. But we moved together out of the clutch of the Fates, inhabitors of a world without doom; with a scratching, licking and chewing of pens, a whisper and passing of jokes, a titter of tickling, a grumble of labour, a vague stare at the wall in a dream . . .

'Oh, miss, please miss, can I go round the back?'

An unwilling nod permits me. I stamp out noisily into a swoop of fresh air and a musical surge of birds. All around me now is the free green world, with Mrs Birt hanging out her washing. I take stock of myself for a moment, alone. I hear the schoolroom's beehive hum. Of course I don't really belong to that lot at all; I know I'm something special, a young king perhaps placed secretly here in order to mix with the commoners. There is clearly a mystery about my birth, I feel so unique and majestic. One day, I know, the secret will be told. A coach with footmen will appear suddenly at our cottage, and Mother (my mother?) will weep. The family will stand vey solemn and respectful, and I shall drive off to take up my throne. I'll be generous, of course, not proud at all; for my brothers there shall be no dungeons. Rather will I feed them on cakes and jellies, and I'll provide all my sisters with princes. Sovereign mercy shall be their portion, little though they deserve it . . .

I return to the school room and Miss Wardley scowls (she shall curtsy when I am king). But all this is forgotten when Walt Kerry leans over and demands the results of my sums. 'Yes, Walt. Of course, Walt. Here, copy them out. They ain't hard – I done 'em all.' He takes them, the bully, as his tributary right, and I'm proud enough to give them. The little Jim Fern, sitting beside me, looks up from his ruined pages. 'Ain't you a good scholar! You and your Jack. I wish I was a good scholar like thee.' He gives me a sad, adoring look, and I begin to feel much better.

Playtime comes and we charge outdoors, releasing our steamed-up cries. Somebody punches a head. Somebody bloodies their knees. Boys cluster together like bees. 'Let's go round the back then, shall us, eh?' To the dark narrow alley, rich with our mysteries, we make our clattering way. Over the wall is the girl's own place, quite close, and we shout them greetings.

'I 'eard you, Bill Timbrell! I 'eard what you said! You be careful, I'll tell our teacher!'

Flushed and refreshed, we stream back to our playground, whistling, indivisibly male.

'D'you 'ear what I said then? Did you then, eh? I told 'em! They 'alf didn't squeal!'

We all double up; we can't speak for laughing, we can't laugh without hitting each other.

Miss Wardley was patient, but we weren't very bright. Our books showed a squalor of blots and scratches as though monkeys were being taught to write. We sang in sweet choirs, and drew like cavemen, but most other faculties escaped us. Apart from poetry, of course, which gave no trouble at all. I can remember Miss Wardley, with her squeaking chalk, scrawling the blackboard like a shopping list:

'Write a poem – which must scan – on one or more of the following; A Kitten. Fairies. My Holidays. An Old Tinker. Charity. Sea Wrack . . .' ('What's that, miss?')

But it was easy in those days, one wrote a dozen an hour, one simply didn't hesitate, just began at the beginning and worked steadily through the subjects, ticking them off with indefatigable rhymes.

Sometimes there was a beating, which nobody minded – except an occasional red-faced mother. Sometimes a man came and took out our teeth. ('My mum says you ain't to take out any double-'uns . . .' '. . . Fourteen, fifteen, sixteen, seventeen . . .' 'Is they all double-'uns?' 'Shut up, you little horror.') Sometimes the Squire would pay us a visit, hand out prizes, and make a misty-eyed speech. Sometimes an Inspector arrived on a bicycle and counted our heads and departed. Meanwhile Miss Wardley moved jingling amongst us, instructing, appealing, despairing:

'You're a grub, Walter Kerry. You have the wits of a hen. You're a great hulking lout of an oaf. You can just stay behind and do it over again. You can all stay behind, the lot of you.'

When lessons grew too tiresome, or too insoluble, we had our traditional ways of avoiding them.

'Please, miss, I got to stay 'ome tomorrow, to 'elp with the washing – the pigs – me dad's sick.'

'I dunno, miss; you never learned us that.'

'I 'ad me book stole, miss. Carry Burdock pinched it.'

'Please, miss, I got a gurt 'eadache.'

Sometimes these worked, sometimes they didn't. But once, when some tests hung over our heads, a group of us boys evaded them entirely by stinging our hands with horseflies. The task took all day, but the results were spectacular – our hands swelled like elephants' trunks. ''Twas a swarm, please, miss. They set on us. We run, but they stung us awful.' I remember how we groaned, and that we couldn't hold our pens, but I don't remember the pain.

At other times, of course, we forged notes from our mothers, or made ourselves sick with berries, or claimed to be relations of the corpse at funerals (the churchyard lay only next door). It was easy to start wailing when the hearse passed by, 'It's my aunty, miss – it's my cousin Wilf – can I go miss, please miss, can I?'

Many a lone coffin was followed to its grave by a straggle of long—faced children, pinched, solemn, raggedly dressed, all strangers to the astonished bereaved.

So our school work was done – or where would we be today? We would be as we are; watching a loom or driving a tractor, and counting in images of fives and tens. This was as much as we seemed to need, and Miss Wardley did not add to the burden. What we learned in her care were the less formal truths – the names of flowers, the habits of birds, the intimacy of objects in being set to draw them, the treacherous innocence of boys, the sly charm of girls, the idiot's soaring fancies, and the tongue-tied dunce's informed authority when it came to talking about stoats. We were as merciless and cruel as most primitives are. But we learned at that school the private nature of cruelty; and our inborn hatred for freaks and outcasts was tempered by meeting them daily.

There was Nick and Edna from up near the Cross, the children of that brother and sister – the boy was strong and the girl was beautiful, and it was not at school that we learned to condemn them. And there was the gipsy boy Rosso, who lived up the quarry where his tribe had encamped for the summer. He had a chocolate-smooth face and crisp black curls, and at first we cold-shouldered him. He was a real outsider (they ate snails, it was said) and his slant Indian eyes repelled us. Then one day, out of hunger, he stole some sandwiches and was given the cane by Miss Wardley. Whatever the rights and wrongs of the case, that made him one of us.

We saw him run out of school, grizzling from the beating, and kneel down to tie up his boots. The shopkeeper's wife, passing by at that moment, stopped to preach him a little sermon. 'You didn't have to steal, even if you was that hungry. Why didn't you come to me?' The boy gave her a look, picked himself up, and ran off without a word. He knew, as we did, the answer to that one: we set our dogs on the gipsies here. As we walked back home to our cabbage dinners we were all of us filled with compassion. We pictured poor Rosso climbing back to his quarry, hungry to his miserable tents, with nothing but mud and puddles to sit in and the sour banks to scavenge for food. Gipsies no longer seemed either sinister or strange. No wonder they eat snails, we thought.

The narrow school was just a conveyor belt along which the short years drew us. We entered the door marked 'Infants', moved gradually to the other, and were then handed back to the world. Lucky, lucky point of time; our eyes were on it always. Meanwhile we had moved to grander desks, saw our juniors multiplying in number, Miss Wardley suddenly began to ask our advice and to spoil us as though we were dying. There was no more to be done, no more to be learned. We began to look round the schoolroom with nostalgia and impatience. During playtime in the road we walked about gravely, patronizing the younger creatures. No longer the trembling, white-faced battles, the flights, the buttering-up of bullies; just a punch here and there to show our authority, then a sober stroll with our peers.

At last Miss Wardley was wringing our hands, tender and deferential. 'Goodbye, old chaps, and jolly good luck! Don't forget to come back and see me.' She gave each one of us a coy sad glance. She knew that we never would.

4

The Kitchen

Our house, and our life in it, is something of which I still constantly dream, helplessly bidden, night after night, to return to its tranquillity and nightmares: to the heavy shadows of its stone-walled rooms creviced between bank and yew trees, to its boarded ceilings and gaping mattresses, its blood-shot geranium windows, its smells of damp pepper and mushroom growths, its chaos, and rule of women.

We boys never knew any male authority. My father left us when I was three, and apart from some rare and fugitive visits he did not live with us again. He was a knowing, brisk, elusive man, the son and the grandson of sailors, but having himself no stomach for the sea he had determined to make good on land. In his miniature way he succeeded in this. He became, while still in his middle teens, a grocer's assistant, a local church organist, an expert photographer, and a dandy. Certain portraits he took of himself at that time show a handsome though threadbare lad, tall and slender, and much addicted to gloves, high-collars, and courtly poses. He was clearly a cut above the average, in charms as well as ambition. By the age of twenty he had married the beautiful daughter of a local merchant, and she bore him eight children – of whom five survived – before dying herself still young. Then he married his housekeeper, who bore him four more, three surviving, of which I was one. At the time of this second marriage he was still a grocer's assistant, and earning nineteen shillings a week. But his dearest wish was to become a Civil Servant, and he studied each night to this end. The First World War gave him the chance he wanted, and though properly distrustful of arms and battle he instantly sacrificed both himself and his family, applied for a post in the Army Pay Corps, went off to Greenwich in a bullet-proof vest, and never permanently lived with us again.

He was a natural fixer, my father was, and things worked out pretty smoothly. He survived his clerk-stool war with a War Office pension (for nervous rash, I believe), then entered the Civil Service, as he had planned to do, and settled in London for good. Thus enabling my Mother to raise both his families, which she did out of love and pity, out of unreasoning loyalty and a fixed belief that he would one day return to her . . .

Meanwhile, we lived where he had left us; a relic of his provincial youth; a sprawling, cumbersome, countrified brood too incongruous to carry with him. He sent us money and we grew up without him; and I, for one, scarcely missed him. I was perfectly content in this world of women, muddle-headed though it might be, to be bullied and tumbled through the hand-to-mouth days, patched or dressed-up, scolded, admired, swept off my feet in sudden passions of kisses, or dumped forgotten among the unwashed pots.

My three half-sisters shared much of Mother's burden, and were the good fortune of our lives. Generous, indulgent, warm-blooded, and dotty, these girls were not hard to admire. They seemed wrapped as it were in a perpetual bloom, the glamour of their grown-up teens, and expressed for us boys all that women should be in beauty, style, and artifice.

For there was no doubt at all about their beauty, or the naturalness with which they wore it. Marjorie, the eldest, a blonde Aphrodite, appeared quite unconscious of the rarity of herself, moving always to measures of oblivious grace and wearing her beauty like a kind of sleep. She was tall, long-haired, and dreamily gentle, and her voice was low and slow. I never knew her to lose her temper, or to claim any personal justice. But I knew her to weep, usually for others, quietly, with large blue tears. She was a natural mother, and skilled with her needle, making clothes for us all when needed. With her constant beauty and balanced nature she was the tranquil night-light of our fears, a steady flame reassuring always, whose very shadows seemed thrown for our comfort.

Dorothy, the next one, was a wispy imp, pretty and perilous as a firework. Compounded equally of curiosity and cheek, a spark and tinder for boys, her quick dark body seemed writ with warnings that her admirers did well to observe. 'Not to be held in the hand,' it said. 'Light the touch-paper, but retire immediately.' She was an active forager who lived on thrills, provoked adventure, and brought home gossip. Marjorie's were the ears to which most of it came, making her pause in her sewing, open wide her eyes, and shake her head at each new revelation. 'You don't mean it, Doth! He *never*! No! . . .' was all I seemed ever to hear.

Dorothy was as agile as a jungle cat, quick-limbed, entrancing, noisy. And she protected us boys with fire and spirit, and brought us treasures from the outside world. When I think of her now she is a coil of smoke, a giggling splutter, a reek of cordite. In repose she was also something else: a fairy-tale girl, blue as a plum, tender, and sentimental.

The youngest of the three was cool, quiet Phyllis, a tobacco-haired, fragile girl, who carried her good looks with an air of apology, being the junior and somewhat shadowed. Marjorie and Dorothy shared a natural intimacy, being closer together in age, so Phyllis was the odd one, an unclassified solitary, compelled to her own devices. This she endured with a modest simplicity, quick to admire and slow to complain. Her favourite chore was putting us boys to bed, when she emerged in a strange light of her own, revealing a devout almost old-fashioned watchfulness, and gravely singing us to sleep with hymns.

Sad Phyllis, lit by a summer night, her tangled hair aglow, quietly sitting beside our beds, hands folded, eyes far away, singing and singing of 'Happy Eden' alone with her care over us – how often to this did I drop into sleep, feel the warmth of its tide engulf me, steered by her young hoarse hymning voice and tuneless reveries . . .

These half-sisters I cherished; and apart from them I had two half-brothers also. Reggie, the first-born, lived apart with his grandmother; but young Harold, he lived with us. Harold was handsome, bony, and secretive, and he loved our absent father. He stood somewhat apart, laughed down his nose, and was unhappy more often than not. Though younger than the girls, he seemed a generation older, was clever with his hands, but lost.

My own true brothers were Jack and Tony, and we three came at the end of the line. We were of Dad's second marriage, before he flew, and were born within the space of four years. Jack was the eldest, Tony the youngest, and myself the protected centre. Jack was the sharp one, bright as a knife, and was also my close companion. We played together, fought and ratted, built a private structure around us, shared the same bed till I finally left home, and lived off each other's brains. Tony, the baby – strange and beautiful waif – was a brooding, imaginative solitary. Like Phyllis he suffered from being the odd one of three; worse still, he was the odd one of seven. He was always either running to keep up with the rest of us or sitting alone in the mud. His curious, crooked, suffering face had at times the radiance of a saint, at others the blank watchfulness of an insect. He could walk by himself or keep very still, get lost or appear at wrong moments. He drew like an artist, wouldn't read or write, swallowed beads by the boxful, sang and danced, was quite without fear, had secret friends, and was prey to terrible nightmares. Tony was the one true visionary amongst us, the tiny hermit no one quite understood . . .

With our Mother, then, we made eight in that cottage and disposed of its three large floors. There was the huge white attic which ran the length of the house, where the girls slept on fat striped mattresses; an ancient, plaster-crumbling room whose sloping ceilings bulged like tent-cloths. The roof was so thin that rain and bats filtered through, and you could hear a bird land on the tiles. Mother and Tony shared a bedroom below; Jack, Harold, and I the other. But the house, since its building, had been so patched and parcelled that it was now almost impossible to get to one's room without first passing through someone else's. So each night saw a procession of pallid ghosts, sleepily seeking their beds, till the candle-snuffed darkness laid us out in rows, filed away in our allotted sheets, while snores and whistles shook the old house like a roundabout getting up steam.

But our waking life, and our growing years, were for the most part spent in the kitchen, and until we married, or ran away, it was the common room we shared. Here we lived and fed in a family fug, not minding the little space, trod on each other like birds in a hole, elbowed our ways without spite, all talking at once or all silent at once, or crying against each other, but never I think feeling overcrowded, being as separate as notes in a scale.

That kitchen, worn by our boots and lives, was scruffy, warm, and low, whose fuss of furniture seemed never the same but was shuffled around each day. A black grate crackled with coal and beech-twigs; towels toasted on the guard; the mantel was littered with fine old china, horse brasses, and freak potatoes. On the floor were strips of muddy matting, the windows were choked with plants, the walls supported stopped clocks and calendars, and smoky fungus ran over the ceilings. There were also six tables of different sizes, some armchairs gapingly stuffed, boxes, stools, and unravelling baskets, books and papers on every chair, a sofa for cats, a harmonium for coats, and a piano for dust and photographs. These were the shapes of our kitchen landscape, the rocks of our submarine life, each object worn smooth by our constant nuzzling, or encrusted by lively barnacles, relics of birthdays and dead relations, wrecks of furniture long since foundered, all silted deep by Mother's newspapers which the years piled round on the floor.

Waking up in the morning I saw squirrels in the yew trees nibbling at the moist red berries. Between the trees and the window hung a cloud of gold air composed of floating seeds and spiders. Farmers called to their cows on the other side of the valley and moorhens piped from the ponds. Brother Jack, as always, was the first to move, while I pulled on my boots in bed. We both stood at last on the bare-wood floor scratching and saying our prayers. Too stiff and manly to say them out loud, we stood back to back and muttered them, and if an audible plea should slip out by chance one just burst into song to cover it.

Singing and whistling were useful face-savers, especially when confounded by argument. We used the trick readily, one might say monotonously, and this morning it was Jack who began it.

'What's the name of the King, then?' he said, groping for his trousers.

'Albert.'

'No, it's not. It's George.'

'That's what I said you, didn't I? George.'

'No you never. You don't know. You're feeble.'

'Not so feeble as you be, any road.'

'You're balmy. You got brains of a bed-bug.'

'Da-da-di-da-da.'

'I said you're brainless. You can't even count.'

'Turrelee-turrelee . . . Didn't hear you.'

'Yes you did then, blockhead. Fat and lazy. Big faa –'

'Dum-di-dah! . . . Can't hear . . . Hey nonnie! . . .'

Well, that was all right; honours even, as usual. We broke the sleep from our eyes and dressed quickly.

Walking downstairs there was a smell of floorboards, of rags, sour lemons, old spices. The smoky kitchen was in its morning muddle, from which breakfast would presently emerge. Mother stirred the porridge in a soot-black pot. Tony was carving bread with a ruler, the girls in their mackintoshes were laying the table, and the cats were eating the butter. I cleaned some boots and pumped up some fresh water; Jack went for a jug of skimmed milk.

'I'm all behind,' Mother said to the fire. 'This wretched coal's all slack.'

She snatched up an oil-can and threw it all on the fire. A belch of flame roared up the chimney. Mother gave a loud scream, as she always did, and went on stirring the porridge.

'If only I had a proper stove,' she said. 'It's a trial getting you off each day.'

I sprinkled some sugar on a slice of bread and bolted it down while I could. How different again looked the kitchen this morning, swirling with smoke and sunlight. Some cut-glass vases threw jagged rainbows across the piano's field of dust, while Father in his pince-nez up on the wall looked down like a scandalized god.

At last the porridge was dabbed on our plates from a thick and steaming spoon. I covered the smoky lumps with treacle and began to eat from the sides to the middle. The girls round the table chewed moonishly, wrapped in their morning stupor. Still sick with sleep, their mouths moved slow, hung slack while their spoons came up; then they paused for a moment, spoon to lip, collected their wits, and ate. Their vacant eyes stared straight before them, glazed at the sight of the day. Pink and glowing from their dreamy beds, from who knows what arms of heroes, they seemed like mute spirits hauled back to the earth after paradise feasts of love.

'Golly!' cried Doth. 'Have you seen the time?'

They began to jump to their feet.

'Goodness, it's late.'

'I got to be off.'

'Me too.'

'Lord, where's my things?'

'Well, ta-ta Ma; ta boys – be good.'

'Anything you want up from the Stores . . .?'

They hitched up their stockings, patted their hats, and went running up the bank. This was the hour when walkers and bicyclists flowed down the long hills to Stroud, when the hooters called through the morning dews and factories puffed out their plumes. From each crooked corner of Stroud's five valleys girls were running to shops and looms, with sleep in their eyes, and eggy cheeks, and in their ears night voices fading. Marjorie was off to her Milliners' Store, Phyllis to her Boots-and-Shoes, Dorothy to her job as junior clerk in a decayed cloth-mill by a stream. As for Harold, he'd started work already, his day began at six, when he'd leave the house with an angry shout for the lathe-work he really loved.

But what should we boys do, now they had all gone? If it was school-time, we pushed off next. If not, we dodged up the bank to play, ran snail races along the walls, or dug in the garden and found potatoes and cooked them in tins on the rubbish heap. We were always hungry, always calling for food, always seeking it in cupboards and hedges. But holiday mornings were a time of risk, there might be housework or errands to do. Mother would be ironing, or tidying-up, or reading books on the floor. So if we hung around the yard we kept our ears cocked; if she caught us, the game was up.

'Ah, there you are, son. I'm needing some salt. Pop to Vick's for a lump, there's a dear.'

Or: 'See if Granny Trill's got a screw of tea – only ask her nicely, mind.'

Or: 'Run up to Miss Turk and try to borrow half-crown; I didn't know I'd got so low.'

'Ask our Jack, our Mother! I borrowed the bacon. It's blummin'-well his turn now.'

But Jack had slid off like an eel through the grass, making his sly get-away as usual. He was jumpy, shifty, and quick off the mark, an electric flex of nerves, skinny compared with the rest of us, or what farmers might call a 'poor doer'. If they had, in fact, they would have been quite wrong, for Jack did himself very well. He had developed a mealtime strategy which ensured that he ate for two. Speed and guile were the keys to his success, and we hungry ones called him The Slider.

Jack ate against time, that was really his secret; and in our house you had to do it. Imagine us all sitting down to dinner; eight round a pot of stew. It was lentil stew usually, a heavy brown mash made apparently of plastic studs. Though it smelt of hot stables, we were used to it, and it was filling enough – could you get it. But the size of our family outstripped the size of the pot, so there was never quite enough to go round.

When it came to serving, Mother had no method, not even the law of chance – a dab on each plate in any old order and then every man for himself. No grace, no warning, no starting-gun; but the first to finish what he'd had on his plate could claim what was left in the pot. Mother's swooping spoon was breathlessly watched – let the lentils fall where they may. But starving Jack had worked it all out, he followed the spoon with his plate. Absentmindedly Mother would give him first dollop, and very often a second, and as soon as he got it he swallowed it whole, not using his teeth at all. 'More please, I've finished' – the bare plate proved it, so he got the pot-scrapings too. Many the race I've lost to him thus, being just that second slower. But it left me marked with an ugly scar, a twisted, food-crazed nature, so that still I am calling for whole rice puddings and big pots of stew in the night.

The day was over and we had used it, running errands or prowling the fields. When evening came we returned to the kitchen, back to its smoky comfort, in from the rapidly cooling air to its wrappings of warmth and cooking. We boys came first, scuffling down the bank, singly, like homing crows. Long tongues of shadows licked the curves of the fields and the trees turned plump and still. I had been off to Painswick to pay the rates, running fast through the long wet grass, and now I was back, panting hard, the job finished, with hay seeds stuck to my legs. A plate of blue smoke hung above our chimney, flat in the motionless air, and every stone in the path as I ran down home shook my bones with arriving joy.

We chopped wood for the night and carried it in; dry beech sticks as brittle as candy. The baker came down with a basket of bread slung carelessly over his shoulder. Eight quartern loaves, cottage-size, black-crusted, were handed in at the door. A few crisp flakes of pungent crust still clung to his empty basket, so we scooped them up on our spit-wet fingers and laid them upon our tongues. The twilight gathered, the baker shouted good-night, and whistled his way up the bank. Up in the road his black horse waited, the cart lamps smoking red.

Indoors, our Mother was cooking pancakes, her face aglow from the fire. There was a smell of sharp lemon and salty batter, and a burning hiss of oil. The kitchen was dark and convulsive with shadows, no lights had yet been lit. Flames leapt, subsided, corners woke and died, fires burned in a thousand brasses.

'Poke around for the matches, dear boy,' said Mother. 'Damn me if I know where they got to.'

We lit the candles and set them about, each in its proper order: two on the mantelpiece, one on the piano, and one on a plate in the window. Each candle suspended a ball of light, a luminous fragile glow, which swelled and contracted to the spluttering wick or leaned to the moving air. Their flames pushed weakly against the red of the fire, too tenuous to make much headway, revealing our faces more by casts of darkness than by any clear light they threw.

Next we filled and lit the tall iron lamp and placed it on the table. When the wick had warmed and was drawing properly, we turned it up full strength. The flame in the funnel then sprang alive and rose like a pointed flower, began to sing and shudder and grow more radiant, throwing pools of light on the ceiling. Even so, the kitchen remained mostly in shadow, its walls a voluptuous gloom.

The time had come for my violin practice. I began twanging the strings with relish. Mother was still frying and rolling up pancakes; my brothers lowered their heads and sighed. I propped my music on the mantelpiece and sliced through a Russian Dance while sweet smells of resin mixed with lemon and fat as the dust flew in clouds from my bow. Now and then I got a note just right, and then Mother would throw me a glance. A glance of piercing, anxious encouragement as she side-stepped my swinging arm. Plump in her slippers, one hand to her cheek, her pan beating time in the other, her hair falling down about her ears, mouth working to help out the tune – old and tired though she was, her eyes were a girl's, and it was for looks such as these that I played.

'Splendid!' she cried. 'Top-hole! Clap-clap! Now give us another, me lad.'

So I slashed away at 'William Tell', and when I did that, plates jumped; and Mother skipped gaily around the hearth-rug, and even Tony rocked a bit in his chair.

Meanwhile Jack had cleared some boots from the table, and started his inscrutable homework. Tony, in his corner, began to talk to the cat and play with some fragments of cloth. So with the curtains drawn close and the pancakes coming, we settled down to the evening. When the kettle boiled and the toast was made, we gathered and had our tea. We grabbed and dodged and passed and snatched, and packed our mouths like pelicans.

Mother ate always standing up, tearing crusts off the loaf with her fingers, a hand-to-mouth feeding that expressed her vigilance, like that of a wireless-operator at sea. For most of Mother's attention was fixed on the grate, whose fire must never go out. When it threatened to do so she became seized with hysteria, wailing and wringing her hands, pouring on oil and chopping up chairs in a frenzy to keep it alive. In fact it seldom went out completely, though it was very often ill. But Mother nursed it with skill, banking it up every night and blowing hard on the bars every morning. The state of our fire became as important to us as it must have been to a primitive tribe. When it sulked and sank we were filled with dismay; when it blazed all was well with the world; but if – God save us – it went out altogether, then we were clutched by primeval chills. Then it seemed that the very sun had died, that winter had come for ever, that the wolves of the wilderness were gathering near, and that there was no more hope to look for . . .

But tonight the firelight snapped and crackled, and Mother was in full control. She ruled the range and all its equipment with a tireless, nervous touch. Eating with one hand, she threw on wood with the other, raked the ashes, and heated the oven, put on a kettle, stirred the pot, and spread out some more shirts on the guard. As soon as we boys had finished our tea, we pushed all the crockery aside, piled it up roughly at the far end of the table, and settled down under the lamp. Its light was warm and live around us, a kind of puddle of fire of its own. I set up my book and began to draw. Jack worked at his notes and figures. Tony was playing with some cotton reels, pushing them slowly round the table.

All was silent except Tony's voice, softly muttering his cotton reel story.

'. . . So they come out of this big hole see, and the big chap say fie and said we'll kill 'em see, and the pirates was waiting up 'ere, and they had this gurt cannon and they went bang fire and the big chap fell down wheeee! and rolled back in the 'ole and I said we got 'em and I run up the 'ill and this boat see was comin' and I jumped on board woosh cruump and I said now I'm captain see and they said fie and I took me 'atchet 'ack 'ack and they all fell plop in the sea wallop and I sailed the boat round 'ere and round 'ere and up 'ere and round 'ere and down 'ere and up 'ere and round 'ere and down 'ere . . .'

Now the girls arrived home in their belted mackintoshes, flushed from their walk through the dark, and we looked up from our games and said; 'Got anything for us?' and Dorothy gave us some liquorice. Then they all had their supper at one end of the table while we boys carried on at the other. When supper was over and cleared away, the kitchen fitted us all. We drew together round the evening lamp, the vast and easy time . . . Marjorie began to trim a new hat, Dorothy to write a love-letter, Phyllis sat down with some forks and spoons, blew ah! and sleepily rubbed them. Harold, home late, cleaned his bike in a corner. Mother was cutting up newspapers.

We talked in spurts, in lowered voices, scarcely noticing if anyone answered.

'I turned a shaft to a thou' today,' said Harold.

'A what?'

'He said a "thou".'

Chairs creaked awhile as we thought about it . . .

'Charlie Revell's got a brand new suit. He had it made to fit . . .'

'He half fancies himself.'

'Charlie Revell! . . .'

Pause.

'Look, Doth, I got these bits for sixpence. I'm going to stitch 'em all round the top here.'

'Mmmmm. Well. Tccch-tcch. S'all right . . .'

'Dr Green came up to the shop this morning. Wearing corduroy bloomers. Laugh! . . .'

'Look, Ma, look! I've drawn a church on fire. Look Marge, Doth! Hey, look! . . .'

'If x equals x, then y equals z – shut up! – if x is y . . .'

'O Madeline, if you'll be mine, I'll take you o'er the sea, di-dah . . .'

'Look what I've cut for my scrapbook, girls – a Beefeater – isn't he killing?'

'Charlie Revell cheeked his dad today. He called him a dafty. He . . .'

'. . . You know that boy from the Dairy, Marge – the one they call Barnacle Boots? Well, he asked me to go to Spot's with him. I told him to run off home.'

'No, you never!'

'I certainly did. I said I don't go to no pictures with butter-wallopers. You should have seen his face . . .'

'Harry Lazbury smells of chicken-gah. I had to move me desk.'

'Just hark who's talking. Dainty Dick.'

'I'll never be ready by Sunday . . .'

'I've found a lovely snip for my animal page – an old seal – look girls, the expression! . . .'

'So I went round 'ere, and down round 'ere, and he said fie so I went 'ack, 'ack . . .'

'What couldn't I do to a nice cream slice . . .'

'Charlie Revell's had 'is ears syringed . . .'

'D'you remember, Doth, when we went to Spot's, and they said Children in Arms Not Allowed, and we walked little Tone right up the steps and he wasn't even two . . .'

Marge gave her silky, remembering laugh and looked fondly across at Tony. The fire burned clear with a bottle-green light. Their voices grew low and furry. A farm-dog barked far across the valley, fixing the time and distance exactly. Warned by the dog and some hooting owls, I could sense the night valley emptying, stretching in mists of stars and water, growing slowly more secret and late.

The kitchen, warm and murmuring now, vibrated with rosy darkness. My pencil began to wander on the page, my eyes to cloud and clear. I thought I'd stretch myself on the sofa – for a while, for a short while only. The girls' muted chatter went on and on; I struggled to catch the drift. 'Sh! . . . Not now . . . When the boys are in bed . . . You'll die when you hear . . . Not now . . .'

The boards on the ceiling were melting like water. Words broke and went floating away. Chords of smooth music surged up in my head, thick tides of warmth overwhelmed me, I was drowning in languors of feathered seas, spiralling cosily down . . .

Once in a while I was gently roused to a sound amplified by sleep; to the fall of a coal, the sneeze of the cat, or a muted exclamation. 'She couldn't have done such a thing . . . She did . . .' 'Done what? . . . What thing? . . . Tell, tell me . . .' But helpless I glided back to sleep, deep in the creviced seas, the blind waters stilled me, weighed me down, the girls' words floated on top. I lay longer now, and deeper far; heavier weeds were falling on me . . .

'Come on, Loll. Time to go to bed. The boys went up long ago.' The whispering girls bent over me; the kitchen returned upside down. 'Wake up, lamb . . . He's whacked to the wide. Let's try and carry him up.'

Half-waking, half-carried, they got me upstairs. I felt drunk and tattered with dreams. They dragged me stumbling round the bend in the landing, and then I smelt the sweet blankets of bed.

It was cold in the bedroom; there were no fires here. Jack lay open-mouthed, asleep. Shivering, I swayed while the girls undressed me, giggling around my buttons. They left me my shirt and my woollen socks, then stuffed me between the sheets.

Away went the candle down the stairs, boards creaked and the kitchen door shut. Darkness. Shapes returning slow. The window a square of silver. My bed-half was cold – Jack hot as a bird. For a while I lay doubled, teeth-chattering, blowing, warming against him slowly.

'Keep yer knees to yerself,' said Jack, turning over. He woke. 'Say, think of a number!'

''Leven-hundered and two,' I groaned, in a trance.

'Double it,' he hissed in my ear.

Double it ... Twenny-four hundred and what? Can't do it. Something or other ... A dog barked again and swallowed a goose. The kitchen still murmured downstairs. Jack quickly submerged, having fired off his guns, and began snorkling away at my side. Gradually I straightened my rigid limbs and hooked all my fingers together. I felt wide awake now. I thought I'd count to a million. 'One, two ...' I said; that's all.

Grannies in the Wainscot

Our house was seventeenth-century Cotswold, and was handsome as they go. It was built of stone, had hand-carved windows, golden surfaces, moss-flaked tiles, and walls so thick they kept a damp chill inside them whatever the season or weather. Its attics and passages were full of walled-up doors which our fingers longed to open – doors that led to certain echoing chambers now sealed off from us for ever. The place had once been a small country manor, and later a public beerhouse; but it had decayed even further by the time we got to it, and was now three poor cottages in one. The house was shaped like a T, and we lived in the down-stroke. The top-stroke – which bore into the side of the bank like a rusty expended shell – was divided separately among two old ladies, one's portion lying above the other's.

Granny Trill and Granny Wallon were rival ancients and lived on each other's nerves, and their perpetual enmity was like mice in the walls and absorbed much of my early days. With their sickle-bent bodies, pale pink eyes, and wild wisps of hedgerow hair, they looked to me the very images of witches and they were also much alike. In all their time as such close neighbours they never exchanged a word. They communicated instead by means of boots and brooms – jumping on floors and knocking on ceilings. They referred to each other as "Er-Down-Under' and "Er-Up-Atop, the Varmint'; for each to the other was an airy nothing, a local habitation not fit to be named.

'Er-Down-Under, who lived on our level, was perhaps the

smaller of the two, a tiny white shrew who came nibbling through her garden, who clawed squeaking with gossip at our kitchen window, or sat sucking bread in the sun; always mysterious and self-contained and feather-soft in her movements. She had two names, which she changed at will according to the mood of her day. Granny Wallon was her best, and stemmed, we were told, from some distinguished alliance of the past. Behind this crisp and trotting body were certainly rumours of noble blood. But she never spoke of them herself. She was known to have raised a score of children. And she was known to be very poor. She lived on cabbage, bread, and potatoes – but she also made excellent wines.

Granny Wallon's wines were famous in the village, and she spent a large part of her year preparing them. The gathering of the ingredients was the first of the mysteries. At the beginning of April she would go off with her baskets and work round the fields and hedges, and every fine day till the end of summer would find her somewhere out in the valley. One saw her come hobbling home in the evening, bearing her cargoes of crusted flowers, till she had buckets of cowslips, dandelions, elder-blossom crammed into every corner of the house. The elder-flower, drying on her kitchen floor, seemed to cover it with a rancid carpet, a crumbling rime of grey-green blossom fading fast in a dust of summer. Later the tiny grape-cluster of the elderberry itself would be seething in purple vats, with daisies and orchids thrown in to join it, even strands of the dog-rose bush.

What seasons fermented in Granny Wallon's kitchen, what summers were brought to the boil, with limp flower-heads piled around the floor holding fast to their clotted juices – the sharp spiced honey of those cowslips first, then the coppery reeking dandelion, the bitter poppy's whiff of powder, the cat's-breath, death-green elder. Gleanings of days and a dozen pastures, strippings of lanes and hedges – she bore them home to her flag-tiled kitchen, sorted them each from each, built up her fires and loaded her pots, and added her sugar and yeast. The vats boiled daily in suds of sugar, revolving petals in throbbing water, while the air,

aromatic, steamy, embalmed, distilled the hot dews and flowery soups and ran the wine down the dripping walls.

And not only flower-heads went into these brews; the old lady used parsnips, too, potatoes, sloes, crab-apples, quinces, in fact anything she could lay her hands on. Granny Wallon made wine as though demented, out of anything at all; and no doubt, if given enough sugar and yeast, could have made a drink out of a box of old matches.

She never hurried or hoarded her wines, but led them gently through their natural stages. After the boiling they were allowed to settle and to work in the cool of the vats. For several months, using pieces of toast, she scooped off their yeasty sediments. Then she bottled and labelled each liquor in turn and put them away for a year.

At last one was ready, then came the day of distribution. A squeak and a rattle would shake our window, and we'd see the old lady, wispily grinning, waving a large white jug in her hand.

'Hey there, missus! Try this'n, then. It's the first of my last year's cowslip.'

Through the kitchen window she'd fill up our cups and watch us, head cocked, while we drank. The wine in the cups was still and golden, transparent as a pale spring morning. It smelt of ripe grass in some far-away field and its taste was as delicate as air. It seemed so innocent, we would swig away happily and even the youngest guzzled it down. Then a curious rocking would seize the head; tides rose from our feet like a fever, the kitchen walls began to shudder and shift, and we all fell in love with each other.

Very soon we'd be wedged, tight-crammed, in the window, waving our cups for more, while our Mother, bright-eyed, would be mumbling gaily:

'Lord bless you, Granny. Fancy cowsnips and parsney. You must give me the receipt, my dear.'

Granny Wallon would empty the jug in our cups, shake out the last drops on the flowers, then trot off tittering down the garden path, leaving us hugging ourselves in the window.

★

Whatever the small indulgences with which Granny Wallon warmed up her old life, her neighbour, Granny Trill, had none of them. For 'Er-Up-Atop was as frugal as a sparrow and as simple in her ways as a grub. She could sit in her chair for hours without moving, a veil of blackness over her eyes, a suspension like frost on her brittle limbs, with little to show that she lived at all save the gentle motion of her jaws. One of the first things I noticed about old Granny Trill was that she always seemed to be chewing, sliding her folded gums together in a daylong ruminative cud. I took this to be one of the tricks of age, a kind of slowed-up but protracted feasting. I imagined her being delivered a quartern loaf – say, on a Friday night – then packing the lot into her rubbery cheeks and chewing them slowly through the week. In fact, she never ate bread at all – or butter, or meat, or vegetables – she lived entirely on tea and biscuits, and on porridge sent up by the Squire.

Granny Trill had an original sense of time which seemed to obey some vestigial pattern. She breakfasted, for instance, at four in the morning, had dinner at ten, took tea at two-thirty, and was back in her bed at five. This regime never varied either winter or summer, and belonged very likely to her childhood days when she lived in the woods with her father. To me it seemed a monstrous arrangement, upsetting the roots of order. But Granny Trill's time was for God, or the birds, and although she had a clock she kept it simply for the tick, its hands having dropped off years ago.

In contrast to the subterranean, almost cavernous life which Granny Wallon lived down under, Granny Trill's cottage door was always open and her living-room welcomed us daily. Not that she could have avoided us anyway, for she lay at our nimble mercy. Her cottage was just outside our gate and there were geraniums in pots round the door. Her tiny room opened straight on to the bank and was as visible as a last year's bird's-nest. Smells of dry linen and tea-caddies filled it, together with the sweeter tang of old flesh.

'You at home, Granny Trill? You in there, Gran?'

Of course – where else would she be? We heard her creaking sigh from within.

'Well, I'll be bound. That you varmints again?'

'We come on a visit, Gran.'

'Just mind them pots then, or I'll cut you to pieces.'

The three of us clumped indoors. Granny Trill was perched in the windowsill, combing her thin white hair.

'What you doing, Gran?'

'Just biding still. Just biding and combing me bits.'

The room was blue and hazy with woodsmoke. We prowled slowly around its treasures, opening boxes, filling teapots with cotton-reels, skimming plates along the floor. The old lady sat and watched us mildly, taking very little notice, while her dry yellow arm swept up and down, and the black-toothed comb, as it slid through her hair, seemed to be raking the last ash of a fire.

'You going bald, Gran?'

'I still got me bits.'

'It's coming out.'

'No, it ain't.'

'Look at that dead stuff dropping out of yer comb.'

'That's healthy. It makes room for more.'

We didn't think it mattered; it was merely conversation, any subject at all would do. But suddenly the old lady skipped out of her seat and began to leap up and down on the floor.

''Er down there! I got more than 'er! Er's bald as a tater root! Wicked old lump, I'll see 'er gone. 'Er's failing, you mark my words.'

When the spasm was over, she was back in the window, winding her hair into a fragile bun. Beautiful were the motions of her shrunken hands, their movements so long rehearsed; her fingers flew and coiled and pinned, worked blind without aid of a mirror. The result was a structure of tight perfection, a small shining ball of snow.

'Get yer hands from me drawers! Them's female things!'

She sat relaxed now her hair was done, put on her cracked and steel-rimmed glasses, unhooked the almanac from the wall, and began to read bits out aloud. She read in a clear and solemn voice, as though from the Holy Writ.

'"Tragic Intelligence of a Disaster at Sea, in the Region of the Antipoods." That's for June, poor creatures, with their families an' all. "A party of Scientists Will Slip Down a Crevice, With Certain Resultant Fatalities ..." Oh, dear, oh well, if they must poke round them places. "A Murdered Cadaver will be Shockingly Uncovered in a Western Industrial Town." There, what did I tell you! I knew that'd come. I been expecting that.' She began to skip pages, running through the months, but giving weight to the Warnings that struck her. '"Crisis in Parliament" ... "House Struck by Fireball" ... "Riots" ... "A Royal Surprise" ... "Turkish Massacre" ... "Famine" ... "War" ... "The King will Suffer a Slight Infirmity" ...' The catalogue of disasters seemed to give her peace, to confirm her sense of order. In Old Moore's pages she saw the future's worst, saw it and was not dismayed. Such alarms were neither threats nor prophecies but simply repetitions; were comforting, frightful, and familiar, being composed of all that had fashioned her long past, the poisoned cuds she had so patiently chewed, swallowed, and yet survived.

'Ah, well,' she said placidly, as she lay down the book. 'He foresees some monstrous doings. A terrible year it looks to be. And he says we'll have hail on Tuesday ...'

We boys took up the almanac and leafed through the pages, seeking the more ominous pictures. We saw drawings of skies cracked across by lightning, of church towers falling, multitudes drowning, of men in frock-coats shaking warning fingers, of coffins laden with crowns. The drawings were crude but jaggedly vital, like scratches on a prison wall. We relished them much as did Granny Trill, as signs of an apocalypse which could not touch us. In them we saw the whole outside world, split, convulsive, and damned. It had nothing, of course, to do with our village; and we felt like gods, both compassionate and cruel, as we savoured these bloody visions.

Granny Trill used the almanac as an appetizer; now she shifted
to her table for dinner. She sopped a few biscuits in a cup of cold
tea and scooped the wet crumbs into her mouth, then began
grinding away with such an effort of gums one would have
thought she was cracking bones. She wore, as usual, her black
net dress, but her bright old head rising out of it looked like a
flame on a smoking lamp. Her brow was noble, her pink eyes
glittered, her nose swooped down like a finger; only the lower
part of her face was collapsed and rubbery, but then that did all
the work.

'You a hundred yet, Granny?'

'Nigh on – nigh on.'

'Have you got a dad?'

'Bless you, no; he died long since. He was killed by a tree over
Ashcomb.'

She often told us the story of this, and now she told us again.
Her father had been a woodcutter, strong as a giant – he could lift
up a horse and wagon. From the age of five, when she lost her
mother, she lived with him in the woods. They used to sleep in a
tent, or a kind of wigwam of pine branches, and while her father
was tree-felling, the little girl made baskets and sold them around
the village. For ten years they lived together and were perfectly
contented. She grew up into a beautiful young girl – 'Some'ow
I seemed to send men breathless' – but her father was careful,
and when the timber-men came he used to hide her under piles of
sacking.

Then one day – she was fifteen years old at the time – a tree fell
on her father. She heard him shout and ran up the thicket and
found him skewered into the ground with a branch. He was lying
face down and couldn't see her. 'I'm going, Alice,' he'd said. She
clawed a hole with her hands and lay down beside him, and held
him until he died. It took twenty-four hours and she never moved,
nor did he speak again.

When at last some carters discovered them, she was still lying
with the body. She watched them roll the tree off him, and

straighten his limbs, then she ran up the Scrubs and hid. She hid for a week near some fox-holes there, and neither ate nor drank. Then the Squire sent out some men to look for her, and when they found her she fought like a savage. But they managed to carry her down to the Manor, where she was given a bath and a bed. 'That was the first bath I ever had,' said Granny. 'It took six of 'em to get me soaped.' But they nursed her and pacified her, and gave her housework to do, and later married her to George Trill, the gardener. 'He were a good man, too – he settled me. I was about sixteen years at the time. He was much like me dad, only a good bit slower – and a lot older than I, of course.'

When she finished her story her chin was resting in her cup and her features were abstracted and bright. Sharp little veins crackled around her eyes, and her skull pushed hard through the skin. Could she ever have been that strapping Alice whom the carters had chased through the woods? a girl of sixteen whom men washed and married? the age of our sister Dorothy? . . .

'Me dad planted that tree,' she said absently, pointing out through the old cracked window.

The great beech filled at least half the sky and shook shadows all over the house. Its roots clutched the slope like a giant hand, holding the hill in place. Its trunk writhed with power, threw off veils of green dust, rose towering into the air, branched into a thousand shaded alleys, became a city for owls and squirrels. I had thought such trees to be as old as the earth, I never dreamed that a man could make them. Yet it was Granny Trill's dad who had planted this tree, had thrust in the seed with his finger. How old must he have been to leave such a mark? Think of Granny's age, and add his on top, and you were back at the beginning of the world.

'He were a young man then, a-course,' said Granny. 'He set it afore he got married.' She squinted up at the height of the tree, and sat there nodding gently, while a branch of green shadows, thrown by its leaves, moved softly across her face.

'I got to see to summat!' she said abruptly, slipping creakily down from her chair. She left us then, gathered up her skirts, and trotted lightly along to the wood. We saw her squatting among the undergrowth, bright-eyed, like a small black partridge. Old age might compel her to live in a house, but for comfort she still went to the woods.

Granny Trill and Granny Wallon were traditional ancients of a kind we won't see today, the last of that dignity of grandmothers to whom age was its own embellishment. The grandmothers of those days dressed for the part in that curious but endearing uniform which is now known to us only through music-hall. And our two old neighbours, when setting forth on errands, always prepared themselves scrupulously so. They wore high laced boots and long muslin dresses, beaded chokers and candlewick shawls, crowned by tall poke bonnets tied with trailing ribbons and smothered with inky sequins. They looked like starlings, flecked with jet, and they walked in a tinkle of darkness.

Those severe and similar old bodies enthralled me when they dressed that way. When I finally became King (I used to think) I would command a parade of grandmas, and drill them, and march them up and down – rank upon rank of hobbling boots, nodding bonnets, flying shawls, and furious chewing faces. They would be gathered from all the towns and villages and brought to my palace in wagon-loads. No more than a monarch's whim, of course, like eating cocoa or drinking jellies; but far more spectacular any day than those usual trudging guardsmen.

In spite of their formal dressing-up, the two old ladies never went very far – now and again to church for the sermon, and to the village shop once a week. Granny Wallon went for her sugar and yeast; Granny Trill for her tuppence of snuff.

Snuff was Granny T's one horrible vice, and she indulged it with no moderation. A fine brown dust coated all her clothes and she had nostrils like badger-holes. She kept her snuff in a small round box, made of tin and worn smooth as a pebble. She was continually tapping and snapping it open, pinching a nailful, gasping *Ah!*, flicking her fingers and wiping her eyes, and leaving on the air a faint dry cloud like an explosion of fungoid dust.

The snuff-box repelled and excited us boys and we opened its lid with awe. Reeking substance of the underworld, clay-brown dust of decay, of powdered flesh and crushed old bones, rust-scrapings, and the rubbish of graves. How sharp and stinging was this fearful spice, eddying up from its box, animating the air with tingling fumes like a secret breath of witchery. Though we clawed and sniffed it we could not enjoy it, but neither could we leave it alone.

'You at me snuff agen, you boys? I'll skin yer bottoms, I will!'

We looked up guiltily, saw her cackling face, so took a big pinch between us. With choking tears and head-rocking convulsions we rolled across the floor. The old lady regarded us with pleasure; our paroxysms shook the house.

'That'll learn you, I reckon; you thieving mites. Here, give it to me, I'll show 'ee.'

She took up the box and tapped the lid, then elegantly fed her nose. A shudder of ecstasy closed her eyes. She was borne very far away.

One morning our Mother was paring apples, so we boys settled down to the peelings. They lay in green coils upon the table, exuding their tart fresh odours. Slowly we chewed through the juicy ribbons, mumbling our jaws as we went.

'I'm old Granny Trill, a-eating her dinner,' said Jack, sucking peel through his gums. A great joke, this; we chewed and moaned, making much of the toothless labour.

'Don't mock,' said our Mother. 'The poor, poor soul – alone by herself all day.'

We glanced at our sisters to share our wit, but got no encouragement there. They were absorbed as usual in some freakish labour, stitching dead birds on canvas hats.

'The poor lone creature,' our Mother went on, lowering her voice out of charity. 'It's a sin and a shame!' She raised it again.

'That's what it is – a crime! You girls ought to pop up and pay her a visit. You know how she dotes on you all.'

Our sisters had reached the impressive stage; they talked careful and dressed in splendour – as fine, that is, as they were able to do with the remnants that fell to their hands. With a short length here, a bit of tulle there, a feather picked up at a sale, a hedgehog of needles, a mouthful of pins, a lot of measuring, snipping, and arguing – it was remarkable what raiment they managed to conjure considering what little they had.

They were always willing to put on a show, so they accepted Mother's suggestion. They decided to deck themselves out in their best and to give Gran Trill a treat. The attics were ransacked, the cupboards breached, and very soon all was uproar. Quarrelling, snatching, but smoothly efficient, they speedily draped themselves; took a tucket in here, let a gusset out there, spliced a waist or strapped up a bodice; in no time at all they were like paradise birds, and off they minced to see the old lady.

Enthralled as ever by their patchwork glories, I followed them closely behind. Beautiful Marge led the way up the path and rapped elegantly on Granny's door. Meanwhile Doth and Phyl hitched their slipping girdles, pushed the bandeaux out of their eyes, stood hands on hips making light conversation – two jazz-debs bright in the sun.

For once Granny Trill seemed hard of hearing, though the girls had knocked three times. So with a charming shrug and a fastidious sigh Marge swung a great kick at the door.

'Who's that?' came a frightened yelp from within.

'It's only us,' trilled the girls.

They waltzed through the door, apparitions of rose, striking postures straight out of *Home Notes*. 'How do we look then, Gran?' asked Marjorie. 'This line is the mode, you know. We copied it out of that pattern book. It's the rage in Stroud, they say.'

Riffling their feathers, arching their necks, catching coy reflections in mirrors, they paraded the room, three leggy flamingoes, each lit by a golden down. To me they were something out of the sky, airborne visions of fairy light; and with all the enthusiasm they were capable of they gave the old lady the works. Yet all was clearly not going well. There was a definite chill in the air . . .

Granny watched them awhile, then her jaws snapped shut; worse still, her gums stopped chewing. Then she clapped her hands with a terrible crack.

'You baggages! You jumped-up varmints! Be off, or I'll fetch me broom!'

The girls retreated at the dainty double, surprised but in no way insulted. Their sense of fashion was unassailable, for were they not up with the times? How could the old girl know about belts and bandeaux? – after all, she was only a peasant . . .

But later Gran Trill took our Mother aside and spoke grimly of her concern.

'You better watch them gels of yourn. They'll bring shame on us one of these days. Strutting and tennis-playing and aping the gentry – it's carnal and blasphemy. Just you watch 'em, missus; I don't like their doings. Humble gels got to remember their stations.'

Mother, I fancy, was half with her there; but she wouldn't have dreamed of interfering.

For several more years the lives of the two old ladies continued to revolve in intimate enmity around each other. Like cold twin stars, linked but divided, they survived by a mutual balance. Both of them reached back similarly in time, shared the same modes and habits, the same sense of feudal order, the same rampaging terrible God. They were far more alike than unalike, and could not abide each other.

They arranged things therefore so that they never met. They used separate paths when they climbed the bank, they shopped on different days, they relieved themselves in different areas, and staggered their church-going hours. But each one knew always what the other was up to, and passionately disapproved. Granny Wallon worked at her flowering vats, boiling and blending her wines; or crawled through her cabbages; or tapped on our windows, gossiped, complained, or sang. Granny Trill continued to rise in the dark, comb her waxen hair, sit out in the wood, chew, sniff, and suck up porridge, and study her almanac. Yet between them they sustained a mutual awareness based solely on ear and nostril. When Granny Wallon's wines boiled, Granny Trill had convulsions; when Granny Trill took snuff, Granny Wallon had strictures – and neither let the other forget it. So all day they listened, sniffed, and pried, rapping on floors and ceilings, and prowled their rooms with hawking coughs, chivvying each other long-range. It was a tranquil, bitter-pleasant life, perfected by years of custom; and to me they both seemed everlasting, deathless crones of an eternal mythology; they had always been somewhere there in the wainscot and I could imagine no world without them.

Then one day, as Granny Trill was clambering out of her wood, she stumbled and broke her hip. She went to bed then for ever. She lay patient and yellow in a calico coat, her combed hair fine as a girl's. She accepted her doom without complaint, as though some giant authority – Squire, father, or God – had ordered her there to receive it.

'I knowed it was coming,' she told our Mother, 'after that visitation. I saw it last week sitting at the foot of me bed. Some person in white; I dunno . . .'

There was a sharp early rap on our window next morning. Granny Wallon was bobbing outside.

'Did you hear him, missus?' she asked knowingly. 'He been a-screeching around since midnight.' The death-bird was Granny Wallon's private pet and messenger, and she gave a skip as she told us about him. 'He called three-a-four times. Up in them yews. Her's going, you mark my words.'

And that day indeed Granny Trill died, whose bones were too old to mend. Like a delicate pale bubble, blown a little higher and further than the other girls of her generation, she had floated just long enough for us to catch sight of her, had hovered for an instant before our eyes; and then had popped suddenly, and disappeared for ever, leaving nothing on the air but a faint-drying image and the tiniest cloud of snuff.

The little church was packed for her funeral, for the old lady had been a landmark. They carried her coffin along the edge of the wood and then drew it on a cart through the village. Granny Wallon, dressed in a shower of jets, followed some distance behind; and during the service she kept to the back of the church and everybody admired her.

All went well till the lowering of the coffin, when there was a sudden and distressing commotion. Granny Wallon, ribbons flying, her bonnet awry, fought her way to the side of the grave.

'It's a lie!' she screeched, pointing down at the coffin.

'That baggage were younger'n me! Ninety-five she says! – ain't more'n ninety, an' I gone on ninety-two! It's a crime you letting 'er go to 'er Maker got up in such brazen lies! Dig up the old devil! Get 'er brass plate off! It's insulting the living church! . . .'

They carried her away, struggling and crying, kicking out with her steel-sprung boots. Her cries grew fainter and were soon obliterated by the sounds of the grave-diggers' spades. The clump of clay falling on Granny Trill's coffin sealed her with her inscription for ever; for no one knew the truth of her age, there was no one old enough to know.

Granny Wallon had triumphed, she had buried her rival; and now there was no more to do. From then on she faded and diminished daily, kept to her house and would not be seen. Sometimes we heard mysterious knocks in the night, rousing and summoning sounds. But the days were silent, no one walked in the garden, or came skipping to claw at our window. The wine fires sank and died in the kitchen, as did the sweet fires of obsession.

About two weeks later, of no special disease, Granny Wallon gave up in her sleep. She was found on her bed, dressed in bonnet and shawl, and her signalling broom in her hand. Her open eyes were fixed on the ceiling in a listening stare of death. There was nothing in fact to keep her alive; no cause, no bite, no fury. 'Er-Down-Under had joined 'Er-Up-Atop, having lived closer than anyone knew.

6

Public Death, Private Murder

Soon after the First World War a violent event took place in the village which drew us together in a web of silence and cut us off for a while almost entirely from the outside world. I was too young at the time to be surprised by it, but I knew those concerned and learned the whole story early. Though it was seldom discussed – and never with strangers – the facts of that night were familiar to us all, and common consent buried the thing down deep and raked out the tracks around it. So bloody, raw, and sudden it was, it resembled an outbreak of family madness which we took pains to conceal, out of shame and pride, and for the sake of those infected.

The crime occurred a few days before Christmas, on a night of deep snow and homecoming; the time when the families called in their strays for an annual feast of goose. The night was as cold as Cotswold cold can be, with a wind coming straight from the Arctic. We children were in bed blowing hard on our knees; wives toasted their feet by the fires; while the men and youths were along at the pub, drinking hot-pokered cider, cutting cards for crib, and watching their wet boots steam.

But few cards were dealt or played that night. An apparition intervened. The door blew open to a gust of snow and a tall man strode into the bar. He seemed to the drinkers both unknown and familiar; he had a sharp tanned face, a nasal twang, and convinced of his welcome he addressed everyone by name, while they lowered their eyes and nodded. Slapping the bar, he ordered drinks all round, and then he began to talk.

Everyone, save the youths, remembered this man; now they studied the change within him. Years ago, as a pale and bony lad, he had been packed off to one of the Colonies, sent by subscription and the prayers of the Church, as many a poor boy before him. Usually they went, and were never heard from again, and their existence was soon forgotten. Now one of them had returned like a gilded ghost, successful and richly dressed, had come back to taunt the stay-at-homes with his boasting talk and money.

He had landed that morning, he said, at Bristol, from an Auckland mutton-boat. The carriage he'd hired had broken down in the snow, so he was finishing his journey on foot. He was on his way to his parents' cottage to give them a Christmas surprise; another mile up the valley, another mile in the snow – he couldn't pass the old pub, now, could he?

He stood feet apart, his back to the bar, displaying himself to the company. Save for his yelping voice, the pub was silent, and the drinkers watched him closely. He'd done pretty well out there, he said, raised cattle, made a heap of money. It was easy enough if you just had the guts and weren't stuck in the bogs like some . . . The old men listened, and the young men watched, with the oil lamps red in their eyes . . .

He sent round more drinks and the men drank them down. He talked of the world and its width and richness. He lectured the old ones for the waste of their lives and the youths for their dumb contentment. They slogged for the Squire and the tenant-farmers for a miserable twelve bob a week. They lived on potatoes and by touching their caps, they hadn't a sovereign to rub between them, they saw not a thing save muck and each other – and perhaps Stroud on a Saturday night. Did they know what he'd done? what he'd seen? what he'd made? His brown face was aglow with whisky. He spread a sheaf of pound notes along the bar and fished a fat gold watch from his pocket. That's nothing, he said, that's only a part of it. They should see his big farm in New Zealand – horses, carriages, meat every day, and he never said 'sir' to no one.

The old men kept silent, but drank their free drinks and

sniggered every so often. The youths in the shadows just gazed at the man, and gazed at his spinning watch, and as he grew more drunk they looked at each other, then stole away one by one . . .

The weather outside had suddenly hardened into a blizzard of cutting snow; the night shut down to the blinding cold and the village curled up in its sheets. When the public house closed and turned down its lamps, the New Zealander was the last to leave. He refused a lantern, said he was born here, wasn't he? and paid for his bill with gold. Then he buttoned his coat, shouted good-night, and strode up the howling valley. Warm with whisky and nearing home, he went singing up the hill. There were those in their beds who heard his last song, pitched wailing against the storm.

When he reached the stone-cross the young men were waiting, a bunched group, heads down in the wind.

'Well, Vincent?' they said; and he stopped, and stopped singing.

They hit him in turn, beat him down to his knees, beat him bloodily down in the snow. They beat and kicked him for the sake of themselves, as he lay there face down, groaning. Then they ripped off his coat, emptied his pockets, threw him over a wall, and left him. He was insensible now from his wounds and the drink; the storm blew all night across him. He didn't stir again from the place where he lay; and in the morning he was found frozen to death.

The police came, of course, but discovered nothing. Their inquiries were met by stares. But the tale spread quickly from mouth to mouth, was deliberately spread amongst us, was given to everyone, man and child, that we might learn each detail and hide it. The police left at last with the case unsolved; but neither we nor they forgot it . . .

About ten years later an old lady lay dying, and towards the end she grew light-headed. The subject of her wandering leaked out somehow: she seemed to be haunted by a watch. 'The watch,' she kept mumbling, 'they maun find the watch. Tell the boy to get it hid.' A dark-suited stranger, with a notebook in his hand, appeared suddenly at her bedside. While she tossed and muttered, he sat and waited, head bent to her whispering mouth. He was patient, anonymous, and never made any fuss; he just sat by her bed all day, his notebook open, his pencil poised, the blank pages like listening ears.

The old lady at last had a lucid moment and saw the stranger sitting beside her. 'Who's this?' she demanded of her hovering daughter. The girl leaned over the bed. 'It's all right, Mother,' said the daughter distinctly. 'It's only a police-station gentleman. He hasn't come to make any trouble. He just wants to hear about the watch.'

The old lady gave the stranger a sharp clear look and uttered not another word; she just leaned back on the pillow, closed her lips and eyes, folded her hands, and died. It was the end of the weakness that had endangered her sons; and the dark-suited stranger knew it. He rose to his feet, put his notebook in his pocket, and tiptoed out of the room. This old and wandering dying mind had been their final chance. No other leads appeared after that, and the case was never solved.

But the young men who had gathered in that winter ambush continued to live among us. I saw them often about the village: simple jokers, hard-working, mild – the solid heads of families. They were not treated as outcasts, nor did they appear to live under any special stain. They belonged to the village and the village looked after them. They are all of them dead now anyway.

Grief or madness were not so private, though they were kept within the village, playing themselves out before our eyes to the accompaniment of lowered voices. There was the case of Miss Flynn, the Ashcomb suicide, a solitary off-beat beauty, whose mute, distressed, life-abandoned image remains with me till this day.

Miss Flynn lived up on the other side of the valley in a cottage which faced the Severn, a cottage whose rows of tinted windows all burst into flame at sundown. She was tall, consumptive, and pale as thistledown, a flock-haired pre-Raphaelite stunner, and she had a small wind-harp which played tunes to itself by swinging in the boughs of her apple trees. On walks with our Mother we often passed that way, and we always looked out for her. When she saw strangers coming she skipped at the sight of them – into her cellar or into their arms. Mother was evasive when we asked questions about her, and said, 'There are others more wicked, poor soul.'

Miss Flynn liked us boys, and gave us apples and stroked our hair with her long yellow fingers. We liked her too, in an eerie way – her skipping, her hair, her harp in the trees, her curious manners of speech. Her beauty for us was also remarkable, there was no one like her in the district; her long, stone-white and tapering face seemed as cool as a churchyard angel.

I remember the last time we passed her cottage, our eyes cocked as usual for her. She was sitting behind the stained-glass window, her face brooding in many colours. Our Mother called brightly; 'Yoo-hoo, Miss Flynn! Are you home? How you keeping, my dear?'

Miss Flynn came out with a skip to the door, stared down at her hands, then at us.

'Such cheeky boys,' I heard her say. 'The image of Morgan they are.' She lifted one knee and pointed her toe. 'I've been bad, Mrs Er,' she said.

She came swaying towards us, twisting her hair with her fingers and looking white as a daylight moon. Our Mother made a clucking, sympathetic sound, and said the west wind was bad for the nerves.

Miss Flynn embraced Tony with a kind of abstract passion and stared hard over our heads at the distance.

'I've been bad, Mrs Er – for the things I must do. It's my mother again, you know. I've been trying to keep her sick spirit from me. She don't let me alone at nights.'

Quite soon we were hurried off down the lane, although we were loath to go. 'The poor, poor soul,' Mother sighed to herself; 'and she half gentry, too . . .'

A few mornings later we were sitting round the kitchen, waiting for Fred Bates to deliver the milk. It must have been a Sunday because the breakfast was spoilt; and on weekdays that didn't matter. Everybody was grumbling; the porridge was burnt, and we hadn't yet had any tea. When Fred came at last he was an hour and a half late, and he had a milk-wet look in his eyes.

'Where were you, Fred Bates?' our sisters demanded; he'd never been late before. He was a thin, scrubby lad in his middle teens, with a head like a bottle-brush. But the cat didn't coil round his legs this morning, and he made no reply to the girls. He just ladled us out our usual jugful and kept sniffing and muttering 'God dammit'.

'What's up then, Fred?' asked Dorothy.

'Ain't nobody told you?' he asked. His voice was hollow, amazed, yet proud, and it made the girls sit up. They dragged him indoors and poured him a cup of tea and forced him to sit down a minute. Then they all gathered round him with gaping eyes, and I could see they had sniffed an occurrence.

At first Fred could only blow hard on his tea and mutter, '*Who'd* a thought it?' But slowly, insidiously, the girls worked on him, and in the end they got his story . . .

He'd been coming from milking; it was early, first light, and he was just passing Jones's pond. He'd stopped for a minute to chuck a stone at a rat – he got tuppence a tail when he caught one. Down by the lily-weeds he suddenly saw something floating. It was spread out white in the water. He'd thought at first it was a dead swan or something, or at least one of Jones's goats. But when he went down closer, he saw, staring up at him, the white drowned face of Miss Flynn. Her long hair was loose – which had made him think of a swan – and she wasn't wearing a stitch of clothes. Her eyes were wide open and she was staring up through the water like somebody gazing through a window. Well, he'd got such a shock he dropped one of his buckets, and the milk ran into the pond. He'd stood there a bit, thinking, 'That's Miss Flynn'; and there was no one but him around. Then he'd run back to the farm and told them about it, and they'd come and fished her out with a hay-rake. He'd not waited to see any more, not he; he'd got his milk to deliver.

Fred sat for a while, sucking his tea, and we gazed at him with wonder. We all knew Fred Bates, we knew him well, and our girls often said he was soppy; yet only two hours ago, and only just down the lane, he'd seen drowned Miss Flynn with no clothes on. Now he seemed to exude a sort of salty sharpness so that we all wished to touch and taste him; and the excited girls tried to hold him back and make him go through his story again. But he finished his tea, sniffed hard, and left us, saying he'd still got his milk-round to do.

The news soon spread around the village, and women began to gather at their gates.

'Have you heard?'

'No. What?'

'About poor Miss Flynn . . . Been and drowned herself down in the pond.'

'You just can't mean it!'

'Yes. Fred Bates found her.'

'Yes – he just been drinking tea in our kitchen.'

'I can't believe it. I only saw her last week.'

'I know: I saw her just yesterday. I said, "Good morning, Miss Flynn"; and she said, "Good morning, Mrs Ayres," – you know, like she always did.'

'But she was down in the town, only Friday it was! I saw her in the Home-and-Colonial.'

'Poor, sad creature – whatever made her do it?'

'Such a lovely face she had.'

'So good to our boys. She was kindness itself. To think of her lying there.'

'She had a bit of a handicap, so they say.'

'You mean about those fellows?'

'No, more'n that.'

'What was it?'

'Ssssh!'

'Well, not everyone knows, of course . . .'

Miss Flynn was drowned. The women looked at me listening. I stole off and ran down the lane. I was dry with excitement and tight with dread; I just wanted to see the pond. A group of villagers, including my sisters, stood gaping down at the water. The pond was flat and green and empty, and a smudge of milk clung to the reeds. I hid in the rushes, hoping not to be seen, and stared at that seething stain. This was the pond that had choked Miss Flynn. Yet strangely, and not by accident. She had come to it naked, alone in the night, and had slipped into it like a bed; she lay down there, and drew the water over her, and drowned quietly away in the reeds. I gazed at the lily roots coiled deep down, at the spongy weeds around them. That's where she lay, a green foot under, still and all night by herself, looking up through the water as though through a window and waiting for Fred to come by. One of my knees began to quiver; it was easy to see her there, her hair floating out and her white eyes open, exactly as Fred Bates had found her. I saw her clearly, slightly magnified, and heard her vague dry voice: 'I've been bad, Mrs Er. It's my mother's spirit. She won't let me bide at night . . .'

The pond was empty. She'd been carried home on a hurdle, and the women had seen to her body. But for me, as long as I can remember, Miss Flynn remained drowned in that pond.

As for Fred Bates, he enjoyed for a day a welcome wherever he went. He repeated his story over and over again and drank cups of tea by the dozen. But his fame turned bad, very suddenly; for a more sinister sequel followed. The very next day, on a visit to Stroud, he saw a man crushed to death by a wagon.

'Twice in two days,' the villagers said. 'He'll see the Devil next.'

Fred Bates was avoided after that. We crossed roads when we saw him coming. No one would speak to him or look him in the eyes, and he wasn't allowed to deliver milk any more. He was sent off instead to work alone in a quarry, and it took him years to re-establish himself.

★

The murder and the drowning were long ago, but to me they still loom large; the sharp death-taste, tooth-edge of violence, the yielding to the water of that despairing beauty, the indignant blood in the snow. They occurred at a time when the village was the world and its happenings all I knew. The village in fact was like a deep-running cave still linked to its antic past, a cave whose shadows were cluttered by spirits and by laws still vaguely ancestral. This cave that we inhabited looked backwards through chambers that led to our ghostly beginnings; and had not, as yet, been tidied up, or scrubbed clean by electric light, or suburbanized by a Victorian church, or papered by cinema screens.

It was something we just had time to inherit, to inherit and dimly know – the blood and beliefs of generations who had been in this valley since the Stone Age. That continuous contact has at last been broken, the deeper caves sealed off for ever. But arriving, as I did, at the end of that age, I caught whiffs of something old as the glaciers. There were ghosts in the stones, in the trees, and the walls, and each field and hill had several. The elder people knew about these things and would refer to them in personal terms, and there were certain landmarks about the valley – tree-clumps, corners in woods – that bore separate, antique, half-muttered names that were certainly older than Christian. The women in their talk still used these names which are not used now any more. There was also a frank and unfearful attitude to death, and an acceptance of violence as a kind of ritual which no one accused or pardoned.

In our grey stone village, especially in winter, such stories never seemed strange. When I sat at home among my talking sisters, or with an old woman sucking her jaws, and heard the long details of hapless suicides, of fighting men loose in the snow, of witch-doomed widows disembowelled by bulls, of child-eating sows, and so on – I would look through the windows and see the wet walls streaming, the black trees bend in the wind, and I saw these things happening as natural convulsions of our landscape, and though dry-mouthed, I was never astonished.

Being so recently born, birth had no meaning; it was the other extreme that enthralled me. Death was absorbing, and I saw much of it; it was my childhood's continuous fare. Somebody else had gone, they had gone in the night, and nobody tried to hide it. Old women, bright-eyed, came carrying the news; the corpse was praised and buried; while Mother and the girls at their kitchen chorus went over the final hours. 'The poor old thing. She fought to the last. She didn't have the strength left in her.' They wept easily, sniffing, and healthily flushed; they could have been mourning the death of a dog.

Winter, of course, was the worst time for the old ones. Then they curled up like salted snails. We called one Sunday on the old Davies couple who lived along by the shop. It had been a cold wet January, a marrow-bone freezer, during which three old folk, on three successive Saturdays, had been carried off to their graves. Mr and Mrs Davies were ancient too, but they had a stubborn air of survival; and they used to watch each other, as I remember, with the calculating looks of card-players. This morning the women began to discuss the funerals, while we boys sat down by the fire. Mrs Davies was jaunty, naming each of the mourners and examining their bills of health. She rocked her white head, shot her husband a glance, and said she wondered who would be next.

The old man listened, fed some sticks to the fire, then knocked out his pipe on his leggings.

'You best fasten the windows, missus,' he said. 'The Old Bugger seems to snatch 'em weekends.'

He wheezed at that, and coughed a bit, then relapsed into a happy silence. His wife considered him brightly for a moment, and then turned with a sigh to our Mother.

'Once you had to run to keep up with him,' she said. 'You can talk to him now all right. He's no longer the way as I remember. The years have slowed him down.'

Her husband just cackled and stared at the fire-bars as though he'd still a few cards up his sleeve . . .

A week or two later he took to his bed. He was bad and was

said to be wasting. We went up again to the bank-side cottage to inquire how the old man was. Mrs Davies, looking frisky in a new yellow shawl, received us in her box-like kitchen – a tiny smoked cave in which had been gathered a lifetime of fragile trophies, including some oddments of china, an angel clock, a text on a string by the fireplace, a bust of Victoria, some broken tea-pots and pipes, and an engraving of Redcoats at bay.

Mrs Davies was boiling a pot of gruel, her thin back bent like an eel-cage. She bade us sit down, stirred the pot madly, then sank into a wicker chair.

'He's bad,' she said, jerking her head upstairs, 'and you can't really wonder at it. He's had ammonia for years . . . his lungs is like sponges. He don't know it, but we reckon he's sinking.'

She handed us boys some hard peas to chew and settled to talk to our Mother.

'It was like this, Mrs Lee. He took ill on the Friday. I sent for me daughter Madge. We fetched him two doctors, Dr Wills and Dr Packer, but they fell out over the operation. Dr Wills, you see, don't believe in cutting, so he gave him a course of treatment. But Dr Packer, he got into a pet over that, being a rigid one for the knife. But Albert wouldn't be messed about. He said he'd no mind to be butchered. "Give me a bit of boiled bacon and let me bide," he said. I'm with him there of course. It's true, you know – once you've been cut, you're never the same again.'

'Let me finish the gruel,' said Mother, standing up. 'You're trying to do too much.'

Mrs Davies surrendered the ladle vaguely, and shook out her shawl around her.

'D'you know, Mrs Lee, I was setting here last night just count-ing all them as been took; and from Farmer Lusty's up to the Memorial I reckoned 'twere nigh on a hunderd.' She folded her hands into a pious box and settled her eyes on the ceiling. 'Give me the strength to fight the world, and that what's to come upon us . . .'

Later we were allowed to climb up the stairs and visit the old man in his bed. Mr Davies was sinking, that was only too clear. He lay in the ice-cold poky bedroom, his breath coming rough and heavy, his thin brown fingers clutching the sheets like hooks of copper wire. His face was a skull wrapped in yellow paper, pierced by two brilliant holes. His hair had been brushed so that it stuck from his head like frosted grass on a stone.

'I've brought the boys to see you!' cried Mother; but Mr Davies made no answer; he just stared away at some shiny distance, at something we could not see. There was a long, long silence, smelling of cologne and bed-dust, of damp walls and apple-sweet fever. Then the old man sighed and shrank even smaller, a bright wetness against the pillow. He licked his lips, shot a glance at his wife, and gave a wheezy half-giggling cough.

'When I'm gone,' he said, 'see I'm decent, missus. Wrap up me doings in a red silk handkerchief . . .'

The wet winter days seemed at times unending, and quite often they led to self-slaughter. Girls jumped down wells, young men cut their veins, spinsters locked themselves up and starved. There was something spendthrift about such gestures, a scorn of life and complaining, and those who took to them were never censured, but were spoken about in a special voice as though their actions raised them above the living and defeated the misery of the world. Even so such outbursts were often contagious and could lead to waves of throat-cutting; indeed, during one particularly gloomy season even the coroner did himself in.

But if you survived melancholia and rotting lungs it was possible to live long in this valley. Joseph and Hannah Brown, for instance, appeared to be indestructible. For as long as I could remember they had lived together in the same house by the common. They had lived there, it was said, for fifty years; which seemed to me for ever. They had raised a large family and sent them into the world, and had continued to live on alone, with nothing left of their noisy brood save some dog-eared letters and photographs.

The old couple were as absorbed in themselves as lovers, content and self-contained; they never left the village or each other's company, they lived as snug as two podded chestnuts. By day blue smoke curled up from their chimney, at night the red windows glowed; the cottage, when we passed it, said 'Here live the Browns', as though that were part of nature.

Though white and withered, they were active enough, but they ordered their lives without haste. The old woman cooked, and threw grain to the chickens, and hung out her washing on bushes; the old man fetched wood and chopped it with a billhook, did a bit of gardening now and then, or just sat on a seat outside his door and gazed at the valley, or slept. When summer came they bottled fruit, and when winter came they ate it. They did nothing more than was necessary to live, but did it fondly, with skill – then sat together in their clock-ticking kitchen enjoying their half-century of silence. Whoever called to see them was welcomed gravely, be it man or beast or child; and to me they resembled two tawny insects, slow but deft in their movements; a little foraging, some frugal feeding, then any amount of stillness. They spoke to each other without raised voices, in short chirrups as brief as bird-song, and when they moved about in their tiny kitchen they did so smoothly and blind, gliding on worn, familiar rails, never bumping or obstructing each other. They were fond, pink-faced, and alike as cherries, having taken and merged, through their years together, each other's looks and accents.

It seemed that the old Browns belonged for ever, and that the miracle of their survival was made commonplace by the durability of their love – if one should call it love, such a balance. Then suddenly, within the space of two days, feebleness took them both. It was as though two machines, wound up and synchronized, had run down at exactly the same time. Their interdependence was so legendary we didn't notice their plight at first. But after a week, not having been seen about, some neighbours thought it best to call.

They found old Hannah on the kitchen floor feeding her man with a spoon. He was lying in a corner half-covered with matting, and they were both too weak to stand. She had chopped up a plate of peelings, she said, as she hadn't been able to manage the fire. But they were all right really, just a touch of the damp; they'd do, and it didn't matter.

Well, the Authorities were told; the Visiting Spinsters got busy; and it was decided they would have to be moved. They were too frail to help each other now, and their children were too scattered, too busy. There was but one thing to be done; it was for the best; they would have to be moved to the Workhouse.

The old couple were shocked and terrified, and lay clutching each other's hands. 'The Workhouse' – always a word of shame, grey shadow falling on the close of life, most feared by the old (even when called The Infirmary); abhorred more than debt, or prison, or beggary, or even the stain of madness.

Hannah and Joseph thanked the Visiting Spinsters but pleaded to be left at home, to be left as they wanted, to cause no trouble, just simply to stay together. The Workhouse could not give them the mercy they needed, but could only divide them in charity. Much better to hide, or die in a ditch, or to starve in one's familiar kitchen, watched by the objects one's life had gathered – the scrubbed empty table, the plates and saucepans, the cold grate, the white stopped clock . . .

'You'll be well looked after,' the Spinsters said, 'and you'll see each other twice a week.' The bright busy voices cajoled with authority and the old couple were not trained to defy them. So that same afternoon, white and speechless, they were taken away to the Workhouse. Hannah Brown was put to bed in the Women's Wing, and Joseph lay in the Men's. It was the first time, in all their fifty years, that they had ever been separated. They did not see each other again, for in a week they both were dead.

I was haunted by their end as by no other, and by the kind, killing authority that arranged it. Divided, their life went out of them, so they ceased as by mutual agreement. Their cottage stood empty on the edge of the common, its front door locked and soundless. Its stones grew rapidly cold and repellent with its life so suddenly withdrawn. In a year it fell down, first the roof, then the walls, and lay scattered in a tangle of briars. Its decay was so violent and overwhelming, it was as though the old couple had wrecked it themselves.

Soon all that remained of Joe and Hannah Brown, and of their long close life together, were some grass-grown stumps, a garden gone wild, some rusty pots, and a dog-rose.

7

Mother

My Mother was born near Gloucester, in the village of Quedgeley, sometime in the early 1880s. On her own mother's side she was descended from a long static line of Cotswold farmers who had been deprived of their lands through a monotony of disasters in which drink, simplicity, gambling, and robbery played more or less equal parts. Through her father, John Light, the Berkeley coachman, she had some mysterious connection with the Castle, something vague and intimate, half-forgotten, who knows what? but implying a blood-link somewhere. Indeed, it was said that a retainer called Lightly led the murder of Edward II – at least, this was a local scholar's opinion. Mother accepted the theory with both shame and pleasure – as it has similarly confused me since.

But whatever the illicit grandeurs of her forebears, Mother was born to quite ordinary poverty, and was the only sister to a large family of boys, a responsibility she discharged somewhat wildly. The lack of sisters and daughters was something Mother always regretted; brothers and sons being her lifetime's lot.

She was a bright and dreamy child, it seemed, with a curious, hungry mind; and she was given to airs of incongruous elegance which never quite suited her background. She was the pride, none the less, of the village schoolmaster, who did his utmost to protect and develop her. At a time when country schooling was little more than a cane-whacking interlude in which boys picked up facts like bruises and the girls scarcely counted at all, Mr Jolly, the Quedgeley schoolmaster, found this solemn child and her ravenous questioning both rare and irresistible. He was an elderly man who had battered the rudiments of learning into several generations of farm-hands. But in Annie Light he saw a freak of intelligence which he felt bound to nurture and cherish.

'Mr Jolly was really educated,' Mother told us; 'and the pains he took with poor me.' She giggled. 'He used to stop after school to put me through my sums – I was never any good at figures. I can see him now, parading up and down, pulling at his little white whiskers. "Annie," he used to say, "you've got a lovely fist. You write the best essays in class. But you can't do sums ..." And I couldn't, either; they used to tie me in knots inside. But he was patience itself; he *made* me learn; and he used to lend me all his beautiful books. He wanted me to train to be a teacher, you see. But of course Father wouldn't hear of it ...'

When she was about thirteen years old her mother was taken ill, so the girl had to leave school for good. She had her five young brothers and her father to look after, and there was no one else to help. So she put away her books and her modest ambitions as she was naturally expected to do. The schoolmaster was furious and called her father a scoundrel, but was helpless to interfere. 'Poor Mr Jolly,' said Mother, fondly, 'He never seemed to give up. He used to come round home when I was doing the washing and lecture me on Oliver Cromwell. He used to sit there so sad, saying it was a sinful shame, till Father used to dance and swear ...'

There was probably no one less capable of bringing up five husky brothers than this scatter-brained, half-grown girl. But she did what she could, at least. Meanwhile, she grew into tumble-haired adolescence, slap-dashing the housework in fits of abstraction and sliding into trances over the vegetables. She lived by longing rather than domestic law: Mr Jolly and his books had ruined her. During her small leisure hours she would put up her hair, squeeze her body into a tight-boned dress, and either sit by the window, or walk in the fields – getting poetry by heart, or sketching the landscape in a delicate snowflake scribble.

To the other village girls Mother was something of a case, yet they were curiously drawn towards her. Her strain of fantasy, her deranged sense of fun, her invention, satire, and elegance of manner, must have intrigued and perplexed them equally. One gathered that there were also quarrels at times, jealousies, name-callings, and tears. But there existed a coterie among the Quedgeley girls of which Mother was the exasperating centre. Books were passed round, excursions arranged, boys confounded by witty tongues. 'Beatie Thomas, Vi Phillips – the laughs we used to have. The things we did. We were *terrible*.'

When her brothers were big enough to look after themselves, Mother went into domestic service. Wearing her best straw hat and carrying a rope-tied box, seventeen and shapely, half-wistful, half-excited, she set out alone for that world of great houses which in those days absorbed most of her kind. As scullery-maid, housemaid, nursemaid, parlour-maid, in large manors all over the west, she saw luxuries and refinements she could never forget, and to which in some ways she naturally belonged.

The idea of the gentry, like love or the theatre, stayed to haunt her for the rest of her life. It haunted us too, through her. 'Real gentry wouldn't hear of it,' she used to say; 'the gentry always do it like this.' Her tone of voice, when referring to their ways, was reverent, genteel, and longing. It proclaimed standards of culture we could never hope to attain and mourned their impossible perfections.

Sometimes, for instance, faced by a scratch meal in the kitchen, Mother would transform it in a trance of memory. A gleam would come to her hazy eyes and a special stance to her body. Lightly she would deploy a few plates on the table and curl her fingers airily . . .

'For dining, they'd have every place just *so*; personal cruets for every guest . . .' Grimly we settled to our greens and bacon: there was no way to stop her now. 'The silver and napery must be arranged in order, a set for each separate dish . . .' Our old bent forks would be whisked into line, helter-skelter along the table.

'First of all, the butler would bring in the soup (scoop-scoop) and begin by serving the ladies. There'd be river-trout next, or fresh salmon (flick-flick) lightly sprinkled with herbs and sauces. Then some woodcock perhaps, or a guinea-fowl – oh, yes, and a joint as well. And a cold ham on the sideboard, too, if you wished. For the gentlemen only, of course. The ladies never did more than pick at their food –' 'Why not?' '– Oh, it wasn't thought proper. Then Cook would send in some violet cakes, and there'd be walnuts and fruit in brandy. You'd have wine, of course, with every dish, each served in a different glass . . .' Stunned, we would listen, grinding our teeth and swallowing our empty hungers. Meanwhile Mother would have completely forgotten our soup, which then boiled over, and put out the fire.

But there were other stories of Big House life which we found somewhat less affronting. Glimpses of balls and their shimmering company, the chandeliers loaded with light. ('We cleared a barrel of candle-ends next morning.') And then Miss Emily's betrothal. ('What a picture she was – we were allowed a peep from the stairs. A man came from Paris just to do her hair. Her dress had a thousand pearls. There were fiddlers in black perched up in the gallery. The gentlemen all wore uniform. Then the dances – the Polka, the Two-Step, the Schottische – oh, dear, I was carried away. We were all of us up on the top landing, listening; I was wicked in those days, I know. I seized hold of the pantry-boy and said, "Come on Tom", and we danced up and down the passage. Then the Butler found us and boxed our ears. He was a terrible man, Mr Bee . . .')

The long hard days the girls had of it then: rising before dawn, all feathered with sleep, to lay twenty or thirty fires; the sweeping, scrubbing, dusting, and polishing that was done but to be done again; the scouring of pyramids of glass and silver; the scampering up and down stairs; and those irritable little bells that began ringing in tantrums just when you'd managed to put up your feet.

There was a £5-a-year wage, a fourteen-hour day, and a small attic for ravenous sleep: for the rest, the sub-grandees of the servants' hall with a caste-system more rigid than India's.

All the same, below-stairs was a lusty life, an underworld of warmth and plenty, huge meals served cosily cheek-by-jowl, with roast joints and porter for all. Ruled by a despotic or gin-mellow Butler and a severe or fun-fattened Cook, the young country girls and the grooms and the footmen stirred a seething broth together. There were pursuits down the passages, starched love in the laundry, smothered kisses behind green-baize doors – such flights and engagements filled the scrambling hours when the rows of brass bells were silent.

How did Mother fit into all this, I wonder? And those neat-fingered parlour-queens, prim over-housemaids, reigning Cooks, raging Nannies, who ordered her labours – what could they have made of her? Mischievous, muddle-headed, full of brilliant fancies, half witless, half touched with wonder; she was something entirely beyond their ken and must often have been their despair. But she was popular in those halls, a kind of mascot or clown; and she was beautiful, most beautiful at that time. She may not have known it, but her pictures reveal it; she herself seemed astonished to be noticed.

Two of her stories which reflect this astonishment I remember very well. Each is no more than an incident, but when she told them to us they took on a poignancy which prevented us from thinking them stale. I must have heard them many times, right on into her later years, but at each re-telling she flushed and shone, and looked down at her hands in amazement, recalling again those two magic encounters which raised her for a moment from Annie Light the housemaid to a throne of enamelled myrtles.

The first one took place at the end of the century, when Mother was at Gaviston Court. 'It was an old house, you know; very rambling and dark; a bit primitive too in some ways. But they entertained a lot – not just gentry, but all sorts, even black men too at times. The Master had travelled all round the world and he was a very distinguished gentleman. You never quite knew what you were going to run into – it bothered us girls at times.

'Well, one winter's night they had this big house-party and the place was packed right out. It was much too cold to use the outside privy, but there was one just along the passage. The staff wasn't supposed to use it, of course; but I thought, oh, I'll take a chance. Well, I'd just got me hand on the privy door when suddenly it flew wide open. And there, large as life, stood an Indian prince, with a turban, and jewels in his beard. I felt awful, you know – I was only a girl – I wished the ground to swallow me up. I just bobbed him a curtsy and said, "Pardon, your Highness" – I was paralysed, you see. But he only smiled, and then folded his hands, and bowed low, and said "Please madame to enter." So I held up my head, and went in, and sat down. Just like that. I felt like a Queen . . .'

The second encounter Mother always described as though it had never happened – in that special, morning, dream-telling voice that set it apart from all ordinary life. 'I was working at the time in a big red house at a place called Farnhamsurrey. On my Sundays off I used to go into Aldershot to visit my friend Amy Frost – Amy Hawkins that was, from Churchdown you know, before she got married, that is. Well, this particular Sunday I'd dressed up as usual, and I do think I looked a picture. I'd my smart lace-up boots, striped blouse and choker, a new bonnet, and crochet-work gloves. I got into Aldershot far too early so I just walked about for a bit. We'd had rain in the night and the streets were shining, and I was standing quite alone on the pavement. When suddenly round the corner, without any warning, marched a full-dress regiment of soldiers. I stood transfixed; all those men and just me; I didn't know where to look. The officer in front – he had beautiful whiskers – raised his sword and cried out "Eyes right!" Then, would you believe, the drums started rolling, and the bagpipes started to play, and all those wonderful lads as they went swinging by snapped to attention and looked straight in my eyes. I stood all alone in my Sunday dress, it quite took my breath away. All those drums and pipes, and that salute just for me – I just cried, it was so exciting . . .'

★

Later, our grandfather retired from his horses and went into the liquor business. He became host at The Plough, a small Sheepscombe inn, and when Grandmother died, a year or two afterwards, Mother left service to help him. Those were days of rough brews, penny ales, tuppenny rums, home-made cider, the staggers, and violence. Mother didn't altogether approve of the life, but she entered the calling with spirit. 'That's where I learned the frog-march,' she'd say; 'and there were plenty of those who got it! Pug Sollars, for instance; the biggest bully in Sheepscombe – cider used to send him mad. He'd pick up the tables and lay about him like an animal while the chaps hid behind the piano. "Annie!" they'd holler, "for the Lord's sake save us!" I was the only one could handle Pug. Many's the time I've caught him by the collar and run him along the passage. Others, too – if they made me wild, I'd just throw them out in the road. Dad was too easy, so it was me had to do it . . . They smirk when they see me now.'

The Plough Inn was built as one of the smaller stages on the old coach road to Birdlip; but by Mother's time the road had decayed and was no longer the main route to anywhere. One or two carters, impelled by old habits, still used the lane and the inn, and Mother gave them ale and bacon suppers and put them to sleep in the stables. Otherwise, few travellers passed that way, and the lane was mostly silent. So through the long afternoons Mother fell into dreams of idleness, would dress in her best and sit out on the terrace, reading, or copying flowers. She was a lonely young woman, mysteriously detached, graceful in face and figure. Most of the village boys were afraid of her, of her stormy temper, her superior wit, her unpredictable mental exercises.

Mother spent several odd years in that village pub, living her double life, switching from bar-room rages to terrace meditations, and waiting while her twenties passed. Grandfather, on the other hand, spent his time in the cellars playing the fiddle across his boot. He held the landlordship of an inn to be the same as Shaw's definition of marriage – as something combining the maximum of temptation with the maximum of opportunity. So he seldom appeared except late in the evening, when he'd pop up through a hole in the floor, his clothes undone, his face streaming with tears, singing 'The Warrior's Little Boy'.

Mother stuck by him faithfully, handled the drunks, grew older, and awaited deliverance. Then one day she read in a local paper: 'Widower (4 Children) Seeks Housekeeper.' She had had enough of Pug Sollars by now, and of fiddle-tunes in the cellar. She changed into her best, went out on to the terrace, sat down, and answered the advertisement. A reply came back, an appointment was made; and that's how she met my father.

When she moved into his tiny house in Stroud, and took charge of his four small children, Mother was thirty and still quite handsome. She had not, I suppose, met anyone like him before. This rather priggish young man, with his devout gentility, his airs and manners, his music and ambitions, his charm, bright talk, and undeniable good looks, overwhelmed her as soon as she saw him. So she fell in love with him immediately, and remained in love for ever. And herself being comely, sensitive, and adoring, she attracted my father also. And so he married her. And so later he left her – with his children and some more of her own.

When he'd gone, she brought us to the village and waited. She waited for thirty years. I don't think she ever knew what had made him desert her, though the reasons seemed clear enough. She was too honest, too natural for this frightened man; too remote from his tidy laws. She was, after all, a country girl; disordered, hysterical, loving. She was muddled and mischievous as a chimney-jackdaw, she made her nest of rags and jewels, was happy in the sunlight, squawked loudly at danger, pried and was insatiably curious, forgot when to eat or ate all day, and sang when sunsets were red. She lived by the easy laws of the hedgerow, loved the world, and made no plans, had a quick holy eye for natural wonders and couldn't have kept a neat house for her life. What my father wished for was something quite different, something she could never give him – the protective order of an unimpeachable suburbia, which was what he got in the end.

The three or four years Mother spent with my father she fed on for the rest of her life. Her happiness at that time was something she guarded as though it must ensure his eventual return. She would talk about it almost in awe, not that it had ceased but that it had happened at all.

'He was proud of me then. I could make him laugh. "Nance, you're a killer," he'd say. He used to sit on the doorstep quite helpless with giggles at the stories and things I told him. He admired me too; he admired my looks; he really loved me, you know. "Come on, Nance," he'd say. 'Take out your pins. Let your hair down – let's see it shine!' He loved my hair; it had gold lights in it then and it hung right down my back. So I'd sit in the window and shake it over my shoulders – it was so heavy you wouldn't believe – and he'd twist and arrange it so that it caught the sun, and then sit and just gaze and gaze . . .

'Sometimes, when you children were all in bed, he'd clear all his books away – "Come on, Nance," he'd say, "I've had enough of them. Come and sing us a song!" We'd go to the piano, and I'd sit on his lap, and he'd play with his arms around me. And I'd sing him "Killarney" and "Only a Rose". They were both his favourites then . . .'

When she told us these things it was yesterday and she held him again in her enchantment. His later scorns were stripped away and the adored was again adoring. She'd smile and look up the weed-choked path as though she saw him coming back for more.

But it was over all right, he'd gone for good, we were alone and that was that. Mother struggled to keep us clothed and fed, and found it pretty hard going. There was never much money, perhaps just enough, the few pounds that Father sent us; but it was her own muddlehead that Mother was fighting, her panic and innocence, forgetfulness, waste, and the creeping tide of debt. Also her outbursts of wayward extravagance which splendidly ignored our needs. The rent, as I said, was only 3s. 6d. a week, but we were often six months behind. There would be no meat at all from Monday to Saturday, then on Sunday a fabulous goose; no coal or new clothes for the whole of the winter, then she'd take us all to the theatre; Jack, with no boots, would be expensively photographed, a new bedroom suite would arrive; then we'd all be insured for thousands of pounds and the policies would lapse in a month. Suddenly the iron-frost of destitution would clamp down on the house, to be thawed out by another orgy of borrowing, while harsh things were said by our more sensible neighbours and people ran when they saw us coming.

In spite of all this, Mother believed in good fortune, and especially in newspaper competitions. She was also convinced that if you praised a firm's goods they would shower you with free samples and money. She was once paid five shillings for such a tribute which she had addressed to a skin-food firm. From then on she bombarded the market with letters, dashing off several each week. Ecstatically phrased and boasting miraculous cures, they elegantly hinted at new dawns opened up because of, or salvations due only to: headache-powders, limejuice-bottlers, corset-makers, beef-extractors, sausage-stuffers, bust-improvers, eyelash-growers, soap-boilers, love-mongerers, statesmen, corn-plasterers, and kings. She never got another penny from any of these efforts; but such was her style, her passion and conviction, that the letters were often printed. She had bundles of clippings lying all over the house, headed 'Grateful Sufferer' or 'After Years of Torture' or 'I Used to Groan Myself to Sleep till I Stumbled on Your Ointment' ... She used to read them aloud with a flush of pride, quite forgetting their original purpose.

Deserted, debt-ridden, flurried, bewildered, doomed by ambitions that never came off, yet our Mother possessed an indestructible gaiety which welled up like a thermal spring. Her laughing, like her weeping, was instantaneous and childlike, and switched without warning – or memory. Her emotions were entirely without reserve; she clouted you one moment and hugged you the next – to the ruin of one's ragged nerves. If she knocked over a pot, or cut her finger she let out a blood-chilling scream – then forgot about it immediately in a hop and skip or a song. I can still seem to hear her blundering about the kitchen: shrieks and howls of alarm, an occasional oath, a gasp of wonder, a sharp command to things to stay still. A falling coal would set her hair on end, a loud knock make her leap and yell, her world was a maze of small traps and snares acknowledged always by cries of dismay. One couldn't help jumping in sympathy with her, though one learned to ignore these alarms. They were, after all, no more than formal salutes to the devils that dogged her heels.

Often, when working and not actually screaming, Mother kept up an interior monologue. Or she would absentmindedly pick up your last remark and sing it back at you in doggerel. 'Give me some tart,' you might say, for instance. 'Give you some tart? Of course . . . Give me some tart! O give me your heart! Give me your heart to keep! I'll guard it well, my pretty Nell, As the shepherd doth guard his sheep, tra-la . . .'

Whenever there was a pause in the smashing of crockery, and Mother was in the mood, she would make up snap verses about local characters that could stab like a three-pronged fork:

> Mrs Okey
> Makes me choky:
> Hit her with a mallet! – croquet.

This was typical of their edge, economy, and freedom. Mrs Okey was our local postmistress and an amiable, friendly woman; but my Mother would sacrifice anybody for a rhyme.

Mother, like Gran Trill, lived by no clocks, and unpunctuality was bred in her bones. She was particularly offhand where buses were concerned and missed more than she ever caught. In the free-going days when only carrier-carts ran to Stroud she would often hold them up for an hour, but when the motor-bus started she saw no difference and carried on in the same old way. Not till she heard its horn winding down from Sheepscombe did she ever begin to get ready. Then she would cram on her hat and fly round the kitchen with habitual cries and howls.

'Where's my gloves? Where's my handbag? Damn and cuss – where's my shoes? You can't find a thing in this hole! Help me, you idiots – don't just jangle and jarl – you'll all make me miss it, I know. Scream! There it comes! – Laurie, run up and stop it. Tell 'em I won't be a minute . . .'

So I'd tear up the bank, just in time as usual, while the packed bus steamed to a halt.

'. . . Just coming, she says. Got to find her shoes. Won't be a minute, she says . . .'

Misery for me; I stood there blushing; the driver honked his horn, while all the passengers leaned out of the windows and shook their umbrellas crossly.

'Mother Lee again. Lost 'er shoes again. Come on, put a jerk in it there!'

Then sweet and gay from down the bank would come Mother's placating voice.

'I'm coming – yoo-hoo! I Just mislaid my gloves. Wait a second! I'm coming, my dears.'

Puffing and smiling, hat crooked, scarf dangling, clutching her baskets and bags, she'd come hobbling at last through the stinging-nettles and climb hiccuping into her seat . . .

When neither bus nor carrier-cart were running, Mother walked the four miles to the shops, trudging back home with her baskets of groceries and scattering packets of tea in the mud. When she tired of this, she'd borrow Dorothy's bicycle, though she never quite mastered the machine. Happy enough when the thing was in motion, it was stopping and starting that puzzled her. She had to be launched on her way by running parties of villagers; and to stop she rode into a hedge. With the Stroud Co-op Stores, where she was a registered customer, she had come to a special arrangement. This depended for its success upon a quick ear and timing, and was a beautiful operation to watch. As she coasted downhill towards the shop's main entrance she would let out one of her screams; an assistant, specially briefed, would tear through the shop, out the side door, and catch her in his arms. He had to be both young and nimble, for if he missed her she piled up by the police-station.

Our Mother was a buffoon, extravagant and romantic, and was never wholly taken seriously. Yet within her she nourished a delicacy of taste, a sensibility, a brightness of spirit, which though continuously bludgeoned by the cruelties of her luck remained uncrushed and unembittered to the end. Wherever she got it from, God knows – or how she managed to preserve it. But she loved this world and saw it fresh with hopes that never clouded. She was an artist, a light-giver, and an original, and she never for a moment knew it . . .

My first image of my Mother was of a beautiful woman, strong, bounteous, but with a gravity of breeding that was always visible beneath her nervous chatter. She became, in a few years, both bent and worn, her healthy opulence quickly gnawed away by her later trials and hungers. It is in this second stage that I remembered her best, for in this stage she remained the longest. I can see her prowling about the kitchen, dipping a rusk into a cup of tea, with hair loose-tangled, and shedding pins, clothes shapelessly humped around her, eyes peering sharply at some revelation of the light, crying Ah or Oh or There, talking of Tonks or reciting Tennyson and demanding my understanding.

With her love of finery, her unmade beds, her litters of unfinished scrapbooks, her taboos, superstitions, and prudishness, her remarkable dignity, her pity for the persecuted, her awe of the gentry, and her detailed knowledge of the family trees of all the Royal Houses of Europe, she was a disorganized mass of unreconciled denials, a servant girl born to silk. Yet in spite of all this, she fed our oafish wits with steady, imperceptible shocks of beauty. Though she tortured our patience and exhausted our nerves, she was, all the time, building up around us, by the unconscious revelations of her loves, an interpretation of man and the natural world so unpretentious and easy that we never recognized it then, yet so true that we never forgot it.

Nothing now that I ever see that has the edge of gold around it

– the change of a season, a jewelled bird in a bush, the eyes of orchids, water in the evening, a thistle, a picture, a poem – but my pleasure pays some brief duty to her. She tried me at times to the top of my bent. But I absorbed from birth, as now I know, the whole earth through her jaunty spirit.

Not until I left home did I ever live in a house where the rooms were clear and carpeted, where corners were visible and window-seats empty, and where it was possible to sit on a kitchen chair without first turning it up and shaking it. Our Mother was one of those obsessive collectors who spend all their time stuffing the crannies of their lives with a ballast of wayward objects. She collected anything that came to hand, she never threw anything away, every rag and button was carefully hoarded as though to lose it would imperil us all. Two decades of newspapers, yellow as shrouds, was the dead past she clung to, the years saved for my father, maybe something she wished to show him ... Other crackpot symbols also littered the house: chair-springs, boot-lasts, sheets of broken glass, corset-bones, picture-frames, firedogs, top-hats, chess-men, feathers, and statues without heads. Most of these came on the tides of unknowing, and remained as though left by a flood. But in one thing – old china – Mother was a deliberate collector, and in this had an expert's eye.

Old china to Mother was gambling, the bottle, illicit love, all stirred up together; the sensuality of touch and the ornament of a taste she was born to but could never afford. She hunted old china for miles around, though she hadn't the money to do so; haunted shops and sales with wistful passion, and by wheedling, guile, and occasional freaks of chance carried several fine pieces home.

Once, I remember, there was a big auction at Bisley, and Mother couldn't sleep for the thought of its treasures.

'It's a splendid old place,' she kept telling us. 'The Delacourt family, you know. Very cultivated they were – or *she* was, at least. It would be a crime not to go and look.'

When the Sale day arrived, Mother rose right early and dressed in her auction clothes. We had a cold scratch breakfast – she was too nervy to cook – then she edged herself out through the door.

'I shall only be looking. I shan't buy, of course. I just wanted to see their Spode . . .'

Guiltily she met our expressionless eyes, then trotted away through the rain . . .

That evening, just as we were about to have tea, we heard her calling as she came down the bank.

'Boys! Marge – Doth! I'm home! Come and see!'

Mud-stained, flushed, and just a little shifty, she came hobbling through the gate.

'Oh, you *should* have been there. Such china and glass. I never saw anything like it. Dealers, dealers all over the place – but I did 'em all in the eye. Look, isn't it beautiful? I just had to get it . . . and it only cost a few coppers.'

She pulled from her bag a bone cup and saucer, paper-thin, exquisite, and priceless – except that the cup and its handle had parted company, and the saucer lay in two pieces.

'Of course, I could get those bits riveted,' said Mother, holding them up to the sky. The light on her face was as soft and delicate as the egg-shell chips in her hand.

At that moment two carters came staggering down the path with a huge packing-case on their shoulders.

'Put it there,' said Mother, and they dumped it in the yard, took their tip, and departed groaning.

'Oh dear,' she giggled, 'I'd quite forgotten . . . *That* went with the cup and saucer. I had to take it, it was all one lot. But I'm sure we'll find it helpful.'

We broke open the crate with a blow from the chopper and gathered to inspect the contents. Inside was a ball-cock, a bundle of stair-rods, an aigrette, the head of a spade, some broken clay-pipes, a box full of sheep's teeth, and a framed photograph of Leamington Baths . . .

In this way and others, we got some beautiful china, some of it even perfect. I remember a Sèvres clock once, pink-crushed with angels, and a set of Crown Derby in gold, and some airy figures from Dresden or somewhere that were like pieces of bubble-blown sunlight. It was never quite clear how Mother came by them all, but she would stroke and dust them, smiling to herself, and place them in different lights; or just stop and gaze at them, broom in hand, and sigh and shake with pleasure. They were all to her as magic casements, some cracked, some gravelled with faults, but each opening out on that secret world she knew intuitively but could never visit. She couldn't keep any of them long, however. She just had time to look them up in books, to absorb their shapes and histories, then guilt and necessity sent her off to Cheltenham to sell them back to the dealers. Sometimes – but rarely – she made a shilling or two profit, which eased her mind a little. But usually her cry was 'Oh, dear, I *was* foolish! I should really have asked them double . . .'

Mother's father had a touch with horses; she had the same with flowers. She could grow them anywhere, at any time, and they seemed to live longer for her. She grew them with rough, almost slap-dash love, but her hands possessed such an understanding of their needs they seemed to turn to her like another sun. She could snatch a dry root from field or hedgerow, dab it into the garden, give it a shake – and almost immediately it flowered. One felt she could grow roses from a stick or chair-leg, so remarkable was this gift.

Our terraced strip of garden was Mother's monument, and she worked it headstrong, without plan. She would never control or clear this ground, merely cherish whatever was there; and she was as impartial in her encouragement to all that grew as a spell of sweet sunny weather. She would force nothing, graft nothing, nor set things in rows; she welcomed self-seeders, let each have its head, and was the enemy of very few weeds. Consequently our garden was a sprouting jungle and never an inch was wasted. Syringa shot up, laburnum hung down, white roses smothered the apple tree, red flowering-currants (smelling sharply of foxes) spread entirely along one path; such a chaos of blossom as amazed the bees and bewildered the birds in the air. Potatoes and cabbages were planted at random among foxgloves, pansies, and pinks. Often some species would entirely capture the garden – forget-me-nots one year, hollyhocks the next, then a sheet of harvest poppies. Whatever it was, one let it grow. While Mother went creeping around the wilderness, pausing to tap some odd bloom on the head, as indulgent, gracious, amiable and inquisitive as a queen at an orphanage.

Our kitchen extended this outdoor profusion, for it was always crammed with bunches. In the green confines of that shadowy place, stockaded by leaves and flowers, the sun filtered dimly through the plant-screened windows, I often felt like an ant in a jungle overwhelmed by its opulent clusters. Almost anything that caught her wandering eye, Mother gathered and brought indoors. In bottles, teapots, dishes, and jugs, in anything old or beautiful, she'd put roses, beech-boughs, parsley, hellebore, garlic, cornstalks, and rhubarb. She also grew plants in whatever would hold them – saucepans, tea-caddies, or ash tins. Indeed, she once raised a fine crop of geraniums in a cast-iron water-softener. We boys had found it thrown away in a wood – but only she knew what use to give it.

Although there was only one man in my Mother's life – if he could ever be said to have been in it – she often grew sentimental about her girlhood suitors and liked to tell of their vanquished attentions. The postman she rejected because of his wig, the butcher who bled from her scorn, the cowman she'd shoved into Sheepscombe brook to cool his troublesome fires – there seemed many a man up and down the valleys whose love she once had blasted. Sometimes, out walking, or trudging from Stroud with our heads to the blowing rain, some fat whiskered farmer or jobbing builder would go jingling past in his trap. Then Mother would turn and watch him go, and shake the rain from her hat. 'You know, I could have married that man,' she'd murmur; 'if only I'd played my cards right . . .'

Mother's romantic memories may not have all been reliable, for their character frequently changed. But of the stories she told us, about herself and others, the one of the Blacksmith and Toffee-Maker was true . . .

Once, she said, in the village of C—, there lived a lovelorn blacksmith. For years he had loved a local spinster, but he was shy, as most blacksmiths are. The spinster, who eked out a poor existence by boiling and selling toffee, was also lonely, in fact desperate for a husband, but too modest and proud to seek one. With the years the spinster's desperation grew, as did the blacksmith's speechless passion.

Then one day the spinster stole into the church and threw herself down on her knees. 'O Lord!' she prayed, 'please be mindful of me, and send me a man to marry!'

Now the blacksmith by chance was up in the belfry, mending the old church clock. Every breathless word of the spinster's entreaties rose clearly to where he was. When he heard her praying, 'Please send me a man!' he nearly fell off the roof with excitement. But he kept his head, tuned his voice to Jehovah's, and boomed 'Will a blacksmith do?'

'Ern a man's better than nern, dear Lord!' cried the spinster gratefully.

At which the blacksmith ran home, changed into his best, and caught the spinster on her way out of church. He proposed, and they married, and lived forever contented, and used his forge for boiling their toffee.

In trying to recapture the presence of my Mother I am pulling at broken strings. The years run back through the pattern of her confusions. Her flowers and songs, her unshaken fidelities, her attempts at order, her relapses into squalor, her near madness, her crying for light, her almost daily weeping for her dead child-daughter, her frisks and gaieties, her fits of screams, her love of man, her hysterical rages, her justice towards each of us children – all these rode my Mother and sat on her shoulders like a roosting of ravens and doves. Equally I remember her occasional blooming, when she became secretly beautiful and alone. And those summer nights – we boys in bed – when the green of the yew trees filled the quiet kitchen, and she would change into her silk, put on her bits of jewellery, and sit down to play the piano.

She did not play well; her rough fingers stumbled, they trembled to find the notes – yet she carried the music with little rushes of grace, half-faltering surges of feeling, that went rippling out through the kitchen windows like signals from a shuttered cage. Solitary, eyes closed, in her silks and secrets, tearing arpeggios from the yellow keys, yielding, through dusty but golden chords, to the peak of that private moment, it was clearly then, in the twilit tenderness she created, that the man should have returned to her.

I would lie awake in my still-light bedroom and hear the chime of the piano below, a ragged chord, a poignant pause, then a twinkling wagtail run. Brash yet melancholy, coarse yet wistful, it would rise in a jangling burst, then break and shiver as soft as water and lap round my listening head. She would play some waltzes, and of course 'Killarney'; and sometimes I would hear her singing – a cool lone voice, uncertainly rising, addressed to her own reflection. They were sounds of peace, half-edged with sleep, yet disturbing, almost shamefully moving. I wanted to run to her then, and embrace her as she played. But somehow I never did.

As time went on, Mother grew less protesting. She had earned acquiescence and wore it gratefully. But as we children grew up, leaving home in turn, so her idiosyncrasies spread; her plant-pots and newspapers, muddles and scrapbooks extended further throughout the house. She read more now and never went to bed, merely slept upright in a chair. Her nights and days were no longer divided nor harassed by the wants of children. She would sleep for an hour, rise and scrub the floor, or go wooding in the middle of the night. Like Granny Trill, she began to ignore all time and to do what she would when she wished. Even so, whenever we returned for a visit, she was ready, fires burning, to greet us . . .

I remember coming home in the middle of the war, arriving about two in the morning. And there she was, sitting up in her chair, reading a book with a magnifying glass. 'Ah, son,' she said – she didn't know I was coming – 'come here, take a look at this . . .' We examined the book, then I went up to bed and fell into an exhausted sleep. I was roused at some dark cold hour near dawn by Mother climbing the stairs. 'I got you your dinner son,' she said, and planked a great tray on the bed. Aching with sleep, I screwed my eyes open – veg soup, a big stew, and a pudding. The boy had come home and he had to have supper, and she had spent half the night preparing it. She sat on my bed and made me eat it all up – she didn't know it was nearly morning.

So with the family gone, Mother lived as she wished, knowing she'd done what she could: happy to see us, content to be alone, sleeping, gardening, cutting out pictures, writing us letters about the birds, going for bus-rides, visiting friends, reading Ruskin or the lives of the saints. Slowly, snugly, she grew into her background, warm on her grassy bank, poking and peering among the flowery bushes, dishevelled and bright as they. Serenely unkempt were those final years, free from conflict, doubt or dismay, while she reverted gently to a rustic simplicity as a moss-rose reverts to a wild one.

Then suddenly our absent father died – cranking his car in a Morden suburb. And with that, his death, which was also the death of hope, our Mother gave up her life. Their long separation had come to an end, and it was the coldness of that which killed her. She had raised his two families, faithfully and alone: had waited thirty-five years for his praise. And through all that time she had clung to one fantasy – that aged and broken, at last in need, he might one day return to her. His death killed that promise, and also ended her reason. The mellow tranquillity she had latterly grown forsook her then forever. She became frail, simple-minded, and returned to her youth, to that girlhood which had never known him. She never mentioned him again, but spoke to shades, saw visions, and then she died.

We buried her in the village, under the edge of the beechwood, not far from her four-year-old-daughter.

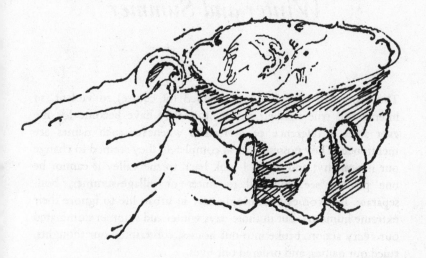

8

Winter and Summer

The seasons of my childhood seemed (of course) so violent, so intense and true to their nature, that they have become for me ever since a reference of perfection whenever such names are mentioned. They possessed us so completely they seemed to change our nationality; and when I look back to the valley it cannot be one place I see, but village-winter or village-summer, both separate. It becomes increasingly easy in urban life to ignore their extreme humours, but in those days winter and summer dominated our every action, broke into our houses, conscripted our thoughts, ruled our games, and ordered our lives.

Winter was no more typical of our valley than summer, it was not even summer's opposite; it was merely that other place. And somehow one never remembered the journey towards it; one arrived, and winter was here. The day came suddenly when all details were different and the village had to be rediscovered. One's nose went dead so that it hurt to breathe, and there were jigsaws of frost on the window. The light filled the house with a green polar glow; while outside – in the invisible world – there was a strange hard silence, or a metallic creaking, a faint throbbing of twigs and wires.

The kitchen that morning would be full of steam, billowing from kettles and pots. The outside pump was frozen again, making a sound like broken crockery, so that the girls tore icicles from the eaves for water and we drank boiled ice in our tea.

'It's wicked,' said Mother. 'The poor, poor birds.' And she flapped her arms with vigour.

She and the girls were wrapped in all they had, coats and scarves and mittens; some had the shivers and some drops on their noses, while poor little Phyllis sat rocking in a chair holding her chilblains like a handful of bees.

There was an iron-shod clatter down the garden path and the milkman pushed open the door. The milk in his pail was frozen solid. He had to break off lumps with a hammer.

'It's murder out,' the milkman said. 'Crows worryin' the sheep. Swans froze in the lake. An' tits droppin' dead in mid-air . . .' He drank his tea while his eyebrows melted, slapped Dorothy's bottom, and left.

'The poor, poor birds,' Mother said again.

They were hopping around the windowsill, calling for bread and fats – robins, blackbirds, woodpeckers, jays, never seen together save now. We fed them for a while, amazed at their tameness, then put on our long wool mufflers.

'Can we go out, Mother?'

'Well, don't catch cold. And remember to get some wood.'

First we found some old cocoa-tins, punched them with holes, then packed them with smouldering rags. If held in the hand and blown on occasionally they would keep hot for several hours. They were warmer than gloves, and smelt better too. In any case, we never wore gloves. So armed with these, and full of hot breakfast, we stepped out into the winter world.

It was a world of glass, sparkling and motionless. Vapours had frozen all over the trees and transformed them into confections of sugar. Everything was rigid, locked-up and sealed, and when we breathed the air it smelt like needles and stabbed our nostrils and made us sneeze.

Having sucked a few icicles, and kicked the water-butt – to hear its solid sound – and breathed through the frost on the window-pane, we ran up into the road. We hung around, waiting for something to happen. A dog trotted past like a ghost in a cloud, panting his aura around him. The distant fields in the low weak sun were crumpled like oyster shells.

Presently some more boys came to join us, wrapped like Russians, with multi-coloured noses. We stood round in a group and just gasped at each other, waiting to get an idea. The thin ones were blue, with hunched up shoulders, hands deep in their pockets, shivering. The fat ones were rosy and blowing like whales; all of us had wet eyes. What should we do? We didn't know. So the fat ones punched the thin ones, who doubled up, saying, 'Sod you.' Then the thin ones punched the fat ones, who half-died coughing. Then we all jumped up and down for a bit, flapped our arms, and blew on our cocoa-tins.

'What we goin' to *do*, then, eh?'

We quietened down to think. A shuddering thin boy, with his lips drawn back, was eating the wind with his teeth. 'Giddy up,' he said suddenly, and sprang into the air and began whipping himself, and whinnying. At that we all galloped away down the road, bucking and snorting, tugging invisible reins, and lashing away at our hindquarters.

Now the winter's day was set in motion and we rode through its crystal kingdom. We examined the village for its freaks of frost, for anything we might use. We saw the frozen spring by the side of the road, huge like a swollen flower. Water-wagtails hovered above it, nonplussed at its silent hardness, and again and again they dropped down to drink, only to go sprawling in a tumble of feathers. We saw the stream in the valley, black and halted, a tarred path threading through the willows. We saw trees lopped-off by their burdens of ice, cow-tracks like pot-holes in rock, quiet lumps of sheep licking the spiky grass with their black and rotting tongues. The church clock had stopped and the weather-cock was frozen, so that both time and the winds were stilled; and nothing, we thought, could be more exciting than this; interference by a hand unknown, the winter's No to routine and laws – sinister, awesome, welcome.

'Let's go an' 'elp Farmer Wells,' said a fat boy.

'You can – I ain't,' said a thin one.

'If you don't, I'll give thee a clip in the yer'ole.'

'Gurt great bully.'

'I ain't.'

'You be.'

So we went to the farm on the lip of the village, a farm built from a long-gone abbey. Wells, the farmer, had a young sick son more beautiful than a girl. He waved from his window as we trooped into the farmyard, and wouldn't live to last out the winter. The farmyard muck was brown and hard, dusted with frost like a baked bread-pudding. From the sheds came the rattle of morning milking, chains and buckets, a cow's deep sigh, stumbling hooves, and a steady munching.

'Wan' any 'elp, Mr Wells?' we asked.

He crossed the yard with two buckets on a yoke; as usual he was dressed in dung. He was small and bald, but had long sweeping arms that seemed stretched from his heavy labours.

'Well, come on,' he said. 'But no playing the goat . . .'

Inside the cowsheds it was warm and voluptuous, smelling sweetly of milky breath, of heaving hides, green dung, and udders, of steam and fermentations. We carried cut hay from the heart of the rick, packed tight as tobacco flake, with grass and wild flowers juicily fossilized within – a whole summer embalmed in our arms.

I took a bucket of milk to feed a calf. I opened its mouth like a hot wet orchid. It began to suck at my fingers, gurgling in its throat and raising its long-lashed eyes. The milk had been skimmed for making butter and the calf drank a bucket a day. We drank the same stuff at home sometimes; Mr Wells sold it for a penny a jug.

When we'd finished the feeding we got a handful of apples and a baked potato each. The apples were so cold they stung the teeth, but the potatoes were hot, with butter. We made a dinner of this, then scuffled back to the village, where we ran into the bully Walt Kerry.

'Wan' a know summat?' he asked.

'What?'

'Shan't tell ya.'

He whistled a bit, and cleaned his ears. He gave out knowledge in very small parcels.

'Well, if you *wan'* a know, I may's well . . .'

We waited in a shivering lump.

'Jones's pond is bearing,' he said at last. 'I bin a-slidin' on it all mornin'. Millions bin comin' wi 'orses an' traps an' skates an' things an' all.'

We tore away down the frosty lane, blood up and elbows well out.

'Remember I told ya. An' I got there fust. An' I'll be back when I've 'ad me tea!'

We left him standing in the low pink sun, small as a cankered rose, spiky, thorny, a thing of dread, only to be encountered with shears.

We could hear the pond as we ran down the hill, the shouts that only water produces, the squeal of skates, the ring of the ice and its hollow heaving grumble. Then we saw it; black and flat as a tray, the skaters rolling round it like marbles. We broke into a shout and charged upon it and fell sprawling in all directions. This magic substance, with its deceptive gifts, was something I could never master. It put wings on my heels and gave me the motions of Mercury, then threw me down on my nose. Yet it chose its own darlings, never the ones you supposed, the dromedary louts of the schoolroom, who came skating past with one leg in the air, who twirled and simpered, and darted like swifts; and never fell once – not they.

I was one of the pedestrians, and we worked up a slide across the polished darkness. So smooth that to step on it was to glide away, while the valley slid past like oil. You could also lie prone and try to swim on the ice, kicking your arms and legs. And you saw deep down, while in that position, little bubbles like cold green stars, jagged ominous cracks, dead ribbons of lilies, drowned bulrushes loaded like rockets.

The frozen pond on such a winter's evening was a very treadmill of pleasure. Time was uncounted; sensations almost sexual; we played ourselves into exhaustion. We ran and slid till we dripped with sweat; our scarves were pearled with our breath. The reeds and horse-tails at the pond's edge smelt as pungent as old men's fingers. Hanging branches of willow, manacled in the ice, bloomed like lilac in the setting sun. Then the frost moon rose through the charcoal trees and we knew that we'd played too long.

We had promised Mother we would fetch some wood. We had to get some each day in winter. Jack and I, hands in pockets, mooched silently up the lane; it was night now, and we were frightened. The beech wood was a cavern of moonlight and shadows, and we kept very close together.

The dead sticks on the ground were easily seen, glittering with the night's new frost. As we ripped them from the earth, scabbed with soil and leaves, our hands began to burn with the cold. The wood was silent and freezing hard, white and smelling of wolves. Such a night as lost hunters must have stared upon when first they wandered north into the Ice Age. We thought of caves, warm skins and fires, grabbed our sticks, and tore off home.

Then there were 'Where've-you-beens?' 'Never-minds', 'Oh-Dears', and 'Come-by-the-fire-you-look-half-dead'. First the long slow torment as our hands thawed out, a quiet agony of returning blood. Worse than toothache it was; I sat there sobbing, but gradually the pain wave passed. Then we had jugs of tea, hot toast and dripping; and later our sisters came.

'It was murder in Stroud. I fell down twice – in the High Street – and tore my stockings. I'm sure I showed everything. It was terrible, Ma. And a horse went through Maypole's window. And old Mr Fowler couldn't get down the hill and had to sit on his bottom and slide. It's freezing harder than ever now. We won't none of us be able to budge tomorrow.'

They sat at their tea and went on talking about it in their sing-song disaster voices. And we boys were content to know the winter had come, total winter, the new occupation . . .

Later, towards Christmas, there was heavy snow, which raised the roads to the top of the hedges. There were millions of tons of the lovely stuff, plastic, pure, all-purpose, which nobody owned, which one could carve or tunnel, eat, or just throw about. It covered the hills and cut off the villages, but nobody thought of rescues; for there was hay in the barns and flour in the kitchens, the women baked bread, the cattle were fed and sheltered – we'd been cut off before, after all.

The week before Christmas, when snow seemed to lie thickest, was the moment for carol-singing; and when I think back to those nights it is to the crunch of snow and to the lights of the lanterns on it. Carol-singing in my village was a special tithe for the boys, the girls had little to do with it. Like hay-making, blackberrying, stone-clearing, and wishing-people-a-happy-Easter, it was one of our seasonal perks.

By instinct we knew just when to begin it; a day too soon and we should have been unwelcome, a day too late and we should have received lean looks from people whose bounty was already exhausted. When the true moment came, exactly balanced, we recognized it and were ready.

So as soon as the wood had been stacked in the oven to dry for the morning fire, we put on our scarves and went out through the streets, calling loudly between our hands, till the various boys who knew the signal ran out from their houses to join us.

One by one they came stumbling over the snow, swinging their lanterns around their heads, shouting and coughing horribly.

'Coming carol-barking then?'

We were the Church Choir, so no answer was necessary. For a year we had praised the Lord out of key, and as a reward for this service – on top of the Outing – we now had the right to visit all the big houses, to sing our carols and collect our tribute.

To work them all in meant a five-mile foot journey over wild and generally snowed-up country. So the first thing we did was to plan our route; a formality, as the route never changed. All the same, we blew on our fingers and argued; and then we chose our leader. This was not binding, for we all fancied ourselves as leaders, and he who started the night in that position usually trailed home with a bloody nose.

Eight of us set out that night. There was Sixpence the Tanner, who had never sung in his life (he just worked his mouth in church); the brothers Horace and Boney, who were always fighting everybody and always getting the worst of it; Clergy Green, the preaching maniac; Walt the bully, and my two brothers. As we went down the lane other boys, from other villages, were already about the hills, bawling 'Kingwenslush', and shouting through keyholes 'Knock on the knocker! Ring at the Bell! Give us a penny for singing so well!' They weren't an approved charity as we were, the Choir; but competition was in the air.

Our first call as usual was the house of the Squire, and we trouped nervously down his drive. For light we had candles in marmalade-jars suspended on loops of string, and they threw pale gleams on the towering snowdrifts that stood on each side of the drive. A blizzard was blowing, but we were well wrapped up, with army puttees on our legs, woollen hats on our heads, and several scarves around our ears.

As we approached the Big House across its white silent lawns, we too grew respectfully silent. The lake near by was stiff and black, the waterfall frozen and still. We arranged ourselves shuffling around the big front door, then knocked and announced the Choir.

A maid bore the tidings of our arrival away into the echoing distances of the house, and while we waited we cleared our throats noisily. Then she came back, and the door was left ajar for us, and we were bidden to begin. We brought no music, the carols were in our heads. 'Let's give 'em "Wild Shepherds",' said Jack. We began in confusion, plunging into a wreckage of keys, of different words and tempo; but we gathered our strength; he who sang loudest took the rest of us with him, and the carol took shape if not sweetness.

This huge stone house, with its ivied walls, was always a mystery to us. What were those gables, those rooms and attics, those

narrow windows veiled by the cedar trees. As we sang 'Wild Shepherds' we craned our necks, gaping into that lamplit hall which we had never entered; staring at the muskets and untenanted chairs, the great tapestries furred by dust – until suddenly, on the stairs, we saw the old Squire himself standing and listening with his head on one side.

He didn't move until we'd finished; then slowly he tottered towards us, dropped two coins in our box with a trembling hand, scratched his name in the book we carried, gave us each a long look with his moist blind eyes, then turned away in silence.

As though released from a spell, we took a few sedate steps, then broke into a run for the gate. We didn't stop till we were out of the grounds. Impatient, at last, to discover the extent of his bounty, we squatted by the cowsheds, held our lanterns over the book, and saw that he had written 'Two Shillings'. This was quite a good start. No one of any worth in the district would dare to give us less than the Squire.

So with money in the box, we pushed on up the valley, pouring scorn on each other's performance. Confident now, we began to consider our quality and whether one carol was not better suited to us than another. Horace, Walt said, shouldn't sing at all; his voice was beginning to break. Horace disputed this and there was a brief token battle – they fought as they walked, kicking up divots of snow, then they forgot it, and Horace still sang.

Steadily we worked through the length of the valley, going from house to house, visiting the lesser and the greater gentry – the farmers, the doctors, the merchants, the majors, and other exalted persons. It was freezing hard and blowing too; yet not for a moment did we feel the cold. The snow blew into our faces, into our eyes and mouths, soaked through our puttees, got into our boots, and dripped from our woollen caps. But we did not care. The collecting-box grew heavier, and the list of names in the book longer and more extravagant, each trying to outdo the other.

Mile after mile we went, fighting against the wind, falling into snowdrifts, and navigating by the lights of the houses. And yet we never saw our audience. We called at house after house; we sang in courtyards and porches, outside windows, or in the damp gloom of hallways; we heard voices from hidden rooms; we smelt rich clothes and strange hot food; we saw maids bearing in dishes or carrying away coffee-cups; we received nuts, cakes, figs, preserved ginger, dates, cough-drops, and money; but we never once saw our patrons. We sang as it were at the castle walls, and apart from the Squire, who had shown himself to prove that he was still alive, we never expected it otherwise.

As the night drew on there was trouble with Boney. 'Noël', for instance, had a rousing harmony which Boney persisted in singing, and singing flat. The others forbade him to sing it at all, and Boney said he would fight us. Picking himself up, he agreed we were right, then he disappeared altogether. He just turned away and walked into the snow and wouldn't answer when we called him back. Much later, as we reached a far point up the valley, somebody said 'Hark!' and we stopped to listen. Far away across the fields from the distant village came the sound of a frail voice singing, singing 'Noël', and singing it flat – it was Boney, branching out on his own.

We approached our last house high up on the hill, the place of Joseph the farmer. For him we had chosen a special carol, which was about the other Joseph, so that we always felt that singing it added a spicy cheek to the night. The last stretch of country to reach his farm was perhaps the most difficult of all. In these rough bare lanes, open to all winds, sheep were buried and wagons lost. Huddled together, we tramped in one another's footsteps, powdered snow blew into our screwed-up eyes, the candles burned low, some blew out altogether, and we talked loudly above the gale.

Crossing, at last, the frozen mill-stream – whose wheel in summer still turned a barren mechanism – we climbed up to Joseph's farm. Sheltered by trees, warm on its bed of snow, it seemed always to be like this. As always it was late; as always this was our final call. The snow had a fine crust upon it, and the old trees sparkled like tinsel.

We grouped ourselves round the farmhouse porch. The sky cleared, and broad streams of stars ran down over the valley and away to Wales. On Slad's white slopes, seen through the black sticks of its woods, some red lamps still burned in the windows.

Everything was quiet; everywhere there was the faint crackling silence of the winter night. We started singing, and we were all moved by the words and the sudden trueness of our voices. Pure, very clear, and breathless we sang:

> As Joseph was a walking
> He heard an angel sing;
> 'This night shall be the birth-time
> Of Christ the Heavenly King.
>
> He neither shall be bornèd
> In Houses nor in hall,
> Nor in a place of paradise
> But in an ox's stall . . .'

And two thousand Christmases became real to us then; the houses, the halls, the places of paradise had all been visited; the stars were bright to guide the kings through the snow; and across the farmyard we could hear the beasts in their stalls. We were given roast apples and hot mince-pies, in our nostrils were spices like myrrh, and in our wooden box, as we headed back for the village, there were golden gifts for everyone.

Summer, June summer, with the green back on earth and the whole world unlocked and seething – like winter, it came suddenly and one knew it in bed, almost before waking up; with cuckoos and pigeons hollowing the woods since daylight and the chirping of tits in the pear-blossom.

On the bedroom ceiling, seen first through sleep, was a pool of expanding sunlight – the lake's reflection thrown up through the trees by the rapidly climbing sun. Still drowsy, I watched on the ceiling above me its glittering image reversed, saw every motion of its somnambulant waves and projections of the life upon it. Arrows ran across it from time to time, followed by the far call of a moorhen; I saw ripples of light around each root of the bulrushes, every detail of the lake seemed there. Then suddenly the whole picture would break into pieces, would be smashed like a molten mirror and run amok in tiny globules of gold, frantic and shivering; and I would hear the great slapping of wings on water, building up a steady crescendo, while across the ceiling passed the shadows of swans taking off into the heavy morning. I would hear their cries pass over the house and watch the chaos of light above me, till it slowly settled and re-collected its stars and resumed the lake's still image.

Watching swans take off from my bedroom ceiling was a regular summer wakening. So I woke and looked out through the open window to a morning of cows and cockerels. The beech trees framing the lake and valley seemed to call for a Royal Hunt; but they served equally well for climbing into, and even in June you could still eat their leaves, a tight-folded salad of juices.

Outdoors, one scarcely knew what had happened or remembered any other time. There had never been rain, or frost, or cloud; it had always been like this. The heat from the ground climbed up one's legs and smote one under the chin. The garden, dizzy with scent and bees, burned all over with hot white flowers, each one so blinding an incandescence that it hurt the eyes to look at them.

The villagers took summer like a kind of punishment. The women never got used to it. Buckets of water were being sluiced down paths, the dust was being laid with grumbles, blankets and mattresses hung like tongues from the windows, panting dogs crouched under the rain-tubs. A man went by and asked 'Hot enough for 'ee?' and was answered by a worn-out shriek.

In the builder's stable, well out of the sun, we helped to groom Brown's horse. We smelt the burning of his coat, the horn of his hooves, his hot leather harness, and dung. We fed him on bran, dry as a desert wind, till both we and the horse half-choked. Mr Brown and his family were going for a drive, so we wheeled the trap into the road, backed the blinkered horse between the shafts, and buckled his jingling straps. The road lay deserted in its layer of dust and not a thing seemed to move in the valley. Mr Brown and his best-dressed wife and daughter, followed by his bowler-hatted son-in-law, climbed one by one into the high sprung trap and sat there with ritual stiffness.

'Where we goin' then, Father?'

'Up the hill, for some air.'

'Up the hill? He'll drop down dead.'

'Bide quiet,' said Mr Brown, already dripping with sweat, 'Another word, and you'll go back 'ome.'

He jerked the reins and gave a flick of the whip and the horse broke into a saunter. The women clutched their hats at the unexpected movement, and we watched them till they were out of sight.

When they were gone there was nothing else to look at, the village slipped back into silence. The untarred road wound away up the valley, innocent as yet of motor cars, wound empty away to other villages, which lay empty too, the hot day long, waiting for the sight of a stranger.

We sat by the roadside and scooped the dust with our hands and made little piles in the gutters. Then we slid through the grass and lay on our backs and just stared at the empty sky. There was nothing to do. Nothing moved or happened, nothing happened at all except summer. Small heated winds blew over our faces, dandelion seeds floated by, burnt sap and roast nettles tingled our nostrils together with the dull rust smell of dry ground. The grass was June high and had come up with a rush, a massed entanglement of species, crested with flowers and spears of wild wheat, and coiled with clambering vetches, the whole of it humming with blundering bees and flickering with scarlet butterflies. Chewing grass on our backs, the grass scaffolding the sky, the summer was all we heard; cuckoos crossed distances on chains of cries, flies buzzed and choked in the ears, and the saw-toothed chatter of mowing-machines drifted on waves of air from the fields.

We moved. We went to the shop and bought sherbet and sucked it through sticks of liquorice. Sucked gently, the sherbet merely dusted the tongue; too hard, and you choked with sweet powders; or if you blew back through the tube the sherbet-bag burst and you disappeared in a blizzard of sugar. Sucking and blowing, coughing and weeping, we scuffled our way down the lane. We drank at the spring to clean our mouths, then threw water at each other and made rainbows. Mr Jones's pond was bubbling with life, and covered with great white lilies – they poured from their leaves like candle-fat, ran molten, then cooled on the water. Moorhens plopped, and dabchicks scooted, insects rowed and skated. New-hatched frogs hopped about like flies, lizards gulped in the grass. The lane itself was crusted with cow-dung, hard baked and smelling good.

We met Sixpence Robinson among the bulrushes, and he said, 'Come and have some fun.' He lived along the lane just past the sheepwash in a farm cottage near a bog. There were five in his family, two girls and three boys, and their names all began with S. There was Sis and Sloppy, Stosher and Sammy, and our good friend Sixpence the Tanner. Sis and Sloppy were both beautiful girls and used to hide from us boys in the gooseberries. It was the brothers we played with: and Sammy, though a cripple, was one of the most agile lads in the village.

Theirs was a good place to be at any time, and they were good to be with. (Like us, they had no father; unlike ours, he was dead.) So today, in the spicy heat of their bog, we sat round on logs and whistled, peeled sticks, played mouth-organs, dammed up the stream, and cut harbours in the cool clay banks. Then we took all the pigeons out of their dovecots and ducked them in the water-butt, held them under till their beaks started bubbling then threw them up in the air. Splashing spray from their wings they flew round the house, then came back to roost like fools. (Sixpence had a one-eyed pigeon called Spike who he boasted could stay under longest, but one day the poor bird, having broken all records, crashed for ever among the cabbages.)

When all this was over, we retired to the paddock and played cricket under the trees. Sammy, in his leg-irons, charged up and down. Hens and guinea-fowl took to the trees. Sammy hopped and bowled like murder at us, and we defended our stumps with our lives. The cracked bat clouting; the cries in the reeds; the smells of fowls and water; the long afternoon with the steep hills around us watched by Sloppy still hid in the gooseberries – it seemed down here that no disasters could happen, that nothing could ever touch us. This was Sammy's and Sixpence's; the place past the sheepwash, the hide-out unspoiled by authority, where drowned pigeons flew and cripples ran free; where it was summer, in some ways, always.

Summer was also the time of these: of sudden plenty, of slow hours and actions, of diamond haze and dust on the eyes, of the valley in post-vernal slumber; of burying birds out of seething corruption; of Mother sleeping heavily at noon; of jazzing wasps and dragonflies, haystooks and thistle-seeds, snows of white butterflies, skylarks' eggs, bee-orchids, and frantic ants; of wolf-cub parades, and boy scouts' bugles; of sweat running down the legs; of boiling potatoes on bramble fires, of flames glass-blue in the sun; of lying naked in the hill-cold stream; begging pennies for bottles of pop; of girls' bare arms and unripe cherries, green apples and liquid walnuts; of fights and falls and new-scabbed knees, sobbing pursuits and flights; of picnics high up in the crumbling quarries, of butter running like oil, of sunstroke, fever, and cucumber peel stuck cool to one's burning brow. All this, and the feeling that it would never end, that such days had come for ever, with the pump drying up and the water-butt crawling, and the chalk ground hard as the moon. All sights twice-brilliant and smells twice-sharp, all game-days twice as long. Double charged as we were, like the meadow ants, with the frenzy of the sun, we used up the light to its last violet drop, and even then couldn't go to bed.

When darkness fell, and the huge moon rose, we stirred to a second life. Then boys went calling along the roads, wild slit-eyed animal calls, Walt Kerry's naked nasal yodel, Boney's jackal scream. As soon as we heard them we crept outdoors, out of our stifling bedrooms, stepped out into moonlight warm as the sun to join our chalk-white, moon-masked gang.

Games in the moon. Games of pursuit and capture. Games that the night demanded. Best of all, Fox and Hounds – go where you like, and the whole of the valley to hunt through. Two chosen boys loped away through the trees and were immediately swallowed in shadow. We gave them five minutes, then set off after them. They had churchyard, farmyard, barns, quarries, hilltops, and woods to run to. They had all night, and the whole of the moon, and five miles of country to hide in . . .

Padding softly, we ran under the melting stars, through sharp garlic woods, through blue blazed fields, following the scent by the game's one rule, the question and answer cry. Every so often, panting for breath, we paused to check on our quarry. Bullet heads lifted, teeth shone in the moon. 'Whistle-or-'OLLER! Or-we-shall-not-FOLLER!' It was a cry on two notes, prolonged. From the other side of the hill, above white fields of mist, the faint fox-cry came back. We were off again then, through the waking night, among sleepless owls and badgers, while our quarry slipped off into another parish and would not be found for hours.

Round about midnight we ran them to earth, exhausted under a haystack. Until then we had chased them through all the world, through jungles, swamps, and tundras, across pampas plains and steppes of wheat and plateaux of shooting stars, while hares made love in the silver grasses, and the large hot moon climbed over us, raising tides in my head of night and summer that move there even yet.

9

Sick Boy

As a child I used to boast the rare distinction of having been christened twice. The second time, which took place in church, was a somewhat rowdy affair; I was three years old and I cheeked the parson and made free with the holy water. But my first anointing was much more solemn and occurred immediately after my birth. I had entered the world in doubt and silence, a frail little lifeless lump; and the midwife, after one look at my worn-out face, said I wouldn't last the day. Everybody agreed, including the doctor, and they just waited for me to die.

My Mother, however, while resigned to my loss, was determined I should enter heaven. She remembered those tiny anonymous graves tucked away under the churchyard laurels, where quick-dying infants – behind the vicar's back – were stowed secretly among the jam-jars. She said the bones of her son should rest in God's own ground and not rot with those pitiful heathens. So she summoned the curate, who came and called out my Adam, baptized me from a tea-cup, admitted me to the Church, and gave me three names to die with.

This flurried christening proved unnecessary, however. Something – who knows what? – some ancestral toughness maybe, saw me safely through the first day. I remained seriously ill for many months, inert, unnoticing, one of life's bad debts, more or less abandoned by all. 'You never moved or cried,' said my Mother. 'You just lay where I put you, like a little image, staring up at the ceiling all day.' In that motionless swoon I was but a clod, a scarce-breathing parcel of flesh. For a year I lay prone to successive invasions, enough to mop up an orphanage – I had diphtheria, whooping-cough, pleurisy, double pneumonia, and congestion of the bleeding lungs. My Mother watched, but could not help me; waited, but could not hope. In those days young children dropped dead like chickens, their diseases not well understood; families were large as though by compensation; at least a quarter were not expected to survive. My father had buried three of his children already, and was quite prepared to do the same by me.

But secretly, silently, aided by unknown forces, I hung on – though it was touch and go. My most perilous moment came when I was eighteen months old, at the hands of Mrs Moore, a neighbour. My Mother was in bed for the birth of my brother – we were all born at home those days. Mrs Moore, a Negress, had been called in to help, to scrub the children and to cook them soups. She was a jolly, eye-bulging, voodoo-like creature who took charge of us with primitive casualness. While still in her care I entered a second bout of pneumonia. What followed I was told much later . . .

It seems that brother Tony was but two days born and Mother just beginning to take notice. Eleven-year-old Dorothy came upstairs to see her, played awhile with the baby, nibbled some biscuits, then sat in the window and whistled.

'How you all getting on?' asked Mother.

'Oh, all right,' said Dorothy.

'You behaving yourselves?'

'Yes, Ma.'

'And what you all up to?'

'Nothing much.'

'Where's Marjorie then?'

'Out in the yard.'

'And Phyllis?'

'She's peeling spuds.'

'What about the others?'

'Harold's cleaning his trolley. And Jack and Frances is sitting on the steps.'

'And Laurie? . . . How's Laurie?'

'Oh, Laurie's dead.'

'What!'

'He turned yellow. They're laying him out . . .'

Giving one of her screams, Mother leapt out of bed.

'No one's going to lay out our Laurie!'

Gasping, she groped her way downstairs and staggered towards the kitchen: and lo, there I was, stretched naked on the table, yellow, just as Dorothy said. Mrs Moore, humming gaily, was sponging my body as though preparing a chicken for dinner.

'What you think you're doing?' my Mother shouted.

'Poor boy, he's gone,' crooned the Negress. 'Gone fled to the angels – thought I'd wash him for the box – just didn't want to bother you, mum.'

'You cruel wicked woman! Our Laurie ain't dead – just look at his healthy colour.'

Mother plucked me from the table, wrapped me up in a blanket, and carried me back to my cot – cursing Mrs Moore for a snatcher of bodies and asking the saints what they thought they were up to. Somehow, I lived – though it was a very near thing, a very near thing indeed. So easy to have succumbed to Mrs Moore's cold sponge. Only Dorothy's boredom saved me.

It was soon after this that my sister Frances died. She was a beautiful, fragile, dark-curled child, and my Mother's only daughter. Though only four, she used to watch me like a nurse, sitting all day beside my cot and talking softly in a special language. Nobody noticed that she was dying herself, they were too much concerned with me. She died suddenly, silently, without complaint, in a chair in the corner of the room. An ignorant death which need never have happened – and I believe that she gave me her life.

But at least she was mourned. Not a day passed afterwards but that Mother shed some tears for her. Mother also grew jealous for the rest of us, more careful that we should survive. So I grew to be, not a pale wasting boy, but sickly in another way, switching regularly from a swaggering plumpness – a tough equality with other boys – to a monotonous return of grey-ghosted illness, hot and cold, ugly-featured and savage. When I was well I could hold my own; no one spared me, because I didn't look delicate. But when I was ill, I just disappeared from the scene and remained out of sight for weeks. If it was summer when the fever caught me, I lay and sweated in my usual bed, never quite sure which of us was ill, me or the steaming weather. But in winter a fire was lit in the bedroom, and then I knew I was ill indeed. Wash-basins could freeze, icicles hang from the ornaments, our bedrooms remained normally unheated; but the lighting of a fire, especially in Mother's room, meant that serious illness had come.

As soon as I recognized the returning face of my sickness – my hands light as feathers, a swaying in the head, and lungs full of pulsing thorns – the first thing I did was to recall my delusions and send messages to the anxious world. As I woke to the fever I thought of my subjects, and their concern always gave me comfort. Signals in morse, tapped out on the bed-rail, conveyed brief and austere intelligences. 'He is ill.' (I imagined the first alarm.) 'He has told his Mother.' (Some relief.) 'He is fighting hard.' (Massed prayers in the churches.) 'He is worse.' (Cries of doom in the streets.) There were times when I was almost moved to tears at the thought of my anxious people, the invisible multitudes up and down the land joined in grief at this threat to their king. How piteously they awaited each sombre bulletin, and how brave I was meanwhile. Certainly I took pains to give them something to be anxious about, but I also bid them be strong. 'He wishes no special arrangements made. Only bands and tanks. A parade or two. And perhaps a three minutes' silence.'

This would occupy my first morning, with the fever still fresh; but by nightfall I was usually raving. My limbs went first, splintering like logs, so that I seemed to grow dozens of arms. Then the bed no longer had limits to it and became a desert of hot wet sand. I began to talk to a second head laid on the pillow, my own head once removed; it never talked back, but just lay there grinning very coldly into my eyes. The walls of the bedroom were the next to go; they began to bulge and ripple and roar, to flap like pastry, melt like sugar, and run bleeding with hideous hues. Then out of the walls, and down from the ceiling, advanced a row of intangible smiles; easy, relaxed, in no way threatening at first, but going on far too long. Even a maniac's smile will finally waver, but these just continued in silence, growing brighter, colder, and ever more humourless till the sick blood roared in my veins. They were Cheshire-cat smiles, with no face or outlines, and I could see the room clearly through them. But they hung above me like a stain on the air, a register of smiles in space, smiles without pity, smiles without love, smiling smiles of un-smiling smileness; not even smiles of strangers but smiles of no one, expanding in brilliant silence, persistent, knowing, going on and on . . . till I was screaming and beating the bed-rails.

At my scream all the walls shook down like a thunderclap and everything was normal again. The kitchen door opened, feet thumped up the stairs, and the girls bustled into the room. 'He's been seeing them faces again,' they whispered. 'It's all right!' they bawled, 'There, there! You won't see any more. Have a nice jug of lemon.' And they mopped me, and picked up the bedclothes. I lay back quietly while they fussed around; but what could I say to them? That I hadn't seen faces – that I'd only seen smiles? I tried that, but it got me nowhere.

Later, as the red night closed upon me, I was only barely conscious. I heard myself singing, groaning, talking, and the sounds were like hands on my body. Blood boiled, flesh crept, teeth chattered and clenched, my knees came up to my mouth; I lay in an evil swamp of sweat which alternately steamed and froze me. My shirt was a kind of enveloping sky wetly wrapping my goosy skin, and across which, at intervals, hot winds from Africa and Arctic blizzards blew. All objects in the room became molten again, and the pictures repainted themselves; things ran about, changed shape, grew monstrous, or trailed off into limitless distances. The flame of the candle threw shadows like cloaks which made everything vanish in turn, or it drew itself up like an ivory saint, or giggled and collapsed in a ball. I heard voices that couldn't control themselves, that either whispered just out of sound, or suddenly boomed some great echoing word, like 'Shovel!' or 'Old-men's-ears!' Such a shout would rouse me with terrible echoes, as though a piano had just been kicked by a horse.

It was myself, no doubt, who spoke these words, and the monologue went on for hours. Sometimes I deliberately answered back, but mostly I lay and listened, watching while the room's dark crevices began to smoke their ash-white nightmares . . . Such a night of fever slowed everything down as though hot rugs had been stuffed in a clock. I went gliding away under the surface of sleep, like a porpoise in tropic seas, heard the dry house echoing through caves of water, followed caverns through acres of dreams, then emerged after fathoms and years of experience, of complex lives and deaths, to find that the moon on the window had not moved an inch, that the world was not a minute older.

Between this sleeping and waking I lived ten generations and grew weak on my long careers, but when I surfaced at last from its endless delirium the real world seemed suddenly dear. While I slept it had been washed of fever and sweetened, and now wrapped me like a bell of glass. For a while, refreshed, I heard its faintest sounds: streams running, trees stirring, birds folding their wings, a hill-sheep's cough, a far gate swinging, the breath of a horse in a field. Below me the kitchen made cosy murmurs, footsteps went up the road, a voice said Good-night, a door creaked and closed – or a boy suddenly hollered, animal-clear in the dark, and was answered far off by another. I lay moved to stupidity by these precious sounds as though I'd just got back from the dead. Then the fever returned as it always did, the room began its whisper and dance, the burnt-down candle spat once and shuddered, and I saw its wick fold and go out . . . Then darkness hit me, a corroding

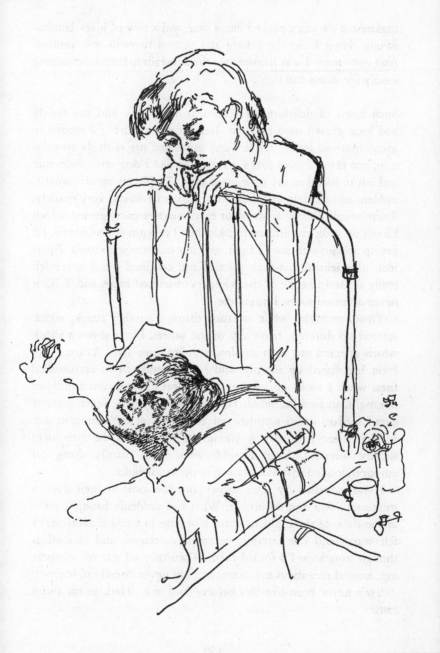

darkness, a darkness packed like a box, and a row of black lanterns swung down from the ceiling and floated towards me, smiling. And once more I was hammering the bed-rails in terror, screaming loudly for sisters and light.

Such bouts of delirium were familiar visitations, and my family had long grown used to them. Jack would inquire if I needed to groan quite so much, while Tony examined me with sly speculation; but for the most part I was treated like a dog with distemper and left to mend in my own good time. The fevers were dramatic, sudden, and soaring, but they burned themselves out very quickly. There would follow a period of easy convalescence, during which I lived on milk custards and rusks; then I'd begin to feel bored, I'd get up and go out, start a fight, and my sickness was closed. Apart from the deliriums, which puzzled and confused me, I never felt really ill; and in spite of the whispers of scarred lungs and T.B., it never occurred to me I might die.

Then one night, while sweating through another attack, which seemed no different from any of the others, I was given a shock which affected me with an almost voluptuous awe. As usual my fever had flared up sharply, and I was tossing in its accustomed fires, when I woke up, clear-headed, somewhere in the middle of the night, to find the whole family round my bed. Seven pairs of eyes stared in dread surmise, not at me but at something in me. Mother stood helplessly wringing her hands, and the girls were silently weeping. Even Harold, who could usually shrug off emotion, looked pale and strained in the candlelight.

I was surprised by their silence and the look in their eyes, a mixture of fear and mourning. What had suddenly brought them in the dark of the night to stand blubbing like this around me? I felt warm and comfortable, completely relaxed, and amused as though somehow I'd fooled them. Then they all started whispering, around me, about me, across me, but never directly to me.

'He's never been like this before,' said one. 'Hark at his awful rattle.'

'He never had that ghastly colour, either.'

'It's cruel – the poor little mite.'

'Such a gay little chap he was, boo-hoo.'

'There, there, Phyl; don't you fret.'

'D'you think the vicar would come at this hour?'

'Someone better run and fetch him.'

'We'd better knock up Jack Halliday, too. He could bike down and fetch the doctor.'

'He'll have to sit up, Ma. His breathing's horrible.'

'Perhaps we should wire his dad . . .'

Perfectly conscious, I heard all this, and was tempted to join in myself. But their strangeness of tone compelled my silence, some peculiar threat in their manner, and a kind of fearful reverence in their eyes and voices as though they saw in me shades of the tomb. It was then that I knew I was very ill; not by pain, for my body felt normal. Silently the girls began to prepare for their vigil, wrapping their shawls around them. 'You go get some rest, Ma – we'll call you later.' They disposed themselves solemnly round the bed, folded their hands in their laps, and sat watching my face with their hollow eyes for the first signs of fatal change. Held by the silence of those waiting figures, in that icy mid-hour of the night, it came to me then, for the first time in my life, that it was possible I might die.

I remember no more of that sombre occasion, I think I just fell asleep – my eyelids closing on a shroud of sisters which might well have been my last sight on earth. When I woke next morning to their surprise, the crisis was apparently over. And save for that midnight visitation, and for the subsequent behaviour of the village, I would never have known my danger.

I remained in Mother's bedroom for many weeks, and a wood-fire burned all day. Schoolfriends, as though on a pilgrimage, came in their best clothes to bring me flowers. Girls sent me hen's-eggs pencilled with kisses; boys brought me their broken toys. Even my schoolteacher (whose heart was of stone) brought me a bagful of sweets and nuts. Finally Jack, unable to keep the secret any longer, told me I'd been prayed for in church, just before the collections, twice, on successive Sundays. My cup was full, I felt immortal; very few had survived that honour.

This time my convalescence was even more indulgent. I lived on Bovril and dry sponge-cakes. I was daily embalmed with camphorated oils and hot-poulticed with Thermogene. Lying swathed in these pungent and peppery vapours, I played through my hours and days, my bed piled high with beads and comics, pressed flowers, old cartridges, jack-knives, sparking-plugs, locusts, and several stuffed linnets.

I took every advantage of my spoiled condition and acted simple when things got tough. Particularly when it came to taking my medicine, a hell-draught of unspeakable vileness.

It was my sisters' job to get this down, and they would woo me with outstretched spoon.

'Now come on, laddie – One! Two! Three! . . .'

'You can clean out the jam-pot after . . .'

'We'll peg up your nose. You won't taste it at all.'

I crossed my eyes and looked vacant.

'Be a good boy. Just this once. Come on.'

'Archie says No,' I said.

'What?'

'Archie,' I said, 'does not want the dose. Archie does not like the dose. And Archie will not have the dose. Says Archie.'

'Who's Archie?' they whispered, shaking their heads at each other. They usually left me then.

After fever my body and head felt light, like a piece of dew-damp vegetable. The illness had emptied me so completely now I seemed bereft of substance. Being so long in that sunless, fever-spent room, I was filled with extraordinary translations. I felt white and blood-drained, empty of organs, transparent to colour and sound, while there passed through my flesh the lights of the window, the dust-changing air, the fire's bright hooks, and the smooth lapping tongues of the candle. Heat, reflection, whispers, shadows, played around me as though I was glass. I seemed to be bodiless, printed flat on the sheets, insubstantial as a net in water. What gross human wastes, dull jellies, slack salts I had been purged of I could not say; but my senses were now tuned to such an excruciating awareness that they vibrated to every move of the world, to every shift and subsidence both outdoors and in, as though I were renewing my entire geography.

When I woke in the mornings, damp with weakness, the daylight was milk of paradise; it came through the windows in beaming tides, in currents of green and blue, bearing debris of bird-song, petals, voices, and the running oils of the sky. Its light washed the room of night and nightmare and showed me the normal day, so that waking was a moment of gratitude that savages must have felt. The bedroom objects removed their witch-masks and appeared almost sheepishly ordinary. The boarded walls shone with grains and knots; the mirror recorded facts; the pictures, framed in the morning's gold, restored me their familiar faces. I sighed and stretched like a washed-up sailor who feels the earth safe beneath him, wild seas wiped away, green leaves around, deliverance miraculously gained.

So each morning at dawn I lay in a trance of thanks. I sniffed the room and smelt its feathers, the water in the wash-jug, the dust in the corners, kind odours of glass and paper, the dry stones facing the windowsills, bees bruising the geranium leaves, the pine in the pencil beside my bed, the dead candle, and the fire in the matchstick. But I also sensed, without needing to look, the state of the early day: the direction of the wind, how the trees were blowing, that there were cows in the fields or not, whether the garden gate was open or shut, whether the hens had yet been fed, the weight of the clouds in the invisible sky, and the exact temperature of the air. As I lay in my bed I could sense the whole valley by the surfaces of my skin, the turn of the hour, the set of the year, the weather, and the life to come. A kind of pantheist grandeur made me one with the village, so that I felt part of its destination; and washed of my fever, ice-cold but alive, it seemed I would never lose it again . . .

Then Mother would come carolling upstairs with my breakfast, bright as a wind-blown lark.

'I've boiled you an egg, and made you a nice cup of cocoa. And cut you some lovely thin bread and butter.'

The fresh boiled egg tasted of sun-warmed manna, the cocoa frothed and steamed, and the bread and butter – cut invalid fashion – was so thin you could see the plate through it. I gobbled it down, looking weak and sorry, while Mother straightened the bed, gave me my pencil and drawing-book, my beads and toys, and chattered of treats to come.

'I'm going to walk into Stroud and buy you a paint-box. And maybe some liquorice allsorts. All kinds of people have been asking about you. Even Miss Cohen! – just fancy that.'

Mother sat on the bed and looked at me proudly. All was love; and I could do no wrong. When I got up I would not have to chop any firewood, and nobody would be cross for a month. Oh, the fatal weakness that engaged me then, to be always and forever ill . . .

Pneumonia was the thing for which I was best known, and made a big drama out of it. But it was not by any means my only weapon; I collected minor diseases also, including, in the space of a few short years, bouts of shingles, chicken-pox, mumps, measles, ring-worm, adenoids, nose-bleed, nits, ear-ache, stomach-ache, wobbles, bends, scarlet-fever, and catarrhal deafness.

Then finally, as though to round the lot off, I suffered concussion of the brain. I was knocked down by a bicycle one pitch-dark night and lay for two days unconscious. By the time I came to, all battered and scabbed, one of my sisters was in love with the bicyclist – a handsome young stranger from Sheepscombe way who had also knocked down my Mother.

But my boyhood career of shocks and fevers confirmed one thing at least: had I been delicate I would surely have died, but there was no doubt about my toughness. Those were the days, as I have already said, when children faded quickly, when there was little to be done, should the lungs be affected, but to burn coal-tar and pray. In those cold valley cottages, with their dripping walls, damp beds, and oozing floors, a child could sicken and die in a year, and it was usually the strongest who went. I was not strong; I was simply tough, self-inoculated by all the plagues. But sometimes, when I stop to think about it, I feel it must have been a very close call.

Strangely enough it was not illness, but the accident, which I believe most profoundly marked me. That blow in the night, which gave me concussion, scarred me, I think, for ever – put a stain of darkness upon my brow and opened a sinister door in my brain, a door through which I am regularly visited by messengers whose words just escape me, by glimpses of worlds I can never quite grasp, by grief, exultation, and panic . . .

10

The Uncles

Our family was large, even by the full-bred standards of those days, and we were especially well-endowed with uncles. Not so much by their numbers as by their qualities of behaviour, which transformed them for us boys into figures of legend, and filled the girls with distress and excitement. Uncle George – our father's brother – was a thin, whiskered rogue, who sold newspapers in the streets, lived for the most part in rags, and was said to have a fortune in gold. But on my Mother's side there were these five more uncles: squat, hard-hitting, heavy-drinking heroes whom we loved and who were the kings of our youth. For the affection we bore them and the pride we took in them, I hope they'll not be displeased by what follows.

Grandfather Light – who had the handsomest legs of any coachman in Gloucestershire – raised his five sons in a world of horses; and they inherited much of his skill. Two of them fought against the Boers; and all five were cavalrymen in the First World War, where they survived the massacres of Mons and Ypres, quickwitted their way through some others, and returned at last to peace and salvation with shrapnel in each of their bodies. I remember them first as khaki ghosts coming home on leave from the fighting, square and huge with their legs in puttees, smelling sweetly of leather and oats. They appeared as warriors stained with battle; they slept like the dead all day; then blackened their boots and Brassoed their buttons and returned again to the war. They were men of great strength, of bloody deeds, a fist of uncles

156

aimed at the foe, riders of hell and apocalypse, each one half-man, half-horse.

Not until after the war did that brotherhood of avengers detach itself in my mind, so that I was able to see each one separate and human and to know at last who they were. The sons of John Light, the five Light brothers, illuminated many a local myth, were admired for their wildness, their force of arms, and for their leisurely, boasting wit. 'We come from the oldest family in the world. We're down in the Book of Genesis. The Almighty said, 'Let there be Light' – and *that* was long afore Adam . . .'

The uncles were all of them bred as coachmen and intended to follow their father; but the Army released them to a different world, and by the time I was old enough to register what they were up to only one worked with horses, the others followed separate careers; one with trees, one with motors, another with ships, and the last building Canadian railways.

Uncle Charlie, the eldest, was most like my grandfather. He had the same long face and shapely gaitered legs, the same tobacco-kippered smell about him, the same slow story-telling voice heavy with Gloucester bass-notes. He told us long tales of war and endurance, of taming horses in Flanders mud, of tricks of survival in the battlefield which scorned conventional heroism. He recounted these histories with stone-faced humour, with a cool self-knowing wryness, so that the surmounting of each of his life-and-death dilemmas sounded no more than a slick win at cards.

Now that he had returned at last from his mysterious wars he had taken up work as a forester, living in the depths of various local woods with a wife and four beautiful children. As he moved around, each cottage he settled in took on the same woody stamp of his calling, putting me in mind of charcoal-burners and the lost forest-huts of Grimm. We boys loved to visit the Uncle Charles family, to track them down in the forest. The house would be wrapped in aromatic smoke, with winter logs piled in the yard, while from eaves and door-posts hung stoats'-tails, fox-skins, crow-bones, gin-traps, and mice. In the kitchen there were axes and guns on the walls, a stone-jar of ginger in the corner, and on the mountainous fire a bubbling stew-pot of pigeon or perhaps a new-skinned hare.

There was some curious riddle about Uncle Charlie's early life which not even our Mother could explain. When the Boer War ended he had worked for a time in a diamond town as a barman. Those were wide open days when a barman's duties included an ability to knock drunks cold. Uncle Charlie was obviously suited to this, for he was a lion of a man in his youth. The miners would descend from their sweating camps, pockets heavy with diamond dust, buy up barrels of whisky, drink themselves crazy, then start to burn down the saloon ... This was where Uncle Charles came in, the king-fish of those swilling bars, whose muscled bottle-swinging arm would then lay them out in rows. But even he was no superman and suffered his share of damage. The men used him one night as a battering-ram to break open a liquor store. He lay for two days with a broken skull, and still had a fine bump to prove it.

Then for two or three years he disappeared completely and went underground in the Johannesburg stews. No letters or news were received during that time, and what happened was never explained. Then suddenly, without warning, he turned up in Stroud, pale and thin and penniless. He wouldn't say where he'd been, or discuss what he'd done, but he'd finished his wanderings, he said. So a girl from our district, handsome Fanny Causon, took him and married him.

He settled then in the local forests and became one of the best woodsmen in the Cotswolds. His employers flattered, cherished, and underpaid him; but he was content among his trees. He raised his family on labourer's pay, fed them on game from the woods, gave his daughters no discipline other than his humour, and taught his sons the skill of his heart.

It was a revelation of mystery to see him at work, somewhere in a cleared spread of the woods, handling seedlings like new-hatched birds, shaking out delicately their fibrous claws, and setting them firmly along the banks and hollows in the nests that his fingers had made. His gestures were caressive yet instinctive with power, and the plants settled ravenously to his touch, seemed to spread their small leaves with immediate life and to become rooted for ever where he left them.

The new woods rising in Horsley now, in Sheepscombe, in Rendcombe and Colne, are the forests my Uncle Charlie planted on thirty-five shillings a week. His are those mansions of summer shade, lifting skylines of leaves and birds, those blocks of new green now climbing our hills to restore their remembered perspectives. He died last year, and so did his wife – they died within a week of each other. But Uncle Charlie has left a mark on our landscape as permanent as he could wish.

The next of the Lights was Uncle Tom, a dark, quiet talker, full of hidden strength, who possessed a way with women. As I first remember him he was coachman-gardener at an old house in Woodchester. He was married by then to my Aunty Minnie – a tiny, pretty, parted-down-the-middle woman who resembled a Cruickshank drawing. Life in their small, neat stable-yard – surrounded by potted ferns, high-stepping ponies, and bright-painted traps and carriages – always seemed to me more toylike than human, and to visit them was to change one's scale and to leave the ponderous world behind.

Uncle Tom was well-mannered, something of a dandy, and he did peculiar things with his eyebrows. He could slide them independently up and down his forehead, and the habit was strangely suggestive. In moments of silence he did it constantly, as though to assure us he wished us well; and to this trick was ascribed much of his success with women – to this and to his dignified presence. As a bachelor he had suffered almost continuous pursuit; but though slow in manner he was fleet of foot and had given the girls a long run. Our Mother was proud of his successes. 'He was a cut above the usual,' she'd say. 'A proper gentleman. Just like King Edward. He thought nothing of spending a pound.'

When he was young, the girls died for him daily and bribed our Mother to plead their cause. They were always inviting her out to tea and things, and sending him messages, and ardent letters, wrapped up in bright scarves for herself. 'I was the most popular girl in the district,' she said. 'Our Tom was so refined . . .'

For years Uncle Tom played a wily game and avoided entanglements. Then he met his match in Effie Mansell, a girl as ruthless as she was plain. According to Mother, Effie M was a monster, six foot high and as strong as a farm horse. No sooner had she decided that she wanted Uncle Tom than she knocked him off his bicycle and told him. The very next morning he ran away to Worcester and took a job as a tram-conductor. He would have done far better to have gone down the mines, for the girl followed hot on his heels. She began to ride up and down all day long on his tram, where she had him at her mercy; and what made it worse, he had to pay her fares: he had never been so humiliated. In the end his nerve broke, he muddled the change, got the sack, and went to hide in a brick-quarry. But the danger passed, Effie married an inspector, and Uncle Tom returned to his horses.

By now he was chastened, and the stables reassured him – you could escape on a horse, not a tram. But what he wished for more than anything was a good woman's protection: he had found the pace too hot. So very soon after, he married the Minnie of his choice, abandoned his bachelor successes, and settled for good with a sigh of relief and a few astonishing runs on his eyebrows.

From then on Uncle Tom lived quietly and gratefully like a prince in deliberate exile, merely dressing his face, from time to time, in those mantles of majesty and charm, those solemn winks and knowing convulsions of the brow which were all that remained of past grandeur . . .

My first encounter with Uncle Ray – prospector, dynamiter, buffalo-fighter, and builder of transcontinental railways – was an occasion of memorable suddenness. One moment he was a legend at the other end of the world, the next he was in my bed. Accustomed only to the satiny bodies of my younger brothers and

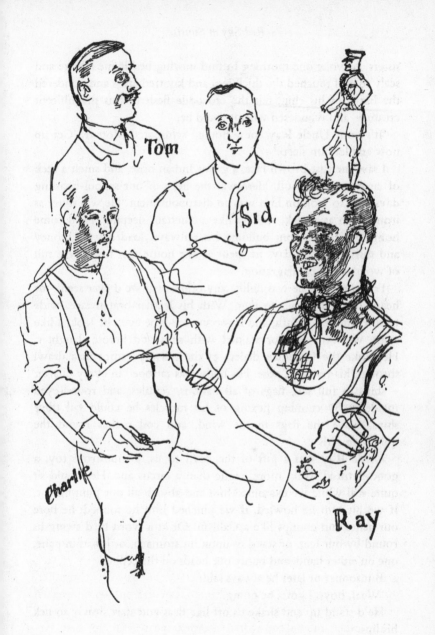

Tom

Sid.

Charlie

Ray

sisters, I awoke one morning to find snoring beside me a huge and scaly man. I touched the thick legs and knotted arms and pondered the barbs of his chin, felt the crocodile flesh of this magnificent creature, and wondered what it could be.

'It's your Uncle Ray come home,' whispered Mother. 'Get up now and let him sleep.'

I saw the rust-brown face, a gaunt Indian nose, and smelt a reek of cigars and train-oil. Here was the hero of our school-boasting days, and to look on him was no disappointment. He was shiny as iron, worn as a rock, and lay like a chieftain sleeping. He'd come home on a visit from building his railways, loaded with money and thirst, and the days he spent at our house that time were full of wonder and conflagration.

For one thing he was unlike any other man we'd ever seen – or heard of, if it comes to that. With his leather-beaten face, wide teeth-crammed mouth, and far-seeing ice-blue eyes, he looked like some wigwam warrior stained with suns and heroic slaughter. He spoke the Canadian dialect of the railway camps in a drawl through his resonant nose. His body was tattooed in every quarter – ships in full sail, flags of all nations, reptiles, and round-eyed maidens. By cunning flexing of his muscles he could sail these ships, wave the flags in the wind, and coil snakes round the quivering girls.

Uncle Ray was a gift of the devil to us, a monstrous toy, a good-natured freak, more exotic than a circus ape. He would sit quite still while we examined him and absorb all our punishment. If we hit him he howled, if we pinched him he sobbed: he bore our aches and cramps like a Caliban. Or at a word he'd swing us round by our feet, or stand us upon his stomach, or lift us in pairs, one on either hand, and bump our heads on the ceiling.

But sooner or later he always said:

'Waal, boys, I gotta be going.'

He'd stand up and shake us off like fleas and start slowly to lick his lips.

'Where you got to go to, Uncle?'

'See a man 'bout a mule.'

'You ain't! Where you going! What for?'

'Get my fingers pressed. Tongue starched. Back oiled.'

'It ain't true! You're fibbing! Uncle! . . .'

'Just *got* to, boys. See you all in the oven. Scrub yer elbows. Be good. So long.'

Off he'd go at a run: though the Lord knew where, *we* couldn't think of any place to go to. Then he'd come back much later, perhaps the following night, wet through, with a dog-like grin. He'd be unable to see properly, couldn't hang up his coat, couldn't find the latch on the door. He'd sit by the fire and steam and sing and flirt with the squawking girls. 'You'd best get to bed,' Mother would say severely: at which he'd burst into theatrical sobs. 'Annie, I can't! I can't move an inch. Got a bone in me leg . . . Mebbe two.'

One night, after he'd been missing for a couple of days, he came home on a bicycle, and rode it straight down the bank in the stormy darkness and crashed into the lavatory door. The girls ran out and fetched him indoors, howling and streaming with blood. They laid him full length on the kitchen table, then took off his boots and washed him. 'What a state he's in,' they giggled, shocked. 'It's whisky or something, Mother.' He began to sing, 'O, Dolly dear . . .' then started to eat the soap. He sang and blew bubbles, and we crowded around him, never having had any man in our house like this.

Word soon got round that Ray Light was home, laden with Canadian gold. He was set on by toughs, hunted by girls, and warned several times by the police. He took most of this in his powerful stride but the girls had him worried at times. A well-bred young seamstress whom he was cuddling in the picture-palace stole his dollar-crammed purse in the dark. Then one morning Beatie Burroughs arrived on our doorstep and announced that he'd promised to marry her. Under the Stroud Brewery arches, she said: just to clinch it. He had to hide for three days in our attic . . .

But drunk or sober, Uncle Ray was the same: a great shaggy animal wagging off to his pleasures: a helpless giant, amiable, naïve, sentimental, and straightforwardly lustful. He startled my sisters, but even so they adored him: as for us boys, what more could we want? He even taught us how to tie him up, boasting that no knots could hold him. So we tied him one night to a kitchen chair, watched him struggle, and then went to bed. Mother found him next morning on his hands and knees, still tied up and fast asleep.

That visit of Uncle Ray's, with its games and exhibitions, was like a prolonged Christmas Day in the house. Routine, discipline, and normal behaviour were suspended during that time. We stayed up late, took liberties, and shared his intoxications: while he bounded about, disappeared on his errands, returned in a tousled daze, fumbled the girls, sang songs, fell down, got up, and handed dollars all round. Mother was prim by turns and indulgent with him, either clicking her tongue or giggling. And the girls were as excited and assailed as we, though in a different, whispering way: saying Would you believe it? I never! How awful! or Did you hear what he said to me then?

When he got through his money he went back to Canada, back to the railway camps, leaving behind him several broken heads, fat innkeepers, and well-set-up girls. Soon after, while working in the snow-capped Rockies, he blew himself up with dynamite. He fell ninety feet down the Kicking Horse Pass and into a frozen lake. A Tamworth schoolteacher – now my Aunt Elsie – travelled four thousand miles to repair him. Having plucked him from the ice and thawed him out, she married him and brought him home. And that was the end of the pioneer days of that bounding prairie dog: without whom the Canadian Pacific Railway would never have reached the Pacific, at least, so we believe.

Moody, majestic Uncle Sid was the fourth, but not least, of the brothers. This small powerful man, at first a champion cricketer, had a history blighted by rheumatism. He was a bus-driver too, after he left the Army, put in charge of our first double-deckers. Those solid-tyred, open-topped, passenger chariots were the leviathans of the roads at that time – staggering siege-towers which often ran wild and got their top-decks caught under bridges. Our Uncle Sid, one of the élite of the bus-drivers, became a famous sight in the district. It was a thing of pride and some alarm to watch him go thundering by, perched up high in his reeking cabin, his face sweating beer and effort, while he wrenched and wrestled at the steering wheel to hold the great bus on its course. Each trip through town destroyed roof-tiles and gutters and shook the gas mantles out of the lamps, but he always took pains to avoid women and children and scarcely ever mounted the pavements. Runaway roarer, freighted with human souls, stampeder of policemen and horses – it was Uncle Sid with his mighty hands who mastered its mad career.

Uncle Sid's story, like Uncle Charlie's, began in the South African War. As a private soldier he had earned a reputation for silence, cunning, and strength. His talent for cricket, learned on the molehills of Sheepscombe, also endowed him with special privileges. Quite soon he was chosen to play for the Army and was being fed on the choicest rations. The hell-bent technique of his village game worked havoc among the officers. On a flat pitch at last, with a scorched dry wicket, after the hillocks and cowdung of home, he was projected straightaway into regions of greatness and broke records and nerves galore. His murderous bowling reduced heroes to panic: they just waved him goodbye and ran: and when he came in to bat men covered their heads and retired piecemeal to the boundaries. I can picture that squat little whizzing man knocking the cricket ball out of the ground, his face congested with brick-red fury, his shoulders bursting out of his braces. I can see him crouch for the next delivery, then spin on his short bowed legs, and clout it again half-way to Johannesburg while he heard far-off Sheepscombe cheer. In an old Transvaal newspaper, hoarded by my Mother, I once found a score-card which went something like this:

Army v. Transvaal. Pretoria 1899

ARMY

Col. 'Tigger' ffoukes–Wyte	1
Brig.-Gen. Fletcher	0
Maj. T. W. G. Staggerton–Hake	12
Capt. V. O. Spillingham	0
Major Lyle (not)	31
Pte S. Light (not)	126
Extras	7
Total (for 4 dec.)	177

TRANSVAAL 21 all out (Pte S. Light 7 for 5)

This was probably the peak of Uncle Sid's glory, the time he would most wish to remember. From then on his tale shows a certain fall – though it still flared up on occasions.

There was, for instance, the day of the Outing, when our village took three charabancs to Clevedon, with Uncle Sid driving the leading one, a crate of beer at his feet. 'Put her in top, Uncle Sid!' we cried, as we roared through the summer country. Guzzling with one hand, steering with the other, he drove through the flying winds, while we bounced and soared above the tops of the hedges, made airborne by this man at the wheel . . .

Then on our way home, at the end of the day, we were stopped by a woman's screams. She stood by the roadside with a child in her arms, cringing from a threatening man. The tableau froze for us all to see; the wild-haired woman, the wailing child, the man with his arm upraised. Our charabancs came to a shuddering halt and we all started shouting at once. We leaned over the sides of our open wagons and berated the man for a scoundrel. Our men from their seats insulted him roundly, suggesting he leave the poor woman alone. But our Uncle Sid just folded his coat, climbed down from his cab without speaking, walked up to the bully, swung back his arm, and knocked the man straight through the hedge. Life to him was black and white and he had reacted to it simply. Scowling with pride, he returned to the wheel and drove us home a hero.

Uncle Sid differed in no way from all his other brothers in chivalry, temper, and drink. He could knock down a man or a glass of beer as readily and as neatly as they. But his job as a bus-driver (and his rheumatism) both increased – and obstructed – his thirst. The result exposed him to official censure, and it was here that the fates laid him low.

When he married my Aunt Alice, and became the father of two children, his job promised to anchor his wildness. But the law was against him and he soon got into scrapes. He was the best double-decker driver in Stroud, without doubt: even safer, more inspired when he drank. Everybody knew this – except the Bus Company. He began to get lectures, admonitions, stern warnings, and finally suspensions without pay.

When this last thing happened, out of respect for Aunt Alice, he always committed suicide. Indeed he committed suicide more than any man I know, but always in the most reasonable manner. If he drowned himself, then the canal was dry: if he jumped down a well, so was that: and when he drank disinfectant there was always an antidote ready, clearly marked, to save everyone trouble. He reasoned, quite rightly, that Aunt Alice's anger, on hearing of another suspension, would be swallowed up by her larger anxiety on finding him again near to death. And Aunty Alice never failed him in this, and forgave him each time he recovered.

The Bus Company were almost equally forgiving: they took him back again and again. Then one night, having brought his bus safely home, they found him fast asleep at the wheel, reeking of malt and stone-jar cider: and they gave him the sack for good.

We were sitting in the kitchen rather late that night, when a loud knock came at the door. A hollow voice called 'Annie! Annie!' and we knew that something had happened. Then the kitchen door crept slowly open and revealed three dark-clad figures. It was Aunty Alice and her two small daughters, each dressed in their Sunday best. They stood at the foot of the kitchen steps, silent as apparitions, and Auntie Alice's face, with its huge drawn eyes, wore a mantle of tragic doom.

'He's done it this time,' she intoned at last. 'That's what. I know he has.'

Her voice had a churchlike incantation which dropped crystals of ice down my back. She held the small pretty girls in a majestic embrace while they squirmed and sniffed and giggled.

'He never came home. They must have given him the sack. Now he's gone off to end it all.'

'No, no,' cried our Mother. 'Come and sit down, my dear.' And she drew her towards the fire.

Aunty Alice sat stiffly, like a Gothic image, still clutching her wriggling children.

'Where else could I go, Annie? He's gone down to Deadcombe. He always told me he would . . .'

She suddenly turned and seized Mother's hands, her dark eyes rolling madly.

'Annie! Annie! He'll do himself in. Your boys – they just *got* to find him! . . .'

So Jack and I put on caps and coats and went out into the half-moon night. From so much emotion I felt light-headed: I wanted to laugh or hide. But Jack was his cool, intrepid self, tight-lipped as a gunboat commander. We were men in a crisis, on secret mission, life and death seemed to hang on our hands. So we stuck close together and trudged up the valley, heading for Deadcombe Wood.

The wood was a waste of rotting silence, transformed by its mask of midnight: a fine rain was falling, wet ferns soaked our legs, leaves shuddered with owls and water. What were we supposed to do? we wondered. Why had we come, anyway? We beat up and down through the dripping trees, calling 'Uncle!' in chill, flat voices. What should we find? Perhaps nothing at all. Or worse, what we had come to seek . . . But we remembered the women, waiting fearfully at home. Our duty, though dismal, was clear.

So we stumbled and splashed through invisible brooks, followed paths, skirted ominous shadows. We poked bits of stick into piles of old leaves, prodded foxholes, searched the length of the wood. There was nothing there but the fungoid darkness, nothing at all but our fear.

We were about to go home, and gladly enough, when suddenly we saw him. He was standing tiptoe under a great dead oak with his braces around his neck. The elastic noose, looped to the branch above him, made him bob up and down like a puppet. We approached the contorted figure with dread; we saw his baleful eye fixed on us.

Our Uncle Sid was in a terrible temper.

'You've been a bloody long time!' he said.

Uncle Sid never drove any buses again but took a job as a gardener in Sheepscombe. All the uncles now, from their wilder beginnings, had resettled their roots near home – all, that is, save Insurance Fred, whom we lost through prosperity and distance. These men reflected many of Mother's qualities, were foolish, fantastical, moody; but in spite of their follies they remained for me the true heroes of my early life. I think of them still in the image they gave me; they were bards and oracles each; like a ring of squat megaliths on some local hill, bruised by weather and scarred with old glories. They were the horsemen and brawlers of another age, and their lives spoke its long farewell. Spoke, too, of campaigns on desert marches, of Kruger's cannon, and Flanders mud; of a world that still moved at the same pace as Caesar's, and of that Empire greater than his – through which they had fought, sharp-eyed and anonymous, and seen the first outposts crumble . . .

11

Outings and Festivals

The year revolved around the village, the festivals round the year, the church round the festivals, the Squire round the church, and the village round the Squire. The Squire was our centre, a crumbling moot tree; and few indeed of our local celebrations could take place without his shade. On the greater occasions he let us loose in his gardens, on the smaller gave us buns and speeches; and at historic moments of national rejoicing – when kings were born, enemies vanquished, or the Conservatives won an election – he ransacked his boxrooms for fancy-dresses that we might rejoice in a proper manner.

The first big festival that I can remember was Peace Day in 1919. It was a day of magical transformations, of tears and dusty sunlight, of bands, processions, and buns by the cartload; and I was so young I thought it normal ...

We had all been provided with fancy-dress, and that seemed normal too. Apart from the Squire's contribution Marjorie had been busy for weeks stitching up glories for ourselves and the neighbours. No makeshift, rag-bag cobbling either; Marjorie had worked as though for a wedding.

On the morning of the feast Poppy Green came to the house to try on her angel's dress. She was five years old and about my size. She had russet curls like apple peelings, a polished pumpkin face, a fruity air of exploding puddings, and a perpetual cheeky squint. I loved her, she was like a portable sweet-shop. This morning I watched my sisters dress her. She was supposed to represent a spirit. They'd made her a short frilly frock, a tinfoil helmet, cardboard wings, and a wand with a star. When they'd clothed her they stood her up on the mantelpiece and had a good look at her. Then they went off awhile on some other business and left us alone together.

'Fly!' I commanded. 'You got wings, ain't you?'

Poppy squirmed and wiggled her shoulders.

I grew impatient and pushed her off the mantelpiece, and she fell with a howl into the fireplace. Looking down at her, smudged with coal and tears, her wand and wings all crumpled, I felt nothing but rage and astonishment. She should have been fluttering round the room.

They sponged and soothed her, and Poppy trotted home, her bent wand clutched in her hand. Then shapes and phantoms began to run through the village, and we started to get ready ourselves. Marge appeared as Queen Elizabeth, with Phyllis her lady-in-waiting. Marjorie, who was sixteen and at her most beautiful, wore a gown of ermine, a brocaded bodice, and a black cap studded with pearls. She filled the kitchen with such a glow of grace that we just stood and gaped at her. It was the first time I had seen Queen Elizabeth, but this was no sharp-faced Tudor. Tender and proud in her majestic robes, she was the Queen of Heaven, risen from the dust, unrecognizable as Marge till she spoke, and her eyes shone down on us from her veils of ermine like emeralds laid in snow. Thirteen-year-old Phyllis, with finery of her own, skipped like a magpie around her, wearing a long chequered dress of black and white velvet, and a hat full of feathers and moths.

The rest of us, whom Marjorie had dressed, were the result of homespun inspirations. Dorothy, as 'Night', was perhaps the most arresting; an apparition of unearthly beauty, a flash of darkness, a strip of nocturnal sky, mysteriously cloaked in veils of black netting entangled with silver paper. A crescent moon lay across her breast, a comet across her brow, and her long dark curls fell in coils of midnight and were sprinkled with tinsel dust. I smelt frost when I saw her and heard a crackling of stars; familiar Dorothy had grown far and disturbing.

Brother Jack had refused to be dressed up at all, unless in some aspect of recognized valour. So they hung him in green, gave him a bow and arrow, and he called himself Robin Hood. Little Tony was dressed as a market-girl, curly-headed and pretty as love, bare-armed and bonneted, carrying a basket of flowers, but so proud we forgave him his frock.

As for me, a squat neck and solid carriage made the part I should play inevitable. I was John Bull – whoever he was – but I quickly surmised his importance. I remember the girls stuffing me into my clothes with many odd squeals and giggles. Gravely I offered an arm or leg, but remained dignified and aloof. Marjorie had assembled the ritual garments with her usual flair and cunning. I wore a top-hat and choker, a union-jack waistcoat, a frock-coat, and pillowcase breeches. But I'd been finished off hurriedly with gaiters of cardboard fastened loosely together with pins – a slovenly makeshift which offended my taste, and which I was never able to forgive.

This Peace Day I remember as a blur of colour, leading from fury to triumph. There was a procession with a band. I walked alone solemnly. Fantastic disguises surrounded me; every single person seemed covered with beards, false-noses, bootblack, and wigs. We had not marched far when my boots fell off, followed by my cardboard gaiters. As I stopped to find them, the procession swept over me. I sat down by the roadside and howled. I howled because I could hear the band disappearing, because I was John Bull and it should not have happened. I was picked up by a carriage, restored to the procession, then placed on a trolley and pulled. Cross-legged on the trolley, bare-footed and gaiterless, I rode like a prince through the village.

Dusty, sweating from its long route-march, the procession snaked round the houses. The old and infirm stood and cheered from the gutters; I nodded back from my trolley. At last we entered the cool beech wood through which the Squire's drive twisted. The brass-band's thunder bounced back from the boughs. Owls hooted and flapped away.

172

We came out of the wood into the Big House gardens, and the sun returned in strength. Doves and pigeons flew out of the cedars. The swans took off from the lake. On the steps of the Manor stood the wet-eyed Squire, already in tears at the sight of us. His mother, in a speech from a basket-chair, mentioned the glory of God, the Empire, us; and said we wasn't to touch the flowers.

With the procession dispersed, I was tipped off the trolley, and I wandered away through the grounds. Flags and roses moved against the sky, bright figures among the bushes. Japanese girls and soot-faced savages grew strangely from banks of lilac. I saw Charlie Chaplin, Peter the Pieman, a collection of upright tigers, a wounded soldier about my age, and a bride on the arm of a monkey.

Later I was given a prize by the Squire and was photographed in a group by a rockery. I still have that picture, all sepia shadows, a leaf ripped from that summer day. Surrounded by girls in butter muslin, by druids and eastern kings, I am a figure rooted in unshakeable confidence, oval substantial, and proud. About two feet high and two feet broad, my breeches like slack balloons, I stand, top-hatted, with a tilted face as severe as on a Roman coin. Others I recognize are gathered round me, all marked by that day's white dust. Tony has lost his basket of flowers, Jack his bow and arrow. Poppy Green has had her wings torn off and is grasping a broken lily. She stands beside me, squinting fiercely, ruffled a bit by the heat, and the silver letters across her helmet – which I couldn't read then – say PEACE.

Our village outings were both sacred and secular, and were also far between. One seldom, in those days, strayed beyond the parish boundaries, except for the annual Choir Outing. In the meantime we had our own tribal wanderings, unsanctified though they were, when a sudden fine morning would send us forth in families for a day's nutting or blackberrying. So up we'd go to the wilder end of the valley, to the bramble-entangled Scrubs, bearing baskets and buckets and flasks of cold tea, like a file of foraging Indians.

Blackberries clustered against the sky, heavy and dark as thunder, which we plucked and gobbled, hour after hour, lips purple, hands stained to the wrists. Or later, mushrooms, appearing like manna, buttoning the shaggy grass, found in the mists of September mornings with the wet threads of spiders on them. They came in the night from nowhere, rootless, like a scattering of rubber balls. Their suckers clung to the roots of grass and broke off with a rubbery snap. The skin rubbed away like the bark of a birch tree, the flesh tasted of something unknown ... At other times there would be wild green damsons, tiny plums, black sloes, pink crab-apples – the free waste of the woods, an unpoliced bounty, which we'd carry back home in bucketfuls. Whether we used them for jam or jellies or pies, or just left them to rot, didn't matter.

Then sometimes there'd be a whole day's outing, perhaps to Sheepscombe to visit relations – a four-mile walk, which to our short legs seemed further, so that we needed all day to do it. We would start out early, with the sun just rising and the valley wrapped in mist ...

'It's going to be hot,' says our Mother brightly, and usually she is right. We climb up slowly towards Bulls Cross, picking at the bushes for birds'-nests. Or we stop to dig holes or to swing on gates while Mother looks back at the view. 'What a picture,' she murmurs. 'Green as green ... And those poppies, red as red.' The mist drags the tree-tops, flies away in the sky, and there is suddenly blue air all round us.

Painswick sprawls white in the other valley, like the skeleton of a foundered mammoth. But active sounds of its working morning – carts and buzz-saws, shouts and hammering – come drifting in gusts towards us. The narrow lane that leads to Sheepscombe bends steeply away on our right. 'Step out, young men!' our Mother says crisply. She begins to teach us a hymn; the kind that cries for some lost land of paradise, and goes well with a tambourine. I've not heard it before (nor ever since), but it entirely enshrines our outing – the remote, shaggy valley in which we find ourselves, the smell of hot straw on the air, dog-roses and distances, dust and spring waters, and the long day's journey, by easy stages, to the sheep-folds of our wild relations.

They are waiting for us with warm ginger-beer, and a dinner of broad beans and bacon. Aunty Fan says, 'Annie, come in out of the sun. You must be ready to drop.' We go indoors and find our Uncle Charlie hacking at the bacon with a bill-hook. Young cousin Edie and her cautious brothers seem to be pondering whether to punch our heads. Our Gramp comes in from his cottage next door, dressed in mould-green corduroy suiting. We sit down and eat, and the cousins kick us under the table, from excitement rather than spite. Then we play with their ferrets, spit down their well, have a fight, and break down a wall. Later we are called for and given a beating, then we climb up the tree by the earth closet. Edie climbs highest, till we bite her legs, then she hangs upside down and screams. It has been a full, far-flung, and satisfactory day; dusk falls, and we say goodbye.

Back down the lane in the thick hot darkness we walk drowsily, heavy with boots. Night odours come drifting from woods and gardens; sweet musks and sharp green acids. In the sky the fat stars bounce up and down, rhythmically, as we trudge along. Glow-worms, brighter than lamps or candles, spike the fields with their lemon fires, while huge horned beetles stumble out of the dark and buzz blindly around our heads.

Then Painswick appears – a starfish of light dilating in a pool of distance. We hurry across the haunted common and come at last to the top of our valley. The village waterfall, still a mile away, lifts its cool, familiar murmur. We are nearing home, we are almost there: Mother starts to recite a poem. 'I remember, I remember, the house where I was born ...' She says it right through, and I tag beside her watching the trees walk past in the sky ...

The first Choir Outing we ever had was a jaunt in a farm-wagon to Gloucester. Only the tenors and basses and the treble boys were included in that particular treat. Later, with the coming of the horse-brake and charabanc, the whole village took part as well. With the help of the powerful new charabanc we even got out of the district altogether, rattling away to the ends of the earth, to Bristol or even further.

One year the Outing was to Weston-super-Mare, and we had saved up for months to be worthy of it. We spent the night before preparing our linen, and the girls got up at dawn to make sandwiches. The first thing I did when I came down that morning was to go out and look at the weather. The sky was black, and Tony was behind the lavatory praying hard through his folded hands. When he saw that I'd seen him he began to scratch and whistle, but the whole thing was a very bad sign.

We couldn't eat breakfast, the porridge was like gravel; so Jack and I ran up the bank to see what was going on. Families were already gathering for the charabancs, so we ran back down again. The girls were ready, and Tony was ready. Mother was raking under the piano with a broomstick.

'Come on, our Mother! They'll go without us!'

'I've just got to find my corsets.'

She found them; then started very slowly to wash, like a duck with all summer to do it. We stood round and nagged her, rigid with nerves.

'Run along – you're under my feet.'

So we left her, and scampered along to the Woolpack. The whole village was waiting by now; mothers with pig-buckets stuffed with picnics, children with cocoa-tin spades, fathers with bulging overcoats lined entirely with clinking bottles. There was little Mrs Tulley collecting the fares and plucking at her nervous cheeks; Mr Vick, the shopkeeper, carrying his keys in a basket; the two dressmakers in unclaimed gowns; and Lily Nelson, a fugitive from her brother, whispering, 'You mustn't tell Arnold – he'd kill me.' The Squire's old gardener had brought a basket of pigeons which he planned to release from the pier. And the postman, having nobody to deliver his letters to, had dumped them, and was coming along too.

Faces looked pale in the early light. Men sniffed and peered at the sky. 'Don't look too good, do it?' 'Can't say it do.' 'Bloody black over Stroud.' 'Might clear though . . .' Teeth were sucked in, heads doubtfully shaken; I felt the doom of storm-sickness on me.

The vicar arrived to see us off – his pyjamas peeping out from his raincoat. 'There's a very nice church near the Promenade . . . I trust you will all spare a moment . . .' He issued each choirboy with his shilling for dinner, then dodged back home to bed. The last to turn up was Herbert the gravedigger, with something queer in a sack. The last, that is, except our Mother, of whom there was still no sign.

Then the charabancs arrived and everyone clambered aboard, fighting each other for seats. We abandoned our Mother and climbed aboard too, feeling guilty and miserable. The charabancs were high, with broad open seats and with folded tarpaulins at the rear, upon which, as choirboys, we were privileged to perch and to fall off and break our necks. We all took our places, people wrapped themselves in blankets, horns sounded, and we were ready. 'Is everyone present?' piped the choirmaster. Shamefully, Jack and I kept silent.

Our Mother, as usual, appeared at that moment, a distant trotting figure, calling and waving her handbags gaily to disarm what impatience there might be. 'Come on, Mother Lee! We near went without you!' Beaming, she climbed aboard. 'I just had to wash out my scarf,' she said, and tied it on the windscreen to dry. And there it blew like a streaming pennant as we finally drove out of the village.

In our file of five charabancs, a charioted army, we swept down the thundering hills. At the speed and height of our vehicles the whole valley took on new dimensions; woods rushed beneath us, and fields and flies were devoured in a gulp of air. We were windborne now by motion and pride, we cheered everything, beast and fowl, and taunted with heavy ironical shouts those unfortunates still working in the fields. We kept this up till we had roared through Stroud, then we entered the stranger's country. It was no longer so easy to impress pedestrians that we were the Annual Slad Choir Outing. So we settled down, and opened our sandwiches, and began to criticize the farming we passed through.

The flatness of the Severn Valley now seemed dull after our swooping hills, the salmon-red sandstone of the Clifton Gorges too florid compared with our chalk. Everything began to appear strange and comic, we hooted at the shapes of the hayricks, laughed at the pitiful condition of the cattle – 'He won't last long – just look at 'is knees.' We began to look round fondly at our familiar selves, drawn close by this alien country. Waves of affection and loyalty embraced us. We started shouting across the seats. 'Harry! Hey, Harry! Say whatcher, Harry! Bit of all right, ain't it, you? Hey, Bert! 'Ow's Bert? 'Ow you doin', ole sparrer? Where's Walt? Hey there, Walt! Watcher!'

Mile after rattling mile we went, under the racing sky, flying neckties and paper kites from the back, eyes screwed in the weeping wind. The elders, protected in front by the windscreen, chewed strips of bacon, or slept. Mother pointed out landmarks and lectured the sleepers on points of historical interest. Then a crawling boy found the basket of pigeons and the coach exploded with screams and wings . . .

The weather cleared as we drove into Weston, and we halted on the Promenade. 'The seaside,' they said: we gazed around us, but we saw no sign of the sea. We saw a vast blue sky and an infinity of mud stretching away to the shadows of Wales. But rousing smells of an invisible ocean astonished our land-locked nostrils: salt, and wet weeds, and fishy oozes; a sharp difference in every breath. Our deep-ditched valley had not been prepared for this, for we had never seen such openness, the blue windy world seemed to have blown quite flat, bringing the sky to the level of our eyebrows. Canvas booths flapped on the edge of the Prom, mouths crammed with shellfish and vinegar; there were rows of prim boarding-houses (each the size of our Vicarage); bathchairs, carriages, and donkeys; and stilted far out on the rippled mud a white pier like a sleeping dragon.

The blue day was ours; we rattled our money and divided up into groups. 'Hey, Jake, Steve; let's go have a wet' – and the men shuffled off down a side-street. 'I'm beat after that, Mrs Jones, ain't you? – there's a clean place down by the bandstand.' The old women nodded, and went seeking their comforts; the young ones to stare at the policemen.

Meanwhile, we boys just picked up and ran; we had a world of mud to deal with. The shops and streets ended suddenly, a frontier to the works of man; and beyond – the mud, salt winds, and birds, a kind of double ration of light, a breathless space neither fenced nor claimed, and far out a horizon of water. We whinnied like horses and charged up and down, every hoof-mark written behind us. If you stamped in this mud, you brought it alive, the footprint began to speak, it sucked and sighed and filled with water, became a foot cut out of the sky. I dug my fingers into a stretch of mud to see how deep it was, felt a hard flat pebble and drew it out and examined it in the palm of my hand. Suddenly, it cracked, and put out two claws; I dropped it in horror, and ran . . .

Half the village now had hired themselves chairs and were bravely facing the wind. Mrs Jones was complaining about Weston tea: 'It's made from the drains, I reckon.' The Squire's old gardener, having lost his pigeons, was trying to catch gulls in a basket; and the gravedigger (who appeared to have brought his spade) was out on the mud digging holes. Then the tide came in like a thick red sludge, and we all went on the pier.

Magic construction striding the waves, loaded with freaks and fancies, water-chutes and crumpled mirrors, and a whole series of nightmares for a penny. One glided secretly to one's favourite machine, the hot coin burning one's hand, to command a murder, a drunk's delirium, a haunted grave, or a Newgate hanging. This last, of course, was my favourite; what dread power one's penny purchased – the painted gallows, the nodding priest, the felon with his face of doom. At a touch they jerked through their ghastly dance, the priest, hangman, and the convict, joined together by rods and each one condemned as it were to perpetual torment. Their ritual motions led to the jerk of the corpse; the figures froze and the lights went out. Another penny restored the lights, brought back life to the cataleptic trio, and dragged the poor felon once more to the gallows to be strangled all over again.

That white pier shining upon the waves seemed a festive charnel house. With our mouths hanging open, sucking gory sticks of rock, we groped hungrily from horror to horror. For there were sideshows too, as well as the machines with hair-raising freaks under glass – including a two-headed Indian, a seven-legged sheep, and a girl's eye with a child coiled inside it.

We spent more time on that turgid pier than anywhere else in Weston. Then the tide went out, and evening fell, and we returned to the waiting charabancs. People came wandering from all directions, with bags full of whelks and seaweed, the gravedigger was dragged from his holes in the sand, and our numbers were checked and counted. Then we were all in our seats, the tarpaulin pulled over us, and with a blast of horns we left.

A long homeward drive through the red twilight, through landscapes already relinquished, the engines humming, the small children sleeping, and the young girls gobbling shrimps. At sunset we stopped at a gaslit pub for the men to have one more drink. This lasted till all of them turned bright pink and started embracing their wives. Then we repacked the charabancs, everyone grew drowsy, and we drove through the darkness beyond Bristol. The last home stretch: someone played a harmonica; we boys groped for women to sleep on, and slept, to the sway and sad roar of the coach and the men's thick boozy singing.

We passed Stroud at last and climbed the valley road, whose every curve our bodies recognized, whose every slant we leaned to, though still half asleep, till we woke to the smell of our houses. We were home, met by lanterns – and the Outing was over. With subdued 'Good-nights' we collected into families, then separated towards our beds. Where soon I lay, my head ringing with sleep, my ears full of motors and organs, my shut eyes printed with the images of the day – mud, and red rock, and hangmen . . .

The Parochial Church Tea and Annual Entertainment was the village's winter treat. It took place in the schoolroom, round about Twelfth Night, and cost us a shilling to go. The Tea was an orgy of communal gluttony, in which everyone took pains to eat more than his money's worth and the helpers ate more than the customers. The Entertainment which followed, home produced and by lamplight, provided us with sufficient catch-phrases for a year.

Regularly, for a few weeks before the night, one witnessed the same scenes in our kitchen, the sisters sitting in various corners of the room, muttering secretly to themselves, smiling, nodding, and making lah-di-dah gestures with a kind of intent and solitary madness. They were rehearsing their sketches for the Entertainment, which I found impossible not to learn too, so that I would be haunted for days by three nightmare monologues full of one-sided unanswered questions.

On the morning of the feast we got the school ready. We built a stage out of trestles and planks. Mr Robinson was in the cloakroom slicing boiled ham, where he'd been for the last three days, and three giggling helpers were now forking the meat and slapping it into sandwiches. Outside in the yard John Barraclough had arrived and set up his old field kitchen, had broken six hurdles across his knee, and filled up the boiler with water. Laid out on the wall were thirty-five teapots, freshly washed and drying in the wind. The feast was preparing; and by carrying chairs, helping with the stage, and fetching water from the spring, Jack and I made ourselves sufficiently noticeable to earn a free ticket each.

Punctually at six, with big eating to be done, we returned to the lighted school. Villagers with lanterns streamed in from all quarters. We heard the bubbling of water in Barraclough's boiler, smelt the sweet wood smoke from his fire, saw his red face lit like a turnip lamp as he crouched to stoke up the flames.

We lined up in the cold, not noticing the cold, waiting for the doors to open. When they did, it was chins and boots and elbows, no queues, we just fought our way in. Lamp-light and decorations had transformed the schoolroom from a prison into a banqueting hall. The long trestle-tables were patterned with food; fly-cake, brown buns, ham sandwiches. The two stoves were roaring, reeking of coke. The helpers had their teapots charged. We sat down stiffly and gazed at the food; fidgeted, coughed, and waited . . .

The stage-curtains parted to reveal the Squire, wearing a cloak and a deer-stalking hat. He cast his dim, wet eyes round the crowded room, then sighed and turned to go. Somebody whispered from behind the curtain; 'Bless me!' said the Squire, and came back.

'The Parochial Church Tea!' he began, then paused. 'Is with us again . . . I suggest. And Entertainment. Another year! Another year comes round! . . . When I see you all gathered together here – once more – when I see – when I think . . . And here you all are! When I see you here – as I'm sure you all are – once again . . . It comes to me, friends! – how time – how you – how all of us here – as it were . . .' His moustache was quivering, tears ran down his face, he groped for the curtains and left.

His place was taken by the snow-haired vicar, who beamed weakly upon us all.

'What is the smallest room in the world?' he asked.

'A mushroom!' we bawled, without hesitation.

'And the largest, may I ask?'

'ROOM FOR IMPROVEMENT!'

'You know it,' he muttered crossly. Recovering himself, he folded his hands: 'And now O bountiful Father . . .'

We barked through grace and got our hands on the food and began to eat it any old order. Cakes, buns, ham, it didn't matter at all, we just worked from one plate to the next. Folks by the fires fanned themselves with sandwiches, a joker fried ham on the stove, steaming brown teapots passed up and down, and we were so busy there was small conversation. Through the lighted windows we could see snow falling, huge feathers against the dark. 'It's old Mother Hawkins a-plucking her geese!' cried someone: an excellent omen. Twelfth Night, and old Mother Hawkins at work, up in the sky with her birds; we loosened our belts and began to nod at each other; it was going to be a year of fat.

We had littered the tables with our messy leavings of cake-crumbs and broken meat; some hands still went through the motions of eating, but clearly we'd had enough. The vicar rose to his feet again, and again we thanked the Lord. 'And now, my friends, comes the – er – feast for the soul. If you would care to – ah – take the air a moment, willing hands are waiting to clear the hall and prepare for the – um – Entertainment . . .'

We crowded outside and huddled in the snow while the tables were taken away. Inside, behind curtains, the actors were making up – and my moment, too, was approaching. The snow whirled about me and I began to sweat, I wanted to run off home. Then the doors reopened and I crouched by the stove, shivering and chattering with nerves. The curtains parted and the Entertainment began with a comic I neither saw nor heard . . .

'For the next item, ladies and gentlemen, we have an instrumental duet, by Miss Brown and – er – young Laurie Lee.'

Smirking with misery I walked to the stage. Eileen's face was as white as a minim. She sat at the piano, placed the music crooked, I straightened it, it fell to the ground. I groped to retrieve it; we looked at one another with hatred; the audience was still as death. Eileen tried to give me an A, but struck B instead, and I tuned up like an ape threading needles. At last we were ready, I raised my fiddle; and Eileen was off like a bolting horse. I caught her up in the middle of the piece – which I believe was a lullaby – and after playing the repeats, only twice as fast, we just stopped, frozen motionless, spent.

Some hearty stamping and whistling followed, and a shout of 'Give us another!' Eileen and I didn't exchange a glance, but we loved each other now. We found the music of 'Danny Boy' and began to give it all our emotion, dawdling dreamily among the fruitier chords and scampering over the high bits; till the audience joined in, using their hymn-singing voices, which showed us the utmost respect. When it was over I returned to my seat by the stove, my body feeling smooth and beautiful. Eileen's mother was weeping into her hat, and so was mine, I think . . .

Now I was free to become one of the audience, and the Entertainment burgeoned before me. What had seemed to me earlier as the capering of demons now became a spectacle of human genius. Turn followed turn in variety and splendour. Mr Crosby, the organist, told jokes and stories as though his very life depended on them, trembling, sweating, never pausing for a laugh, and rolling his eyes at the wings for rescue. We loved him, however, and wouldn't let him go, while he grew more and more hysterical, racing through monologues, gabbling songs about shrimps, skipping, mopping, and jumping up and down, as though humouring a tribe of savages.

Major Doveton came next, with his Indian banjo, which was even harder to tune than my fiddle. He straddled a chair and began wrestling with the keys, cursing us in English and Urdu. Then all the strings broke, and he snarled off the stage and started kicking the banjo round the cloakroom. He was followed by a play in which Marjorie, as Cinderella, sat in a goose-feathered dress in a castle. While waiting for the pumpkin to turn into a coach, she sang 'All alone by the telephone'.

Two ballads came next, and Mrs Pimbury, a widow, sang them both with astonishing spirit. The first invited us to go with her to Canada; the second was addressed to a mushroom:

> Grow! Grow! Grow little mushroom grow!
> Somebody wants you soon.
> I'll call again tomorrow morning –
> See!
> And if you've grown bigger you will just suit ME!
> So Grow! Grow! Grow little mushroom – Grow!

Though we'd not heard this before, it soon became part of our heritage, as did the song of a later lady. This last – the Baroness von Hodenburg – sealed our entertainment with almost professional distinction. She was a guest star from Sheepscombe and her appearance was striking, it enshrined all the mystery of art. She wore a loose green gown like a hospital patient's, and her hair was red and long. 'She writes,' whispered Mother. 'Poems and booklets and that.'

'I am going to sink you,' announced the lady, 'a little ditty I convected myself. Bose vords und music, I may say, is mine – und zey refer to ziss pleasant valleys.'

With that she sat down, arched her beautiful back, raised her bangled wrists over the keyboard, then ripped off some startling runs and trills, and sang with a ringing laugh:

> Elfin volk come over the hill!
> Come und dance, just vere you vill!
> Brink your pipes, und brink your flutes,
> Brink your sveetly soundink notes!
> Come avay-hay! Life is gay-hay!
> Life – Is – Gay!

We thought this song soppy, but we never forgot it. From then on, whenever we saw the Baroness in the lanes we used to bawl the song at her through the hedges. But she would only stop, and cock her head, and smile dreamily to herself . . .

After these songs the night ended with slapstick; rough stuff about babies, chaps dressed as women, broad Gloucester exchanges between yokels and toffs, with the yokels coming off best. We ached with joy, and kicked at the chairs; but we knew the end was coming. The vicar got up, proposed a vote of thanks, and said oranges would be distributed at the gate. The National Anthem was romped through, we all began coughing, then streamed outdoors through the snow.

Back home our sisters discussed their performances till the tears dripped off their noses. But to us boys it was not over, till tomorrow; there was still one squeeze left in the lemon. Tomorrow, very early, we'd go back to the schoolroom, find the baskets of broken food – half-eaten buns, ham coated with cake-crumbs – and together we'd finish the lot.

12

First Bite at the Apple

So quiet was Jo always, so timorous yet eager to please, that she was the one I chose first. There were others, of course, louder and more bouncingly helpful, but it was Jo's cool face, tidy brushed-back hair, thin body, and speechless grace which provided the secretive prettiness I needed. Unknowingly, therefore, she became the pathfinder, the slender taper I carried to the grottoes in whose shadows I now found myself wandering.

I used to seek her out on her way home from school, slyly separate her from the others, watch her brass bracelet dangling. Was I eleven or twelve? I don't know – she was younger. She smiled easily at me from the gutter.

'Where you going then, Jo?'

'Nowhere special.'

'Oh.'

It was all right so long as she didn't move.

'Let's go down the bank then. Shall us? Eh?'

No answer, but no attempt to escape.

'Down the bank. Like before. How about it, Jo?'

Still no answer, no sign or look. She didn't even stop the turning of her bracelet, but she came down the bank all the same. Stepping toe-pointed over the ant-heaps, walking straight and near and silent, she showed no knowledge of what she was going for, only that she was going with me.

Close under the yews, in the heavy green evening, we sat ourselves solemnly down. The old red trees threw arches above us, making tunnels of rusty darkness. Jo, like a slip of yew, was motionless; she neither looked at me nor away. I leaned on one elbow and tossed a stone into the trees, heard it skipping from branch to branch.

'What shall we do then, Jo?' I asked.

She made no reply, as usual.

'What d'you say, Jo?'

'I don't mind.'

'Come on – you tell.'

'No, you.'

The pronouncement had always to come from me. She waited to hear me say it. She waited, head still, staring straight before her, tugging gently at a root of weed.

'Good morning, Mrs Jenkins!' I said breezily. 'What seems to be the trouble?'

Without a blink or a word Jo lay down on the grass and gazed up at the red-berried yews, stretched herself subtly on her green crushed bed, and scratched her calf, and waited. The game was formal and grave in character, its ritual rigidly patterned. Silent as she lay, my hands moved as silently, and even the birds stopped singing.

Her body was pale and milk-green on the grass, like a birch-leaf lying in water, slightly curved like a leaf and veined and glowing, lit faintly from within its flesh. This was not Jo now but the revealed unknown, a labyrinth of naked stalks, stranger than flesh, smoother than candleskins, like something thrown down from the moon. Time passed, and the cool limbs never moved, neither towards me nor yet away; she just turned a grass ring around her fingers and stared blindly away from my eyes. The sun fell slanting and struck the spear-tipped grass, laying tiger-stripes round her hollows, binding her body with crimson bars, and moving slow colours across her.

Night and home seemed far away. We were caught in the rooted trees. Knees wet with dew I pondered in silence all that Jo's acquiescence taught me. She shivered slightly and stirred her hands. A blackbird screamed into a bush . . .

'Well, that'll be all, Mrs Jenkins,' I said. 'I'll be back again to-morrow.'

I rose from my knees, mounted an invisible horse, and cantered away to supper. While Jo dressed quietly and dawdled home, alone among the separate trees.

Of course, they discovered us in the end; we must have thought we were invisible. 'What about it, young lad? You and Jo – last night? Ho, yes! we seen you, arf! arf!' A couple of cowmen had stopped me in the road; I denied it, but I wasn't surprised. Sooner or later one was always caught out, but the thing was as readily forgotten; very little in the village was either secret or shocking, we merely repeated ourselves. Such early sex-games were formal exercises, a hornless charging of calves; but we were certainly lucky to live in a village, the landscape abounded with natural instruction which we imitated as best we could; if anyone saw us they laughed their heads off – and there were no magistrates to define us obscene.

This advantage was shared by young and old, was something no town can know. We knew ourselves to be as corrupt as any other community of our size – as any London street, for instance. But there was no tale-bearing then or ringing up 999; transgressors were dealt with by local opinion, by silence, lampoons, or nicknames. What we were spared from seeing – because the village protected itself – were the crimes of our flesh written cold in a charge sheet, the shady arrest, the police-court autopsy, the headline of magistrate's homilies.

As for us boys, it is certain that most of us, at some stage or other of our growth, would have been rounded up under present law, and quite a few shoved into reform school. Instead we emerged – culpable it's true – but unclassified in criminal record. No wilder or milder than Battersea boys, we were less ensnared by by-laws. If caught in the act, we got a quick bashing; and the fist of the farmer we'd robbed of apples or eggs seemed more natural and just than any cold-mouthed copper adding one more statistic for the book.

It is not crime that has increased, but its definition. The modern city, for youth, is a police-trap.

Our village was clearly no pagan paradise, neither were we conscious of showing tolerance. It was just the way of it. We certainly committed our share of statutory crime. Manslaughter, arson, robbery, rape cropped up regularly throughout the years. Quiet incest flourished where the roads were bad; some found their comfort in beasts; and there were the usual friendships between men and boys who walked through the fields like lovers. Drink, animality, and rustic boredom were responsible for most. The village neither approved nor disapproved, but neither did it complain to authority. Sometimes our sinners were given hell, taunted, and pilloried, but their crimes were absorbed in the local scene and their punishment confined to the parish.

So when, in due time, I breathed the first faint musks of sex, my problem was not one of guilt or concealment but of simple revelation. That early exploration of Jo's spread body was a solitary studying of maps. The signs upon her showed the way I should go, then she was folded and put away. Very soon I caught up with other travellers, all going in the same direction. They received me naturally, the boys and girls of my age, and together we entered the tricky wood. Daylight and an easy lack of shame illuminated our actions. Banks and brakes were our tiring-houses, and curiosity our first concern. We were awkward, convulsed, but never surreptitious, being protected by our long knowledge of each other. And we were all of that green age which could do no wrong, so unformed as yet and coldly innocent we did little more than mime the realities.

The girls played their part of invitation and show, and were rather more assured than we were. They sensed they had come into their own at last. For suddenly they were not creatures to order about any more, not the makeshift boys they had been; they possessed, and they knew it, the clues to secrets more momentous than we could guess. They became slippery and difficult – but far from impossible. Shy, silent Jo scarcely counted now against the challenge of Rosie and Bet. Bet was brazen, Rosie provocative, and together they forced our paces. Bet was big for eleven and shabbily blonde, and her eyes were drowsy with insolence. 'Gis a wine-gum,' she'd say, 'an I'll show ya, if ya want.' (For a wine-gum she would have stripped in church.) Rosie, on the other hand, more devious and sly, had sharp salts of wickedness on her, and she led me a dance round the barns and fowl-houses which often left me parched and trembling. What to do about either – Bet or Rosie – took a considerable time to discover.

Meanwhile, it was as though I had been dipped in hot oil, baked, dried, and hung throbbing on wires. Mysterious senses clicked into play overnight, possessed one in luxuriant order, and one's body seemed tilted out of all recognition by shifts in its balance of power. It was the time when the thighs seemed to burn like dry grass, to cry for cool water and cucumbers, when the emotions swung drowsily between belly and hands, prickled, hungered, moulded the curves of the clouds; and when to lie face downwards in a summer field was to feel the earth's thrust go through you. Brother Jack and I grew suddenly more active, always running or shinning up trees, working ourselves into lathers of exhaustion, whereas till then we'd been inclined to indolence. It was not that we didn't know what was happening to us, we just didn't know what to do with it. And I might have been shinning up trees to this day if it hadn't been for Rosie Burdock . . .

The day Rosie Burdock decided to take me in hand was a motionless day of summer, creamy, hazy, and amber-coloured, with the beech trees standing in heavy sunlight as though clogged with wild wet honey. It was the time of hay-making, so when we came out of school Jack and I went to the farm to help.

The whirr of the mower met us across the stubble, rabbits jumped like firecrackers about the fields, and the hay smelt crisp and sweet. The farmer's men were all hard at work, raking, turning, and loading. Tall, whiskered fellows forked the grass, their chests like bramble patches. The air swung with their forks and the swathes took wing and rose like eagles to the tops of the wagons. The farmer gave us a short fork each and we both pitched in with the rest . . .

I stumbled on Rosie behind a haycock, and she grinned up at me with the sly, glittering eyes of her mother. She wore her tartan frock and cheap brass necklace, and her bare legs were brown with hay-dust.

'Get out a there,' I said. 'Go on.'

Rosie had grown and was hefty now, and I was terrified of her. In her cat-like eyes and curling mouth I saw unnatural wisdoms more threatening than anything I could imagine. The last time we'd met I'd hit her with a cabbage stump. She bore me no grudge, just grinned.

'I got sommat to show ya.'

'You push off,' I said.

I felt dry and dripping, icy hot. Her eyes glinted, and I stood rooted. Her face was wrapped in a pulsating haze and her body seemed to flicker with lightning.

'You thirsty?' she said.

'I ain't, so there.'

'You be,' she said. 'C'mon.'

So I stuck the fork into the ringing ground and followed her, like doom.

We went a long way, to the bottom of the field, where a wagon stood half-loaded. Festoons of untrimmed grass hung down like curtains all around it. We crawled underneath, between the wheels, into a herb-scented cave of darkness. Rosie scratched about, turned over a sack, and revealed a stone jar of cider.

'It's cider,' she said. 'You ain't to drink it though. Not much of it, any rate.'

Huge and squat, the jar lay on the grass like an unexploded bomb. We lifted it up, unscrewed the stopper, and smelt the whiff of fermented apples. I held the jar to my mouth and rolled my eyes sideways, like a beast at a water-hole. 'Go on,' said Rosie. I took a deep breath . . .

Never to be forgotten, that first long secret drink of golden fire, juice of those valleys and of that time, wine of wild orchards, of russet summer, of plump red apples, and Rosie's burning cheeks. Never to be forgotten, or ever tasted again . . .

I put down the jar with a gulp and a gasp. Then I turned to look at Rosie. She was yellow and dusty with buttercups and seemed to be purring in the gloom; her hair was rich as a wild bee's nest and her eyes were full of stings. I did not know what to do about her, nor did I know what not to do. She looked smooth and precious, a thing of unplumbable mysteries, and perilous as quicksand.

'Rosie . . .' I said, on my knees, and shaking.

She crawled with a rustle of grass towards me, quick and superbly assured. Her hand in mine was like a small wet flame which I could neither hold nor throw away. Then Rosie, with a remorseless, reedy strength, pulled me down from my tottering perch, pulled me down, down into her wide green smile and into the deep subaqueous grass.

Then I remember little, and that little, vaguely. Skin drums beat in my head. Rosie was close-up, salty, an invisible touch, too near to be seen or measured. And it seemed that the wagon under which we lay went floating away like a barge, out over the valley where we rocked unseen, swinging on motionless tides.

Then she took off her boots and stuffed them with flowers. She did the same with mine. Her parched voice crackled like flames in my ears. More fires were started. I drank more cider. Rosie told me outrageous fantasies. She liked me, she said, better than Walt, or Ken, Boney Harris, or even the curate. And I admitted to her, in a loud, rough voice, that she was even prettier than Betty Gleed. For a long time we sat with our mouths very close, breathing the same hot air. We kissed, once only, so dry and shy, it was like two leaves colliding in air.

At last the cuckoos stopped singing and slid into the woods. The mowers went home and left us. I heard Jack calling as he went down the lane, calling my name till I heard him no more.

And still we lay in our wagon of grass tugging at each other's hands, while her husky, perilous whisper drugged me and the cider beat gongs in my head . . .

Night came at last, and we crawled out from the wagon and stumbled together towards home. Bright dew and glow-worms shone over the grass, and the heat of the day grew softer. I felt like a giant; I swung from the trees and plunged my arms into nettles just to show her. Whatever I did seemed valiant and easy. Rosie carried her boots, and smiled.

There was something about that evening which dilates the memory, even now. The long hills slavered like Chinese dragons, crimson in the setting sun. The shifting lane lassoed my feet and tried to trip me up. And the lake, as we passed it, rose hissing with waves and tried to drown us among its cannibal fish.

Perhaps I fell in – though I don't remember. But here I lost Rosie for good. I found myself wandering home alone, wet through, and possessed by miracles. I discovered extraordinary tricks of sight. I could make trees move and leapfrog each other, and turn bushes into roaring trains. I could lick up the stars like acid drops and fall flat on my face without pain. I felt magnificent, fateful, and for the first time in my life, invulnerable to the perils of night.

When at last I reached home, still dripping wet, I was bursting with power and pleasure. I sat on the chopping-block and sang 'Fierce Raged the Tempest' and several other hymns of that nature. I went on singing till long after supper-time, bawling alone in the dark. Then Harold and Jack came and frog-marched me to bed. I was never the same again . . .

A year or so later occurred the Brith Wood rape. If it could be said to have occurred. By now I was one of a green-horned gang who went bellowing round the lanes, scuffling, fighting, aimless and dangerous, confused by our strength and boredom. Of course something like this was bound to happen, and it happened on a Sunday.

We planned the rape a week before, up in the builder's stable. The stable's thick air of mouldy chaff, dry leather, and rotting straw, its acid floors and unwashed darkness provided the atmosphere we needed. We met there regularly to play cards and scratch and whistle and talk about girls.

There were about half a dozen of us that morning, including Walt Kerry, Bill Shepherd, Sixpence the Tanner, Boney, and Clergy Green. The valley outside, seen through the open door, was crawling with April rain. We sat round on buckets sucking strips of harness. Then suddenly Bill Shepherd came out with it.

'Here,' he said. 'Listen. I got'n idea . . .'

He dropped his voice into a furry whisper and drew us into a circle.

'You know that Lizzy Berkeley, don't ya?' he said. He was a fat-faced lad, powerful and shifty, with a perpetual caught-in-the-act look. 'She'd do,' he said. 'She's daft in the 'ead. She'd be all right, y'know.'

We thought about Lizzy and it was true enough; she was daft about religion. A short, plump girl of about sixteen, with large, blue-bottle eyes, she used to walk in Brith Wood with a handful of crayons writing texts on the trunks of the beech trees. Huge rainbow letters on the smooth green bark, saying 'JESUS LOVES ME NOW.'

'I seen 'er Sunday,' said Walt, 'an' she was at it then.'

'She's always at it,' said Boney.

'Jerusalem!' said Clergy in his pulpit voice.

'Well, 'ow about it?' said Bill.

We drew closer together, out of earshot of the horse. Bill rolled us in his round red eyes.

'It's like this, see. Blummin'-well simple.' We listened and held our breath. 'After church Sunday mornin' we nips up to the wood. An' when 'er comes back from chapel – we got 'er.'

We all breathed out. We saw it clearly. We saw her coming alone through the Sunday wood, chalk-coloured Lizzy, unsuspecting and holy, in the bundle of her clothes and body. We saw her come walking through her text-chalked trees, blindly, straight into our hands.

'She'd 'oller,' said Boney.

'She's too batty,' said Bill.

'She'd think I was one of the 'possles.'

Clergy gave his whinnying, nervous giggle, and Boney rolled on the floor.

'You all on, then?' Bill whispered. 'Wha's say? 'Ow about it? It'll half be a stunt, you watch.'

We none of us answered, but we all felt committed; soon as planned, the act seemed done. We had seen it so vividly it could have happened already, and there was no more to be said. For the rest of the week we avoided each other, but we lived with our scruffy plan. We thought of little else but that coming encounter; of mad Lizzy and her stumpy, accessible body which we should all of us somehow know . . .

On Sunday morning we trooped from the church and signalled to each other with our eyebrows. The morning was damp with a springtime sun. We nodded, winked, and jerked our heads, then made our separate ways to the wood. When we gathered at last at the point of ambush, the bounce had somehow gone out of us. We were tense and silent; nobody spoke. We lay low as arranged, and waited.

We waited a long time. Birds sang, squirrels chattered, the sun shone; but nobody came. We began to cheer up and giggle.

'She ain't comin',' said someone. 'She seen Bill first.'

'She seen 'im and gone screamin' 'ome.'

''Er's lucky, then. I'd 'ave made 'er 'oller.'

'I'd 'ave run 'er up a tree.'

We were savage and happy, as though we'd won a battle. But we waited a little while longer.

'Sod it!' said Bill. 'Let's push off. Come on.' And we were all of us glad he'd said it.

At that moment we saw her, walking dumpily up the path, solemn in her silly straw hat. Bill and Boney went sickly pale and

watched her in utter misery. She approached us slowly, a small fat doll, shafts of sunlight stroking her dress. None of us moved as she drew level with us, we just looked at Bill and Boney. They returned our looks with a kind of abject despair and slowly got to their feet.

What happened was clumsy, quick, and meaningless; silent, like a very old film. The two boys went loping down the bank and barred the plump girl's way. She came to a halt and they all stared at each other ... The key moment of our fantasy; and trivial. After a gawky pause, Bill shuffled towards her and laid a hand on her shoulder. She hit him twice with her bag of crayons, stiffly, with the jerk of a puppet. Then she turned, fell down, got up, looked round, and trotted away through the trees.

Bill and Boney did nothing to stop her, they slumped and just watched her go. And the last we saw of our virgin Lizzy was a small round figure, like a rubber ball, bouncing downhill out of sight.

After that, we just melted away through the wood, separately, in opposite directions. I dawdled home slowly, whistling aimless tunes and throwing stones at stumps and gateposts. What had happened that morning was impossible to say. But we never spoke of it again.

As for our leaders, those red-fanged ravishers of innocence – what happened to them in the end? Boney was raped himself soon afterwards; and married his attacker, a rich farm-widow, who worked him to death in her bed and barnyard. Bill Shepherd met a girl who trapped him neatly by stealing his Post Office Savings Book. Walt went to sea and won prizes for cooking, then married into the fish-frying business. The others married too, raised large families, and became members of the Parish Church Council.

Of the little girls who had been our victims and educators, and who led us through those days: pretty Jo grew fat with a Painswick baker, lusty Bet went to breed in Australia, and Rosie, having baptized me with her cidrous kisses, married a soldier and I lost her for ever.

13

Last Days

The last days of my childhood were also the last days of the village. I belonged to that generation which saw, by chance, the end of a thousand years' life. The change came late to our Cotswold valley, didn't really show itself till the late 1920s; I was twelve by then, but during that handful of years I witnessed the whole thing happen.

Myself, my family, my generation, were born in a world of silence; a world of hard work and necessary patience, of backs bent to the ground, hands massaging the crops, of waiting on weather and growth; of villages like ships in the empty landscapes and the long walking distances between them; of white narrow roads, rutted by hooves and cartwheels, innocent of oil or petrol, down which people passed rarely, and almost never for pleasure, and the horse was the fastest thing moving. Man and horse were all the power we had – abetted by levers and pulleys. But the horse was king, and almost everything grew around him: fodder, smithies, stables, paddocks, distances, and the rhythm of our days. His eight miles an hour was the limit of our movements, as it had been since the days of the Romans. That eight miles an hour was life and death, the size of our world, our prison.

This was what we were born to, and all we knew at first. Then, to the scream of the horse, the change began. The brass-lamped motor car came coughing up the road, followed by the clamorous charabanc; the solid-tyred bus climbed the dusty hills and more people came and went. Chickens and dogs were the early sacrifices, falling demented beneath the wheels. The old folk, too, had strokes and seizures, faced by speeds beyond comprehension. Then scarlet motor-bikes, the size of five-barred gates, began to appear in the village, on which our youths roared like rockets up the two-minute hills, then spent weeks making repairs and adjustments.

These appearances did not immediately alter our lives; the cars were freaks and rarely seen, the motor-bikes mostly in pieces, we used the charabancs only once a year, and our buses at first were experiments. Meanwhile Lew Ayres, wearing a bowler-hat, ran his wagonette to Stroud twice a week. The carriage held six, and the fare was twopence, but most people preferred to walk. Mr West, from Sheepscombe, ran a cart every day, and would carry your parcels for a penny. But most of us still did the journey on foot, heads down to the wet Welsh winds, ignoring the carters – whom we thought extortionate – and spending a long hard day at our shopping.

But the car-shying horses with their rolling eyes gave signs of the hysteria to come. Soon the village would break, dissolve, and scatter, become no more than a place for pensioners. It had a few years left, the last of its thousand, and they passed almost without our knowing. They passed quickly, painlessly, in motor-bike jaunts, in the shadows of the new picture-palace, in quick trips to Gloucester (once a foreign city) to gape at the jazzy shops. Yet right to the end, like the false strength that precedes death, the old life seemed as lusty as ever.

The church, for instance, had never appeared more powerful. Its confident bell rang out each Sunday; the village heard it, asked no questions, put on satin and serge, filed into the pews, bobbed and nodded, frowned at its children, crouched and prayed, bawled or quavered through hymns, and sat in blank rows or jerkily slept while the curate reeled off those literary sermons which he had hired from the ecclesiastical library.

Sunday, far from being a day of rest, was in some ways tougher than a weekday; it was never torpid and it gave one a lift, being a combination of both indulgence and discipline. On that one day in seven – having bathed the night before – we were clean, wore our best, and ate meat. The discipline was Sunday School, learning the Collect, and worship both morning and evening. Neither mood nor inclination had any say in the matter, nor had doubt occurred to us yet.

Sunday mornings at home were the usual rush – chaos in the kitchen, shrill orders to wash, and everyone's eyes on the clock. We polished our hair with grease and water, and scrubbed ourselves under the pump. Being Sunday, there was a pound of large sausages for breakfast, fried black and bursting with fat. One dipped them in pepper and ate them in haste, an open prayer-book propped up by the plate.

'Heavens alive, you'll be late, our lad.'

Gobble, mumble, and choke.

'What *are* you up to? Get a move on do.'

'Leave off – I'm learning the Collect.'

'What's that you say?'

'I-Gotta-Learn-Me-Collect!'

'Hurry up and learn it then.'

'I can't hurry up! Not if you keep on! . . .'

But it was really not difficult at all; ten inscrutable lines absorbed between mouthfuls, and usually on the run. Up the bank, down the road, the greasy prayer-book in one hand, the remains of the sausage in the other: 'Almighty and Most Merciful Father, who alone worketh Great Marvels . . .' In five minutes it was all in my head.

At Sunday School Miss Bagnall, polishing her nose, said: 'The Collect – now who will oblige . . .' I would jump to my feet and gabble, word perfect, the half page of sonorous syllables. It came in through the eyes and out through the mouth, and left no trace of its passing. Except that I can never read a Collect today without tasting a crisp burnt sausage . . .

After an hour of Sunday School we all went to the church, the choir going straight to the vestry. Here we huddled ourselves into our grimy robes, which only got washed at Easter. The parson lined us up and gave us a short, sharp prayer; then we filed into the stalls, took our privileged places, and studied the congregation. The Sunday School infants packed the bleak north wing, heads fuzzy as frosted flowers. The rest of the church was black with adults, solemn in cat's-fur and feathers. Most were arranged in family groups, but here and there a young couple, newly engaged, sat red in the neck and hands. The leading benches contained our gentry, their pews marked with visiting cards: the Lords of the Manor, Squire Jones and the Croomes; then the Army, the Carvossos and Dovetons; the rich and settled spinsters, the Misses Abels and Bagnalls; and finally the wealthier farmers. All were neatly arranged by protocol, with the Squire up front by the pulpit. Through prayers and psalms and rackety hymns he slept like a beaming child, save when a visiting preacher took some rhetorical flight, when he'd wake with a loud, 'God damn!'

Morning service began with an organ voluntary, perhaps a Strauss waltz played very slow. The organ was old, and its creaks and sighs were often louder than the music itself. The organ was blown by an ordinary pump-handle which made the process equally rowdy; and Rex Brown, the blower, hidden away in his box – and only visible to us in the choir – enlivened the service by parodying it in mime or by carving girls' names on the woodwork.

But in the packed congregation solemnity ruled. There was power, lamentation, full-throated singing, heavy prayers, and public repentance. No one in the village stayed away without reason, and no one yet wished to do so. We had come to the church because it was Sunday, just as we washed our clothes on Monday. There was also God taking terrible notes – a kind of Squire-archical rent-collector, ever ready to record the tenants' backsliding and to evict them if their dues weren't paid.

This morning service was also something else. It was a return to the Ark of all our species in the face of the ever-threatening flood. We are free of that need now and when the flood does come shall drown proud and alone, no doubt. As it was, the lion knelt down with the lamb, the dove perched on the neck of the hawk, sheep nuzzled wolf, we drew warmth from each other and knew ourselves beasts of one kingdom . . .

That was Sunday morning. With the service over, there was gossip among the gravestones, a slow walk home to roasted dinners, then a nap with the *News of the World*. The elders dozed sexily through the fat afternoon, while the young went again to Sunday School. Later came Evensong, which was as different from Matins as a tryst from a Trafalgar Square rally. The atmosphere was gentler, moonier, more private; the service was considered to be voluntary. We choirboys, of course, were compelled to go, but for the rest they went who would.

The church at night, in the dark of the churchyard, was just a strip of red-fired windows. Inside, the oil-lamps and motionless candles narrowed the place with shadows. The display of the morning was absent now; the nave was intimate, and sleepy. Only a few solitary worshippers were present this time, each cloaked in a separate absorption: a Miss Bagnall, Widow White, the church-cleaning woman, a widower, and the postman at the back. The service was almost a reverie, our hymns nocturnal and quiet, the psalms traditional and never varying so that one could sing them without a book. The scattered faithful, half-obscured by darkness, sang them as though to themselves. 'Lord, now lettest Thou Thy servant depart in peace . . .' It was sung, eyes closed, in trembling tones. It could not have been sung in the morning.

From our seats in the choir we watched the year turn: Christmas, Easter and Whitsun, Rogation Sunday and prayers for rain, the Church following the plough very close. Harvest Festival perhaps was the one we liked best, the one that came nearest home. Then how heavily and abundantly was our small church loaded; the cream of the valley was used to decorate it. Everyone brought of his best from field and garden; and to enter the church on Harvest morning was like crawling head first into a horn of plenty, a bursting granary, a vegetable stall, a grotto of bright flowers. The normally bare walls sprouted leaves and fruits, the altar great stooks of wheat, and ornamental loaves as big as cartwheels stood parked by the communion rails. Bunches of grapes, from the Squire's own vines, hung blue from the lips of the pulpit. Gigantic and useless marrows abounded, leeks and onions festooned the pews, there were eggs and butter on the lectern shelves, the windows were heaped with apples, and the fat round pillars which divided the church were skirted with oats and barley.

Almost everyone in the congregation had some hand in these things. Square-rumped farmers and ploughmen in chokers, old gardeners and poultry-keepers, they nodded and pointed and prodded each other to draw attention to what they had brought. The church was older than its one foundation, was as old as man's life on earth. The seed of these fruits, and the seed of these men, still came from the same one bowl; confined to this valley and renewing itself here, it went back to the days of the Ice. Pride, placation, and the continuity of growth were what we had come to praise. And even where we sang, 'All is safely gathered in', knowing full well that some of Farmer Lusty's oats still lay rotting in the fields, the discrepancy didn't seem important.

I remember one particular Harvest Festival which perfectly summed up this feeling. I was not old enough then to be in the choir, and I was sitting beside Tony, who was three. It was his first Harvest Festival, but he'd heard much about it and his expectations were huge. The choir, with banners, was fidgeting in the doorway, ready to start its procession. Tony gazed with glittering eyes around him, sniffing the juicy splendours. Then, in a moment of silence, just before the organ crashed into the hymn, he asked loudly, 'Is there going to be drums?'

It was a natural question, innocent and true. For neither drums, nor cymbals, nor trumpets of brass would have seemed out of place at that time.

The death of the Squire was not the death of the church, though they drew to their end together. He died, and the Big House was sold by auction and became a Home for Invalids. The lake silted up, the swans flew away, and the great pike choked in the reeds. With the Squire's hand removed, we fell apart – though we were about to do so anyway. His servants dispersed and went into the factories. His nephew broke up the estate.

Fragmentation, free thought, and new excitements, came now to intrigue and perplex us. The first young couple to get married in a registry office were roundly denounced from the pulpit. 'They who play with fire shall be consumed by fire!' stormed the vicar. 'Ye mark my words!' Later he caught me reading *Sons and Lovers* and took it away and destroyed it. This may well have been one of his last authoritative gestures. A young apologist succeeded him soon.

Meanwhile the old people just dropped away – the white-whiskered, gaitered, booted and bonneted, ancient-tongued last of their world, who thee'd and thou'd both man and beast, called young girls 'damsels', young boys 'squires', old men 'masters', the Squire himself 'He', and who remembered the Birdlip stagecoach. Kicker Harris, the old coachman, with his top-hat and leggings, blew away like a torn-out page. Lottie Escourt, peasant shoot of a Norman lord, curled up in her relics and died. Others departed with hardly a sound. There was old Mrs Clissold, who sometimes called us for errands: 'Thee come up our court a minute, squire; I wants thee to do I a mission.' One ran to the shop to buy her a packet of bull's-eyes and was rewarded in the customary way. Bull's-eye in cheek, she'd sink back in her chair and dismiss one with a sleepy nod. 'I ain't nurn a aypence about I just now – but Mrs Crissole'll recollect 'ee ...' We wrote her off as the day's good deed, and she died still recollecting us.

Now the last days of my family, too, drew near, beginning with the courting of the girls.

I remember very clearly how it started. It was summer, and we boys were sitting on the bank watching a great cloud of smoke in the sky.

A man jumped off his bike and cried, 'It's the boiler-works!' and we ran up the hill to see it.

There was a fire at the boiler-works almost every year. When we got there we found it a particularly good one. The warehouse, as usual, was sheathed in flame, ceilings and floors fell in, firemen shouted, windows melted like icicles, and from inside the building one heard thundering booms as the boilers started crashing about. We used up a lot of the day at this, cheering each toppling chimney.

When we got back to the village, much later in the evening, we saw a strange man down in our garden. We studied him from a distance with some feeling of shock. No one but neighbours and visiting relations had ever walked there before. Yet this ominous stranger was not only wandering free, he was being accompanied by all our women.

We rushed down the bank and burst roughly upon them, to find everyone crack-jawed with politeness. Our sisters cried La! when they saw us coming, and made us welcome as though we'd been round the world. Marjorie was particularly soft and loving, the others beamed anxiously at us; Mother, though not smart, was in her best black dress, and the stranger was twisting his hat.

'These are our brothers,' said Marjorie, grabbing two of us close to her bosom. 'This is Jackie and Loll, and that one's Tone. They're all of them terrible bad.'

There was nervous laughter and relief at this, as though several dark ghosts had been laid. We smirked and wriggled, aped and showed off, but couldn't think what was going on. In fact, the day of that boiler-works fire marked a beacon in the life of our girls. It was the day when their first young man came courting, and this stranger was he, and he was Marjorie's, and he opened a path through the garden.

He was handsome, curly-haired, a builder of barges, very strong, and entirely acceptable. His name was Maurice, and we boys soon approved him and gave him the run of the place. He was followed quite quickly by two other young men, one each for Dorothy and

Phyllis. Dorothy got Leslie, who was a shy local scoutmaster, at least until he met her; Phyllis in turn produced Harold the Bootmaker, who had fine Latin looks, played the piano by ear, and sang songs about old-fashioned mothers. Then Harold, our brother, got the infection too, mended our chairs, re-upholstered the furniture, and brought home a girl for himself.

At these strokes our home life changed for ever; new manners and notions crept in; instead of eight in the kitchen there were now a round dozen, and so it stayed till the girls started marrying. The young men called nightly, with candles in jars, falling headlong down our precipitous bank; or came pushing their bikes on summer evenings, loitering with the girls in the lanes; or sat round the fire talking slowly of work; or sat silent, just being there; while the sewing-machine hummed, and Mother rambled, and warm ripples of nothing lapped round them. They were wary of Mother, unsure of her temper, though her outbursts were at the world, not people. Leslie was tactful and diffident, giving short sharp laughs at her jokes. Maurice often lectured her on 'The Working Man Today', which robbed her of all understanding. Phyl's Harold would sometimes draw up to the piano, strike the keys with the strength of ten, then charm us all by bawling 'Because' or 'An Old Lady Passing By'.

Then there was cheese and cocoa, and 'Good-night all', and the first one got up to leave. There followed long farewells by the back-kitchen door, each couple taking their turn. Those waiting inside had to bide their time. 'Our Doth! Ain't you finished yet?' 'Shan't be a minute.' Yum-yum, kiss-kiss. 'Well, hurry up do! You're awful.' Five more minutes of silence outside, then Marge shakes the latch on the door. 'How much longer, our Doth? You been there all night. There's some got to work tomorrow,' 'All right, don't get ratty. He's just off now. Night-night, my beautiful bab.' One by one they departed; we turned down the lights, and the girls heaved themselves to bed.

Sundays, or Bank Holidays, were day-long courtships, and then the lovers were all over us. When it rained it was hopeless and we

just played cards, or the boyfriends modelled for dress-making.
When fine perhaps Mother would plan a small treat, like a picnic
in the woods.

I remember a sweltering August Sunday. Mother said it would
be nice to go out. We would walk a short mile to a nice green
spot and boil a kettle under the trees. It sounded simple enough,
but we knew better. For Mother's picnics were planned on a tribal
scale, with huge preparations beforehand. She flew round the
kitchen issuing orders and the young men stood appalled at the
work. There were sliced cucumbers and pots of paste, radishes,
pepper and salt, cakes and buns and macaroons, soup-plates of
bread and butter, jam, treacle, jugs of milk, and several fresh-
made jellies.

The young men didn't approve of this at all, and muttered it
was blooming mad. But with a 'You carry that now, there's a
dear boy', each of us carried something. So we set off at last like a
frieze of Greeks bearing gifts to some woodland god – Mother,
with a tea-cloth over her head, gathering flowers as she went
along, the sisters following with cakes and bread, Jack with the
kettle, Tony with the salt, myself with a jug of milk; then the
scowling youths in their blue serge suits carrying the jellies in
open basins – jellies which rapidly melted in the sun and splashed
them with yellow and rose. The young men swapped curses under
their breath, brother Harold hung back in shame, while Mother
led the way with prattling songs determined to make the thing go.

She knew soon enough when people turned sour and moved
mountains to charm them out of it, and showed that she knew by
a desperate gaiety and by noisy attacks on silence.

'Now come along, Maurice, best foot forward, mind how you
go, tee-hee. Leslie! just look at those pretty what-d'you-call'-ems –
those what's-is – *aren't* they a picture? I said Leslie, look, aren't
they pretty, my dear? Funny you don't know the name. Oh, isn't
it a scrumptious day, tra-la? Boys, isn't it a scrumptious day?'

Wordy, flustered, but undefeated, she got us to the woods at
last. We were ordered to scatter and gather sticks and to build a

fire for the kettle. The fire smoked glumly and stung our eyes, the young men sat round like martyrs, the milk turned sour, the butter fried on the bread, cake crumbs got stuck to the cucumber, wasps seized the treacle, the kettle wouldn't boil, and we ended by drinking the jellies.

As we boys would eat anything, anywhere, none of this bothered us much. But the young courting men sat on their spread silk handkerchiefs and gazed at the meal in horror. 'No thanks, Mrs Lee. I don't think I could. I've just had me dinner, ta.'

They were none of them used to such disorder, didn't care much for open-air picnics – but most of all they were wishing to be away with their girls, away in some field or gully, where summer and love would be food enough, and an absence of us entirely.

When the girls got engaged heavy blushes followed as the rings were shown to the family. 'It's a cluster of brilliants. Cost more than two pounds. He got it at Gloucester Market.' Now that things were official, there was more sitting in the dark and a visible increase in tensions. The girls were now grown and they wished to be gone. They were in love and had found their men. Meanwhile, impatience nagged at them all, till in one case it suddenly exploded . . .

It was evening. I was drawing at the kitchen table. One of the girls was late. When she came at last we had finished supper. She arrived with her boy, which seemed unusual, as it wasn't his calling-night.

'Well, take your coat off,' said Mother. 'Sit down.'

'No, thank you,' he answered frozenly.

'Don't just stand there – stiff as stiff can be.'

'I'm all right, Mrs Lee, I assure you.'

'Ma, we've been thinking –' the sister began. Her voice was level and loud.

I always went still at the sound of trouble, and didn't turn round or look. I just worked at my drawing, and each line and detail became inscribed with the growing argument. A pencilled leaf, the crook of a branch, each carried a clinging phrase: 'Don't talk so daft ... You're acting very funny ... You don't none of you know what I feel ... It's cruel to hear you talk like that ... I never had a proper chance ... Oh, come and sit down and don't act so silly ... It's no good, we made up our minds ... She's just about had enough, Mrs Lee, it's time she was out of it all ...' My pencil paused; what did they mean?

The other girls were indignant, Mother sad and lost, the argument rose and fell. 'Well, that's what *we* think, anyway. It's a scandal, you coming like this. What about him? – he just walks in – who does he think he is? What about *you*, if it comes to that? Well, what about us? We're listening. You think the whole place is just run for you. We don't! You do! We never! Well, come on girl, I've had enough!' Shocked pause, aghast. 'You dare!'

I was listening with every nerve and muscle of my back. Nothing happened; words flared and died. At last we boys went up to bed, undressed, and lay in the dark. As we lay, still listening, the kitchen grew quieter, the trouble seemed to fade to a murmur ... Suddenly, there was uproar, the girls screaming, Mother howling, and a scuffling and crashing of furniture. Jack and I sprang instantly from our beds and tore downstairs in our shirts. We found Mother and two sisters at the young man's throat, bouncing him against the wall. The other girl was trying to pull them away. The whole was a scene of chaos. Without hesitation, and in spite of the congestion, we sprang at the young man too.

But by the time we reached him the battle was over, the women had broken off. The young man stood panting, alone in the corner. I gave him a shove, he gave me a swipe, then he bent down to look for his hat.

He had tried to carry off our willing sister and we had all of us very near killed him. Now, just as suddenly, everybody was kissing each other, weeping, embracing, forgiving. Mother put her arm round the young man's neck and nearly strangled him afresh with affection. The whole party moved out into the dark back-kitchen, sniffing, and murmuring; 'There, there. It's all right. We're all friends now, aren't we? Dear boy ... Oh, Mother ... There, there ...'

A moment before I'd been blind with anger, ready to slay for the family. Now the rage was over, cancelled, let down. I turned in disgust from their billing and cooing; went up to the fire, lifted my nightshirt, and warmed my bare loins on the fire-guard ...

The girls were to marry; the Squire was dead; buses ran and the towns were nearer. We began to shrug off the valley and look more to the world, where pleasures were more anonymous and tasty. They were coming fast, and we were nearly ready for them. Each week Miss Bagnall held her penny dances where girls' shapes grew more familiar. For a penny one could swing them through Lancers and Two-Steps across the resinous floor of the Hut – but if one swung them entirely off their feet then Miss B locked the piano and went home ...

Time squared itself, and the village shrank, and distances crept nearer. The sun and moon, which once rose from our hill, rose from London now in the east. One's body was no longer a punch-ing ball, to be thrown against trees and banks, but a telescoping totem crying strange demands few of which we could yet supply. In the faces of the villagers one could see one's change, and in their habits their own change also. The horses had died; few people kept pigs any more but spent their spare time buried in engines. The flutes and cornets, the gramophones with horns, the wind harps were thrown away – now wireless aerials searched the electric sky for the music of the Savoy Orpheans. Old men in the pubs sang, 'As I Walked Out', then walked out and never came back. Our Mother was grey now, and a shade more light-headed, talking of mansions she would never build.

As for me – for me, the grass grew longer, and more sorrowful, and the trees were surfaced like flesh, and girls were no longer to be treated lightly but were creatures of commanding sadness, and all journeys through the valley were now made alone, with passion in every bush, and the motions of wind and cloud and stars were suddenly for myself alone, and voices elected me of all men living and called me to deliver the world, and I groaned from solitude, blushed when I stumbled, loved strangers and bread and butter, and made long trips through the rain on my bicycle, stared wretchedly through lighted windows, grinned wryly to think how little I was known, and lived in a state of raging excitement.

The sisters, as I said, were about to get married. Harold was working at a factory lathe. Brother Jack was at Grammar School, and his grammar was excellent; and Tony still had a fine treble voice. My Mother half-knew me, but could not help, I felt doomed, and of all things wonderful.

It was then that I began to sit on my bed and stare out at the nibbling squirrels, and to make up poems from intense abstraction, hour after unmarked hour, imagination scarcely faltering once, rhythm hardly skipping a beat, while sisters called me, suns rose and fell, and the poems I made, which I never remembered, were the first and last of that time . . .

As I Walked Out One Midsummer Morning

Illustrated by Leonard Rosoman

To T. S. Matthews

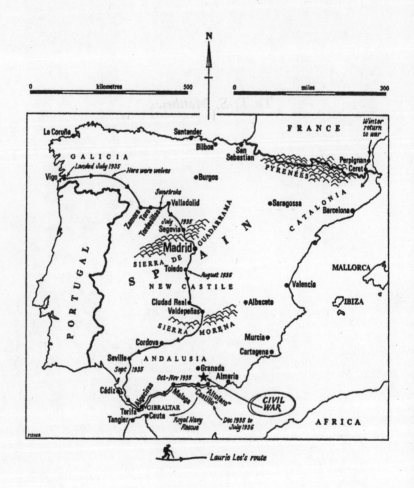

Laurie Lee's route

Contents

Just before the Spanish Civil War, I lived in a small fishing village in Andalucia whose Mayor has since erected a small monument on the sea-front proclaiming that 'The grand writer Laurie Lee once passed this way and immortalized the town in his work *As I Walked Out One Midsummer Morning* and *A Rose for Winter*.' I originally concealed the name of the town for political reasons and referred to it as 'Castillo'. Fortunately, that reticence no longer applies, and I am now able to give the town its real name of 'Almuñécar'.

Laurie Lee
March 1995

1

London Road

The stooping figure of my mother, waist-deep in the grass and caught there like a piece of sheep's wool, was the last I saw of my country home as I left it to discover the world. She stood old and bent at the top of the bank, silently watching me go, one gnarled red hand raised in farewell and blessing, not questioning why I went. At the bend of the road I looked back again and saw the gold light die behind her; then I turned the corner, passed the village school, and closed that part of my life for ever.

It was a bright Sunday morning in early June, the right time to be leaving home. My three sisters and a brother had already gone before me; two other brothers had yet to make up their minds. They were still sleeping that morning, but my mother had got up early and cooked me a heavy breakfast, had stood wordlessly while I ate it, her hand on my chair, and had then helped me pack up my few belongings. There had been no fuss, no appeals, no attempts at advice or persuasion, only a long and searching look. Then, with my bags on my back, I'd gone out into the early sunshine and climbed through the long wet grass to the road.

It was 1934. I was nineteen years old, still soft at the edges, but with a confident belief in good fortune. I carried a small rolled-up tent, a violin in a blanket, a change of clothes, a tin of treacle biscuits, and some cheese. I was excited, vainglorious, knowing I had far to go; but not, as yet, how far. As I left home that morning and walked away from the sleeping village, it never occurred to me that others had done this before me.

I was propelled, of course, by the traditional forces that had sent many generations along this road – by the small tight valley closing in around one, stifling the breath with its mossy mouth, the cottage walls narrowing like the arms of an iron maiden, the local girls whispering, 'Marry, and settle down.' Months of restless unease, leading to this inevitable moment, had been spent wandering about the hills, mournfully whistling, and watching the high open fields stepping away eastwards under gigantic clouds . . .

And now I was on my journey, in a pair of thick boots and with a hazel stick in my hand. Naturally, I was going to London, which lay a hundred miles to the east; and it seemed equally obvious that I should go on foot. But first, as I'd never yet seen the sea, I thought I'd walk to the coast and find it. This would add another hundred miles to my journey, going by way of Southampton. But I had all the summer and all time to spend.

That first day alone – and now I was really alone at last – steadily declined in excitement and vigour. As I tramped through the dust towards the Wiltshire Downs a growing reluctance weighed me down. White elder-blossom and dog-roses hung in the hedges, blank as unwritten paper, and the hot empty road – there were few motor cars then – reflected Sunday's waste and indifference. High sulky summer sucked me towards it, and I offered no resistance at all. Through the solitary morning and afternoon I found myself longing for some opposition or rescue, for the sound of hurrying footsteps coming after me and family voices calling me back.

None came. I was free. I was affronted by freedom. The day's silence said, Go where you will. It's all yours. You asked for it. It's up to you now. You're on your own, and nobody's going to stop you. As I walked, I was taunted by echoes of home, by the tinkling sounds of the kitchen, shafts of sun from the windows falling across the familiar furniture, across the bedroom and the bed I had left.

When I judged it to be tea-time I sat on an old stone wall and opened my tin of treacle biscuits As I ate them I could hear mother banging the kettle on the hob and my brothers rattling their tea-cups. The biscuits tasted sweetly of the honeyed squalor of home – still only a dozen miles away.

I might have turned back then if it hadn't been for my brothers, but I couldn't have borne the look on their faces. So I got off the wall and went on my way. The long evening shadows pointed to folded villages, homing cows, and after-church walkers. I tramped the edge of the road, watching my dusty feet, not stopping again for a couple of hours.

When darkness came, full of moths and beetles, I was too weary to put up the tent. So I lay myself down in the middle of a field and stared up at the brilliant stars. I was oppressed by the velvety emptiness of the world and the swathes of soft grass I lay on. Then the fumes of the night finally put me to sleep – my first night without a roof or bed.

I was woken soon after midnight by drizzling rain on my face, the sky black and the stars all gone Two cows stood over me, windily sighing, and the wretchedness of that moment haunts me still. I crawled into a ditch and lay awake till dawn, soaking alone in that nameless field. But when the sun rose in the morning the feeling of desolation was over. Birds sang, and the grass steamed warmly. I got up and shook myself, ate a piece of cheese, and turned again to the south.

Now I came down through Wiltshire, burning my roots behind me and slowly getting my second wind; taking it easy, idling through towns and villages, and knowing what it was like not to have to go to work. Four years as a junior in that gaslit office in Stroud had kept me pretty closely tied. Now I was tasting the extravagant quality of being free on a weekday, say at eleven o'clock in the morning, able to scuff down a side-road and watch a man herding sheep, or a stalking cat in the grass, or to beg a screw of tea from a housewife and carry it into a wood and spend an hour boiling a can of spring water.

As for this pocket of England through which I found myself

walking, it seemed to me immense. A motor car, of course, could have crossed it in a couple of hours, but it took me the best part of a week, treading it slowly, smelling its different soils, spending a whole morning working round a hill. I was lucky, I know, to have been setting out at that time, in a landscape not yet bulldozed for speed. Many of the country roads still followed their original tracks, drawn by packhorse or lumbering cartwheel, hugging the curve of a valley or yielding to a promontory like the wandering line of a stream. It was not, after all, so very long ago, but no one could make that journey today. Most of the old roads have gone, and the motor car, since then, has begun to cut the landscape to pieces, through which the hunched-up traveller races at gutter height, seeing less than a dog in a ditch.

But for me, at that time, everything I saw was new, and I could pass it slowly through the hours of the day. While still only a day's march from home, coming through Malmesbury and Chippenham, already I noticed different shades of speech. Then a day or so later I passed down the Wylye Valley and came out on to a vast and rolling plain – a sweep of old dry land covered with shaggy grass which looked as though it had just been cropped by mammoths. Still vague about places, I was unprepared for the delicate spire that rose suddenly out of the empty plain. As I walked, it went before me, gliding behind the curve of the hill and giving no hint of the city beneath it.

Just a spire in the grass: my first view of Salisbury, and the better for not being expected. When I entered the city I found it was market day, the square crowded with bone-thin sheep. Farmers stood round in groups talking sideways to each other and all looking in opposite directions. The pubs were bursting with dealers counting out crumpled money. Shepherds and dogs sat around on the pavements. Supreme above all towered the misty cathedral, still prince of the horizontal town, throwing its slow shifting shade across the market square and jingling handfuls of bells like coins.

*

After a week on the road I finally arrived at Southampton, where I'd been told I would see the sea. Instead, I saw a few rusty cranes and a compressed looking liner wedged tightly between some houses; also some sad allotments fringing a muddy river which they said was Southampton Water.

Southampton Town, on the other hand, came up to all expectations, proving to be salty and shifty in turns, like some ship-jumping sailor who'd turned his back on the sea in a desperate attempt to make good on land. The streets near the water appeared to be jammed with shops designed more for entertainment than profit, including tattooists, ear-piercers, bump-readers, fortune-tellers, whelk-bars, and pudding-boilers. There were also shops selling kites and Chinese paper dragons, coloured sands and tropical birds; and lots of little step-down taverns panelled with rum-soaked timbers and reeking of pickled eggs and onions.

As I'd been sleeping in fields for a week, I thought it was time I tried a bed again, so I went to a doss-house down by the docks. The landlady, an old hag with a tooth like a tin-opener, said it would cost me a shilling a night, demanded the money in advance, treated me to a tumblerful of whisky, then showed me up to the attic.

Early next morning she brought me a cup of tea and some water in a wooden bucket. She looked at me vaguely and asked what ship I was from, and only grunted when I said I'd come from Stroud. Then she spotted my violin hanging on the end of the bed and gave it a twang with her long blue nails.

'Well, hey diddle diddle. I reckon,' she muttered, and skipped nimbly out of the room.

Presently I got up and dressed, stuck my violin under my jacket, and went out into the streets to try my luck. It was now or never. I must face it now, or pack up and go back home. I wandered about for an hour looking for a likely spot, feeling as though I were about to commit a crime. Then I stopped at last under a bridge near the station and decided to have a go.

I felt tense and shaky. It was the first time, after all. I drew the violin from my coat like a gun. It was here, in Southampton, with trains rattling overhead, that I was about to declare myself. One moment I was part of the hurrying crowds, the next I stood nakedly apart, my back to the wall, my hat on the pavement before me, the violin under my chin.

The first notes I played were loud and raw, like a hoarse declaration of protest, then they settled down and began to run more smoothly and to stay more or less in tune. To my surprise, I was neither arrested nor told to shut up. Indeed, nobody took any notice at all. Then an old man, without stopping, surreptitiously tossed a penny into my hat as though getting rid of some guilty evidence.

Other pennies followed, slowly but steadily, dropped by shadows who appeared not to see or hear me. It was as though the note of the fiddle touched some subconscious nerve that had to be answered – like a baby's cry. When I'd finished the first tune there was over a shilling in my hat: it seemed too easy, like a confidence trick. But I was elated now; I felt that wherever I went from here this was a trick I could always live by.

I worked the streets of Southampton for several days, gradually acquiring the truths of the trade. Obvious enough to oldtimers, and simple, once learned, I had to get them by trial and error. It was not a good thing, for instance, to let the hat fill up with money – the sight could discourage the patron; nor was it wise to empty it completely, which could also confuse him, giving him no hint as to where to drop his money. Placing a couple of pennies in the hat to start the thing going soon became an unvarying ritual; making sure, between tunes, to take off the cream, but always leaving two pennies behind.

Slow melodies were best, encouraging people to dawdle (Irish jigs sent them whizzing past); but it also seemed wise to play as well as one was able rather than to ape the dirge of the professional waif. To arouse pity or guilt was always good for a penny, but that was as far as it got you; while a tuneful appeal to the ear, played with sober zest, might often be rewarded with silver.

Old ladies were most generous, and so were women with children, shopgirls, typists, and barmaids. As for the men: heavy drinkers were always receptive, so were big chaps with muscles, bookies, and punters. But never a man with a bowler, briefcase, or dog; respectable types were the tightest of all. Except for retired army officers, who would bark, 'Why aren't you working, young man?'and then over-tip to hide their confusion.

Certain tunes, I discovered, always raised a response, while others touched off nothing at all. The most fruitful were invariably the tea-room classics and certain of the juicier national ballads. 'Loch Lomond', 'Wales! Wales!', and 'The Rose of Tralee' called up their supporters from any crowd – as did 'Largo', 'Ave Maria', Toselli's 'Serenade', and 'The Whistler and His Dog'. The least rewarding, as I said, was anything quick or flashy, such as 'The Devil's Trill' or 'Picking up Sticks', which seemed to throw the pedestrian right out of his stride and completely shatter his charitable rhythm.

All in all, my apprenticeship proved profitable and easy, and I soon lost my pavement nerves. It became a greedy pleasure to go out into the streets, to take up my stand by the station or market, and start sawing away at some moony melody and watch the pennies and halfpennies grow. Those first days in Southampton were a kind of obsession; I was out in the streets from morning till night, moving from pitch to pitch in a gold-dust fever, playing till the tips of my fingers burned.

When I judged Southampton to have taken about as much as it could, I decided to move on eastwards. Already I felt like a veteran, and on my way out of town I went into a booth to have my photograph taken. The picture was developed in a bucket in less than a minute, and has lasted over thirty years. I still have a copy before me of that summer ghost – a pale, oleaginous shade, posed daintily before a landscape of tattered canvas, his old clothes powdered with dust. He wears a sloppy slouch hat, heavy boots, baggy trousers, tent and fiddle slung over his shoulders, and from the long empty face gaze a pair of egg-shell eyes, unhatched, and unrecognizable now.

*

A few miles from Southampton I saw the real sea at last, head on, a sudden end to the land, a great sweep of curved nothing rolling out to the invisible horizon and revealing more distance than I'd ever seen before. It was green, and heaved gently like the skin of a frog, and carried drowsy little ships like flies. Compared with the land, it appeared to be a huge hypnotic blank, putting everything to sleep that touched it.

As I pushed along the shore I was soon absorbed by its atmosphere, new, mysterious, alien: the gritty edge on the wind, the taste of tar and salt, the smell of stale sea-shells, damp roads, and mackintoshes, and the sight of the quick summer storms sliding in front of the water like sheets of dirty glass.

The South Coast, even so, was not what I'd been led to expect – from reading Hardy and Jeffery Farnol – for already it had begun to develop that shabby shoreline suburbia which was part of the whimsical rot of the Thirties. Here were the seashanty-towns, sprawled like a rubbishy tidemark, the scattered litter of land and ocean – miles of tea-shacks and bungalows, apparently built out of wreckage, and called 'Spindrift' or 'Sprite O' The Waves'. Here and there, bearded men sat on broken verandas painting water-colours of boats and sunsets, while big women with dogs, all glistening with teeth, policed parcels of private sand. I liked the seedy disorder of this melancholy coast, unvisited as yet by prosperity, and looking as though everything about it had been thrown together by the winds, and might at any moment be blown away again.

I spent a week by the sea, slowly edging towards the east, sleeping on the shore and working the towns. I remember it as a blur of summer, indolent and vague, broken occasionally by some odd encounter. At Gosport I performed at a barrack-room concert in return for a ration of army beef. In front of Chichester Cathedral I played 'Bless this House', and was moved on at once by the police. At Bognor Regis I camped out on the sands where I met a fluid young girl of sixteen, who hugged me steadily throughout one long hot day with only a gymslip on her sea-wet body. At

Littlehampton, I'd just collected about eighteen pence when I was moved on again by the police. 'Not here. Try Worthing,' the officer said. I did so, and was amply rewarded.

Worthing at that time was a kind of Cheltenham-on-Sea, full of rich, pearl-chokered invalids. Each afternoon they came out in their high-wheeled chairs and were pushed round the park by small hired men. Standing at the gate of the park, in the mainstream of these ladies, I played a selection of spiritual airs, and in little over an hour collected thirty-eight shillings – which was more than a farm-labourer earned in a week.

Worthing was an end to that chapter, a junction in the journey, and as far along the coast as I wished to go. So I turned my back on the sea and headed north for London, still over fifty miles away. It was the third week in June, and the landscape was frosty with pollen and still coated with elder-blossom. The wide-open Downs, the sheep-nibbled grass, the beech hangers on the edge of the valleys, the smell of chalk, purple orchids, blue butterflies, and thistles recalled the Cotswolds I'd so carelessly left. Indeed Chanctonbury Ring, where I slept that night, could have been any of the beacons round Painswick or Haresfield; yet I felt farther from home, by the very familiarity of my surroundings, than I ever did later in a foreign country.

But next day, getting back on to the London road, I forgot everything but the way ahead. I walked steadily, effortlessly, hour after hour, in a kind of swinging, weightless dream. I was at that age which feels neither strain nor friction, when the body burns magic fuels, so that it seems to glide in warm air, about a foot off the ground, smoothly obeying its intuitions. Even exhaustion, when it came, had a voluptuous quality, and sleep was caressive and deep, like oil. It was the peak of the curve of the body's total extravagance, before the accounts start coming in.

I was living at that time on pressed dates and biscuits, rationing them daily, as though crossing a desert. Sussex, of course, offered other diets, but I preferred to stick to this affectation. I pretended I was T. E. Lawrence, engaged in some self-punishing odyssey, burning up my youth in some pitless Hadhramaut, eyes narrowing to the sandstorms blowing out of the wadis of Godalming in a mirage of solitary endurance.

But I was not the only one on the road; I soon noticed there were many others, all trudging northwards in a sombre procession. Some, of course, were professional tramps, but the majority belonged to that host of unemployed who wandered aimlessly about England at that time.

One could pick out the professionals; they brewed tea by the roadside, took it easy, and studied their feet. But the others, the majority, went on their way like somnambulists, walking alone and seldom speaking to each other. There seemed to be more of them inland than on the coast – maybe the police had seen to that. They were like a broken army walking away from a war, cheeks sunken, eyes dead with fatigue. Some carried bags of tools, or shabby cardboard suitcases; some wore the ghosts of city suits; some, when they stopped to rest, carefully removed their shoes and polished them vaguely with handfuls of grass. Among them were carpenters, clerks, engineers from the Midlands; many had been on the road for months, walking up and down the country in a maze of jobless refusals, the treadmill of the mid-Thirties . . .

Then, for a couple of days, I got a companion. I was picked up by the veteran Alf. I'd turned off the road to set up camp for the night, when he came filtering through the bushes.

I'd seen him before; he was about five feet high and was clearly one of the brotherhood. He wore a deerstalker hat, so sodden and shredded it looked like a helping of breakfast food, and round the waist of his mackintosh, which was belted with string, hung a collection of pots and spoons.

Rattling like a dustbin, he sat down beside me and began pulling off his boots.

'Well,' he said, eyeing my dates with disgust, 'you're a poor little bleeder, 'ent you?'

He shook out his boots and put them on again, then gave my supper another look.

'You can't live on terrible tack like that – you'll depress the lot of us. What you want is a billy. A-boil yerself up. 'Ere, 'ang on – jus' wait a minute . . .'

Rummaging through the hardware around his waist, he produced a battered can, the kind of thing my uncles brought home from the war – square, with a triangular handle. It was a miniature cauldron, smoke-blackened outside and dark, tannin-stained within.

''Ere, take it,' he said. 'You make me miserable.' He started to build a fire. 'I'm goin' to boil you a bit of tea and tatters.' And that is what he did.

We stayed together as far as Guildford, and I shared more of his pungent brews. He was a tramp to his bones, always wrapping and unwrapping himself, and picking over his bits and pieces. He wasn't looking for work; this was simply his life, and he carefully rationed his energies – never passing a patch of grass that looked good for a shakedown, nor a cottage that seemed ripe for charity. He said his name was Alf, but one couldn't be sure, as he called me Alf, and everyone else. 'Couple of Alfs got jugged in this town last year,' he'd say. 'Hookin' the shops – you know, with fish-hooks.' Or: 'An Alf I knew used to do twenty-mile a day. One of the looniest Alfs on the road. Said he got round it quicker. And so he did. But folks got sick of his face.'

Alf talked all day, but was garrulously secretive, and never revealed his origins. I suppose that in the shared exposure of the open road he needed this loose verbal hedge around him. At the same time, he never asked me about myself, though he took it for granted that I was a greenhorn, and gave me careful advice about insulation from weather, flannelling housewives, and dodging the cops.

As for his own technique of roadwork, he wasn't slow out of laziness but because he moved to a deliberate timetable, making his professional grand tour in a twelve-months' rhythm, which seemed to him fast enough. During the winter he'd hole up in a London doss-house, then restart his leisurely cycle of England, turning up every year in each particular district with the regularity of the seasons. Thus he was the spring tramp of the Midlands, the summer bird of the south, the first touch of autumn to the Kentish Weald – indeed, I think he firmly believed that his constancy of motion spread a kind of reassurance among the housewives, so that he was looked for and welcomed as one of the recurring phenomena of nature, and was suitably rewarded therefore.

Certainly his begging was profitable, and he never popped through a gate without returning with fistfuls of food – screws of tea, sugar, meat bones, and cake, which he'd then boil in one awful mess. He was clean, down-at-heel, warm-hearted, and cunning; and he showed me genuine if supercilious kindness. 'You're a bleedin' disgrace,' he used to say, 'a miserable little burden.'

Alf had one strange habit – a passion for nursery rhymes, which he'd mutter as he walked along.

> Sing a song of sixpence,
> Pocketful of rye,
> Four-an'-twenny blackbirds
> Baked in an oven.
>
> Ba-ba, black sheep,
> Have you any wool?
> Yes, sir, yes, sir,
> I got plenty . . .

The effect of a dozen of these, left hanging in the air, was enough to dislocate the senses.

At Guildford we parted, Alf turning east for the Weald, which for him still lay three months away.

'So long, Alf,' I said.

'So long, Alf,' he answered. 'Try not to be too much of a nuisance.'

He passed under the railway bridge and out of my life, a shuffling rattle of old tin cans, looking very small and triangular with his pointed hat on his head, and black mackintosh trailing the ground.

London was now quite near, not more than a two-days' walk, but I was still in no particular hurry. So I turned north-west and began a detour round it, rather like a wasp sidling up to a jam jar. After leaving Guildford, I slept on Bagshot Heath – all birches, sand, and horseflies – which to me seemed a sinister and wasted place like some vast dead land of Russia. Then next morning, only a few miles farther up the road, everything suddenly changed back again, and I was walking through parkland as green as a fable, smothered with beeches and creamy grass.

Every motor car on the road was now either a Rolls-Royce or a Daimler – a gliding succession of silver sighs – their crystal interiors packed with girls and hampers and erect top-hatted men. Previously, I'd not seen more than two such cars in my life; now they seemed to be the only kind in the world, and I began to wonder if they were intimations of treasures to come, whether all London was as rich as this.

Tramping in the dust of this splendour, I wasn't surprised when one of the Daimlers pulled up and an arm beckoned to me from the window. I hurried towards it, thinking it might be full of long-lost relations, but in fact there was no one I knew. 'Want a pheasant, my man?' asked a voice from inside. 'We just knocked over a beauty a hundred yards back.'

A quarter of an hour later I arrived at Ascot. It was race week, and I'd walked right into it. White pavilions and flags; little grooms and jockeys dodging among the long glossy legs of thoroughbreds; and the pedigree owners dipping their long cool necks into baskets of paté and gulls' eggs.

I went round to the entrance, thinking I might get in, but was stared at by a couple of policemen. So I stared, in turn, at a beautiful woman by the gate, who for a moment paused dazzlingly near me – her face as silkily finished as a Persian miniature, her body sheathed in swathes like a tulip, and her sandalled feet wrapped in a kind of transparent rice-paper so that I could count every clean little separate toe.

Wealth and beauty were the common order of things now, and I felt I had entered another realm. It would have been no good busking or touting here, indeed outlandish in such a place. Alf, and the tattered lines of the workless, were far away in another country ... So I left Ascot, and came presently to another park, full of oak trees and grazing deer, and saw Windsor Castle standing on its green-baize hill like a battered silver cruet. I slept that stifling night in a field near Stoke Poges, having spent the evening in the village churchyard, sitting on a mossy gravestone and listening to the rooks, and wondering why the place seemed so familiar.

A few mornings later, coming out of a wood near Beaconsfield, I suddenly saw London at last – a long smoky skyline hazed by the morning sun and filling the whole of the eastern horizon. Dry, rusty-red, it lay like a huge flat crust, like ash from some spent volcano, simmering gently in the summer morning and emitting a faint, metallic roar.

No architectural glories, no towers or palaces, just a creeping insidious presence, its vast horizontal broken here and there by a gas-holder or factory chimney. Even so, I could already feel its intense radiation – an electric charge in the sky – that rose from its million roofs in a quivering mirage, magnetically, almost visibly, dilating.

Cleo, my girl-friend, was somewhere out there; hoarding my letters (I hoped) and waiting. Also mystery, promise, chance, and fortune – all I had come to this city to find. I hurried towards it, impatient now, its sulphur stinging my nostrils. I had been a month on the road, and the suburbs were long and empty. In the end I took a tube.

2

London

My village, my home-town, each had a kind of duck-pond centre, but London had no centre at all – just squat little streets endlessly proliferating themselves like ripples in estuary mud. I arrived at Paddington in the early evening, and walked around for a while. The sky was different here, high, wide, and still, rosy with smoke, and the westering sun. There was a smell of rank oil, rotting fish and vegetables, hot pavements and trodden tar; and a sense of surging pressure, the heavy used-up air of the cheek-by-jowl life around me – the families fermenting behind slack-coloured curtains, above shops and in resounding tenements, sons changing their shirts, daughters drying their hair, waistcoated fathers staring at their tea, and in the streets the packed buses grinding nose to tail and the great night coming on.

I was excited, having got here, but also unprepared, and I wasn't sure what I was going to do. But I had Cleo's address – I didn't know anyone else – so I thought this was the time to use it. I'd met Cleo in the spring, in a Tolstoyan settlement near Stroud, where she was living in a borrowed caravan, together with her handsome father – an eagle-nosed left-wing agitator – and her distressed and well-born mother.

Their origins were uncertain, but they'd recently fled from America, where I suspect the father had been in some political trouble. The sixteen-year-old girl was not the kind I'd been used to, and her beauty had knocked me silly. She'd had a husky, nutty Anglo-American accent, huge brown eyes flecked like crumbled honey, a smooth leggy figure, lithe as an Indian pony; and we'd pretended to be in love.

The family were penniless, but they had connections, and friends were always lending them houses; and the address of the last one – somewhere on Putney Heath – sounded very grand indeed. When I finally got there, having walked several miles through the dusk, the house appeared to have been hit by a bomb – only half a wing and the main staircase still standing in a huge garden of churned-up roots.

They were sitting on the staircase, which was open to the sky, and seemed rather surprised to see me – except for lovely Cleo, who cried 'I knew it!' and ran down the steps to meet me. She had kept up superbly with my memories of her, and looked even better than I expected, her body packed beautifully into her shirt and shorts, and her skin the colour of rosewood.

'You walked it, didn't you? – I *told* you, Daddy.' She led me proudly up the eroded staircase, then took me to her room and showed me my bundle of letters which lay wrapped in her scented nightdress.

So I was invited to stay. Cleo burned my clothes and fitted me out with some of her father's. The mansion was being torn down to make room for a block of flats, and the father had a job with the builders; meanwhile, with the half-ruin to live in, they were temporarily secure, and the mother was slowly recovering her senses.

I slept on the floor in the remaining fragment of ballroom, and ate with the family in the Victorian kitchen, whose tall Gothic windows looked from the lip of the Heath across London to the Hampstead hills. I was in luck, and I knew it, and took it easy at first. It seemed a nice soft spot to be in. Sometimes the father, in his loud public voice, would lecture me on the theory of anarchy, on the necessity for political and personal freedom, and on his contempt for the moral law. When he was out, the mother, pale and damp round the eyes, would talk about her childhood home in the shires, and lament the scruffy world of conspiratorial garrets through which this attractive bounder had led her. At other times the daughter, heart-stoppingly voluptuous in her tight Californian pants, would lead me by the hand through the ruined garden, to the last clump of still-rooted myrtles, then crouch, bare-kneed, and pull me down beside her, and demand to know my ideological convictions.

Beautiful Cleo; she never knew what she did to me, her eyes slanting under the myrtle leaves, her coiled russet limbs like something from a Rousseau jungle, her chatter never still for a moment. But not of what I expected; never a word about love, or my hunger, or the summer night. The funeral baked meats of her father's mind were all she seemed able to serve me. He was the one, of course, and I was not old enough to replace him. I thought her the most ravishing and wasted child in the world.

Then one night I took her out on to the twilit Heath, where lovers lay thick as sheaves. We walked miles round the common, and Cleo never drew breath; her lovely mouth was a political megaphone. Finally I pushed her against a tree and desperately kissed her. She lent me her lips like an improving book. 'But I *must* have the Movement. You understand, don't you? You *must* join the Party,' she said.

I didn't give up. I made one last try. After all, I was in considerable torment. So next morning, at dawn, I fetched one of the builder's ladders and climbed through her bedroom window. She lay easily sleeping in her rose-coloured nightdress, a soft breathing heap of love. The hushed dawn, the first birds, and me in my black Russian pyjamas – surely she must melt to this magic moment. As I slipped into her bed she rolled drowsily into my arms, then woke, and her body froze. 'If Daddy knew about this, he'd murder you,' she said. It was no idle figure of speech.

Scrambling back down the ladder in the dawn's early light, I realized that blood could be thicker than theory. Later that day, Cleo's father got me a job with the builders, and gave me the address of some Putney lodgings. I don't know what she had told him, but he'd acted swiftly. It seemed a reasonable compromise between New Thought and the horsewhip.

On my own once again, I found a snug little room over an

eating-house in the Lower Richmond Road – a shambling second-floor back which overhung the railway and rocked all day to the passing trains, while the hot meaty steam of boiling pies filtered up through cracks in the floor.

The café downstairs was a shadowy tunnel lined with high-backed wooden pews, carbolic-scrubbed and exclusively male, with all the comforts of a medieval refectory. My rent of twenty-five shillings a week included the furnished room and three café meals a day – a *carte blanche* arrangement which I exploited fully and which introduced me to new ways of eating. The blackboard menu, propped on the pavement outside, offered a list as immutable as the elements: 'Bubble. Squeak. Liver and B. Toad-in-the-Hole. Meat Pudding or Pie.' My favourite was the pie – a little basin of meat wrapped in a caul of suety dough which was kept boiling all day in a copper cauldron in a cupboard under the stairs. Turned out on the plate, it steamed like a sodden napkin, emitting a mournful odour of laundries; but once pricked with the fork it exploded magnificently with a rich lava of beefy juices. There must have been over a pound of meat in each separate pie – a complete working-man's meal, for sixpence. And remembering the thin days at home, when meat was only for Sundays, I ate at least one of them every day. Otherwise I was encouraged to ring the changes on the house's limited permutations – Squeak, Toad, Liver and B; or as a privilege, an occasional herring. A mug of tea at each meal was of course served without asking, and was so strong you could trot a mouse on it. As for afters, there was a postscript at the foot of the menu which seemed to be painted in permanent enamel. 'During the Present Hot Spell Why Not Try a Cold Sweet?' Winter and summer, it was custard and prunes.

Arnold, the proprietor – who was also my landlord – was a man in his early thirties, a rounded dandy with heavy cream-white jowls and delicate parboiled hands. He did all the work alone, both the cooking and serving, and moved with the rolling dignity of a eunuch, dressed in tight cotton gowns, buttoned up to the throat, which also gave him the appearance of one of his cloth-wrapped pies. He was bald, large-headed, red-lipped and corseted, and was given to abstractions, silence and reveries; and he seemed clearly to be a cut above his clients, though if he thought so, he never showed it. Each day, before breakfast, he padded around the tables laying out the morning newspapers like hymn-sheets; and these again were scrupulously changed in the evening. The customers also had the benefit of his soft-voiced summaries. I've never known a man who gave to this particular job such a sense of modest almost priest-like dedication, advising and serving the labourers at his table and taking their coppers like a church collection.

In fact, this ascetic purveyor of gross Toads and Squeaks was something of a mystery. One might have imagined him to have chosen the job as a purge, an act of self-abasement; but certainly not for the money. I lived for six months in his house, but I never knew him – though I knew he had another life. I knew, for instance, about the two pretty children who visited him briefly each Saturday night. And that in his first-floor back he kept in careful seclusion a young and beautiful wife. Sometimes as I climbed to my room, I saw her standing in her half-open doorway, a tantalizing strip of voluptuous boredom, her hair piled high and elaborately set, her eyes burning like landing lights. She wore a white silk wrap buttoned up to the throat, and her toe-nails were painted green. She was about my own age, but she never spoke. Nor did Arnold ever mention her.

My job at the buildings took it out of me at first, and I lived at a pitch of healthy exhaustion. All day I pushed barrows of wet cement till my muscles stretched and burned. At night, I returned to the steaming café, ate my pie, then climbed to my backstairs room, where I sat half-dozing at the window table, gazing down at the long green trains.

It was the first time in my life I'd had a room of my own, uncluttered with sisters and brothers, and I spread all over it, throwing my clothes about, and keeping the door well locked and bolted. Grateful for privacy at last, I was content just to sit there, lord of the room and its chromium furniture, spending the long summer evenings nodding alone at the table, or drawing girls, or writing short sleepy poems. London waited outside – a stubby plateau of chimneys, a low mutter of dragging sound; but at the beginning there was little I could do about it. My body was too used up.

It took a little while to get toughened-up to the job, to the stiff hours of blistering labour, which wore my hands into holes and pulled my muscles about into new and unaccustomed contortions. I was dead-beat at first, and walked in a tottering daze; but I was young, and I hardened fast. Soon my palms had callouses rough as salted leather, which I could rub together with pride. At last I could get home in the evening without falling into a stupor. I could even begin to look about me.

Of course, I'd not much identity with the city yet; it was just rooftops and a changing sky, a thump of radios coming from open windows, and the summer yelp of the back-street children. And the frail cord with my family was still uncut. Boot-boxes of flowers came by post from my mother, sweet slipshod gatherings from the fields and hedges, wrapped in damp moss and ivy leaves.

Then I made a small breakthrough. I won a poetry prize in a weekly competition organized by a newspaper, *The Sunday Referee*, for a poem I'd dashed off with a sixpenny postal order and never expected to hear of again. Arnold showed it to me one morning, his red mouth twitching; and it was the first of mine I'd ever seen printed. 'Is this really you?' he asked fastidiously. 'I wasn't aware you had such beautiful thoughts.'

Soon after this, I met Philip O'Connor distributing leaflets on Putney Common – a quick ready youth with a fine hungry face and a shock of thick obsidian curls. We were both of us living alone at that time, scribbling poetry in neighbouring streets, so for a while we visited each other quite often, establishing a defensive minority of two. To me, he had an adolescent mystery about him, a frenetic melancholy, like a schoolboy Hamlet; and his poems were the most extravagant I'd read until then, rhapsodic eruptions of surrealist fantasy. I was impressed by his poems; he thought little of mine. I was the older; he was paternal. He used to lie on my bed, nervously scratching his curls, and switching his dark eyes on and off, reciting his latest verses in clear cold tones, snappy and rather bitter. 'You and I are the only true voices left alive in the world,' he'd say. When using my room, his manners were perfect. Not so on his own home ground, when his claims were more self-centred. But he had a nice sense of territory.

Another friend of that period was six-foot Billy, who ate regularly in the café downstairs – a stranded Negro sailor from Troy, Missouri, who had either jumped ship or had lost his way. I never knew where he slept, or how he lived, but every evening he'd be there in his pew, dropping great lumps of butter into his hot strong tea and carefully stripping the bones from a kipper. His huge fat cheeks were lightly scarred by knives, and the marks of knuckledusters ran across his eyebrows. But he was sleepily gentle, never raised his voice, and his favourite diversions seemed to be tea and gossip. Billy was an excellent listener, and it seemed impossible to bore him. He'd salute the dullest story with the most flattering attention. 'Waal, ah'll go slash mah wrists, if that ain't sumpin',' he'd murmur. 'You may hang me up by mah entrails.' Sometimes he'd disappear for a few days, then pop up, beaming. 'Gouge mah eyes, shuh good to see you.' Then we'd go next door for a game of billiards, which he played with a velvet touch. But he didn't last long. They finally caught up with him. A dozen coppers with rolled-up macs. Stepping gingerly into the café, expecting a struggle. But he went with them like a child.

Then my days with Arnold, too, were numbered. A girl came to live on the floor above me. She moved into the attic cupboard just under the roof, which till then had only stored potatoes. The girl seemed to do no work, though occasionally I'd hear her gramophone playing and the sound of her bare feet dancing. Sometimes we'd meet on the stairs and have to struggle together to get round the bend in the banisters. A couple of inches from mine, her eyes never blinked. Her hair smelt of pies and doughnuts. 'D'you see that film called *The Rat*?' she asked me one day.

'You're his bleedin' image, you are.' Her friends came in the evening, and left in the morning. Then Arnold would take her breakfast up on a tray. At last, apologetically, he said he'd be wanting my room. It seemed he was extending the business.

The next lodging I found was somewhat more secure, with a half-Cockney, half-Irish family, who lived in a compact little set-up a dozen yards from the High Street in a squat row of Victorian villas. Here, for twenty-five shillings a week, I got a ground-floor room, meals and laundry and a bright coal fire, the use of the parlour on Sundays, and the warmth of the basement kitchen whenever I felt like extra company.

Mrs Flynn, my landlady, was a valiant blonde, with something of the twilight beauty of Gloria Swanson – a kind of smooth open face that was tough yet wistful, backed by a garrulous and romantic fancy. There seemed to be two Mrs Flynns: one girlish and easy, the other born to furious protest. Mornings saw her most angry, a chain-smoking sweeper of rooms, a tousled mop in a dressing-gown; then at night, after supper, she emerged in laminated gold, with silkily reconditioned hair, to engage the world in a monologue of bubbling non-sequiturs, full of giggles, regrets, and yearnings. Sleekly bent to her cocoa, splendidly robed and corseted, she would then tackle any subject on earth. She'd describe the deer out at Richmond, wearing their beautiful antelopes. She'd give her views on the Russian revulsion. She'd warn me never to get married; she'd married too young, a mistake, she'd been much too impressive. But she liked men with thick lips, the curling rose-bud type – she always thought they looked so essential . . .

Mrs Flynn was Cockney, her absent husband Irish. But there was another somewhere lost in her life. He had been Irish too, a Celtic prince, now gone. She'd mention him tragically, then hoot with laughter. It was that robust, good-natured hunger about her that balanced her bouts of frenzy. Together with those easy tears and sudden giggles of self-mockery. She must have been younger than I thought at the time.

The rest of the family consisted of Mrs Flynn's two children, who were as different as night from day – black-eyed Patsy, a sexily confident child of eight, and blond Mike, a speechless lad of eleven. There was also Beth, the landlady's unmarried sister, a fey, self-effacing spirit, who moved in the background like an anxious guardian and held the whole house together. She watched over us all, worked in an office by day, cooked the supper and scrubbed clothes in the evening, reflected her sister's moods like a seismograph, and shyly explained and excused. The women were much alike, though Beth was the older and took pains to conceal the likeness, having suppressed her own beauty, like a nerve-failed actress, to become her sister's dresser and shadow.

I soon fitted into the house, and was enveloped by it. My room was small, just the kind I prefer. There was a bed, a chair, a coloured print of Killarney, and a barred window looking out on a wall. With winter coming on, I could have done much worse. The place was snug as a badger's hole. And the women treated me well, like a fragile exotic, as though fattening me up for a prize. In the morning young Mike brought me breakfast in bed, together with a fat wad of sandwiches for work. When I returned in the evening the coal fire was blazing and the room whirling with sulphurous smoke. At six, a huge meal on a copper tray was brought in by the pigtailed Patsy, who then sat on the floor, her bare knees to her chin, and mercilessly watched me eat. She'd pay another brief visit before going to bed. 'Ma says anything else you want?' Squirming, coy, a strip of striped pyjamas, Miss Sweater Girl of ten years later – already she knew how to stand, how to snuggle against the doorpost, how to frame her flannel-dressed limbs in the lamplight.

Once the children were in bed, other sounds took over, mysterious but soon familiar. Beth down at the sink, mangling the evening's wash or chopping up piles of sandwiches for the morning. Mrs Flynn, in pale fur, leaving for the Wembley dogs, or stranded alone for the night in the basement, banging her head on the table or laughing the whole thing off with a half-pint bottle of stout. Then sometimes, quite late, from away in the attic, one might hear a succession of howls and groans, reverberating alarms pitched in a sepulchral baritone like the complaining of Hamlet's ghost. But it was only Mr Willow, Mrs Flynn's other lodger, an old actor long since retired, who liked to fill up his solitude by repeating the lines of his one-time triumph: *The Curse of Dr Fu Manchu*.

Otherwise, when home, I spent self-contained evenings, writing by the fire, or playing the fiddle, till just before bed Beth brought me a large tray of supper and perhaps something she'd copied for me to read. It was like being in a family again, except that these knocked on my door and didn't ask me to help with the housework. And when I was ill they looked after me, reduced the rent, and Mrs Flynn brought me bottles of Guinness. 'That Laurie,' she'd say. 'No wonder he goes like that. He burdens his brain too much.' She didn't know much about me, nor did she try to find out. It seemed enough that I made a change.

As for the great spread of London, which I'd come to discover, I don't think I even began to get the feel of it then. Its dimensions were all wrong for my country-grown mind, too out-of-scale for my experience to cope with. In any case I was twenty, when environment plays tricks, and my portholes were fogged by illusion. I just floated around in a capsule of self-absorption, sealed in with my own private weather.

But I can remember the presence of London, its physical toughness at that time, its home-spun, knock-about air. There was more life in the streets (it cost money inside) and people thronged outdoors in the evenings. One saw them standing on corners, in the doorways of pubs, talking in groups, eating from paper bags. And the streets themselves had an almost rustic confusion – Edwardian transport in all its last-ditch vigour: rattling old buses, coster ponies and traps, prim little taxis like upright pianos, and huge dray wagons laden with beer and flour and drawn by teams of magnificent horses. Then on fine Sunday mornings, while the horses rested, Putney High Street filled up with bicycles – buxom girls in white shorts chased by puffing young men, old straw-hatted gents in blazers, whole families on tandems carrying their babies in baskets, and all heading for the open country. Private cars were few, and were often a sign of ill-omen, particularly when parked in a side-street, where the sight of a car outside a terraced house might well mean the doctor or death.

Yet to me, when off duty, London offered a well-heeled idleness, even on £2 5s 0d a week. After paying for my lodgings I had £1 to spend, which could be broken up in a hundred ways. A tot of whisky cost sixpence, a pint of beer fourpence-half-penny, cigarettes were elevenpence for twenty. The best seats in the cinema cost ninepence to a shilling, or I could climb to the gallery for threepence. Then there were fairs and music-halls, Russian ballet at the Alhambra, Queen's Hall concerts – seldom more than a shilling. Suits made to measure for fifty bob, sixpenny dances, ninepenny suppers – life may have been no cheaper, considering what I was earning, but it seemed so, and I paid no taxes.

It was a time of rootless enjoyment, and also luxurious melancholy which I took care to spin out and nourish. Walking almost everywhere, and most often alone, I studied my shadow, my face in the windows, acknowledging the thrust of London and what it demanded of me – fame and fortune at the very least. This was what I was here for, and what they expected back home. Yet my head was idle and empty.

So I did what I could, short of coming to grips; staring at the river, or playing billiards, and waiting. Writing, destroying, confident of time, wandering the heath, not particularly troubled; or picking up servant girls from the last great houses, gnawing at the chicken-wings they brought me, lying taut among the bushes in the broken lamplight and fancying myself with grander loves.

But mostly I wandered, seeking the spacious exhaustion of brooding energies going to waste. Sometimes, on a day off, I'd walk into the City, along the Embankment and up the Strand, pausing at the Victorian chop-houses to sniff the red sides of beef hanging on hooks in the steaming windows. To me such food was like a mountain of Sundays, or the hot gravied kiss of Mammon, strictly reserved for plump brokers and bankers – it never occurred to me that *I* might eat it.

The City itself, with its courtyards and passages, was familiar, like odd corners of Stroud – faded brass plates nailed to flaking doorways, ancient messengers in mould-green coats, tottering porters carrying coal to stuffy clerk-filled attics, an air of wet biscuits and crumbling parchment. But hooded, cramped, and slyly unrecognizable as the counting-house of the treasuries of the world. And not at all what I expected. It made me uneasy. I always expected to run into my father.

After these trips to the City I'd try a change of style, and turn back into Charing Cross Road, then round off the evening in a Soho café smoking coal-black Mexican cigars. Here, darkly international in my crumpled raincoat, and surrounded by soft-tongued Greeks, I'd open the *Heraldo de Madrid*, which I couldn't read, and order Turkish coffee, which I couldn't drink . . .

Half my time, of course, was spent on the buildings, submerged by its mindless, invigorating routine. For almost a year, every weekday morning, I put on my lime-caked clothes, walked up Putney Hill, left my lunch with the tea-boy, and climbed into the windswept scaffolding. I was one of a gang of wheelbarrow-pushers, supplying newly-mixed cement for the floors, rhythmically shuttling to and fro across the springing duckboards and slowly rising as the buildings grew.

For eleven hard months, on the site of that elegant mansion, we raised three unbeautiful blocks of flats – squat, complacent, with mean leaded windows, bogus balconies, and imitation baronials. They were the only things I ever had a hand in building, and I still think of them with some affection, and return there occasionally, even today, to stare amazed at their cramped pretensions.

As builders' labourers, we were the villeins of industry and came at the bottom of the hierarchy of the workers. Unskilled, insecure, poorly paid, often dangerous, the job recruited what it could get; and many of my mates were the kind of city-bred dwarf who must have been the result of centuries of thin blood and compression. The type is rarer now, but can still be seen sometimes, perhaps in a Battersea or Wandsworth pub, crouching chin to table with a diminutive wife, feet barely touching the floor. In my day such men were the millstones of labour, ground small by its wasting demands. Yet they were tough, uncomplaining, almost fatalistic, and ageless in look and manner. Physically cramped and hard, with squashed-up limbs, crop-headed and muffler-choked, they spat Cockney from mouths like ruined quarries, and were the natural users of rhyming slang.

This slang seemed still to be the underworld *argot*, a secretive and evasive language, and had not, at that time, been self-consciously elevated into a saloon-bar affectation. When slang was not used, my mates seemed to suffer a curious inhibition, a reluctance to name people and things. ''Ere, what's-yer-name, mate. Chuck us over that what-d'ya-call-it, will yer? Got to make a what's-it fer this thingummy-jig.' I don't think it was laziness or lack of vocabulary, but rather an instinctive concealment which giving names might betray.

At least half of us, certainly, had been recruited from the underworld, apparently a normal practice of the times – we had old lags and con-men temporarily defeated by crime, skilled cracksmen lying low between jobs, and others who had confessed, under pressure, to a wish to reform and seemed to be required to push barrows to prove it. I found myself working with men straight from the Moor, with its gangrenous pallor still on them, and who moved with that head-down shuffle, passive and blind, as though their world was still a walled-in circle. Most of them were natives of Wandsworth and Fulham, reticent but nostalgic men, who would sometimes loosen up with tales of crime and punishment as though ruminating about the war.

In my gang, I remember, we had a little of everything: safe-breakers, cat-men, dopers, a forger ruined by rheumatism, a bigamist past his prime, and a specialist who picked locks with his celluloid shirt collar. On the fringe there was also a sad little clerk who'd served time for raping his daughter, and who no one forgave but condemned to the perpetual torment of sadistic practical jokes. But it was clear that crime had fattened none of them; they were shrivelled by years of attrition, by the staleness of poverty, doubt and suspicion, and by the diminishing returns of jail.

Yet on the whole there was a natural comradeship; there were no cliques and no self-pity. We were in this together and parcelled the job among us, sharing its profit and loss. We covered up for each other if one of our members was ill, or when the foreman was looking for blood. When it rained, we hid, and played pitch-and-toss in the cellars; when fine, we worked by turns, spinning out illusionary jobs in a mime of activity so that no one should be thought redundant. During the lunch-hour we gathered in an old tin shed, ate our scrappy grub off our knees, rolled cigarettes for each other, worked up a fug, and gambled at crown-and-anchor. Gambling was religion, our wages were mortgaged, and piles of notes changed hands, but though some of us flourished, honour was strictly observed, and it was doubtful if anyone cheated. The old lags particularly were the guardians of honour, implacable as Indian chiefs, their black teeth clamped round their tiny pipes, merciless to any back-sliding.

Off the job, walking home, we appeared to be natural targets for old ladies and local policemen. The police always treated us with truculent aggression: the old ladies gave us pennies and crusts. It may have been an instinctive reaction to our caps and mufflers, a hangover from the pages of *Punch*. Anyway, we accepted it, both the kicks and the charity, as part of the traditional perks of our trade. Certainly we were habitual pilferers – though on a job like ours there was little of value that was portable. I, myself, got the habit of carrying off little bits of copper tubing, which I hid down the legs of my trousers. They were smooth, well-turned, and prettily burnished; but I never knew what to do with them.

On the job, as I said, we labourers were the goons, the untouchable fetchers and carriers. Between us and the craftsmen there existed a gulf of caste almost as extreme as anything in India. The bricklayers, carpenters, plasterers and plumbers treated us with the casual contempt of Brahmins, and even at lunchtime they sat by themselves, rigidly wrapped in their status skills. Consequently we hardened ourselves into a compact little group, even more exclusive and cagey than theirs. The use of solidarity was the only skill we had, and I think we would have slain for each other.

There were two exceptions, however, two lonely outsiders who, though labourers, we never admitted. One was the middle-aged rapist, our haltered scapegoat, who we reserved for special torment. The other was the old head-gardener, whose garden had disappeared with the house, but who had been allowed to stay on by sufferance, and who was now ending his life tipping barrows of cement over the roots of his ruined roses.

Then in early spring, with the flats half-finished, something happened which threw us all together; something ordinary in itself, but for me an occasion which had much of the punitive, rasping air of the Thirties.

It began one morning with the discovery that some non-union men had been smuggled on to the job by the manager – provocation enough to lower for a moment, at least, the sacred barriers between the trades. Someone sounded the alarm by beating on an iron triangle, and everyone immediately stopped work. Cement mixers coughed and came to a halt; the men swarmed off the rooftops and scrambled down the scaffolding as though abandoning a stricken battleship.

We massed in the open outside the manager's office, our tempers suddenly transformed – over five hundred men huddled in the raw cold wind, waiting for our ranks to throw up a leader. At first we were lost; sporadic meetings broke out, voices shouted against each other. 'Brothers! – Comrades! – We got to stand solid on this – Chuck 'em out – Put our demands to the bosses.' The loaded phrases touched off little bush-fires of anger which flickered across the crowd, then died. Finally the manager sent a message ordering us to return to work. He'd discuss nothing. We could take it or leave it.

Just then a tall stoop-backed labourer pushed his way to the front and climbed up on to a pile of timber, and as soon as he turned to address us we knew that he'd do, and that the vacuum was filled.

This man was later to become one of the legends of the Thirties, part of its myth of class struggle and protest – a lean powerful figure with dangling arms, big fists, and a square bitter face. His face, in fact, was almost the perfect prototype of the worker-hero of early Soviet posters – proud, passionate, merciless, and fanatic, yet deeply scarred by hardship. He was still in his twenties but already had a history, he'd been jailed after a naval mutiny, and now as he towered above us, his voice mangled and eloquent, his finger stabbing the cold spring air, he stood enlarged on a screen that seemed giant-sized, a figure straight out of *Potemkin*.

He spoke briefly, with savage almost contemptuous dignity, and the other gabblers round the ground fell silent. With a few iron words he raised the level of our grievance to the heights of cosmic revolution. We had been vague and wavering; now we had no doubts. We voted for immediate strike.

The manager had been listening at the door of his office, smirking, and playing with his trilby. When he heard our decision he went pink with rage and began to bounce up and down like a baby.

'Outside!' he screamed. 'Everyone out this instant! Outside – or I'll have you arrested for trespassing!'

We filed through the gates and sat down on the Heath, five hundred men in the rain, and watched as the gates were locked behind us, and a little later, the police arrived. The half-finished buildings stood wet and empty, with a look of sudden death. An hour ago we'd been in there, swarming all over them, now a row of black-caped cops stood between us. Such a narrow gap between consent and dispute. We were outlaws now all right. When we approached the police, expecting a bit of traditional banter, they seemed just as livid as the manager.

The strike lasted two weeks – a fortnight of back-street agitation during which I tasted the first sweet whiff of revolution. Without work or status, we lived an underground existence, cut off from the rule of law, meeting in cafés and basements, drawing up manifestoes, planning demonstrations, painting placards and posters. In this hazy ghetto of ideological struggle it was easy to lose our dimensions, and the immediate aims of the strike became so blurred that we felt ready to take on the world. It was then, for the first time, that I experienced hallucinations of communism, naïve and innocent as water, a physical sensation rather than an intellectual one, like a weekend at a holiday camp. I began to see visions of the day when the workers would triumph, and we would be running with flags through the streets, the bosses in flight, the temples of privilege falling, other workers waiting to join us, to inherit a scrubbed new world of open-necked shirts, bare arms flexed in common labour, with perhaps a hint of free love shared with our prettier comrades, and communal nurseries crammed with our gold-haired offspring.

Then, suddenly, the strike was over, closed by a grudging agreement, and we were back at work again; back at dodging the foreman and gambling in corners, unchanged except for two weeks' hunger.

Now I'd been nearly a year in London, and had little to show for it except calloused hands and one printed poem. Life at Mrs Flynn's was a little odder, but as comfortable as ever, and she had a new boy-friend who increased the amenities.

One of these was Clara, an orphan from Battersea, who he'd hired to help with the cleaning – a thin rakey child of about fifteen who never spoke when grown-ups were around. She would gossip and play with little Patsy, but otherwise she worked in silence, a fugitive figure of fits and starts in constant agony of being noticed. I never knew Clara, but she seemed to have her private consolations, and also ways of making herself known. Sometimes I'd come home at night and turn on the switch in my room to find that she'd removed all the electric light-bulbs. 'Is that you, Laurie?' shrieked Mrs Flynn from the basement. 'Don't worry, the poor love can't 'elp it.' Then I'd find the electric bulbs in my bed, arranged like a nest of eggs, with one of her shoes or perhaps an old doll of Patsy's.

Patsy herself had grown more torrid with the months and had begun to practise with paint and lipstick, appearing suddenly at my door with scarified mouth and cheeks like Shakespeare's apparition of a bloody child. Shadowy Beth continued to pamper me, and to feed me on large late suppers, hovering with a tight tired smile to see that I had all I wanted, or to explain that Patsy was growing up. Mrs Flynn, more valiantly blonde then ever, and temporarily airborne by social success, regularly returned half my rent with gifts of beer and tobacco, and kept insisting that no one get married. In fact I was pampered by all of them, wrapped in a deep cushioned groove and guarded like some exotic lemur. There seemed to be no good reason why I shouldn't make a life of it here, except that I didn't want to end up in the attic, like Mr Willow.

By early summer the flats were almost completed, and I knew I would soon be out of a job. There was no prospect of another, but I wasn't worried; I never felt so beefily strong in my life. I remember standing one morning on the windy roof-top, and looking round at the racing sky, and suddenly realizing that once the job was finished I could go anywhere I liked in the world.

There was nothing to stop me, I would be penniless, free, and could just pack up and walk away. I was a young man whose time coincided with the last years of peace, and so was perhaps luckier than any generation since. Europe at least was wide open, a place of casual frontiers, few questions and almost no travellers.

So where should I go? It was just a question of getting there – France? Italy? Greece? I knew nothing at all about any of them, they were just names with vaguely operatic flavours I knew no languages either, so felt I could arrive new-born wherever I chose to go. Then I remembered that somewhere or other I'd picked up a phrase in Spanish for 'Will you please give me a glass of water?'

and it was probably this rudimentary bit of lifeline that finally made up my mind. I decided I'd go to Spain.

So as soon as I was sacked from the buildings, at the beginning of June, I bought a one-way ticket to Vigo. I remember it cost £4, which left me with a handful of shillings to see me safely into Spain. I didn't bother to wonder what would happen then, for already I saw myself there, brown as an apostle, walking the white dust roads through the orange groves.

The ship wasn't due to sail for a couple of weeks, so I spent my last days in London with a girl called Nell, who I'd found in a cinema. She came from Balham, and we used to meet on the Heath and then sometimes go to my room. She was soft and nervous, creamily pretty, buxom, yet plaintively chaste. Intoxicated by idleness – she was out of work too – and by the aura of incipient farewell, she used to lie in my arms in the summer dusk, struggling to save us both from sin. She wore the loose peasant blouse that was the fashion of the day, a panting bundle of creviced cotton, and as our time grew shorter she grew larger and softer as though all her frontiers were melting away. Then our last night came: 'Perhaps you could tie my hands. Then I couldn't say nothing, could I?' Finally: 'Take me with you. I wouldn't be any trouble.' I felt light-headed, detached, and heart-less. 'Take me with you' was something I was also hearing from other girls, who seemed not to have noticed me till now. For the first time I was learning how much easier it was to leave than to stay behind and love.

The morning came for departure, and the children helped me pack and Mike gave me his pocket jack-knife. Beth had gone off to work, leaving me a note of farewell, and Mrs Flynn was still asleep. Patsy walked half-way to the station with me, and we stopped on Putney Bridge. It was a fine chill morning, with a light mist on the river and the tide running fast to the sea. Patsy stood on tip-toe and grabbed hold of my ear and pulled it down to her paint-smeared mouth. 'Take me with you,' she said, then gave a quick snort of laughter, waved goodbye, and ran back home.

3

Into Spain

It was early and still almost dark when our ship reached the harbour, and when out of the unconscious rocking of sea and sleep I was simultaneously woken and hooked to the coast of Spain by the rattling anchor going over the side.

Lying safe in the old ship's blowsy care, I didn't want to move at first. I'd enjoyed the two slow days coming down the English Channel and across the Bay of Biscay, smelling the soft Gulf winds blowing in from the Atlantic and feeling the deep easy roll of the ship. But this was Vigo, the name on my ticket, and as far as its protection would take me. So I lay for a while in the anchored silence and listened to the first faint sounds of Spain – a howling dog, the gasping spasms of a donkey, the thin sharp cry of a cockerel. Then I packed and went up on to the shining deck, and the Spanish sun rose too, and for the first time in my life I saw, looped round the bay, the shape of a foreign city.

I'd known nothing till then but the smoother surfaces of England, and Vigo struck me like an apparition. It seemed to rise from the sea like some rust-corroded wreck, as old and bleached as the rocks around it. There was no smoke or movement among the houses. Everything looked barnacled, rotting, and deathly quiet, as though awaiting the return of the Flood. I landed in a town submerged by wet green sunlight and smelling of the waste of the sea. People lay sleeping in doorways, or sprawled on the ground, like bodies washed up by the tide.

But I was in Spain, and the new life beginning. I had a few

shillings in my pocket and no return ticket; I had a knapsack, blanket, spare shirt, and a fiddle, and enough words to ask for a glass of water. So the chill of dawn left me and I began to feel better. The drowned men rose from the pavements and stretched their arms, lit cigarettes, and shook the night from their clothes. Bootblacks appeared, banging their brushes together, and strange vivid girls went down the streets, with hair like coils of dripping tar and large mouths, red and savage.

Still a little off balance I looked about me, saw obscure dark eyes and incomprehensible faces, crumbling walls scribbled with mysterious graffiti, an armed policeman sitting on the Town Hall steps, and a photograph of Marx in a barber's window. Nothing I knew was here, and perhaps there was a moment of panic – anyway I suddenly felt the urge to get moving. So I cut the last cord and changed my shillings for pesetas, bought some bread and fruit, left the seaport behind me and headed straight for the open country.

I spent the rest of the day climbing a steep terraced valley, then camped for the night on a craggy hilltop. Some primitive instinct had forced me to leave the road and climb to this rock tower, which commanded an eagle's view of the distant harbour and all the hills and lagoons around it. Here, sitting on a stone, about six miles inland, I could look out in all directions, see where I was in the landscape, where I'd been that day, and much of the country still to come. Wild and silent, like a picture of western Ireland, it rolled rhythmically and desolately away, and faced with its alien magnificence I felt a last pang of homesickness, and the first twinge of uneasy excitement.

The Galician night came quickly, the hills turned purple and the valleys flooded with heavy shadow. The jagged coastline below, now dark and glittering, looked like sweepings of broken glass. Vigo was cold and dim, an'unlighted ruin, already smothered in the dead blue dusk. Only the sky and the ocean stayed alive, running with immense streams of flame. Then as the sun went down it seemed to drag the whole sky with it like the shreds of a burning curtain, leaving rags of bright water that went on smoking and smouldering along the estuaries and around the many islands. I saw the small white ship, my last link with home, flare like a taper and die away in the darkness; then I was alone at last, sitting on a hilltop, my teeth chattering as the night wind rose.

I found a rough little hollow out of the wind, a miniature crater among the rocks, ate some bread and dates, unrolled the blanket and wrapped myself inside it. I laid the fiddle beside me, used the knapsack as a pillow, and stretched out on the bed of stones; then folded my hands, hooked my little fingers together, shut my eyes and prepared to sleep.

But I slept little that night: I was attacked by wild dogs – or they may have been Galician wolves. They came slinking and snarling along the ridge of my crater, hackles bristling against the moon, and only by shouting, throwing stones, and flashing my torch in their eyes was I able to keep them at bay. Not till early dawn did they finally leave me and run yelping away down the hillside, when I fell at last into a nightmare doze, feeling their hot yellow teeth in my bones.

When I awoke next morning it was already light, and voices were screaming at one another in the valley. I looked at my watch and it was six o'clock, and I was heavily drenched in dew. I wriggled out of the blanket, crawled on to the ridge and lay in the rising sun, and was met by the resinous smell of drying bushes, peppery herbs, and stones. As I warmed my stiff limbs, I looked down the valley from which the sharp hard cries were coming, and saw a group of old women, as black as charcoal, slapping out sheets along the banks of a stream. Galician peasants, women *and* Spanish, unknown and doubly inscrutable – their thin bent bodies knelt over the water, jerking up and down like drinking hens, and as they worked they shrieked, firing off metallic bursts of speech that bounced off the rocks like bullets.

I lay on my belly, the warm earth against me, and forgot the cold dew and the wolves of the night. I felt it was for this I had come: to wake at dawn on a hillside and look out on a world for which I had no words; to start at the beginning, speechless and without plan, in a place that still had no memories for me.

For as I woke that second morning, with the whole of Spain to walk through, I was in a country of which I knew nothing. The names of Velázquez, Goya, El Greco, Lope de Vega, Juan de la Cruz were unknown to me; I'd never heard of the Cordoban Moors or the Catholic kings; nor of the Alhambra or the Escorial; or that Trafalgar was a Spanish Cape, Gibraltar a Spanish rock, or that it was from here that Columbus had sailed for America. My small country school, always generous with its information as to the exports of Queensland and the fate of Jenkins's ear, had provided me with nothing more tangible or useful about Spain than that Seville had a barber, and Barcelona nuts.

But I was innocent then of my ignorance, and so untroubled by it. My clothes steamed and dried as the sun grew stronger. The distant sea shone white, a clean morning freshness after last night's smoky fires. The rising hills before me went stepping away inland, fiercely shaped under the great blue sky. I nibbled some bread and fruit, rolled my things in a bundle, and washed my head and feet in a spring. Then shouldering my burden, and still avoiding the road, I took a track south-east for Zamora.

For three or four days I followed the track through the hills, but saw only occasional signs of life – sometimes a shepherd's hut, or a distant man walking, or a solitary boy with a flock of goats; otherwise no sound or movement except the eagles overhead and the springs gushing out of the rocks. The track climbed higher into the clear cold air, and I just followed it, hoping to keep direction. When twilight came, I curled up where I was, too exhausted to mind the cold. One night I took shelter in a ruined castle which I found piled on top of a crag – a gaunt roofless fortress tufted with the nests of ravens and scattered with abandoned fires. The skeleton of a sheep stood propped in one corner, picked clean, like a wicker basket; and drawings of women and horses were scratched round the walls. An obvious refuge, I thought, for bandits. But I slept well enough in the tottering place, in spite of its audible darkness, the rustling in the walls, the squeaks and twitters, and the sighing of the mountain wind.

Otherwise all I remember of those first days from Vigo is a deliriously sharpening hunger, an appetite so keen it seemed almost a pity to satisfy it, so voluptuous it was.

By the second day I'd finished my bread and dates, but I found a few wild grapes and ate them green, and also the remains of a patch of beans.

Then I remember coming out of a gorge one early evening and seeing my first real village. I remember it well, because it was like all Spain, and it was also my first encounter. It stood on a bare brown rock in the sinking sun – a pile of squat houses like cubes of pink sugar. In the centre rose a tower from which a great black bell sent out cracked jerking gusts of vibration. I'd had enough of the hills and lying around in wet bracken, and now I smelt fires and a sweet tang of cooking. I climbed the steep road into the village, and black-robed women, standing in doorways, made soft exclamations as I went by.

In the village square I came on a great studded door bearing the sign: 'Posada de Nuestra Señora.' I pushed the door open and entered a whitewashed courtyard hanging with geraniums and crowded with mules and asses. There was bedlam in the courtyard – mules stamping, asses braying, chickens cackling, and children fighting. A fat old crone, crouching by the fire in the corner, was stirring soup in a large black cauldron, and as she seemed to be in charge I went up to her and made a sign for food. Without a word she lifted a ladleful of the soup and held it up to my mouth. I tasted and choked; it was hot, strong, and acrid with smoke and herbs. The old lady peered at me sharply through the fumes of the fire. She was bent, leather-skinned, bearded and fanged, and looked like a watchful moose. I wiped my burnt mouth, nodded my head, and said 'Good' in clear loud English. She took a long pull herself, her moustached lips working, her eyes rolling back in her skull. Then she spat briskly into the fire, turned her head abruptly and roared out in a deep hoarse voice – and a barefooted boy, dressed only in a shirt, came and tugged my sleeve and led me to see the bedrooms.

Later I was sitting in the courtyard under the swinging light-bulbs, hungrily watching the supper cooking, when the innkeeper came out, a towel round his waist, and began to scrub his young son in the horse-trough. The infant screamed, the old crone roared, the father shouted, sang, and lathered. Then suddenly, as by a whim, he shoved the child under the water and left him to see what he'd do. The screams were cut off as though by a knife, while the old woman and the father watched him. In a fierce choking silence the child fought the water, kicking and struggling like a small brown frog, eyes open, mouth working, his whole body grappling with the sudden inexplicable threat of death. He was about one year old, but for a moment seemed ageless, facing terror alone and dumb. Then just as he was about to give in, the woman picked up a bucket and threw it at the father's head, and at that he snatched up the child, tossed him in the air, smothered him with kisses, and carried him away.

Supper was laid at last on the long wooden table set out under the open sky. When it was ready the innkeeper, with a sweep of his arm, invited me to join them. Carters and drovers gathered quickly round the table, and a girl dealt out loaves to each of us, and we ate the stew from a common dish, scooping it up with our bread. The old woman sat beside me and roared at me continuously, pinching my legs and thumping me in the belly and urging me on to eat.

Half-way through supper we were joined by two shifty-eyed men who came in carrying a new-skinned lamb. They looked starved, desperate, and poor as dogs, and their shirts hung in rags from their shoulders. They approached us in silence and nobody greeted them, nor did they seem to expect it. They dropped the bleeding lamb at the far end of the table, threw themselves down, and called for wine. Then they began to tear at the carcass, cramming the meat in their mouths and darting fugitive looks over their shoulders. Their movements had all the sharp snapping nervousness of beasts at a kill, crouching low and cracking the bones with their teeth. When a girl had brought them their wine, they were left to themselves – their meal was their own secret business.

At our end of the table, supper was prolonged and noisy, and I didn't know whether it was night or morning. By now I was gorged with stew and warmed to idiocy by wine; I was the stranger, but I felt at home. In each face around me I seemed to recognize characters from my own village: the carters, innkeepers, the dust-covered farmboys, grandmothers, and girls, they were all here. I felt like a child crawling on the edge of some rousing family life which I had yet to grow to understand. And I think they felt it too, for they treated me like a child – grinning, shouting, acting dumb-shows to please me, and smoothing my way with continual tit-bits and indulgencies.

At last supper was over. The women swept the dishes away, and the carters curled up on the ground to sleep. The two outcasts lay snoring across their end of the table, their faces buried in a debris of bones. I rose from my chair and stumbled away to my room, where I found six beds, full of men and fleas. Fowls were roosting in the rafters, and an old man lay fully clothed on the floor, fast asleep, with a goat tethered to his ankle. The room was stifling, but the straw bed was soft. And there I slept, my head roaring with Spain.

That was just one night, an early one on my journey, and also my first inn, like many others to come. From then on the days merged into a continuous movement of sun and shadow, hunger and thirst, fatigue and sleep, all fused and welded into one coloured mass by the violent heat of that Spanish summer.

I had come now out of the hills of Galicia, along high bare tracks overhanging the sheltered valleys where thick grass grew and herds of panting sheep gathered at noon by white-pebbled streams. I had skirted the mountains of León, coming through shaded oak-woods and groves of fig and almond, along great shelves of rock where wooden ox-carts laboured and boys in broad hats went leaping up the hillsides pursuing their scattered flocks. I'd come through poor stone villages, full of wind and dust, where mobs of children convoyed me through the streets, and where priests and women quickly crossed themselves when they saw me, and there was nothing to buy except sunflower seeds. And I'd come down at last to the rich plain of the Douro, with its fields of copper earth, its violent outcrops of poppies running in bloodstained bandannas across acres of rasping wheat.

After the green of the hills the light here was lethal; it thumped the head and screwed up the eyes. I was burnt by the sun, and bug-ridden from the inns – but I was also slowly beginning to pick up the language. Listening to people on the road I noticed that their guttural flow had begun to break up and detach into words and phrases: 'good', 'bad', 'bread and wine', 'how much?' 'too much; shame . . .' So without more inhibition I started talking to everyone, offering anything that came to mind, and many a sombre patriarch jogging towards me on his mule would be met by some stumbling salutation, and would raise a stiff grave hand in defence and greeting, and bid me go with God.

I finally reached Zamora early one Saturday evening, after a blistering day through the wheatfields. The town stood neatly stacked on its rocky hill, a ripple of orange roofs and walls, somewhat decrepit now, but still giving off something of the medieval sternness and isolated watchfulness of its past. Around its rocky site curled the track of the Douro, a leathery arm of wrinkled mud, laced down the middle with a vein of green water in which some half-naked boys were bathing.

Brick-red with road-dust I padded into the square and sat down under a shady plane tree. After the long day's walk my back was sheeted with sweat and my bag was like a load of stones. I slipped it to the ground and sucked in the hot still air; the evening was thunderous and swimming with flies. There was almost no one in the square except a few old women and a man selling mineral water. Seeing my parched condition, he came and gave me a bottle, but refused to take any payment. The pink scented juice tasted like effervescent hair-oil, but it instantly revived me.

As I sat there, scratching, and wondering where I would spend the night, I suddenly heard the sound of music coming from a nearby street – not the Spanish kind, but waltzy gusts of Strauss played on accordion, flute, and fiddle. Curious, I went off to have a look, and found three blond young men bashing out a back-street concert in the midst of a crowd of wide-mouthed children. Men had halted their mules, women stood listening in doorways or hung from balconies overhead. The syrupy beer-hall strains of 'Vienna Woods' swept incongruously round the Spanish houses, but the boys were doing well – pennies tumbled from windows or were tossed over the heads of the children, to be caught with a flourish in the fiddler's hat with heavily accented thanks.

It was a significant moment, and I was cheered by the sight, as this was how I, too, hoped to live. It seemed that I'd come to the right country, poor as it was; the pennies were few, but they were generously given. And music was clearly welcome in this Spanish street, the faces softened with pleasure as they listened.

When they'd finished their playing, the boys spotted me in the crowd, nodded gaily, and addressed me in German. I explained where I came from, which wasn't what they expected, then we sat on the pavement and chattered in broken English. They were about my own age, and displayed a highstrung energy, busy eyes, and a kind of canine sharpness. They were from Hamburg, they said, and had been in Spain two years, had circled it twice and were planning to circle it again. They called themselves students, and said there were a large number in the country, playing instruments and living rough – partly for fun, and partly to get out of Germany: I was the first 'student' they'd met from England. Meanwhile, they introduced themselves – Artur, Rudi, and Heinrich – and invited me to spend the evening with them.

After I, in turn, had given them an account of myself, and they had examined my clothes and blisters, they took me to a shop to buy some cool light sandals, and picked out a beggar on whom to bestow my boots. Then we went to a bar to count out the concert money and drink some of the thin warm, local beer. Artur was full of advice, and seemed to know Zamora well. 'Is beaudival place, but poor as church rats. Tomorrow is going away.'

Germans, of course, had been the folk-devils of my childhood, the bogies of all our games. These ragged young lads, noisily sucking their beer, were the first real Germans I'd ever met. Artur was their leader, and played the violin. He was tall, curly with a long mobile throat, sunken cheeks, and feverish blue eyes. He talked with a jerking vitality that seemed close to hysteria, face sweating, eyes rolling, his speech often broken into by jagged rasps of consumptive coughing. Rudi was young and quieter, and sat stroking his accordion and humming tunes through his fat red lips. Heinrich, the flautist, was as agreeable as a dog, and sat panting at Artur's feet – strung-up, on edge, and watching him intently, ready for any game or change of humour. He was a clown, if needed, and poured Artur's beer, and carried his supply of paper handkerchiefs.

'Now for the danze!' cried Artur. Night had fallen already, and the boys had a job at the local dance-hall. 'Are making the music,' he said. 'Ya, one – two – three! Are drinking the beer and coming many girls. Afterwards good essen, and you can be sleeping in our room, very cheap, you can imagine.'

So we took my things to the lodging house, then headed for the dance-hall down by the river. The town was palely lit by naked yellow bulbs which gave an impression of curried moonlight. As we went down the narrow cobble-stepped streets, Rudi struck up on his accordion, playing wild banshee scales designed to advertise the dance and to summon the youth of the town. He succeeded too: sleeping pigeons took off, dogs barked, and windows flew open, and very soon we had a procession of well-brushed customers hurrying along behind us.

'Look, I say!' cried Artur excitedly, gripping my arm and

sawing the air with it. 'See are coming many boys and girls. You shall make danze with them all, nothing forbidden, you understand.'

The dance-hall was a kind of broken-down warehouse propped up on the river bank, just a bare wooden shack dressed with a few old chairs and some primitive decorations. When you stepped on the floorboards they went off like fireworks, raising little puffballs of peppery dust, and there were holes in the roof through which you could see the stars whenever the dust allowed it. Around the walls hung pictures of half-naked women, clenching roses in desperate teeth, and wearing loose cardboard flaps round their ample loins which the curious could raise to reveal slogans for beer. There was also an improvised bar, some strings of paper carnations, and a platform draped with the Spanish flag.

As they poured into the room, the dancers immediately segregated themselves, girls down one side, boys down the other. Considerably quieter now than they had been in the street, the boys looked pale and anxious, rubbing their hands on their knees, tapping their neat little feet, and gazing at the girls with potent gloom. The girls were far more self-possessed, knowing their worth on such occasions, settling plump in their chairs like bags of sweets, stickily scented and tied with ribbons.

The band tuned up noisily, then Artur swayed to his feet and announced a pasodoble. The barriers fell at once, and the dancing began and the noise it made was soon as loud as the band. The boys stamped like bulls, the girls twirled and shuffled, dust rose, and the floorboards jumped. Caught face to face, away from their neutral corners, the dancers grappled in passionate strife – but as soon as the music ended, the girls turned chastely away, leaving the boys flatfooted.

For an hour or so I sat on the platform with the band sharing their gifts of bottled beer. It was warm, scummy, and rather sour, but it had a lively effect on Artur. Soon his fiddle was soaring above the sounds of the flute, departing on a life of its own, playing thin little tunes of Bavarian extraction which only he and

I could hear. For a while, eyes closed, he was no longer with us, he was away in the forest snows.

Suddenly he looked at me.

'Is not good time?' he shouted. 'But why is not danzing, yah?' He looked round the room, spotted an unused girl, and called her over to join me.

What with my blistered feet, and the beer in my head, it was as much as I could do to stand up. But the girl took charge – she just wrapped her damp arms round me, propped me snugly erect with her bosom, and away we went over the flapping floorboards as though skating on Venetian blinds. This stumbling movement, together with the unexpected nearness of the girl, did nothing to lessen my feeling of drunkenness. Several times I would have fallen, but the girl was like scaffolding, like a straitjacket of cushioned bones. Helpless, half-crippled, half-anaesthetized by her scent, I scuffled after her, praying for the end. She was tough and beautiful, but I could think of nothing to say to her – except Help, I feel sick and hungry. Finally the waltz was over, and the girl led me back to my chair and seated me carefully in it. As she left me she drew her finger down the length of my body as though sealing an envelope.

It was long after midnight before the dancers went home, fading crushed and bruised into the darkness. Suddenly there was no one in the hall but the Germans and myself, and the waiters picking up empty bottles. The floor was littered with paper carnations, and white dust covered everything like frost.

'Eating now,' croaked Artur. He leaned exhausted against the wall, bathed in sweat, trembling like a race-horse. Heinrich took off his jacket and threw it round Artur's shoulders, and we went out into the starlit street. As soon as the cold air met us, Artur's coughing began, and we followed it like a deathknell up through the silent town to the café where supper was waiting.

Artur had fixed it: roast kid and beans – a miracle at this hour of the morning. We slumped round the table, weary and famished, and an old woman brought us some wine. Then we gorged ourselves, using our fingers and winking at one another. The meat had a flavour and tenderness I shall never forget, it came off the bone like petals from a rose.

It seemed that nothing could quieten Artur now. He giggled, whinnied, and coughed out his lungs; his eyes rolled and his lips were flecked. But gradually the food and the wine composed and drowsed him. Heinrich held him by the shoulders and cradled his head. Rudi sang softly at the other end of the table. It was nearly dawn, but no one wished to move. We felt pitiful and sentimental.

We carried Artur like a corpse to the room upstairs, which had four beds, but no light or windows. Someone found a candle, and we lay Artur down, took off his boots, and Heinrich wiped his forehead. Nobody spoke any more, or even whispered; we went to our beds and Rudi blew out the candle. I lay sleepless for a while in the death-room darkness, my first and last night in Zamora, listening to the choking rattle of Artur's breath, and the sound of Heinrich weeping.

4

Zamora–Toro

It was a short sleep and a brutal waking, roused by Artur's reluctant resurrection. While he sat swaying on his bed racked by paroxysms of coughing, his face the colour of crumpled pewter.

We revived him slowly in the tavern below, and then decided that it was time for us to leave. One night of music and dance had emptied the coffers of the city so far as the German boys were concerned. 'Is poor as church rats,' repeated Artur painfully. 'Is better going, you can imagine.'

At midday we packed and walked out of the town and paused for a moment at a fork in the road – one way leading north to León and Oviedo, and the other eastward to Valladolid. This was where we parted. The boys were going to León, where they would join some other 'students', while I'd chosen Valladolid, not because I knew anything about it, but because I liked the sound of its syllables.

At the waste edge of Zamora, a dismal litter of dust with donkeys grazing among bones and bottles, the boys formally shook my hand. The bare tight-laced city rose moodily behind us, its twelfth-century cathedral looking bleached like driftwood.

'Goodbye,' spluttered Artur. 'We see you again and again.' We went our different ways.

Almost immediately I regretted the cool alleys of the town, the scrubbed taverns and frothy fruit-drinks. By the afternoon I was out in the plain, in an electric haze of heat, walking a white dust road as straight as a canal, banked by shimmering wheat and poppies. For mile after mile I saw neither man nor beast; the world seemed to be burnt out, drained and dead; and the blinding white road, narrowing away to the horizon, began to fill me with curious illusions. I felt I was treading the rim of a burning wheel, kicking it behind me step by step, feet scorched and blistered, yet not advancing an inch, pinned for ever at this sweltering spot. For hours, it seemed, I had the same poppy beside me, the same cluster of brittle wheat, the same goldleaf lizard flickering around my toes, the same ant-hill under the bank. The thick silent dust, lifted by shudders of heat rather than by the presence of any wind, crept into my sandals and between my toes, stuck like rime to my lips and eyelashes, and dropped into the breathless cups of the roadside poppies to fill them with a cool white mirage of snow. All around me was silence, deep and dazed, except for the gritty rustle of the wheat. I walked head down, not daring to look at the sky, which by now seemed to be one huge sun.

That Zamoran wheat-plain was my first taste of Spanish heat – the brass-taloned lion which licks the afternoon ground ready to consume anyone not wise enough to take cover. Exposed to its rasping tongue, I learned soon enough one of the obvious truths of summer, that no man, beast, or bird – and indeed very few insects – moved much at that time of the day.

About five o'clock, after some four hours on the road, I at last saw a break in the landscape – a red clay village, dry as the earth around it and compact as a termite's nest. I have forgotten its name, and can find nothing marked there on the map, but it occured at just the right moment.

I stumbled out of the wheatfield on to this evening village to find it in the drowsy grip of harvest. The sun was low already and a coppery dust filled the air, slashed by smouldering shafts of light. In a cleared space by the roadside the menfolk were threshing, driving little sleigh-carts over the scattered sheaves, each drawn by a mule wearing garlands of leaves to keep off the sleepy flies. Women and girls, in broad hats and veils, looking as mysterious as Minoan dancers, stood in graceful circles winnowing the grain in the wind, tossing and catching it in its drifts of gold.

Rhythmically working at their various jobs, and gilded from head to foot with chaff, the villagers clustered together round the threshing floor like a swarm of summer-laden bees.

Some of them shouted a greeting as I approached, while the women paused to line up and stare; then children ran from the alleys and encircled me and ushered me noisily into the village.

'Look at the foreigner!' they cried, as though they had made me up. 'Look at the rubio who's come today.' They aped my walk, and grinned and beckoned, and finally led me to the village inn.

It was much like the others, with a great oak door. The children pushed it open and stood courteously aside. Nodding and beaming, with brilliant smiles of reassurance, they gestured for me to go in.

So I went inside, and found the usual spacious barn hanging with freshly watered flowers. A few low chairs stood around the walls, and there was a table and tiled stove in the corner. All was cool and bare. Chickens pecked at the floor and swallows flashed from the high arched ceiling.

A middle-aged woman sat just inside the door, stitching at a piece of lace. She was fleshy, but handsome, with the strong brooding eyes and confident mouth of the matriarch. The children crowded the doorway, watching me expectantly as though I was a firework just about to go off, while the small ones at the back jumped up and down in order to get a better view. 'Doña Maria!' they shouted. 'We have brought you a Frenchman. Doña Maria, look at him!'

The woman put down her sewing and thanked them politely, then let out a screech that sent them scattering up the street. After which she considered me for a moment over the top of her steel-rimmed spectacles, then said: 'Rest, and I'll get you some food.'

I slumped down at the table and lay with my head in my arms, listening voluptuously to the woman's movements: the rattle of the pan on the fire, the crack of an eggshell, the hiss of frying oil. Sweat dripped from my hair and ran over my hands, and my head was swimming with heat, with throbbing visions of the white dust road and the brassy glare of the fields.

Presently the woman pushed some fried eggs before me, and poured me a glass of purple wine. Then she returned to her sewing and was joined by a girl, and together they sat and watched me. In that great bare room under the diving swallows, I ate the honoured meal of the stranger, while the women murmured together in low furred voices, their needles darting like silver fish.

At dusk an old man came in from threshing, shaking the chaff from his hair. He poured himself some wine and sat down at the table.

'What have we?' he asked the woman.

She dropped her hands in her lap, and looked at me again, sharply but protectively.

'Ah,' she said. 'He comes from somewhere away. A poor devil who is walking the world.'

The man filled up my glass and jerked his thumb to his mouth. 'Drink, and may it give you strength.'

'You want to sleep here tonight?' asked Doña Maria after a while.

'How much?'

'For a straw sack – two pennies.'

'Good,' I said. 'Then I will sleep with you.'

'No – you will sleep on the sack.'

The old man wheezed, the girl covered her face, and the woman piled her sewing on top of her head. Then with a click of her tongue she heaved her bulk from the chair and skipped lightly towards the stove.

Two dusty young men came through the open door, leading a pig and a sheep on a rope. 'My sons,' said the woman. They poured water over their heads, then filled up the trough for the animals. Mother and daughter set the table for supper, while the old man continued to pour me wine. Then with formal excuses and requests for forgiveness, the family began its meal.

The evening now was close and smoky. The lamp was lit, and the great doors shut. I was getting used to this pattern of Spanish life, which could have been that of England two centuries earlier. This house, like so many others I'd seen already, held nothing more than was useful for living – no fuss of furniture and unneces-sary decoration – being as self-contained as the Ark. Pots, pans, the chairs and tables, the manger and drinking-trough, all were of wood, stone, or potter's clay, simply shaped and polished like tools. At the end of the day, the doors and windows admitted all the creatures of the family: father, son, daughter, cousin, the donkey, the pig, the hen, even the harvest mouse and the nesting swallow, bedded together at the fall of darkness.

So it was with us in this nameless village; night found us wrapped in this glowing barn, family and stranger gathered round the long bare table to a smell of woodsmoke, food, and animals. Across the whitewashed walls the shadows of man and beast flickered huge like ancestral ghosts, which since the days of the caves have haunted the corners of fantasy, but which the electric light has killed.

We sat close together, the men drinking and smoking, elbows at rest among the empty plates. It was the short drowsy space between work and sleep, with nothing left of the day but gossip. Doña Maria, who was cobbling a piece of tattered harness, dominated the table with her thick warm voice, telling tales which to me were inscrutable, alas, but which to the others seemed vaguely familiar. The old man was a motionless mask in the shadows, though he showed a tooth in an occasional cackle. The sons sat near me, nudging me politely in the ribs and nodding their heads whenever the mother made a joke. The daughter, sitting close to the only lamp, buried her fingers in her sewing and listened, raising her huge Arab eyes every moment or so, to meet my glance of dumb conjecture.

I was half drunk now; in fact I felt like a bonfire, full of dull smoke and hot congestion. My eyes were hopelessly moored to those small neat breasts, rocking sadly to their rise and fall, till she seemed to be floating before me on waves of breath, naked as a Negress in her tight black dress.

But the brothers surrounded me, and Doña Maria crouched near, watching me with warm but suspicious indulgence. So I sat and swayed in my drowsy conflagration, fitting sentences together

275

in my mind, then producing them slowly, like a string of ill-knotted flags, for the family's polite astonishment.

Suddenly, one of the sons spotted my rolled-up blanket with the violin sticking out of it. 'Música!' he cried, and went and fetched the bundle and laid it gingerly on the table before me.

'Yes, man,' said the mother. 'Come, divert us a little. Touch us a little tune.' The old man woke up, and the daughter put down her sewing, lifted her head, and even smiled.

There was nothing else for it. I sat down on the ground and tore drunkenly into an Irish reel. They listened, open-mouthed, unable to make head or tail of it; I might have been playing a Tibetan prayer-wheel. Then I tried a woozy fandango which I'd picked up in Zamora, and comprehension jerked them to life. The girl stiffened her body, the boys grabbed a handful of spoons and began slapping them across their knees, and the woman leapt to her feet and started stamping the ground, raising great clouds of dust around me. Not to be outdone, the old man left the shadows, struck a posture, and faced the woman. Doña Maria all flesh, he thin as a straw, together they began a dance of merciless contest, while the boys thumped their spoons, the woman shouted 'Ha!' and the hens flew squawking under the table.

It was no longer just a moment of middle-aged horseplay. The old man danced as if his life was at stake. While the woman was suddenly transformed, her great lumpen body becoming a thing of controlled and savage power. Moving with majestic assurance, her head thrown back, her feet pawing the ground like an animal, she stamped and postured round her small hopping husband as if she would tread him into oblivion. The dance was soon over, but while it lasted she was a woman unsheathed and terrible. The old man fell back, threw up his hands in defeat, and retired gasping to the safety of the walls.

The woman was left alone, and the mantle fell from her, and she stood like a girl, mopping her face and giggling, deprecating her performance with little hen-like cluckings and surprised shakings of her head.

'This is not for an old woman. My bones ache,' she said.

'Egyptian!' hissed the man from the shadows.

The sons asked me for another tune, and this time they danced together, with linked arms, rather sedate and formal. The daughter came quietly and sat on the floor beside me, watching my fingers as I played. The scent of her nearness swam troublesomely around me with a mixture of pig's lard and sharp clean lavender.

The evening's routine had been broken, and no one seemed eager to sleep. So some further celebration was possible. The girl was asked to sing, and she did as she was told, in a flat unaffected voice. The songs were simple and moving, and probably local; anyway. I've never heard them since. She sang them innocently, without art, taking breath like a child, often in the middle of a word. Staring blankly before her,' without movement or expression, she simply went through each one, then stopped – as though she'd really no idea what the songs were about, only that they were using her to be heard.

With the singing over, we sat in silence for a while, hearing only the trembling sound of the lamp. Then the woman grunted and spoke, and the boys got up from the table and fetched the mattresses and laid them down by the wall.

'You sleep there,' said the mother. 'My sons will watch you.' She pulled knowingly at one of her eyelids. 'Come then,' she added, and the girl rose from her knees and followed her quickly to another part of the house, while the husband's crinkled old face simply disappeared from the air, soundlessly, like a snuffed-out candle.

I was ready for sleep, and stretched myself out on the floor while the boys went and bolted the door Then they came, fully-clothed, and lay down on each side of me, settling their limbs with little grunts.

The boys were up early, at about half past four, coughing and stamping around the barn. The doors were thrown open to let in the cold pink dawn, and the animals were driven out to the fields. I was still heavy with wine and would have liked more sleep, but it was made clear that the day had started, and soon the girl was about with her birch-twig broom sweeping the chickens across my face.

So I got up from the floor and shook the straw from my clothes, and the girl kicked my mattress into the corner. Then she led me out into the yard, showed me how to use the pump, went through the motions of lathering her face, gave me a piece of soap as hard as a stone, and then departed to light the stove.

Breakfast was a wedge of dry bread and a bowl of soup-thick coffee floating with fatty gobs of goat's milk. By the time I'd swallowed it, it was six o'clock, and all the village was on the move. Framed in the open doorway great golden wagons went swaying down the cobbled street, followed by soft-padding strings of tasselled donkeys, the sun shining red through their ears.

As I stood ready to leave. I heard a shout behind me: 'Where is he? Where is the stranger?' – and Doña Maria strode forth, wildly disarrayed from her bed, and thrust a handful of figs into my shirt. 'Say nothing of that. Nothing at all,' she growled. 'What a night the old one had.' I gave her the coppers I owed her, and she considered them distractedly for a moment, weighing them in her hand as if about to return them. Then she changed her mind, popped them under her skirt, slapped me on the back, and wished me goodbye.

Down by the river, under an olive tree, a group of girls were drawing water. The girl from the inn was among them, and their voices rang sharp, like a clashing of knives on stone. As I came down the lane their chattering stopped, and they turned their heads all together to watch me. Caught in this alert, surprised, almost pastoral attitude, they offered me an unblinking cluster of eyes, intent and expressionless as the eyes of calves, and desolating too. I padded past quickly, and nobody moved, but their eyes followed me like the eyes in a painting. I remember their blank shining pupils, like pebbles in water. The girl from the inn gave no sign that she knew me.

Out in the plain once more, head down to the dust, I walked

fast to make the most of the morning. Not that I'd any particular need to hurry, but the girls had unsettled me to the point of believing that a little hard walking would balance the mind. After a couple of hours or so, still in the grip of a romantic melancholy, I stopped by a little roadside shrine, which announced that a boy, aged ten, had been killed on this spot by a madman, and asked travellers to pray for them both.

I ate the cool green figs which Doña Maria had given me, then walked on for another hour. The monotony of the plain, and the height of the wheat around me, restricted the view to only a few yards, so that I was unprepared for the sudden appearance of Toro – an ancient, eroded, red-walled town spread along the top of a huge flat boulder. The plain ended here in a series of geological convulsions that had thrown up gigantic shelves of rock, raw red in colour and the size of islands, rising abruptly to several hundred feet. Perched on one of the sharpest of these, and scattered along its crumbling edge, Toro looked like dried blood on a rusty sword. The cliff dropped sheer to the bed of the river and was littered with the debris of generations.

Clambering up to the town, in the hard noon silence, I was ready to find it deserted, or to see some Pompeii-like waste long blasted by doom and inhabited only by cats and asses. On the contrary – half-ruined though it certainly was – the town was buzzing with life, with whitewashed hovels brimming with rackety families, children running through holes in the walls, busy shops and café flourishing behind broken-down doors, and the streets crowded with elegant walkers.

I sat in a chair outside the Café Español and watched the parade go by. Each strolling young man was a pocket dandy, carefully buttoned in spite of the heat; each girl a crisp, freshly laundered doll, flamboyantly lacy around neck and knees; and it was curious to see so much almost Edwardian fashion blooming on such an arid shelf of rock. A public show of clothes was obviously the first thing here, in spite of the poverty and ruin of the place, where the poorest tin shack seemed to produce its immaculate debutante, picking her way casually among the offal, superbly dressed for display by a busy task-force of aunts sewing and ironing behind the scenes.

As I sat there watching I was approached by a thin young man who snatched off his beret and bowed.

'I am Billette, mister – at your orders,' he said; then he stood by my chair and waited. He wore a tattered blue suit which seemed to cover his limbs like a cobweb, and his hand clutched a sheaf of tickets.

I offered him a drink, and he sat down beside me, apologizing for any derangement. Then, with a twopenny beer in his hand, he became officially my friend and interpreter of the scene before me. Speaking slowly, carefully, with icy detachment, he indicated the passing dandies.

'Señoritos!' he said. 'From the University of Valladolid. Lawyers and doctors every one. We have many of them. But it makes no difference. We are still ruined, and die.'

Clutching his glass with long spatulate fingers, he shivered and blinked at the sunlight. Why had I come to Toro? I had the right, of course. The world was free for young 'Frenchmen' like me. Tonight, he said, the town would hold a holy procession; I ought to see it, but I should forgive him for mentioning it.

Then he pulled himself together. 'We are the strongest city in the plain,' he said, 'and also very holy. We have saints in the church more beautiful than anybody. The people lead sacred lives ... Look there, for instance.' He jerked his head dolefully and pointed up the street.

I saw a ten-year-old child, dressed like a bride, come mincing along the pavement – a wedding-cake toy capped with a halo of flowers and carrying lilies in her white-gloved hands. She advanced with jaunty solemnity, eyes demurely composed, accompanied by two large women in black, and when the sun fell on her she suddenly blazed like a starshell with a brilliant incandescent light.

'See her,' said Billette. 'Another virgin for the Carmelites. We offer one up almost every day.'

All down the street the child was embraced and saluted, while she dropped her eyes and tried to suppress her excitement; old men doffed their hats, mothers held babies towards her, children ran up and kissed her cheek.

'We are a holy town, as you see,' said my companion. 'Our girls marry Christ from the cradle. Where do they go? Into the caverns of the Church. We shan't see this one again.'

He may have been pulling my leg, of course; it was probably nothing more than her first communion. Yet as the child danced away among her dark attendants she seemed to leave an unhealthy flush behind her.

Throughout the afternoon I drowsed behind the café curtains, hiding from the worst of the heat. The streets were empty now except for a few thin dogs hugging the walls for an inch of shade. All else was silence, blinding white, while the sun moved high over the town, destroyer, putrifier, scavenger of the hovels and breeder of swarming ills.

At the first breath of evening I went off with Billette to look at the castle on the edge of the town. 'Morisco,' he explained; a bit of infidel terrorism now rapidly returning to dust ... He led me nimbly among the eroded dungeons – 'the sepulchres of the Cristianos' – whose bones, he said, were now in the church (and seemed to be lavishly surrounded with excrement).

Here I was approached by another young man who had been poking distractedly among the ruins – a slim womanish figure, wielding a gold-topped cane and carrying a portfolio under his arm. He spoke in a delicate dancing language of his own, a kind of two-step between French and English. He was not from Toro, oh no! – a brutish place. (Billette stood listening with jealous incomprehension.) No, he was an art-master from Valencia, and exploited his leisure by executing ornamental lettering for churches. 'Regard!' he said sharply, and opened the portfolio to reveal some particularly lurid examples of his art. 'At this, I am known to be a master. But today I flower in a desert ...'

Leaning against the crumbling ramparts and gazing at the river below us, he worked himself into a lather of bitterness, bewailing the age of profanity in which he was doomed to live, together with the cowardice of the modern Church. There was no taste, no reverence for ornamental lettering any more, at least not for such devotional work as his. They preferred the gaudy shams of the cheap printers of Madrid, which the Church was buying in bulk like stamps. Where were the bishops and cardinals of old? he cried, those patrons of artistic piety? the holy princes of Christendom whose sainted hands once raised the artist to the floors of Heaven?

Billette was clearly impressed by the noise the other was making and watched him with shining eyes, while the young man sighed, panted, and twisted his eloquent limbs into shuddering postures of outrage. How could he possibly live under such shame and neglect, and continue to keep up his little house in Valencia? Soon he would be reduced to such crimes as mottoes and calendars, which would kill his aged mother.

All this was in French and English. Billette gaped with admiration, recognizing the other's passion, if not the sense. Accepting the sound of protest as something he must obviously share, he touched the young man's arm and began to quieten and console him. A curious calm descended as they whispered together, leaning close in the setting sun. Then with an excuse they left me, and wandered off hand in hand, brothers of a momentary confusion.

Back in Toro the evening deepened with a hot green light as the town prepared for the coming procession. Huge banners and shawls swung down from the balconies, all decorated in Grand Guignol fashion, some stitched with black crosses, others tied at the corners with gigantic bows of crêpe. Townsfolk, and stove-hatted peasants from the plain, were already crowding along the pavements, some with small buttoned cushions and stools to kneel on, all gazing in silence up the street.

The bells, which for an hour had been crashing out a jangle of discords, suddenly stopped with a humming abruptness. At this signal the multitude went quite still, fixing its eyes on the distant church. A heap of gold at noon, it was now a dark blue shadow, hanging in the air like a wisp of incense. The silence increased, and even the cries of the children began instinctively to smother themselves. Then the doors were thrown open on to a sparkling darkness, like a cave full of summer fireflies, as several hundred candles streamed away from the altar and came fluttering towards the street.

Slowly, to the sound of a drum and trumpet, the shuffling procession emerged, and the crush of spectators standing nearest the church fell to their knees as though they'd been sprayed with bullets. The dry beat of the drum and naked wail of the trumpet sounded as alien as I could wish, conjuring up in the glow of this semi-African twilight an extraordinary feeling of fear and magic.

Was it the death of their saint they were so lugubriously celebrating with their black banners and dripping candles? Her image came riding high in the heart of the procession, a glittering figure of painted wood, bobbing her crowned head stiffly, left and right, to the kneeling crowds in the gutters. Her bearers sweated under their jewelled load, grunting patiently into their lacy shirt-fronts, while two lines of young women scuffled along behind, nasally chanting some tuneless dirge.

As the image approached us, protestations and tears rose spontaneously from the crowd around me. Then the saint drew level and I saw her face, rose-tinted, pretty as a sugared sweet, with the smooth head perched on a little doll-like body heavily tented in robes of velvet.

Whoever she was, this prim painted mannikin dominated the town with an undeniable presence, and as she passed on her way she seemed to trail behind a gigantic swathe of absolution. Praise, thanks, and supplication followed her, passionately uttered by young and old. Clearly, to all eyes, she was the living Saint, Sister of the Virgin, Intimate of Christ, Eternal Mediator with the Ghost of God and Compassionate Mother of Toro.

With a dying cry in the distance the image passed from sight, the drum and the trumpet faded, and the last of the girls shuffled by, their candles wilting and guttering, leaving behind in the street the spent faces of the peasants, a smell of wax, burnt wick, and exhaustion. There was a short hushed pause, then the heavy soul-laden blanket was lifted like a cloud from the town. Suddenly everyone was nodding and smiling at one another, gathering up their children and cushions, and remarking how well the Saint had looked today – so comely, so linda, such an excellent colour – and making ready to enjoy themselves.

The solemn wake was over. The streets filled immediately with promenaders spreading from wall to wall. The lights were switched on – strings of small coloured bulbs that looped everywhere like skeins of fruit – and all the life of Toro began to pass beneath them, up and down and around, friend shown to friend, foe to foe, wife to lover, each to all. For a while I wandered invisibly among them, submerged by their self-absorption; and suddenly found myself wishing for a face I knew, for Stroud on a Saturday night . . .

The next day I remember only vaguely. It was one of the hottest of that Spanish summer. No doubt I should have stayed at the inn till the worst was over, but the journey had become a habit.

Toro was deserted when I left it, its shutters still drawn, and a brassy glare hung over the plain. The road ran through the wheat as straight as a meridian, like a knife-cut through a russet apple, and I followed it east towards the morning sun, which was already huge and bloated. After a while, being outdoors became a hallucination, and one felt there was no longer any air to breathe, only clinkered fumes and blasts of sulphur that seemed to rise through cracks in the ground. I remember stopping for water at silent farms where even the dogs were too exhausted to snarl, and where the water was scooped up from wells and irrigation ditches and handed to me warm and green.

The violence of the heat seemed to bruise the whole earth and turn its crust into one huge scar. One's blood dried up and all juices vanished; the sun struck upwards, sideways, and down, while the wheat went buckling across the fields like a solid sheet of copper. I kept on walking because there was no shade to hide in, and because it seemed to be the only way to agitate the air around me. I began to forget what I was doing on the road at all; I walked on as though keeping a vow, till I was conscious only of the hot red dust grinding like pepper between my toes.

By mid-morning I was in a state of developing madness, possessed by pounding deliriums of thirst, my brain running and reeling through all the usual obsessions that are said to accompany the man in the desert. Fantasies of water rose up and wrapped me in cool wet leaves, or pressed the thought of cucumber peel across my stinging eyes and filled my mouth with dripping moss. I began to drink monsoons and winter mists, to lick up the first fat drops of thunder, to lie down naked on deep-sea sponges and rub my lips against the scales of fish. I saw the steamy, damp-uddered cows of home planting their pink-lily mouths in the brook, then standing, knee-deep among dragonflies, whipping the reeds with their tasselled tails. Images bubbled up green from valleys of shining rain and fields of storm-crushed grass, with streams running down from the lime-cold hills into buttery swamps of flowers. I heard my mother again in her summer kitchen splashing water on garden salads, heard the gulping gush of the garden pump and swans' wings beating the lake . . .

The rest of the day was a blur. I remember seeing the spire of a church rising from the plain like the jet of a fountain. Then there was a shower of eucalyptus trees brushing against a roadside tavern, and I was at a bar calling for bottles of pop.

'No, no! You mustn't drink. You will fall down dead.' The woman threw up her hands at the sight of me, then turned, alarmed, to shout at a couple of well-dressed gentlemen eating radishes at a table in the corner.

The older man bowed '*Alemán? Francais?* The lady is right – you are too hot for drinking.'

'He will drop at our feet. Just look at his face.' Everybody tutted and shook their heads.

I could only stand there croaking, desperate with thirst. Somebody gave me some ice to suck. Then I was told to rest and cool off, while they asked me the usual questions: where I came from, where I was going.

At my reply, the woman threw up her hands again. 'On foot? It is not to be thought of!' The gentlemen started an argument, spitting out radishes at each other like furious exclamations. 'If he's English, he's the first walking Englishman I've seen,' said one. 'They walk all over the place,' said the other. 'Up and down mountainsides. Round and round the poles.' 'Yes, yes – but they do not walk in Spain.'

I heard their voices fading and booming around me. My head felt feverish, tight, and bursting. Then someone was leaning over me. 'Enough of the excremental walking. Holy Mother of God, give the young man a little drink. If he lives, and still wishes to go to the city, we will take him in the car.'

The first mouthful of mineral water burst in my throat and cascaded like frosted stars. Then I was given a plate of ham, several glasses of sherry, and a deep languor spread through my limbs. I remember no more of my benefactors, or what they said; only the drowsy glories of drinking. Later, much later, I was lifted to my feet and half-led, half-carried outside. Then, stretched fast asleep in the back of the car, I was driven like a corpse to Valladolid.

5

Valladolid

Valladolid: a dark square city hard as its syllables – a shut box, full of the pious dust and preserved breath of its dead whose expended passions once ruled a world which now seemed of no importance. The motor car had dropped me in the middle of it, on this evening of red stale dust, to find myself surrounded by churches and crypt-like streets bound by the rigidity of sixteenth-century stone. There was little life to be seen in the listless alleys, and the street lamps were hooded by a mysterious thickness of the light. I felt once again the unease of arriving at night in an unknown city – that faint sour panic which seems to cling to a place until one has found oneself a bed.

I stood for a while in the plaza, resting my knapsack against a wall and recovering from the fevered stupors of the day. Silent rope-soled creatures passed shadowless by. I was oppressed by the heavy vacuum around me. This was one of the major cities of Castilla la Vieja – a name ringing with cold chisels and chains. It was here, a priest told me later, that Marghanita de Jarandilla looked from her prison tower and wept tears of gold into the laps of beggars; and it was here, to the altar of San Martin, that a poor cripple from Vallaverde crawled with his severed leg and carved a magnificent crucifix out of the bone. A city of expired fanaticisms and murdered adorations – of the delicate and elaborate Moors, of Ferdinand and Isabella, of the deceived Columbus, and the gentle, crispbrained Cervantes. Against the lives of all these rose the present darkness, the gloom of the drawn oven, the cold closed lamp.

Night was on this city, and upon me too. So I went off to look for a bed. Down a narrow lane I suddenly came on the barracks – a great pile of medieval granite. Groups of ragged young conscripts lay about on the pavement, crouching in hazy circles of lamplight, scratching, spitting, playing tattered cards, and passing their penniless time. I asked them where I might find a lodging, and they pointed across the road.

'Try the Borracho,' said one.

'An ogre,' said another.

'But don't mind him. He's got beds of brass.'

I found the Borracho sitting in a filthy room swilling wine from a goat-skin bag. A naked child lay asleep on the table beside him with its head pillowed in a half-cut pumpkin. The Borracho had spiky grey hair and the looks of a second murderer. His face was as dark and greasy as a pickled walnut and a moustache curled round his lip like an adder.

I asked for a bed, and he just glowered at me.

'Go sleep in the river,' he said.

He took another loud drink, wiped the wine-bag across his mouth, slumped in his chair, and closed his eyes. When he opened them again and saw me still standing there, he struck the table, flapped his arms, and cried: 'Shoo!'

But I wouldn't budge. It was almost midnight now, and all I wanted to do was sleep. I repeated my question and the man suddenly crumpled up and quite childishly began to cry. His fleshy lips curled back and he grizzled like an infant, looking piteously about him for comfort. I offered him a cigarette and he took it between his long black nails, without looking at it, and ripped it down the middle. Then rolling tobacco and paper into a neat little ball, he popped them into his mouth.

'What about a bed then?' I asked.

He looked at me with hatred, but eventually got to his feet.

'There's only one,' he said. 'And may you be pleased to die in it.' And he jerked his head towards the door.

The narrow stairs dripped with greasy mysterious oils and had a feverish rotten smell. They seemed specially designed to lead the visitor to some act of depressed or despairing madness. I climbed them with a mixture of obstinacy and dread, the Borracho wheezing behind me. Half-way up, in a recess, another small pale child sat carving a potato into the shape of a doll, and as we approached she turned, gave us a quick look of panic, and bit off its little head.

The brass bed was magnificent, as the soldiers had promised, and stood about six feet high, with knobs on. It was the only piece of furniture in a room which otherwise seemed to have been devastated by violent tenants. The light from the street lamps decorated the walls with liquid dilating shapes, and the young soldiers were still visible on the pavement outside, some of them fast asleep. The Borracho had recovered his truculence and threw the key at my feet, demanding the rent in advance. Then he fished in his pocket, gave me a candle-end, and said he didn't mind if I burned down the house.

When he'd gone, I sat on the bed and swung my feet and ate my last bit of bread and cheese. I was feeling easier now, in spite of the savagery of the place. I was established. I had a room in this city.

I was awakened next morning by the high clear voice of a boy singing in the street below The sound lifted me gradually with a swaying motion as though I was being cradled on silken cords. It was cool crisp singing, full-throated and pure, and surely the most painless way to be wakened – and as I lay there listening, with the sun filtering across me. I thought this was how it should always be. To be charmed from sleep by a voice like this, eased softly back into life, rather than by the customary brutalities of shouts, knocking, and alarm-bells like blows on the head. The borders of consciousness are anxious enough, raw and desperate places; we shouldn't be dragged across them like struggling thieves as if sleep was a felony.

The boy was leaning against a lamp-post beneath the barrack

walls and carrying a basket slung over his shoulders. He was about twelve years old, thin, and scrub-headed, and was obviously singing for what he could get. But he sang with the whole of his body, his eyes tight-closed, his bare throat rippling in the sunlight, and his voice had a nasal wail that obliterated the city around him – the voice of Islam, aimed at the sky and pitched to an empty landscape. Unshaven soldiers, half-dressed and quiet, leaned listening from the barrack windows. Some of them threw him bits of bread and slices of orange, and when he'd finished he gathered them up in the basket.

Valladolid had a better face this morning. The mask of red dust had been wiped away in the night and an innocent radiance glittered over the heavy buildings. The sky was a blank hard blue, almost chemically bright, stretched for another day of heat. I bought a handful of fruit and collected some letters from the post office, then found a café down by the fishmarket. As I ate my breakfast I opened my letters, which were the first I'd received in Spain. I was surrounded by stale odours of melting ice, by housewives with dripping baskets, by banks of prawns and the dead eyes of fish, each one an ocean sealed and sunless. My letters from home spoke of whist-drives and marrows, of serene and distant gossip. But none of them called me back and it looked as though I was here for good. The time had come for me to make some money.

I'd been told that street-fiddlers in Spain would need a licence – though not every city demanded it. So off I went, after breakfast, to the city hall, which looked like a bankrupt casino. Soldiers with fixed bayonets sat around on the stairs, and hungry dogs ran in and out like messengers, while the usual motionless queues of silent peasants waited for officials who would never appear. Doubting that there would be a queue for fiddlers that morning, I climbed the stairs and opened the first door I came to.

The room inside was large and crowded with heavy presidential furniture. At a desk by the window sat a reed-thin man – or rather he inclined himself parallel to it, his feet on a cabinet, a cigar in his mouth, and a chessboard across his knees. I could see his long hooked profile, like a Leonardo drawing, and one pensive downcast eye. He moved a few pawns and hummed a little, then swung in his chair towards me – and his face, seen front-on, almost disappeared from view, so unusually thin he was. I was aware of two raised eyebrows and an expression of courtly inquiry which seemed entirely unsupported by flesh.

'You are lost, perhaps?'

'I'd like to see the Mayor,' I said.

'So would I. So would all the world.'

'Is he away?'

The man giggled, and a convulsion ran up his body like an air-bubble up a spout.

'Yes, he's away. He's gone to the madhouse.'

I said I was sorry, but he raised his hand.

'Oh, no. He is happy. Who wouldn't be in such a place? Biscuits and chocolate at all hours of the day. Nuns to talk to, and coloured wool to play with . . . At least, so they say.' He looked secretively at his cigar. 'But you see me here. If I can help . . .'

When I told him what I wanted, he gave a little musical squeak and his eyebrows jumped with pleasure.

'How charming,' he murmured. 'But of course you shall. One moment – Manolo, please!'

A swarthy young man, dressed in trousers and pyjama-top, entered softly from another room.

'Find me a licence, Manolito.'

'What kind of licence?'

'Oh, any kind. Only make it a nice one.'

'Then permit me, Don Ignacio.' The young man grasped his chief by the legs, hoisted them from the cabinet, and searched the papers beneath them. Meanwhile Don Ignacio reclined indolently, his legs stuck in the air, beaming upon me and singing 'rumpty-dum-diddle'.

'To sell water,' murmured the clerk. 'To erect a small tomb . . . to beat gold . . . to press juniper berries . . . ah, here we have it, I do believe. Don Ignacio, with your permission . . .'

He replaced his chief's legs on the cabinet and handed him a kind of finely engraved cheque-book, together with pen and ink. Don Ignacio doubled up and began to write, rolling his tongue and grunting with effort. Delicate scrolls and decorations ran over the paper, feathery tendrils in violet ink; then the thing was finished, dusted and sealed, and signed with a delicious flourish.

'There,' said Don Ignacio. 'The city is yours. Rumpty-dum-diddle-de-ay.'

I studied my licence and was pleased with it. It looked like a Royal Charter. Headed with an engraving of lions and a scarlet seal, it formally proclaimed: 'THAT, by using the powers attributed to and conferred upon the Mayorality, and by virtue of the precepts of the Municipal Bye-laws and the appropriate tariffs due to the said most Excellent Ayuntamiento; a licence is hereby granted to Don Lorenzo Le, that he may walk and offer concerts through the streets of this City, and the public squares of the same, PROVIDED ALWAYS that he does not in any manner cause riot, demonstrations, or prejudice the free movement of traffic and persons . . .'

'That will be half a peseta,' said Don Ignacio mildly, swinging his feet back on to the top of the desk. Then he invited me to join him in a game of chess, the question of the fee was forgotten.

Later, armed with my licence, I went back to the Borracho's to fetch my violin and get to work. A woman was scrubbing the courtyard, and she straightened up as I entered and raised an arm to push back her hair. Her handsome, muddy, exhausted face showed that she was expecting someone else. 'Have you seen him?' she asked. I shook my head, and her eyes went grey and listless. To get to my room I had to step over three naked children who sat weeping in pools of water. Even in his absence the deadly stench of the Borracho permeated the place like gas.

After repairing my fiddle, and dusting off the new straw hat which I'd bought in Zamora market, I went out – for the first time in a Spanish town – to try my luck in the streets. I found a busy lane, placed my hat on the ground, and struck up a rusty tune. According to my experience in England, money should then have dropped into the hat; but it didn't work out that way here. No sooner had I started to play than everybody stopped what they were doing and gathered round me in a silent mass, blocking the traffic, blotting out the sun, and treading my new hat into the ground. Again and again I fished it from under their feet, straightened it out, and moved somewhere else. But as soon as I struck up afresh, the crowd re-formed and encircled me, and I saw in their scorched brown faces an expression I was soon to know well – a soft relaxed childishness and staring pleasure, an abandonment of time to a moment's spectacle.

This was all very well, but I was making no money – and there was scarcely room even to swing my arm. Every so often I was compelled to break off, and to attempt a wheedling speech, begging the multitude to have the kindness to walk up and down just a little, or at least to draw back and reveal my hat. A number of lounging soldiers, half-understanding, began to shout what I said at the others. The others screamed back, telling them to shut up and listen. In the meantime, nobody moved.

Presently a policeman appeared, his unbuttoned tunic revealing a damp and hairy chest. He had a dirty rifle slung over his shoulder and was sucking a yellow toothpick.

'German?'

'No, English.'

'Licence?'

'Yes.'

He gave it a slumberous, heavy-lidded glance. Then, shifting his gun to his other shoulder, he hooked my hat on to the toe of his boot, kicked it high in the air, caught it, shook it, and turned crossly upon the crowd.

'Have you no shame?' he demanded. 'Or are you beggars of this town? Look, not a penny, not a dried garbanzo. Have you no dignity to be standing her? Either pay, or go.'

Giggling uneasily, the crowd backed away. There was the tinkle of a coin on the pavement. The policeman picked it up, dropped it into the hat, and handed it to me with a bow.

'Milk from dry udders,' he said loftily. 'You are welcome. Now please continue . . .'

I did so for a while, not made too happy by his support, while he held back the crowd with his gun. But from then on I used the trick which I'd learned in Southampton – I made sure the hat was properly baited beforehand. Nobody kicked over a hat with pennies in it, they just stood delicately around the brim. I learned some other lessons, too. That men were less responsive than women – unless approached in a café, when they paid with the gestures of noblemen. That any Spanish tune worked immediately, and called up ready smiles, while any other kind of music – Schubert excepted – was met by blank stares and bewilderment. Most important of all, I learned when to stop and move on, to spread myself around – a lesson taught me by a bootblack no higher than my knee who had been on the edge of the crowd all morning.

'You play much,' he said finally.

'Why, is it no good?'

'Good enough – but much, too much. Play less for the money. A couple of strophes will do. Then you will reach more people during the day.'

He was right, of course, especially where pavement cafés were concerned, whose clients liked a continuously changing scene. It was enough to make oneself known, followed by a quick whip round, and then to go off somewhere else.

At midday I stopped, having made about three pesetas. The heat by now was driving everyone indoors. So I bought a bottle of wine and a bag of plums and took them down by the river. There, under the mulberry trees, where some thin grass grew, I sat watching the slow green flow of the water. The shade from the trees lay on my hands and legs like pieces of cool wet velvet, and all sounds ceased, save for the piercing stutter of the cicadas which seemed to be nailing the heat to the ground.

I drowsed off presently with a half-eaten plum in my hand, and the bottle of wine untasted. Spanish afternoon-sleep was new to me, and I woke dazed, my limbs glutted with stupor. It was about five o'clock. A girl was wading in the river, her brown legs shining like caramel; while on the opposite bank, in a cloud of red dust, a boy was driving some mules to drink.

The hours had been eaten away, and evening had started, but I was content to lie where I was, to watch the drinking mules, and the girl in the river, and the boy, who was watching the girl. She walked gracefully, thigh-deep, balancing some washing on her head, while the boy stood on one leg leaning against a stick. He began to call out and taunt her, and the girl answered back, and their voices were sharp as the cries of moorhens. The cries continued for a while, bouncing hard on the water, almost visible in the dark red light; then suddenly the shouting ceased, and the girl turned in the river and began to cross to the other side, wading strong and deep towards the waiting boy, her short legs stockinged with mud . . .

I went back to the town that evening in a mood of gauzy unreality, of vague unthinking enchantment. I remember kicking a melon along the street and feeling the air brush round my body. I wandered idly about in a state of aimless benignity, loving all things, even this baleful city – with its rancid shadows and scabby dogs, sweating pavements and offal-filled gutters; its blue-smocked ancients, remote as coolies; its children dozing in doorways, and its women surrounded by aromas of cooking fat, lemons, and chemical violets. I played no music that night, but went from bar to bar, drinking glasses of clotted wine. I was feverish, drowsy, and sentimental. I still had a touch of the sun.

The following morning the light-headedness continued, a curious suspension of focus. I returned to the market for breakfast, among sudden uproars and silences, with churchbells kicking in the throbbing towers. Eating bread and sausage, my back to the church wall, I was aware only of this point of time, the arrested moment of casual detail, the unsorted rubbish of now. I felt the heat of the sun dampened by draughts of ice blowing from fish-boxes stacked near by. I remember a yawning cat – a pin-cushion of teeth and whiskers – sitting on a palm leaf in the gutter. A man said 'Good morning' and passed out of my life, stepping on a petal as though extinguishing a match. I saw an empty wine-barrel roll out of a tavern door, turn slowly, and roll back in again. I saw a hole in the road suddenly wink like a cyclops as a shadow flowered in and out of it. A boy lifted his shirt and scratched his belly, a housewife picked up and put down an orange, and a mule stopped in the road, looked straight into my face, and wrinkled up his wet brown-papery nostrils.

For several more days the city moved somnambulantly before me, like a series of engravings seen through watery glass. I worked the streets and cafés, and made a few pesetas, but I knew I would not stay long. Its alternate elations and leaden ugliness set up uneasy hallucinations. Particularly of the poverty and waste symbolized by that mass of young conscripts gasping away their summer in the city barracks.

Locked up all day, peering from the narrow windows, or drilled to exhaustion on the burning square, in the evenings they were released in stupefied droves to possess the half-empty town. Across the plaza – an arena of silted tramlines – they shuffled like clowns in their crumpled khaki, circling, heads down, with nothing to spend or do, imprisoned by ennui and simple lust. In their cardboard boots they clumped up and down, kicking idly at invisible obstructions. Some languished in groups under the feeble lamps, sucking dead fags among the whirling flies. A few, the lucky ones, stood with tense sick faces fingering the tin jewellery around the necks of their girls. But the rest, the majority, without cigarettes or girls, just stood where they were and whistled – making that sad thin sound which is the sign of young soldiers everywhere, standing about in shut streets on rainy Sundays, on midnight platforms where no trains come, guarding forgotten dumps in abandoned bases or empty petrol-tins in a desert – the sound of their wish to be anywhere but there, the breath of the pointless hours expiring.

Living at the Borracho's, across the street from the barracks, I saw much of these scarecrow troops. I saw the garbage they fed on, the way their youth was humbled, the way they were condemned to spend their time. Bug-hunting, stealing, gambling with thirds of a farthing, quarrelling, bled grey with boredom – sometimes, perhaps, soothed by a lucky friendship, stretched quietly with another boy; or seeking solitary relief in a jog-trot of poetry, or a sudden ejaculation of sex-choked song. Or, when pressures grew too great, going down in the dark to the river to press a whore to the hard wet gravel, then returning barefooted, ready for jail, having paid with their cardboard boots.

Soldiers, priests, and an outer fringe of beggars – three silent and separate categories; there were times at night, with the red dust blowing in from the plain, when there seemed to be no one else but these in the city. The soldiers and beggars groped among the great blank buildings, invisible to each other's miseries, invisible also to the sleek black priests slipping down alleys like padded cats.

But the beggars I remember as something special to Valladolid, something it had nursed to a peak of malformation and horror. One saw little of them by day; they seemed to be let out only at night, surreptitiously, like mad relations. Then limping, scuffling, hopping, and creeping, they came slowly out of the shadows, advancing towards one at pavement-level to a rhythmic chanting of moans and whispers. Here were old men, youths and shrivelled children; creatures of every imaginable curse and deformity – blind, dumb, without hands, without feet, covered with sores, dragging their bodies like sacks.

There was almost nothing for them in the streets except to act out their mutilations, sightlessly begging the empty air, holding up stumps of arms, pointing to empty eye-sockets, wrapping and unwrapping the worst of their sores. The children were especially quiet, mute concentrations of martyrdom, unable to envisage the stretch of doom ahead. They stood numbly apart, gazing through red-filmed eyes and holding out tiny wrinkled palms.

Young and old were like emanations of the stifling medievalism of this pious and cloistered city; infected by its stones, like the pock-marked effigies of its churches, and part of one of the more general blasphemies of Spain.

My last night in Valladolid sustained the sick fever of the place. Too hot to sleep, I stayed late in the bars and got rid of most of my money; then, about two in the morning, I went back to the inn to find it in a state of uproar.

The huge front door had been ripped from its hinges and lay in splinters across the street. The three youngest children were huddled inside, half naked, moaning with fear – while the Borracho's wife, storm centre of the scene, stood screaming at the foot of the stairs. Previously I'd only seen her as a listless drudge, now she was roused to a terrible stature, brandishing a spade in her hand like a two-edged sword, her eyes mad-yellow and full of sparks.

She turned towards me as I entered and made a blind gesture of fury, holding the spade out in front of her.

'I will kill him!' she cried. 'He is bad – bad!'

One of the children ran towards her, pressing against her legs, and she looked down at it with a squinting, distracted gaze as though she'd never seen it before.

'He comes home like a pig, and I lock him out. But he breaks down the door and tries to love Elvira – ELVIRA!' She turned suddenly and screamed out the name, beating the ground with the flat of the spade. 'Daughter! Daughter! . . .' The spade rang like a bell. 'I will smash his cojones against his teeth!'

'Where is he?' I said.

She looked savagely up the stairs and went mad again, beating the walls with frenzy

'Are you dead yet?' she screamed. 'You prince of pigs! Shame of fathers throughout the world . . .'

She stood there shaking, her face green in the lamplight, the sweat glistening in her tangled hair. I took the spade from her hands, and was surprised how easily she surrendered it. Then left her and went upstairs.

I found the Borracho on the landing, about half-way up, sprawled on his back, wet with blood and wine. He lay like a slaughtered bull, breathing in painful gasps and weeping to himself in the dark.

'Help me,' he whimpered.

I dragged him across to my room, and lit a candle. One side of his face was smashed and bleeding. I sponged and cleaned him as best I could, covered him with a coat, and went to bed.

The room, the house, the whole of the city, seemed suddenly corroded with misery. The Borracho lay on the floor, phlegm bubbling in his throat, drunkenly whispering his daughter's name.

6

Segovia–Madrid

There are certain places one leaves never expecting to see again, and I don't ever wish to return to that city. I rose at dawn and went to the patio pump and washed it from my hands and face. Then with my bags on my back I passed through the damp flushed streets and entered once more into the open country.

Where should I go now? It didn't matter. Anywhere south would do. Segovia, Madrid, the heart of Castile lay before me, and that was the direction I took. After the shuttered town, the landscape seemed to have broken from prison and rolled free and glittering away. Green oaks like rocks lay scattered among the cornfields, with peasants chest-deep in the wheat. It was the peak of harvest, and figures of extraordinary brilliance were spread across the fields like butterflies, working alone or in clusters, and dressed to the pitch of the light – blue shirts and trousers, and with broad gold hats tied with green and scarlet cloths. Submerged in the wheat, sickles flickered like fish, with rhythmic flashes of blue and silver; and, as I passed, men straightened and shielded their eyes, silently watching me go, or a hand was raised in salute, showing among its sun-black fingers the glittering sickle like a curved sixth nail.

After the cramped shames of the city it was like a gulp of pure water to be back in this open landscape, in the rustling silence of the naked plain, its heaving solitude of raw burnt light.

Then, towards evening. I came to a village of mud – little more than a tumble of earth in a gulley. Few of the houses were whole,

few had glass in their windows, most of the roofs were stuffed with sacking. They stood broken and bandaged, half-supporting each other like survivors from an old lost war.

The door of the inn this time was simply patched with a sheep-hurdle, and a wolfhound lay across the threshold. When the innkeeper appeared I asked if I could stay the night.

'The world is free,' he said. 'Why not?'

He gave me a loaf, and a rusty tin of sardines which I cut open with my knife. Two shabby Civil Guards were playing cards in a corner, their guns spread out on the table. Fat pink faces, small black eyes, cheating and quarrelling, they watched me darkly. When I'd finished my supper I began to write some notes, which they seemed to consider an act of reckless defiance. Throwing down their cards and picking up their guns they strode noisily across to my table. The notebook was snatched from my hand, sniffed at, shaken, thumped hard, and held upside down. A volley of questions followed, baffled and truculent. What was all this? they asked. They didn't like the look of it. Where was I from? – and where were my documents? Speak up! I had much to answer for. A muddy half-hour was spent in this oafish wrangle, while the innkeeper watched us from a hole in the wall. Finally my indecipherable writing, and the stupidity of my replies, drove them glowering back to their corner.

I had already learned to be wary of the Civil Guards, who were the poison dwarfs of Spain. They would suddenly ride down upon you on their sleek black horses, far out in the open country, and crowd around you, all leather and guns, and put you through a bullying interrogation. Most of them were afraid, and lived in a social vacuum which could only be filled with violence; they had few friends in this country and were suspicious of strangers and indeed of anyone on the road. When challenged by one of them, I took deliberate pains never to allow the issue to become clear between us; for they were alarmed by confusion, and by their superiors, and could usually be relied on to melt away rather than be caught in a complicated situation with a foreigner.

So for the rest of the night these two left me alone. I wrote, and they drank and quarrelled. Finally the landlord brought me over a glass of brandy, and said that the world was free and he only wished he could write. An innocent remark, but made with a twisted mouth, and loud enough for the Guards to hear.

I'd been almost a month on the road since I landed at Vigo, and was now finding the going better. At first I'd hobbled, but my blisters had hardened and at last I could walk without pain. I developed a long loping stride which covered some twenty miles a day, an easy monotonous pace – slightly faster than the mule-trains strung along the route, though slower than trotting asses. On these straight Spanish roads, so empty of motor cars, we moved between horizons like ships at sea, often remaining for hours within sight of each other, gradually losing or gaining ground. The mule-trains at that time were the caravans of Castile, one of the threads of the country's life – teams of small tasselled animals drawing high blue carts brightly painted with vines and flowers. As gaudy as barges or wedding floats, mounted on squealing five-foot wheels, they worked from city to city at three miles an hour – a rhythm unchanged since the days of Hannibal – carrying charcoal, firewood, wineskins, olives, oil, old iron, and gossip. The drivers were a race apart, born and bred on the road, and recognizable by their flat, almost Siberian faces. With long whips and short legs, they travelled like Arabs, some with boys to look after their comforts, and slept at noon in hammocks slung between the wheels, rocking gently to the pace of the mules, and then spent their nights round fires among the open rocks or wrapped in harness in the courtyards of inns. They were the hereditary newsbearers of the Spanish plains, old as the wheel and separate in their ways as gypsies.

I followed this straight southern track for several days, living on figs and ears of wheat. Sometimes I'd hide from the sun under the wayside poplars, face downwards, watching the ants. There was really no hurry. I was going nowhere. Nowhere at all but here.

Close to the spicy warmth of this foreign ground a few inches away from my face. Never in my life had I felt so fat with time, so free of the need to be moving or doing. For hours I could watch some manic ant dragging a piece of orange peel through the grass, pushing and pulling against impossible barriers in a confused and directionless frenzy.

Then one day I noticed a long low cloud lifting slowly above the southern horizon, a purple haze above the quivering plain – the first sign of the approaching Sierras. After the monotonous wheatfields it was like a landfall, the distant coastline of another country, and as I walked, it climbed steadily till it filled half the sky – the immense east-west barrier of the Guadarramas.

Already cool winds were blowing down from its peaks, and the plain was lifting into little hills, and by the next afternoon I'd left the wheat behind me and entered a world of Nordic pinewoods. Here I slipped off the heat like a sweat-soaked shirt and slept an hour among the resinous trees – a fresh green smell as sweet as menthol compared with the animal reek of the plain. I noticed that each tree, slashed with a pattern of fishbone cuts, was bleeding gum into little cups. The wounded trunks seemed to be running with drops of amber, stinging the air with their piercing scent, while some of the older trees, bled dry and abandoned, curled in spirals like burning paper. But it was a good place to sleep; the wood was empty of flies, who had learned to avoid its sticky snares, and the afternoon sun sucked up the flavour of each tree till the whole wood swam in incense like a church.

The villages in the foothills were full of flowers and fountains, but none of them had any food. I remember Cuéllar, Shulomonon, and Naval de Oro – places of steep craggy lanes and leaf-smothered towers and old doors pitted with gigantic keyholes. But all I got to eat from the lot of them was a piece of goat's cheese as hard as a stone.

I remember coming to one village whose streets were black with priests, and its taverns full of seething atheists. Some stood in a doorway heaving stones at the church, others sang obscenities about the bishop. Then a group cornered me in a tavern to complain about their Roman fountain – a naked goddess carved from local marble. Once, they said, she lay in the square, and jets of water sprang out of her breasts. Most beautiful to behold – but the priests had smashed her with hammers and buried her remains in the hills.

They were only shepherds, they said, but theirs was an artistic village; and they pointed out two pictures hanging on the tavern wall. Each was an original, painted on canvas, and the colour of uncooked meat: one was of a broken puppet, labelled 'The Show is Ended'; and the other of a sedate Victorian family, father, mother, and beribboned little girl, watching a dog bleed to death on the carpet. 'We love art, my beauty,' said one of the shepherds. Later, he tried to kiss me.

The wine in Shulomonon was raw and bitter, but cost less than a penny a glass. While sipping some of this, I met an English woman from Walsall, who had just spent five weeks touring Morocco with her husband. She looked worn out and bewildered. Her husband was asleep in the street. She asked for news of the Royal Family.

Early one evening I left the last of these villages and headed for Segovia, about six miles away. As I climbed the hill I saw some girls sitting in the mouth of a cave, facing the sunset, sewing and singing. 'My boy is sharp as salt,' they sang, 'with a house full of gold and silver.'

At this point I got a lift in a farmer's cart, which was loaded with sacks of chaff. As we lumbered along, the farmer talked about work and looked at my hands out of the corner of his eyes. 'It is different in some countries, I believe,' he said. 'But God gave us a country we must fight like a lion.' Suddenly he gave a loud cry, lashed the mules with his whip, and aimed the cart straight up the hillside, leaving the road altogether to follow some ancient track which climbed sheer among the boulders. The mules kicked and slithered, dug their hind-legs into the ground, and spread their haunches like thin black frogs, panting and straining, while the cart rocked like a ship and I clung to the farmer's belt. Half an hour later, with the wheels bouncing off rocks and the mules in a lather of sweat, we reached the top of the rise and saw the city below us, and the farmer locked the wheels for the downhill slide.

Segovia was a city in a valley of stones – a compact, half-forgotten heap of architectural splendours built for the glory of some other time. Here were churches, castles, and medieval walls standing sharp in the evening light, but all dwarfed by that extra-ordinary phenomenon of masonry, the Roman aqueduct, which overshadowed the whole. It came looping from the hills in a series of arches, some rising to over a hundred feet, and composed of blocks of granite weighing several tons and held together by their weight alone. This imperial gesture, built to carry water from a spring ten miles away, still strode across the valley with massive grace, a hundred vistas framed by its soaring arches, to enter the city at last high above the rooftops, stepping like a mammoth among the houses.

'The Aqueduct,' said the farmer, pointing with his whip, in case by chance I had failed to notice it. But to me, not having heard about it before, it came as a unique and visual shock.

'It's like a bridge,' he went on. 'You could drive across it. I once crossed it with a coach and horses.'

'Wouldn't it be too narrow?' I asked.

He looked at me sharply.

'I drove across it in a narrow coach.'

Entering the city by the Puerto de Santiago, the farmer gave me some carobs and wished me a good night's rest. I found an inn tucked away under the aqueduct, conveniently roofed by one of its arches – a vast cave-like place of naked granite smelling warmly of pigs and horses.

Segovia was mounted on rock and still partly boxed in by its Roman-Iberian walls, a small snug city of steep-stepping streets which seemed to ignore the invention of the wheel. There was time before supper to explore some of these alleys, dappled with pools of warm red lamplight, where naked children darted into their tattered houses like pheasants into nests of bracken. At close quarters, the aqueduct seemed both benevolent and mad, its jets of masonry vaulting the sky, and the huge blocked feet coming down on the town and throwing everything out of scale.

After a supper of beans and mutton, served in a cloud of woodsmoke, I was invited out into the plaza to watch a midnight ciné. Here, once again, the aqueduct came into use, with a cotton sheet strung from one of its pillars, on to which a pale beam of light, filtering from an opposite window, projected an ancient and jittery melodrama. Half the town, it seemed, had turned out for the show, carrying footstools and little chairs, while children swarmed on the rooftops and hung in clusters from the trees, their dark heads shining like elderberries.

The film's epic simplicity flickered across the Roman wall, vague and dim as a legend, but each turn of the plot was followed with gusto, people jumping up and down in their seats, bombarding the distant shadows with advice and warning, mixed with occasional shouts of outrage. The appearance of the villain was met by darts and stones, the doltish hero by exasperation, while a tide of seething concern was reserved for the plight of the heroine who spent a vigorously distressful time. During most of the film she hung from ropes in a tower, subject to the tireless affronts of the villain, but when the hero finally bestirred himself and disembowelled the villain with a knife, the audience was satisfied and went to bed.

I was not long in Segovia, and haven't been back there since, but I still recall some of its quieter melancholies – the cool depths of the cathedral, clean and bare, full of wide and curving spaces, and the huge stained-glass windows hanging like hazed chrysanthemums in the amber distances of its height. Also the small black pigs running in and out of shop doorways – often apparently the only customers; and the storks roosting gravely on the chimney-pots, gazing across the valley like bony Arabs.

Then one afternoon, just outside the city walls, I found the little church of the local Virgin, a macabre memorial lying at the foot of the Peña Grajera – the desolate 'Cliff of Crows'. This granite rock, smothered with croaking birds, was also Segovia's cliff of blood, one of the many such places of easy death to be found on the edge of Spanish towns. From here, in the past, Segovia had been in the habit of tossing into the gorge its felons, adulterers, and heretics; thus suiting poverty and indolence by saving the price of a bullet or the extra effort of a sword-thrust. A strolling priest took pains to give me these local tit-bits, as well as to explain the significance of the birds on the cliff; pointing out that the slain, in any case, belonged to the world of the damned and that the crows were the ghosts of their godless souls.

The priest seemed drawn to this noisome place, and stayed with me for a while, gazing with a soft little smile at the fouled-up cliff where the birds rustled and flapped like bats. He mentioned the thirteenth-century heroine, Maria del Salto, a beautiful Jewess accused of adultery. 'Having been cast from the rock in the usual manner,' he said, 'she called on the Virgin to prove her innocence, and was compassionately halted while still in mid-air and allowed to float unhurt to the ground.' The little church in the gorge was built to commemorate the miracle – with no effect on later victims, apparently. But what I remember now is not the sedate little church, but the rock like a bruise above it, its bloodstained face and exhausted crevices haunted by the harsh dry voices of the birds.

Segovia left me with the echo of that carrion-infested place, together with the hollow reverberations of the aqueduct. And with one other, the last, as I walked out of the town and passed the silent and shuttered bullring, and saw a white-faced matador being carried to his car, weeping softly, attended by whispering friends . . .

A few miles south of Segovia, at the foot of the Sierras, I came on the royal gardens of La Granja – acres of writhing statues, walks, and fountains rising from the dust like a mirage. It was a grandiose folly, as large as Versailles and even more extravagant, and I found it in the peak of bloom and entirely deserted except for a few old gardeners with brooms.

A hundred fountains were playing, filling the sky with rainbows and creating an extraordinary dreamlike clamour. Marble gods and wood-nymphs, dolphins and dragons, their anatomies studded with pipes and nozzles, directed complex cascades at one another or shot them high above the flowering trees. Everything that could be done with water seemed to be going on here, almost to the point of hydromania. Lakes, pools, jets, and falls, flooded grottoes and exotic canals, all throbbed and surged at different levels, reflecting classical arbours, paths, and terraces, or running like cooling milk down the statuary.

Yet there was nobody to see it. Nobody but me – except, of course, for the gardeners, who went shuffling about as though under some timeless instruction, preparing for the return of some long-dead queen.

I stayed in the gardens for an hour or more, furtively paddling among the trickling leaves. The fountains, I learned later, played only on rare occasions, and I don't know why they played that day. It was like the winding-up of some monarch's toy, of which the owner had rapidly tired, and which now lay abandoned at the foot of the mountain together with its aged keepers. The fact was that La Granja, when looked at closely, was more than a little vulgar – a royal inflation of a suburban mind, a costly exercise with gnomes and toadstools.

It took me two days to cross the Sierra Guadarrama, as through another season and another country, climbing a magnificent road of granite blocks to a point almost two miles high. Here were racing brooks, great shadowy forests, and fallen boulders covered with flowering creepers. It seemed already autumn here; clouds rolled down the summits, dropping cool intermittent showers, while shepherds scrambled about, followed by wolf-like dogs, and the air smelt freshly of resin and honey.

I spent the first night in a grove of oak trees, lying on leaves as wet as Wales, under a heavy dew and a cold sharp moon and surrounded by the continuous bells of sheep. In the morning I woke shivering to eat a breakfast of goat's cheese, which the night had soaked and softened, then watched the sunlight move slowly down the trunks of the pine trees, dark red, as though they bled from the top. Near by was a waterfall pouring into a bowl of rock, where I stripped and took a short sharp bathe. It was snow-cold, brutal, and revivifying, secluded among the trees, and when I'd finished I sat naked on a mossy stone, slowly drying in the rising sun. I seemed to be in a pocket of northern Europe, full of the cold splendour of Finnish gods. A green haze of pine-dust floated in shafts of sunlight and squirrels swung and chattered above me. Gulping the fine dry air and sniffing the pitch-pine mountain, I was perhaps never so alive and so alone again.

By midday I'd climbed to the six thousand feet pass of Puerto de Navacerrado, where I rested awhile under towering peaks that were dusted with summer snow. Great banks of cloud rolled up the northern slopes, broke over the ridges, and disappeared; while before me, through the pass, I saw a new country emerge – the immense plain of La Mancha, stretching flat as a cowhide and smudged like a sore with distant Madrid.

Crossing the Sierra was not just a stage on my journey, in spite of the physical barrier. It was also one of those sudden, jerky advances in life, which once made closes the past for ever. It was a frontier for me in more ways than one, and not till I'd passed it did I feel really involved in Spain.

The Sierra, like the moon, had two distinct faces: the north one aloof and cold in its shadow, a place of green thickets and alpine silence, while to the south the mountain was just a raw burnt rock, the cliffs stripped bare by the sun – which Madrid seemed to use as a kind of backyard wall on which to scribble slogans for coñac and nightclubs. The north side had a pastoral stillness, a veiled purity and calm; while the blistered south, though at least ten miles from the city, already reeked of the waste of the streets.

Even so, I was impatient to reach Madrid, and hurried my way towards it, stumbling down pathways of broken shale, naked of grass or trees, while the peaks of the mountains slipped back into the clouds, sealing off all I had been till then. One more night on the slopes, then I reached the main road – a clutter of cafés, shacks, and tyre-dumps. And here I was given a lift by two racy young booksellers who were driving a van loaded with Latin missals. The young men, very gay, presented me with their cards and pointed out all the brothels as we bowled into Madrid; where they dropped me at last, at about ten in the morning, in the heart of the city, the heart of Spain.

Madrid struck me at first as being all tram-bells and wire, false marble and dilapidation. Counting London, it was only the second major city I'd seen, and I slipped into it as into the jaws of a lion. It had a lion's breath, too; something fetid and spicy, mixed with straw and the decayed juices of meat. The Gran Via itself had a lion's roar, though inflated, like a circus animal's – wide, self-conscious, and somewhat seedy, and lined with buildings like broken teeth.

These wide show-streets displayed all that pomp and vacuity one associated with Latin-America – political parade-grounds driven between wedding-cake mansions and bearing the names of presidents, historical dates, and virtues. Close behind them, however, ran the living lanes of the city, narrow alleys stuffed with carts and beggars, with thin little housemaids and tubercular children, beautiful and covered with sores.

I went first to the post office to collect my letters, which I found filed under 'E' for 'Esquire' – one from a newspaper with a third prize for a poem, and one from my mother hoping my feet were dry. Then I walked round the back-streets near the Puerta del Sol, looking for a likely inn, and found one at last, as old as Chaucer, with a cowshed in the cellar. The proprietor wrote my name in a big black book, copying it from my mother's envelope, then handed me a door-key as large as a spade and said my room would cost sixpence a night.

By now it was noon, with almost everyone under cover, in the bars and moistly shaded cafés, at this hour when Madrid properly came into its own – a dewdrop on the grid-iron plain. Most other capitals, in such heat, would still have been an inferno of duty, full of damp shopgirls and exhausted clerks. But not here, for Madrid knew when to say No, and draw its shutters against the sun.

This, of course, was also the habit in other Spanish cities; but here it had reached a peak of particular genius. For Madrid at that time, if not today, was a city of a thousand exquisite taverns – water-cooled, barrel-lined, and cavernously spacious, cheap and affectionately run, in whose traditional shade the men, at least, spent a half of their waking time.

Stepping in from the torrid street, you met a band of cool air like fruit-peel pressed to your brow, and entered a cloistered grotto laden with the tang of shellfish, wet tiles, and wine-soaked wood. There was no waiting, no crowding; the place was yours; pot-boys took your orders with ringing cries; and men stood at their ease holding goblets of sherry, with plenty of time to drink them, while piled round the counters – succulently arranged in dishes or enthroned on great blocks of ice – lay banquets of seafood: craggy oysters, crabs, calamares heaped in golden rings, fresh lobsters twitching on beds of palm-leaves, bowls of mussels, and feathery shrimps. Also on offer would be the little sizzling saucers of kidney or roasted sparrow, snails, fried squid, hot prawns in garlic, stewed pork or belly of lamb. Nobody drank without eating – it would have been thought uncivilized (and may have been one of the reasons why no one was drunk). But then this seafood, after all, was some of the best in the world, land-locked Madrid's particular miracle, freshly gathered that morning from the far-away shores – the Mediterranean, Biscay, Atlantic – and rushed to the capital in special trains which pushed everything else into the sidings.

That's how I remember it: under the terracotta roofs, a proliferation of caves of ice. With carters, porters, watchmen, taxi-drivers, sleek dandies, and plump officials sipping their golden wines, fastidiously peeling a prawn, biting into the tart pink flesh of a lobster, tasting the living brine of half-forgotten seas, of half-remembered empires, while the surge of conversation continued like bubbling water under the framed pictures of bulls and heroes. It was a way of life evolved like a honeycomb and buried away from the burning sky; and perhaps no other city at that time had so successfully come to terms with this particular priority of pleasure.

But I think my most lasting impression was still the unhurried dignity and noblesse with which the Spaniard handled his drink. He never gulped, panicked, pleaded with the barman, or let himself be shouted into the street. Drink, for him, was one of the natural privileges of living, rather than the temporary suicide it so often is for others. But then it was lightly taxed here, and there were no licensing laws; and under such conditions one could take one's time.

I felt that Madrid was a city where I might make some money, so I went to the Town Hall to get the usual permission. The man examined my violin, hummed a few bars of *Il Trovatore*, and said I should go to the Commissariat of Police. This was in another part of the city and got me nowhere, for I was passed on immediately to the Ministry of Agriculture. The officials were drowsily kind, rolled me cigarettes and asked me what I thought of Madrid, but although they seemed to approve of the idea of concerts in the streets, none of them could find the necessary form to permit it. But in the end it didn't matter; I was thanked for making the proper approaches and it was suggested I could go ahead without it.

So when the air cooled that evening, I went to the older part of the city, to the teeming cliffs above the Manzanares. There was scarcely any traffic; streets were intimate as courtyards, with lamplit arches smelling of wine and woodsmoke. And all were alive with that dense coming and going of a people too poor really to be going anywhere, content to walk up and down within sight of their neighbours, chewing carobs and sunflower seeds.

I melted easily enough into the evening crowds, playing alone but not entirely ignored. People walked from the shops to give me an apple or orange, and women threw paper-wrapped gifts from the balconies. 'Regard the young man. Find him a morsel, for Jesus' – and pennies and biscuits came scattering down.

Givers and receivers seemed to be equal here. It was a world of exchanges rather than charity. Stallholders swapped with their neighbours, or ate their own wares, and barmen poured out drinks for each other. Beggars were everywhere, sitting propped against walls, carefully inspecting one another's parcels, while around them ran rouged and painted children wearing their mothers' skirts and shoes.

This was a part of Madrid where I spent much of my time, especially those nights when nobody slept, sitting around till dawn on their little pavement chairs waiting for a breath of air from the Sierras. All was snug, drowsy, and closely wrapped, like life in some public bed. I remember the cries and conversations that rose and fell, looping from door to door:

'I buy ropes and iron, cottons and silks! I buy saucepans, nails, and keys!'

'Paco's no value. He's a mala lengua. He knows nothing but to sell old eggs.'

'She comes from Genoa – or her people did. He's from Burgos. He spies for the Guardia ...'

'I have fritas, gambas, and pajaritos – fresh little mouthfuls, gentlemen ...'

'Immaculada! – whore, where have you been all night? Whose mattress you been pressing then? ...'

There seemed no programme to life in these narrow alleys; nothing stopped and all hours were the same: always some mumbling old woman buying a half-litre of beans, a girl at a window, a child at the breast, some boy down a side-street silently torturing another, some family round a table eating ...

And whenever I returned to my inn, no matter how late it

might be, most of the carters would still be awake. The innkeeper would give me some coppers, or a glass of brandy, and suggest I play them a tune

One night, I remember, a gentleman in a grey frock-coat came down from his room to listen, and stood close behind me, nodding and smiling to the music and sticking long silver pins through his throat.

Another night as I played, an old clock in the courtyard suddenly shuddered and struck fourteen.

'It's gone mad,' said the innkeeper. 'It hasn't struck for years.' And he went over and hit it with a bottle.

My bedroom was a cell without any windows, and had bedbugs as big as beetles. Lying down was to be ridden, racked, and eaten, to scratch and fight for breath. It was clear why everyone stayed awake in this city. Only in the streets and courtyards could one breathe at night, and the heat brought the beds alive.

Mornings, however, were miracles of renewal, well worth the short night's inferno. Then the sky was an infinity of bubble-blue, pure as a diamond seen through water, restoring to life the sleepless sufferers who emerged with faces shining like plates. Washed stones and wet dung scented the morning streets, together with the delicate tang of pine. Raised close to the sky, the city sparkled, as though among the first to receive its light. Indeed Madrid, the highest capital in Europe, was a crystal platform at this early hour, and the clarity of the air may have been the cause of a number of local obsessions – the people's concern for truth, their naked and pitiless mysticism, their fascination with pleasure and death. They were certainly lofty in their love of the city, putting it first among the many proverbs. 'From the provinces to Madrid – but from Madrid to the sky,' said one with ascending pride. Also: 'When I die, please God, let me go to Heaven, but have a little window to look back on Madrid.' Standing on its mile-high plateau their city was considered to be the top rung of a ladder reaching just this side of paradise.

Mornings in the posada were the best time of the day, with the walls dripping with watered flowers, I used to sit in the doorway, facing the street, while the girl Concha went to buy my breakfast; then when she returned she'd squat on the bench beside me and start pinning and curling her hair. Concha was a husky young widow from Aranjuez and spent most of the daytime idling about, waiting for the return of her boy-friend from the Asturias who brought her presents of jam and butter. In the meantime she was willing to do my marketing for me, so long as she could keep back a bit for herself.

She was in her ripe middle twenties, and I thought her mature and beautiful – though well out of reach of my years. Her heavy gold hair looked like a load of straw, and would have looked even better if she'd dyed it more often. She would ask me the usual questions. 'Why are you alone? Have you no wife or piccaneeky?' Sometimes she'd pour some fish-oil into the palms of my hands and get me to massage her hair with it. I'd be content to sit out the morning at this indolent task, while the carts rattled past in the street, and feel her leaning against me, heavy and silent, oblivious to the passing cries of the carters . . .

Finally, one morning, towards the end of my stay, I noticed her hot lazy eyes wandering over me. My clothes, she said, were without class or dignity and not proper for an Englishman. What I needed, at least, was a new pair of trousers, and she said she'd get some from a gentleman she knew. 'You will have them tonight, I promise you. Then you will be able to walk in the street with honour.'

That evening, in fact, I did well with the fiddle and spent the rest of the night in the bars. The hot still air sharpened the taste of the wine and sent me wandering from street to street, glad to be alone in this open city with all the benefits of no identity.

I began at the Calle Echegaray – a raffish little lane, half Goya, half Edwardian plush, with café-brothels full of painted mirrors, crippled minstrels, and lacquered girls. The narrow ditch-like alley was crowded with gypsies, watchmen, touts, and lechers, and with youths gazing aghast at the girls in the windows, without the money to buy them. Inside, the lucky ones – the paunchy bald clubmen, and spoiled señoritos spending their mothers' pin-money – had beer and prawns, a girl at each shoulder, a bootblack crouched at their feet, buying the fat court-life for a few pesetas in the midst of a clamour of crones and beggars.

I found a less brassy bar at the end of the street, one designed for quieter, more twilit drinking – but voluptuously furnished and decorated throughout with a Victorian amalgam of blood and sex. Varnished posters on the walls, the colour of old smoked salmon, announced: 'Toros en Valencia, 1911'; or showed Theda Bara-type beauties in black lace mantillas, roses pressed to their naked bosoms, sensuously posturing to a background of dying bull-fighters, and choking bulls stretched on crimson sands.

In this bar the wine was poured from a great stone jar, and served by an old man who'd lost a leg in the bullring. He carried his grumbles and miseries like a guttering candle from one group of drinkers to another.

Someone mentioned Belmonte and Domingo Ortega, the two rival stars of the day.

'They are nothing,' he growled. 'Thieves and catch-pennies both. Don't speak of them to me. There are no men or bulls alive in Spain any more. Only pretty little boys with kittens.'

The wine was thick and strong, and I was still not used to it. The bar began to change dimensions. I was suddenly aware of the beauty of my finger-nail, of people who addressed me, then disappeared.

A little man by my side was boasting in a sing-song voice of his home in the north of Spain. He was short, like a Welshman, with a sad chapel face, and was clearly enjoying his exile. He hated the void of Castile, the burnt-up desert; he came from a land of plenty. 'In the Asturias,' he was saying, while his companions giggled, 'there are three special kinds of green. The dark green of night, the clear green of water, and the pale fresh green of a corpse . . .'

Another man near by suddenly spun round upon me and thrust his red butcher-face at mine.

'Long live Spain and Germany!' he said, raising his fist. 'Death to America! And long live Napoleon!'

'Napoleon's dead,' I said primly.

He gave me a cunning look

'Oh, no; we believe he's alive.' He raised his fist again. 'But death to France too! – and if you're a Frenchman, excuse me . . .'

Then I was in another bar. It was quieter now. People were settling down to the middle hours of the night. Four men by the counter stood with their heads together, hands resting on one another's shoulders, intimate, hushed, middle-aged, and oblivious, taking turns to sing the verse of a song. Each one sang in a distant, ghostly falsetto, while the rest bent their heads to the words, and their long jowled faces, intent and listening, were creased in silent pleasure. Such a group, heads joined in an English pub, would have been known to be swapping dirty jokes; and the songs these men were singing were also sex-jokes in a way, but polished by a thousand anonymous poets – stinging rhymes about passion, the decay of powers, seduction, defeat, and death.

I ended that night, my last in Madrid, with a visit to the Bar Chicote – not the prophylactic night-spot it later became for tourists, but a place of unassumingly local indulgence. More like a private room than a public tavern, it had an atmosphere of exhausted eroticism, and the girls sat quietly in the shadows, subdued but glowing, like daughters waiting to run away from home.

The clients included a few priestly old men and a handful of worn-out dandies, all scrupulously dressed and sprawled at their drinks as if the furniture had been fitted round them. On a stool in one corner a fox-like guitarist whistled through his teeth as he played, and there was a diminutive singer, anxious and hungry, who gave sudden little yelping laughs, and who sat, when not singing, with his lips at the ready, folded back round his shining gums.

Having a few pesetas left, I found a table, and soon there was a girl beside me, whispering wooingly in broken English, full of instant charm and lies. I remember the small gypsy face, fine as an Indian dancer's, and the chaste white buttoned-up blouse. She told me she had a gentleman-friend in America who sent her a hundred dollars a month. 'But I am a bad girl – Lowry – much too bad.' She stroked my arm with her purple fingers. 'Because how romantic I am. How just poetic. I am for nothing but the heart, you know.' She had summed me up quickly. 'I love England, Lowry. I love Cardiff and Hartlepool. I would go with you anywhere.' She ordered more drinks, her head a few inches from mine, energy lighting her face like water. Whispering across her glass: 'My friend in America, he has four, five children. He sends me their photographs. He won't come back. How just romantic I am. Lowry, you take me with you. I wouldn't be bad against you . . .'

Another drink, and I was imagining this girl barefooted, walking beside me, rolled in my blanket at night. But suddenly there was a racket at the door, followed by one of those theatrical entrances – a minor bullfighter with his court of gypsies. Shouts, embraces, a busy stir at the bar, a yelp of song from the awakened singer. And I was alone again, watching the girl's empty glass rolling sideways across the table.

I walked back through the streets with a rocking head, thinking simple ironic thoughts. It was long past midnight, almost dawn, and for once Madrid seemed deserted. The posada was closed, but the door opened to my shoulder and cats darted across the yard like lizards.

As I stumbled upstairs a hand touched mine in the darkness and drew me into a jumbled moonlit room. 'I've got your clothes,' said Concha. She stood close against me, holding my shoulder-blades, and I could smell her peppery flesh. 'Man,' she whispered. I swayed on my feet, full of hazy, unthinking dumbness. Somewhere in the room a child called 'Mama', and the woman paused to give it a spoonful of jam. Then she took off my boots and helped me to bed. Before she joined me she made the sign of the cross.

7

Toledo

Two days later I walked into Toledo, about forty miles to the south, and there the Castilian sun caught up with me at last and struck me down with a twenty-four-hour fever.

I'd found a brilliant white inn just inside the city gate, so dazzling it seemed to be carved from salt, but the bruising impact it made on the eyes soon warned me that something was wrong.

I remember climbing into the town, hugging the narrow shadows and accompanied by rainbow hallucinations, then staggering into a wineshop for a glass of water and dropping unconscious on the floor. When I recovered, I remembered two men carrying me back to the inn and laying me down by a water-trough. Racked with icy heat, I pressed my face to the stone, grateful for the smell of its damp green mould, and dimly aware of the crackle of female voices discussing my poor condition.

They sat in a circle around me, a group of thin old women, pyramids of black against the shimmering walls, carefully keeping their distance but watching me closely with a mixture of concern and exasperation. 'Ay! ... It's his head ... He walks without a hat ... The foolish ... The sad young man ...' Meanwhile I was left alone to sweat and sleep, and not even the dogs approached me.

I was still lying out there in the middle of the night, still lying where the men had put me. I could feel the stone of the water-trough against my cheek, and there was a cold white moon overhead. Everybody else was asleep, and the courtyard was empty, but someone had covered me with a sack.

By noon next day the fever suddenly went, leaving me purged and ravenously hungry. The women were back on their chairs, knees spread, hands folded, grouped silently around the walls. Seeing me sit up, one of them brought me some food and told me not to be such a fool in future. The others nodded in chorus, pointing their fingers at the sun and shrinking away in postures of dread. 'Bad! bad!' they cried, drawing their scarves across their faces till only their eyes and knuckles were showing.

That evening I was back on the job, playing to the open-air cafés in the Plaza de Zocodover – a sloping square of uneven cobbles which was the town's main centre. No traffic, no radios – only the sun-down crowds quietly sitting and watching each other, the waiters mostly idle or flicking at flies with slow caressive movements.

I'd not been there long when a special party arrived and made their way to a nearby table – a curiously striking group and immediately noticeable in the ponderous summer twilight. There were four of them: a woman in dazzling white, a tall man wearing a broad black hat, a jaunty young girl with a rose in her hair, followed by a pretty lacy child.

They were clearly not Spanish, yet they had a Spanish air. I thought they might possibly have been Portuguese. The man sat at the table with a distinguished stoop, while his companions arranged themselves gracefully beside him, spreading their shawls on the chairs and beaming round the darkening square as though in a box at the opera. I finished my last tune and began to take a collection, which brought me at last to their table. The woman asked me in French if I was German, and I replied in Spanish that I was English. 'Ah,' she smiled. 'And so am I.' And she invited me to join them.

The man shifted and coughed. He had a long scorched face and the eyes of a burnt-out eagle. He offered me a strong but shaky hand. 'Roy Campbell,' he said. 'South African poet. Er – reasonably well known in your country.'

323

His voice was musically hoarse, yet broken and interrupted as though being transmitted on faulty wires, and it seemed to quaver between bursts of sudden belligerence and the most humble of hesitations.

In a series of stuttering phrases he rapidly let it be known that he hated England, that all his friends were English, that English literature was an unburied corpse, that he was in Spain because England had no manhood any more; and was I broke and could he help me at all?

The diatribe was short, all over in a moment, like a quick shuffling of totem-masks. Then with affectionate dignity he introduced his companions, inclining his long broad back to each. Mary, his wife, his small daughter Anna, and their Catalan friend, Amelia.

It was the poet's saint's-day, and the party had dressed in his honour and were drinking his health in fizzy pop. Campbell himself drank wine in long shuddering gasps, and suggested I do the same. I was more than satisfied by this encounter, which had come so unexpectedly out of the evening, pleased to have arrived on foot in this foreign city in time to be elected to this poet's table. All things were as they should be – the artist in exile, generous and defiant in mood, his red eyes glittering like broken glass as the phrases came stumbling forth. Still tense and light-headed from my recent fever, I felt the glory of the Word around me, and accepted the stature of the man without surprise, imagining all poets to be made like this.

Then Mary Campbell inquired how long I'd been in Toledo, and whether I was on my own. 'D'you like rissotto?' she asked, and said she was sure there was more than enough if I cared to go home with them for supper.

The Campbells had rented a house under the wall of the cathedral, in Cardinal Cisneros – a typically bare-fronted place with an elegant patio inside surrounded by a gallery of little rooms.

Supper was served in the patio under the open sky, with several bottles of local wine, and I found myself sitting down to a well-laid table for the first time in almost two months. The young girls were excited and ready to make the most of the feast-day, and they dressed up as gypsies to entertain us – dancing and weaving among the old stone pillars to the fluttering light of candles. Little Anna, who was about five years old, had blue eyes and thick black hair, and she danced like a firefly, floating over the flagstones with a precocious, iridescent skill.

Afterwards, they changed again and acted out a shrill Spanish play – aided by the housemaid dressed up as a hag. The epic was long, in dialect, and devoted to the complications of jealousy, during which Roy and I fell asleep.

When the girls had gone to bed, we woke up again and talked until early morning. Roy also read a few poems in his thick trembling voice, monotonous, yet curiously moving, and nothing could have suited me better at that hour, and at that place and time of my life. I was young, full of wine, and in love with poetry, and was hearing it now from the poet's mouth. It came out in agony, bruised yet alive, and each line seemed to shake his body. He read some of his shorter poems. 'Horses on the Camargue', 'The Sisters', 'Choosing a Mast', and the words seemed to flare at the nostrils, whinny and thunder, and rise like steam in the air.

Half-dazed with sleep, I felt my eyelids falling, printed with succulent images: sisters called to their horses, naked in the dark, and met them with silken thighs; a rich Zulu nipple plugged the mouth of a child; mares went rolling beneath the hooves of stallions ... What had I read till then? – cartloads of Augustan whimsy: this, I felt, was the stuff for me.

Presently he finished reading and began to talk and gossip, swaying to and fro in his chair. He spoke of his friends and enemies, pinning scandals to most of them, boasting of quarrels, feuds, and fights. The scene, as he described it, was of a six-foot South African striding contemptuously among the pygmies. Famous names were set up to be torn apart, somewhat confusing to me at the time – Eliot, A. E. Coppard, Wyndham Lewis, Marie Corelli, Jacob Epstein, T. E. Lawrence, the Sitwells. 'Osbert Sitwell? – knocked him down in – ah – Charlotte Street. Him and his coronet . . . Didn't like Coppard – I kicked his ass. Mary will tell you. That's the truth now, isn't it?'

Mary sat listening and saying nothing, cool and white in her dress. In fact it was T. E. Lawrence, he admitted, who had helped to place him as a poet, bringing his first book to the critics' attention. He was one of the few of his friends for whom he had a good word that night – apart from Augustus John.

The Campbells had first met John, Roy told me, before they were married, when they were living in the south of France, at Martigues – a village on a lagoon near the mouth of the Rhône, full of bad water and drink-crazed fishermen. John had adopted the lovers, as well he might, for they must have been an unusually handsome pair: and had helped, in due course, to arrange their wedding, which took place in the wilderness of the Camargue. It had been a 'gypsy' affair, designed like an early John canvas, with caravans, campfires, ceremonial mixings of blood, heavy drinking, and trials of strength, reaching its climax when the couple mounted a couple of horses and galloped away across the midnight plain. (This was a typical Roy fantasy: in fact he met Mary in London, married her soon after, and they spent their honeymoon with the Johns in Dorset. True, there had been a loud 'gypsy' party – held in a pub near Parkstone – and later indeed they had gone to live in Martigues.)

But John would have picked out the poet and his black-haired girl anywhere as though he himself had created them – Mary, with her violet-eyed Celtic beauty, and Roy the deep-browed giant wildly bearded like a lustier Yeats. This was only a few years back, but trembling Roy, as he talked, became again the hero of Martigues, towering in his strength above the small blue fishermen, their brawling champion at arms, out-sailing, out-rowing, out-drinking them – then spending inexhaustible nights of love.

'We never grew tired of it, did we, girl? We must have broken half the beds in the town.'

'Roy – please,' his wife murmured, touching her lavender lips. 'I'm sure he doesn't want to hear all that.'

They asked me to stay the night, and I slept in a little room off the patio, on a mattress propped up by books. Other books lay scattered across the floor, together with sheaves of unfinished poems. I remember peering at one of them, a single line in the candlelight – something about storm-hornets snoring in the wind . . .

Nobody stirred the next morning, except the carolling housemaid, who brought me some breakfast and took my shirt to wash. I got up and wandered about the deserted patio, where I found a note suggesting I stay on if I wished; so I went back to the inn, collected my bags from the old ladies, and returned gratefully to the book-filled room. Roy reappeared at lunch, still tousled with sleep, and talked brokenly throughout the meal, shaking about him as he ate tattered plumes of nerves but slowly regaining his claims to glory.

He'd sailed whalers, swum Hellesponts, broken horses on the Camargues, fought bulls, and caught sharks barehanded. He'd stirred up two hemispheres, as well as the olive-belt between, and restored blood and muscle to poetry. His voice, growing hoarser as though blown through a shell, continued to boom like an ancient mariner's, not so much determined. I felt, to convince me of the truth of these legends as hoping to suggest that this was how a man should live.

In fact, there was something curiously inoffensive about his boasting, it was warm-hearted and even childlike, breathless, confidential, as though he wished you to share in the secret – that anyone on earth could have done such things if only they'd been lucky like him.

After lunch, and the long tidal flow of wine, Roy staggered off to have another sleep. But Mary and I sat on through the hot afternoon while she instructed me about religion. It was only then that I noticed the crucifixes in the house, decorated with knots of jasmine, and recalled where the Campbells had chosen to live, in this street pressed close to the walls of the cathedral, wrapped in its mantle of bells and incense. I was a heretic, of course, and opinionated; jaunty with my lack of belief. But Mary Campbell, soft-voiced and shining-eyed, reproved me with gentle calm. And in her, for the first time, I saw the banked-up voluptuousness of a young and beautiful convert, holding to this single passion in which all hungers were answered and all doubts quietly put away. Here, romantic love was kept on ice, sealed by an unfaltering spiritual flame, and accompanied by a vocabulary of torment, physical denial and ecstacy which promised an eternity of sensuous reward.

It may also have been the first, and most dangerous, time – as I sat with the poet's wife through that hushed afternoon, watching her finger her beads in the airless shade – that I felt the pull of that seductive faith.

But I argued against it – at that age I wanted action, not the devout pause before some deferred consummation; I wanted the excitement of doubt, the satisfaction of mortality, the freedom to make love here and now on earth. Beautiful Mary would have none of it; she sat among her pin-up icons, smiling quietly, unshakably contained. 'Don't you see?' she kept saying (we were damned if we didn't). 'You can't *imagine* the utter peace . . .'

I stayed with the Campbells for about a week, and was treated with a matter-of-fact kindness which surprised and charmed me. I'd arrived from nowhere, but nobody bothered me with questions; I was simply accepted and given the run of the house.

During most of the daylight hours Roy lay low and slept, appearing at nightfall like some ruffled sea-bird, leaning against a pillar with his arms stretched wide as though drying his salt-wet wings. One saw him gathering his wits in great gulps of breath, after which he would be ready for anything.

Mary and little Anna lived in an intimate calm of their own, quietly busy with their spiritual chores, and could be seen in the morning going off to Mass, veiled and modest as shadows, and so native in appearance that when I met them in the street I often forgot and addressed them in Spanish. When they returned from their devotions they would come back transformed, light-footed and chirpy with gossip, their early silence now swept away, and their eyes sparkling, as though they'd been to a party.

One evening, to keep my hand in, I played for an hour in the streets and made over seven pesetas, in copper. I carried it back to the house and poured it out on the table, to the delight of the astonished girls. We bought a few litres of wine and went up on to the roof, where there was a terrace with a view of the city. It was still light, and the humped little red-tiled houses, scaled and patchy, clustered around us like crabs.

We ate supper and drank, and as the evening darkened, Roy coughed and began to sing, croaking the corny laments and border ballads that were near to his expatriate heart. His voice was blurred as usual, and rough as a sailor's, yet deeply charged with feeling; more than that, he sang with a poet's care, renewing the worn, familiar words. 'Scots Wa Hae', 'The Bonnie Earl of Murray', sounded as if they'd just been written – with the blood of the slain still wet. To me, until then, they'd just been songs of the schoolroom, now I heard them fresh and bitter, while Roy sat with hunched shoulders, rocking backwards and forwards, often at the point of tears.

Suddenly the maid, from somewhere down in the house, hearing his singing, started up too – not a brash interruption, but like a night-bird answering to the husky call of another. Sad Castilian airs, harsh but haunting, came floating up the well of the stairs. Each new song from Roy would call up another from the girl, rising like bubbles of grief in the darkness, not clashing with his but hovering round the edges, offering a compassionate echo.

Later, the night grew cold, and we huddled under furs and blankets, talking till nearly dawn. Summer lightning and shooting stars lit up the Toledo sky with little soundless conflagrations, flickering across the cathedral and over the faces of the poet and his wife like ripples of phosphorescence.

Roy drank four and a half litres of wine a day, he said – thin, sharp stuff, lobster pink in colour, and one of the consolations of living in Toledo. Another, for him, was the paintings of El Greco, which were stacked all over the town. 'Never seen him? You must. Bloody marvellous, boy. Wake me up tomorrow, and I'll take you round.'

We began by going to the Museo de San Vicente, to see the 'Annunciation'. Campbell stood quietly before it, bare-headed, slightly bowed, his eyes blinking beneath their sun-bleached lashes; and I first saw the canvas as it were through him, by his physical stance and silence. Then muttering, without jargon, but with a kind of groping reverence, he explained what the painting meant to him. 'A bloody miracle, that hand. And look at that light in the sky. Pure Toledo – only he was the first bugger to see it.'

Then we went higher up the town to El Greco's house – still preserved in its sloping garden; a beautiful, shaggy, intimate little villa, full of dead flowers and idiot guides. Inside were the paintings; colours I'd never seen before, weeping purples, lime greens, bitter yellows; the long skulls of the saints and their sunken eyelids, eyes coated with ecstatic denials, limbs and faces drawn upwards like spires ascending, robes flickering like tapered flames – compared with the robust flesh-painting I'd seen in Madrid, these seemed to be reduced to the fevered bone.

El Greco exhausted us both. It was torrid noon, so we spent the rest of the day in the bars. Roy had started out that morning with a trembling melancholy, walking unsteadily, stuttering with weakness. As we drank, he grew stronger, taller, happy, embracing and singing, full of intimate asides. 'Marvellous girl, that Mary. Wonderful wife. She keeps her thoughts to herself. She's got more genuine saintliness in her little finger than the whole of this god-damn town.'

But it was clear that he was known with affection in Toledo –

at least, by the men in the bars. Leathery hands reached up to lean on his shoulders, processions of dwarfs brought him tumblers of wine. Heads were raised, slightly cocked, to hear what he had to say. Meanwhile he introduced me to everyone.

'A champion, this boy. Walked all the way from Vigo. He walks a thousand miles a week. It's true, by God ...' Dwarfs brought me wine, too. Roy kept repeating: 'The funny thing is – he's English.'

During the long afternoon, amidst waves of euphoria, Roy would also be visited by brief moments of panic. He'd suddenly say it was midnight, and that he'd got to go to Mass, and start searching his pockets for a collar and tie. The shepherds would take him by the arm, lead him out into the street, and show him the position of the sun – at which he would blink and nod, say 'Bless my soul', and return relieved to his drinking.

In the evening we drank brandy. I don't know where we were, but we were sitting on barrels in a kind of cave. The brandy was smooth and warm, straight from the cask, and had a flavour of muscatels. Roy talked about his career and was surprised at it. He spoke of his poetry with humility. Edith Sitwell had written to a paper to say he would make a likely Poet Laureate, and this had amused him and also helped his sales. He told me how much money he'd been paid by various publishers for books he would never write. This amused him too. And so did his autobiography. *Broken Record*, which he'd recently published and which he said was largely a spoof to confuse his enemies.

That night, mixing drinks, he also mixed his emotions, swinging between love and hatred – singing, cursing, offering to lend me money, shaking with pleasure at some success of his youth, praising God, the Virgin Mary, and Mary his wife, and punching out satirical couplets. He loved the Afrikaans language and described its primitive vigour. He hated Amelia for going to Mass dressed like a whore. He hated socialism, dog-lovers, and English dons. He loved fighting, heroism, and pain.

Yet for all his verbal arrogance, chest-beating, and boasting, I found him a curiously gentle companion. 'Look, I must get you some books. You don't mind, do you? And I've got a razor you can have . . .' His manner to those he accepted was warm, modest, and at times almost haltingly apologetic, and the locals we drank with that night treated him not as a joke foreigner to be fleeced, but as a poet and man of their own.

I spent my last morning at the Campbells' shaking the brandy fumes from my head and enjoying the final luxuries of the house. The maid scrubbed and sang. Mary carried roses to the church. Little Anna ran about watering the flower pots. Roy slept, while Amelia sat sewing near by and darting angry glances at his door.

At midday there was a meal of stuffed marrow and salad, accompanied by bottles of Málaga wine. I was packed and ready. 'Don't go in the heat,' they said. Anna said, 'You don't have to go at all.' So I lingered through the afternoon in another metaphysical exercise with Mary, ending with tea and sugared cakes. Snatches of England – flowered china and silver teaspoons – haunted the heavy Spanish air.

Roy woke up in time to take me down to the bridge, by which I would cross the gorge of the Tagus. Here we said goodbye. 'Write if you get short of money,' he said, looking down at me like some puzzled and anxious parent. 'Come back if you want to. Er – we might have gone to Mexico – but we'll always be glad to see you . . .' He coughed and shook hands. Crossing the bridge I looked back and saw him still standing in the road, legs astride, shoulders hunched, head drooping. He raised his wide-brimmed hat and held it high for a moment, then turned and stumbled back into the town.

8

To the Sea

Now it was the end of September and I'd reached the sea, having taken almost three months to come down through Spain. Cádiz, from a distance, was a city of sharp incandescence, a scribble of white on a sheet of blue glass, lying curved on the bay like a scimitar and sparkling with African light.

In fact it was a shut-in city, a kind of Levantine ghetto almost entirely surrounded by sea – a heap of squat cubist hovels enclosed by medieval ramparts and joined to the mainland by a dirty thread of sand.

I lived in an evil old posada whose galleries were packed with sailors, beggars, and pimps; and there was little to do all day except sit round in the dust while the scorching winds blew in from the Atlantic.

The police said it was forbidden to play music in the streets for money, so sometimes I played for nothing. Or I went round the cafés with a blind brother and sister who helped out my fiddle with a couple of goat-skin drums. When we were lucky we were rewarded with a few scraps of food, otherwise we played to amuse ourselves, or simply sat round talking, drinking from cracked tin cups, and eating prawns out of screws of paper.

I seemed to meet no one in Cádiz except the blind and the crippled, the diseased, the deaf and dumb, whose condition was so hopeless they scarcely bothered to complain but treated it all as a twisted joke. They told me tittering tales of others even more wretched than themselves – the homeless who lived in the Arab drains, who lay down at night among rats and excrement and were washed out to sea twice a year by the floods. They told me of families who scraped the tavern floors for shellfish and took it home to boil for soup, and of others who lived by trapping cats and dogs and roasting them on fires of driftwood. They even took me one night to a tenement near the cathedral and pointed out a howling man on the rooftop, who was pretending to be a ghost in order to terrorize the landlord and thereby reduce the rents.

I'd been travelling through Spain in a romantic haze, but as I came south the taste grew more bitter. Cádiz at that time was nothing but a rotting hulk on the edge of a disease-ridden tropic sea; its people dismayed, half-mad, consoled only by vicious humour, prisoners rather than citizens.

Since I left the Campbells in Toledo I'd been almost a month on the road; a month of vintage September weather; travelling in easy stages through autumnal landscapes which seemed to be moistly wrapped in fruit-skins. I'd been glad to be back on my solitary marches, edging mindlessly from village to town, sleeping in thickets, in oases of rushes, under tall reeds, to the smell of water. South of Toledo there was green country still – green trees against brick-red earth, trees so intense they seemed to throw green shade and turn the dust around them to grass.

There were purple evenings, juicy as grapes, the thin moon cutting a cloud like a knife; and dawns of quick sudden thunder when I'd wake in the dark to splashes of rain pouring from cracks of lightning, then walk on to a village to sit cold and alone, waiting for it to wake and sell me some bread, watching the grey light lifting, a man opening a stable, the first girls coming to the square for water.

Out in the open country it grew dark early, and then there was nothing to do but sleep. As the sun went down, I'd turn into a field and curl up like a roosting bird, then wake in the morning soaked with dew, before the first farmer or the sun was up, and take to the road to get warm, through a smell of damp herbs, with the bent dawn moon still shining.

In the valley of the Guadiana I saw herds of black bulls grazing in fields of orange dust, and square white farms, like desert strongholds, protected by packs of savage dogs. Somewhere here, in a barn, under a roof crusted with swallows' nests, a mother and daughter cooked me a supper of eggs, while a horse watched me eating, chickens walked on the table, and an old man in the hay lay dying.

Then as I approached Valdepeñas a carter offered me a lift, exclaiming that no stranger should walk while he rode, and proudly answered my gift of a cigarette by giving me in exchange a miniature cucumber. On our way to the town we stopped at a village fair and watched the performance of an open-air circus, which consisted of a monkey, a camel, an Arab, a snake, and two painted little boys with trumpets.

Valdepeñas was a surprise: a small graceful town surrounded by rich vineyards and prosperous villas – a pocket of good fortune which seemed to produce without effort some of the most genial wines in Spain. The town had an air of privileged well-being, like an oil-well in a desert of hardship; the old men and children had extra flesh on their bones, and even the dogs seemed to shine with fat.

It was also a friendly town, where people welcomed my violin and encouraged me to play as though I'd come to a wedding, drawing back their shutters, leaning over their balconies, and rewarding me with food and money. I remember playing in the evenings to houses of blue and white, while women approached me with cups of wine, and the pork-fattened shopkeepers broke off from kissing their children to bring me parcels of ham and olives.

Then one night, as I was having my supper in the square, three young men invited me to a brothel. They addressed me as 'Maestro', and introduced themselves formally: Antonio, Amistad, and Julio. I would be doing them a bounty, they said, and led me off through the town, waving their arms and making spry little dances.

Somewhere out in the suburbs we came to an old dark house, windowless, with a heavy door. The boys kicked it delicately with their pointed shoes and made low-pitched animal cries. Their teeth shone as they waited, and heat seemed to rise from the ground. The house appeared to be empty. Then the door was opened at last by a girl in a dressing-gown, sleepily eating chips.

'Guapos,' she said, in a warm flat voice, holding her arm across the doorway.

'We've brought music,' said Julio. 'Let us in, Consuelito.'

'Why not?' yawned the girl, and we entered.

Inside was a bare little patio roofed by a trellis of vines and hung with a string of coloured light-bulbs. 'We are always expected, you understand,' said Julio. 'But they will be diverted if you play a little.'

A half-dressed young girl sat at the foot of the stairs polishing her toenails with a hairbrush. Two others were sprawled at a table poring over the pages of a comic. The patio wore an air of low-lit ennui.

Consuelito bolted the door, took another mouthful of chips, then threw back her head and shrieked 'Grandpa!' at which a giggling old greybeard trotted immediately from the kitchen bearing a trayful of wine and food.

He gave us a frisky welcome, fussily filling our glasses, beating off the flies as if they were ravens, calling us masters, dukes, princes, kings, and commanding his granddaughters to stiffen their backs.

When we were comfortably settled, the old man took the violin from my hands and returned it with a little bow. 'Enchant us,' he said, and slipped me some money. The girls rose slowly to their feet and joined us.

I remember the whoosh of the wine going through my limbs, the throbbing and familiar fires, as I sat with my feet across the table scraping out waltzes and pasodobles. Julio beat time with a couple of spoons, Antonio tapped his teeth with a knife, while Amistad, already as pink as a prawn, sang away in a sickly tenor.

Business steadily grew brisker as the night advanced; the front door was increasingly kicked; there were whispers, shadowy figures stumbling their way upstairs, the sounds of boots and bare feet overhead. Grandpa found an accordion, which he gave to Antonio, and together we kept up our wheezy concert. Meanwhile the beaming old man half-drowned us with wine and said we were an honour to the house.

During short intervals of quiet the girls rejoined us, yawning and re-settling their hair, nibbling our food and chattering together in voices that were hoarse and furry with sleep. They were sturdy girls, with ruddy hands and faces, and strong absentminded bodies, and judging from their appearance one might have thought they earned their bread in the fields rather than in this breathless and shuttered house. Two were sisters, the other two cousins, and they were all in their early teens. We seemed to be the youngest visitors they had that night, most of the others being middle-aged farmers.

The four girls and Grandpa made up an intimate establishment which for a brothel appeared strangely muted. I'd expected noise, livid flesh, drunken voices, obscenities, or a kind of hang-dog, ravenous shame. Instead there was this casual atmosphere of neighbourly visiting, hosted by these vague and sleepy girls: subdued talk, a little music, an air of domestic eroticism, with unhurried comings and goings.

At last there was silence in the house, and a gleam of dawn in the patio. I sat fuddled with wine in my chair. The boys were asleep at the table, and Grandpa lay asleep on the floor, curled up like a wrinkled child. The youngest of the cotton-wrapped girls came and shook him by the arm. 'Grandpa, the farmers have gone,' she said. The old man woke up, whispered something in her ear, winked at me, and went to sleep again.

The girl shrugged, yawned, and came across to my table. I felt her lean soft and drowsily against me. She put a long brown finger to the neck of my shirt and drew it slowly down my body. Little shocks ran through me, see-saw surges of feeling, warm vaultings of sleepy comfort. The girl's wandering finger, tipped with precocious cunning, seemed the only thing left alive in the world, and moved absently about me, loosening knots in my flesh, then tying them up again.

A few days later, in a village south of Valdepeñas, I ran into Romero, a young tramp like myself, who was carrying his goods wrapped in a bundle of sailcloth and explained that he was on the road for his health. When he heard what I was doing he threw up his arms and said that was just the thing. He would go with me anywhere, he said, collect the money when I played, scrounge me food, and show me the country.

As I'd been alone for some time it seemed a good idea, so we left the village together – Romero prancing beside me, talking of ways to make money, boasting of his spectacular skill as a cook, of the various tricks he knew of enticing fowls from farmers, and of begging from nuns in convents. He was a handsome young man, witty and unscrupulous, and I felt he had some useful things to teach me. We camped the first night on a threshing floor – a circle of flagstones in the middle of a field – and lay side by side under a single blanket watching the large red sun go down. I still remember the moment: the sun huge on the horizon and the silhouette of a horseman passing slowly across it, with Romero whispering and rolling me cigarettes, and his warmth as the evening cooled.

My pleasure in his company lasted about three days, then soured and diminished quickly. No longer could I imagine myself prince of the road, the lone ranger my fancy preferred. I'd developed an ingrowing taste for the vanity of solitude, and Romero's presence cut into this sharply. Besides, he was sluggish and lazy, was always whining for vino and complaining about his feet. Certainly he detested walking, and after a mile or so would throw himself down and kick like a baby; so after lunch one day, while he was sleeping by the roadside, I put some money in his shoe and left him.

It was an extraordinary relief to be on my own again, and I

made for the hills as fast as I could. But he must have awoken soon after, for presently I heard a distant shout, and there he was, coming in furious pursuit. Throughout the rest of the day I caught glimpses of him in the distance, a small toiling figure, head down and determined, scurrying indignantly along in the dust. Feeling both guilty and hunted, I quickened my pace, and gradually he fell away. There was one last cry, as from an abandoned wife, and I never saw him again.

Then I came to the Sierra Morena – one more of those east-west ramparts which go ranging across Spain and divide its people into separate races. Behind me was Old Castile and the Gothic north; beyond, the Sierra the spiced blur of Andalusia.

A peasant stopped me in the foothills (a twinge of agony on his face at the sight of my road-worn feet) and piled my bags on his mule, gave me a stick, and said he would show me the way up the mountain. We climbed for three hours, up a rope-ladder of goat tracks which led up through a wilderness of rocks – a great jumble of boulders, large as houses, which seemed to have been thrown about by giants. The mule and I stumbled, but my guide climbed ahead of us, light-footed, never looking back. Sometimes he nodded towards the crags and made a reference to bandits. Occasionally we saw a goat-herd sitting brown and alone.

At last we pushed through the peaks and came to a misty plateau with a chill breeze blowing across it. Here was my companion's village – a huddle of rough-stone hovels, primitively rounded and tufted with dripping moss. A few diseased-looking sheep, with ribs like radiators, wandered in and out of the houses.

When they heard us coming the villagers gathered in the mist and waited for my companion to explain who I was. After he'd done this briefly, as best he could, they gave me a meal of bread and curds. Then, with a muted apology, my guide took the violin from its bag and handed it to me delicately, like a new-born lamb. I was now used to this reception – the ritual gift of food, followed by the offered instrument and the expectant silence.

I remember the villagers as they listened, blankets held to their throats, dribbles of damp lying along their eyebrows. I felt I could have been with some lost tribal remnant of seventeenth-century Scotland, during one of their pauses between famine and massacre – the children standing barefooted in puddles of dew, old women wrapped in their rancid sheepskins, and the short shaggy men whose squinting faces seemed stuck between a smile and a snarl.

When I'd finished playing, they filled my bottle with wine and stuffed some stone-hard cheese in my pocket. Then we said good-bye, and I left them standing on the ridge of the plateau like a cluster of wind-bent thorn bushes.

South of the Sierra the mists rolled away, and I met a new kind of heat, brutal and hard, carrying the smell of another continent. As I came down the mountain this heat piled up, pushing against me with blasts of sand, so that I walked half-blind, my tongue dry as a carob bean, obsessed once again by thirst. These were ominous days of nerve-bending sirocco, with peasants wrapped up to the eyes, during which I was savagely bitten by a demented dog with eyes like yellow gas. The southern slopes of the Sierras were flaking in the wind, parched as a rusty furnace, but far down in the valley, running in slow green coils, I could see at last the tree-lined Guadalquivir. Viewed from the blistered heights it was a mirage-river, which I remember putting into a short rough poem:

> Rinsed sweat from the bare Sierras
> courses a curled furrow in the dust
>
> a sun-dazed wanderer
> staggering to the sea . . .

When I reached the river at sundown I found it red, not green – shallow red water running between banks of red earth under a heavy scarlet sky, with flocks of red goats coming down to drink in clouds of vermilion dust. Naked boys, with bodies like copper pennies, splashed about in the shining mud, and all around was the rich and water-fed valley – shimmering eucalyptus, gardens of figs and peaches, orchards of plums fringed by tropical cacti, with loads of fat blackberries along the side of the road which I picked and ate for supper.

Entering the province of Andalusia through fields of ripening melons, I saw the first signs of the southern people: men in tall Cordobese hats, blue shirts, scarlet waistbands, and girls with smouldering Arab faces. Villages had Moorish names – Andújar, Pedro Abad – and an air of proud though listless anarchy. In the main square of one fully exposed to the populace, I saw two prisoners in an iron cage, puffing cheerily at cigarettes, blowing smoke through the bars, and shouting obscenities at the passers-by.

At this point on the road I might have continued south to Granada, which was only two or three days away. Instead I turned west and followed the Guadalquivir, which added several months to my journey, and took me to the sea the roundabout way and affected everything that was later to happen to me.

Ever since childhood I'd imagined myself walking down a white dusty road through groves of orange trees to a city called Seville. This fantasy may have been induced by the Cotswold damp, or by something my mother had told me, but it was one of several such clichés which had brought me to Spain, and now as I approached the city on this autumn morning it was as though I was simply following some old direction.

In fact there was no white road, not even a gold-clustered orange tree, but Seville itself was dazzling – a creamy crustation of flower-banked houses fanning out from each bank of the river. The Moorish occupation had bequeathed the affection for water around which so many of even the poorest dwellings were built – a thousand miniature patios set with inexhaustible fountains which fell trickling upon ferns and leaves, each a nest of green repeated in endless variations around this theme of domestic oasis. Here the rippling of water replaced the coal fire of the north as a symbol of home and comfort, while its whispering presence, seen through grilles and doorways, gave an impression of perpetual afternoon, each house turning its back on the blazing street outside to lie coiled around its moss-cool centre.

Seville was no paradise; even so. There was the customary squalor behind it – children and beggars sleeping out in the gutters under a coating of disease and filth. By day their condition seemed somewhat less intolerable, and they presented a jaunty face to the world. All were part of the city – the adored Seville – to which even the beggars claimed pride of belonging, and where ragged little girls would raise their thin brown arms and dance rapturously at the least excuse. It was a city of traditional alegria, where gaiety was almost a civic duty, something which rich and poor wore with arrogant finesse simply because the rest of Spain expected it. Like the Viennese, the Sevillanas lived under this burden of legend, and were forced into carefree excesses, compelled to flounce and swagger as the embodiment of Andalusia in spite of frequent attacks of liverish exhaustion.

I lived in Seville on fruit and dried fish, and slept at night in a yard in Triana – that ramshackle barrio on the north bank of the river which was once a gypsy ghetto. In my day it still had a seedy vigour, full of tile-makers and free-range poultry, of medieval stables bursting with panniered donkeys, squabbling wives and cooking pots. Stately cockerels with brilliant combs and feathers strutted like Aztecs about the rooftops, while from my yard I could hear the incessant throb of guitars being practised in shuttered rooms.

Seville in the morning was white and gold, the gold-lit river reflecting the Toro de Oro, with flashes of sun striking the Giralda Tower and the spires of the prostrate cathedral. The interior of the cathedral was a bronze half-light, a huge cavern of private penance, with an occasional old woman hobbling about on her knees, mumbling a string of prayers, or some transfixed girl standing in a posture of agony, arms stretched before the bleeding Christ.

At the morning market I bought cactus fruit, dripping with

juice and shot full of seeds, sold by a garrulous old man who entertained his customers with long histories about the rivers of Spain. But his tales, told in dialect, were less intelligible to me than those of the deaf-mute boy Alonso, who I also met in the market and whose restless face and body built up images like a silent movie. He described his family in mime, patting their several heads, and suddenly one could see them in a row beside him – his handsome father, his coughing consumptive mother, fighting brothers, and sly young sister. There was also a sickly baby, its head lolling back, and two dead ones, packed into little boxes – the boy set their limbs stiffly, sprinkled them with prayers, closed their eyes, and laid them away with a shrug.

In the market, too, I met Queipo, a beggar, whose hand had been bitten off by a mad dog in Madrid. Sometimes he'd lift up the red and wrinkled stump, bare his teeth, and bark at it savagely. Otherwise he was a rational companion, and showed me round the town and introduced me to the cheapest cafés. We used to meet at midday, count out our money, and spend it on wine and fishballs, then go down to the quayside, climb into a half-sunken boat, and doze through the afternoon.

The Seville quays were unpretentious, and seemed no more nautical than a coal-wharf in Birmingham. The Guadalquivir, at this point, was rather like the Thames at Richmond, and was about as busy as the Paddington Canal. Yet it was from this narrow river, fifty miles from the sea, that Columbus sailed to discover America, followed a few years later by the leaking caravelles of Magellan, one of which was the first to encircle the world. Indeed, the waterfront at Seville, with its paddling boys and orange-boats, and its mossy provincial stones, was for almost five hundred years – till the coming of space-aimed rockets – history's most significant launching-pad.

Queipo loved the quays. He wanted to go to Honolulu, he said. He pointed to his stump. 'But I can only swim in circles.' He had a family of fourteen, who lived in a cave in the country, and there was another child on the way. He spoke of his ageing wife with awe and impatience; she defeated all his attempts at control. 'I knew it was no good,' he growled, 'when she put that lace on her camisole.' She was over fifty, but still boundingly fertile. Two of his younger sons came into the city each day carrying a bucket wired to a pole, which Quiepo filled with meat-hash and orange skins and other scraps he'd begged from the cafés.

At night, when Queipo had returned to his cave, I'd walk back across the bridge to Triana, and sit on the cool flat roof of the Café Faro, and eat chips and gaze at the river. It seemed to be the only place in the city's bowl of heat where there was the slightest movement of air. The lights on the river collapsed, distended, and coiled hotly like electric eels. Sounds rose from the streets: the shouts of the sleepless children, the throb of music, an occasional scream. This was a city absorbed in a boxed life of its own; strangers were few and almost ignored. Seville lived for itself, split into two halves, one riding on the back of the other.

Until now, I'd accepted this country without question, as though visiting a half-crazed family. I'd seen the fat bug-eyed rich gazing glassily from their clubs, men scrabbling for scraps in the market, dainty upper-class virgins riding to church in carriages, beggar-women giving birth in doorways. Naïve and uncritical, I'd thought it part of the scene, not asking whether it was right or wrong. But it was in Seville, on the bridge, watching the river at midnight, that I got the first hint of coming trouble. A young sailor approached me with a 'Hello, Johnny', and asked for a cigarette. He spoke the kind of English he'd learned on a Cardiff coal boat, spitting it out as though it hurt his tongue. 'I don't know who you are,' he said, 'but if you want to see blood, stick around – you're going to see plenty.'

9

East to Málaga

Life in Cádiz was too acrid to hold me for long, so after a few days I left it and turned eastwards at last, heading along the bare coastal shelf of Andalusia.

Behind me the white fish-hook bay impaled the last tides of the Atlantic, still smelling of herring shoals, but the milky green waves swept steadily towards the Straits through which the Mediterranean would presently bloom. Already a generation old, I was still ignorant of the sea, unused to this sudden unearthly neutrality, and the dizzy sweep of the water gave me a feeling of vertigo, so that I kept carefully to the middle of the road.

Between the mountains and the sea, the country was a dried-up prairie, dun-coloured, smoking with dust. Thin wiry grass bent to the day-long winds which covered them with a ghostly film of salt, while far away to the north one could see the black dots of bulls wandering over the plain like buffaloes.

I spent almost a week in this Arizona-type landscape. It seemed forsaken, and most of the time I was alone. Sometimes I met a solitary horseman, or a veiled woman on a donkey who raised her hand to avert my evil eye. Or I would pass some roadside villagers treading the dregs of their grapes in the sour tail-end of the vintage. It was a joyless scene – the men and girls, bare-legged, circling together in a kind of trance, stamping the scummy vats with their blue-stained feet and uttering little grunts and cries of exhaustion.

I remember sleeping one night in a hill-top cemetery, my face stroked by the beams of a lighthouse, then taking breakfast next

347

morning in a village wineshop where I heard the first talk of war. The faces of the fishermen were dull and grey as they rolled the harsh dry word between them. They spoke of war in Abyssinia; meaningless to me, who hadn't seen a newspaper for almost three months.

Past Cape Trafalgar, the Straits narrowed visibly, the winds died, and the sea grew calmer. Then Africa appeared, and the skeins of the currents grew closer, crawling with little ships. Between the jaws of two continents they met and mingled, slowly filtering in and out, some heading back into the Mediterranean's calm blue womb, others breaking out into the grey Atlantic.

I arrived at Tarifa, the southernmost point of Europe, to find it still skulking behind its Arab walls. Once a Barbary stronghold and master of the Straits, it now lay stranded, a bit of washed-up Africa, a decayed abstraction of Casbah-like alleys wandering among blind and shuttered houses.

I found a café on the beach where I watched the sun go down, almost audibly, into a gulf of purple. The bar was crowded with fishermen, morose and silent, all gazing across the Straits. In the distant dusk one saw the orange smudge of Tangier break into little lights, then the night's heavy heat closed in upon us, prickling the face and hands.

The young fisherman at my table accepted a drink, and I asked him about the town. At first he was formal. 'It is very handsome,' he said; 'very historic, as you can see.' But he couldn't keep it up, and soon relaxed into truculence. 'It's like all the world. We have no work, no boats. The women prostrate themselves.'

We were joined quite soon by a mysterious dandy who invited us to share his bottle of whisky. He had rings on his fingers, wore a white silk shirt, and spoke English with an American accent. 'I am Cuban,' he said. 'You know the type. We are very wild kind of men. All we are innerested in is dames and revolutions – OK?' He wriggled with self-delight.

Suddenly he turned to the young fisherman, handed him a carton of cigarettes, and spoke to him in a rapid whisper. The fisherman listened, spat, shrugged his shoulders, then got up and went to the door. He whistled twice, and from the shadow of an upturned boat another shadow detached itself. The Cuban left the half-bottle of whisky behind him and went to the waiting girl on the beach.

The country east of Tarifa was high, bare, and brown as a mangy lion, with kites and vultures turning slowly overhead, square-winged, like electric fans. It was a scrub-covered wilderness, rippling with wind, but heartless, empty of life, except for occasional hunters who appeared suddenly with muskets, fired at nothing, then went away.

All day, as I climbed the twisting road, I heard the explosions rolling round the hills, the echoing crack of a gun followed by long empty silences like the fag-end of a war. At the top of the rise the country levelled into a kind of platform – a lofty gallery above the Straits – from which one could watch the slow blue currents of the Mediterranean snaking towards the Atlantic's green forked tongue. Africa was now so near one could see the veins in the rocks running up the massive face of Morocco, with the afternoon sun peeling away the shadows to reveal deep and mysterious crevices. From Tangier, the panorama swept east to Ceuta and back into the mint-green hills of the Rif – the Barbary Coast, inscrutable threshold of violence, which made me feel capable of extreme adventures.

Instead I slept for an hour in the withered gorse, and woke to find a gunman standing over me. 'How d'you do?' I said foolishly, flustered, in English. The man giggled, and crept away.

Later the mountain road dropped into a narrow valley full of sea-mist and stunted cork trees, where flocks of damp sheep with long Cotswold faces wandered among strands of glittering cobwebs. The place was green and chill, curiously familiar, like a pocket of western England. And sure enough, as I climbed to the next high peak, there was Gibraltar crouching low in the distance.

Africa, Spain, and the great sweep of the bay, all shone with a fierce bronze light. But not Gibraltar: it lay apart like an interloper, as though it had been towed out from Portsmouth and anchored offshore still wearing its own grey roof of weather. Slate-coloured, aloof, surrounded by a scattering of warships and fringed by its dockyard cranes, the Rock lay shadowed beneath a plate of cloud, immersed in a private rainstorm.

I went no farther that night, but camped out on the hilltop, content to stay where I was. The vista below me spread from Ronda to the Rif, a classical arrangement of sea and rock, with the mouth of the Mediterranean pierced by the wash of ships tracing a course as old as Homer. Kites and kestrels swung silently overhead, smouldering in the evening sun; and as twilight approached, the Pillars of Hercules turned purple and the sea poured between them in a flush of lavender. Alone, with my back to a sun-warmed rock, I finished the last of my food, gazing where Africa and Europe touched fingertips in this merging of day and night.

Suddenly it was dark, and Gibraltar became a heap of diamonds, and Algeciras stretched out claws of light. Then a huge moon rose straight out of the sea, and hung motionless, like a frozen bloom. The wind rose too, funnelling from the Atlantic, and I wrapped in my blanket, shivering with cold.

The Port of Algeciras had a potency and charm which I'd found nowhere else till then. It was a scruffy little town built round an open drain and smelling of fruit skins and rotten fish. There were a few brawling bars and modest brothels; otherwise the chief activity was smuggling. At most street-corners one would be offered exotic items of merchandise unavailable anywhere else in Spain – mouldy chocolate, laddered stockings, damp American cigarettes, leaky Parkers, and fake Swiss watches.

But for all its disreputable purposes and confidence-trickery, it seemed to be a town entirely free of malice, and even the worst of its crooks were so untrained in malevolence that no one was expected to take them seriously. In its position as a bridge between Europe and Morocco, the port could have equalled Marseilles in evil, but its heart wasn't in it, in spite of the opportunities, and it preferred small transgressions with lesser rewards.

Algeciras was a clearing-house for odds and ends, and I stayed there about two weeks. I remember the fishing boats at dawn bringing in tunny from the Azores, the markets full of melons and butterflies, the international freaks drinking themselves into multi-lingual stupors, the sly yachts running gold to Tangier . . . I spent part of my time with a gang of youths who earned their living spiking handbags with fish-hooks, who got rid of their loot in the bars and brothels, and begged their meals at the local convent. The leader of the gang was a 'globe-trotter' from Lisbon, who claimed to be walking round the world. But he was always slipping back home to fetch something he'd forgotten and had taken two years to get as far as this.

For myself, I thought it best to stick to the fiddle, and here the town was rewarding enough. My patrons were varied, and their approach was direct. I was often taken aside and asked for a favourite tune. Schubert, for some reason, was most popular here, followed by local ballads of mystical sex. One night I was taken to a boat to play to a Chinese cook, who baked me a bag of biscuits in return. I was also asked for 'On With the Motley' by a Cardiff stoker, and 'Ave Maria' by a party of drunken priests. Another night a young smuggler invited me to serenade his invalid mistress, after which I was rewarded with a wrist-watch which ticked madly for an hour and then exploded in a shower of wheels.

I was half in love with Algeciras and its miniature villainies, and felt I could have stayed on there indefinitely. But part of my plan at that time was still to follow the coast round Spain, so I had to leave it and get on to Málaga.

But first of all there remained the question of Gibraltar, only twenty minutes across the bay. Too near to resist, I thought I'd drop in for the afternoon, present my passport, and have some tea. The old paddle-wheel ferry carried me across the water, smooth as oil and leaping with dolphins, while I enjoyed the boat's brief passage of tax-free drinking, with brandy a penny a glass.

To travellers from England, Gibraltar is an oriental bazaar, but coming in from Spain I found it more like Torquay – the same helmeted police, tall angular women, and a cosy smell of provincial groceries. I'd forgotten how much the atmosphere of home depended on white bread, soap, and soup-squares. Even in this conclave of Maltese–Genoese–Indians, one sensed the pressure of cooking-steam.

My welcome at the colony was not what I expected. The port officials looked me up and down with doubt. The rest of the travellers were passed briskly through the barrier while I was put on one side like an infected apple. Clipped phone calls were made to remoter authorities, warily seeking advice. 'Oh, his passport's all right. No, he's not broke, exactly. Well, you know. Well, sort of . . . Yes . . .'

Finally I was taken in a truck to see the Chief of Police, a worried but kindly man. 'But who *are* you?' he kept saying. 'It's rather difficult here. You must try to realize our position. It doesn't *do*, you know – if you'll forgive my saying so. Nothing personal, you understand . . .'

Anyway, it was agreed that I could stay for a day or two, if I slept in the police station, where they could keep an eye on me. So I was given a clean little cell, a cake of soap, and I played dominoes with the prisoners in the evenings. I wasn't under arrest, exactly; I was allowed out in the daytime so long as I reported back at night. But the restriction was tedious, and after a few days of bacon and eggs, a policeman conducted me back to the frontier.

Leaving Gibraltar was like escaping from an elder brother in charge of an open jail. I crossed the land-bridge at La Linea and climbed up to San Roque – exiled home of the Spanish mayors of Gibraltar. Looking back, I could see the Rock still capped by its cloud, grey as a gun-turret, dripping with mist – while the mainland around lay under the beating sun, jagged with mountains as blue as clinkers. Spain enclosed me once more with its anarchic indifference, asking no discipline but the discipline of manners. I was back on the road, cushioned by its unswept dust, and by my anonymity, which would raise no eyebrows.

It took five days to Málaga, walking the switch-back road between the mountains and the sea, five days pushing on through the dazzling light to a reek of hot seaweed, thyme, and shellfish. I passed through occasional cork-woods smoking with the camp-fires of gypsies squatting by little streams, through scented beanfields rushing with milky water and villages screened under veils of fishnets. Ruined watch-towers, some fluttering with sleepy ravens, marked the headlands along the way, while below them the rocks and the sea lay motionless, locked together in a fume of heat.

Nothing moved inland except the running channels of water laid out by the Moors eight centuries before. The road rippled before me, and distant villages in the mountains shone like pinches of salt on silk. Sometimes, leaving the road, I would walk into the sea and pull it voluptuously over my head, and stand momentarily drowned in the cool blind silence, in a salt-stung neutral nowhere.

When twilight came I slept where I was, on the shore or some rock-strewn headland, and woke to the copper glow of the rising sun coming slowly across the sea. Mornings were pure resurrection, which I could watch sitting up, still wrapped like a corpse in my blanket, seeing the blood-warm light soak back into the Sierras, slowly re-animating their ash-grey cheeks, and feeling the cold of the ground drain away beneath me as the sunrise reached my body.

Then from far out to sea, through the melting mist, would emerge a white-sailed fishing fleet, voiceless, timeless, quiet as air, drifting inshore like bits of paper. But they were often ships of despair; they brought little with them, perhaps a few baskets of poor sardines. The women waited, then turned and went away in silence. The red-eyed fishermen threw themselves down on the sand.

The road to Málaga followed a beautiful but exhausted shore, seemingly forgotten by the world. I remember the names – San Pedro, Estepona, Marbella, and Fuengirola ... They were saltfish villages, thin-ribbed, sea-hating, cursing their place in the sun. At that time one could have bought the whole coast for a shilling. Not Emperors could buy it now.

From its name, I expected Málaga to be a kind of turreted stronghold, half Saracen, half Corsair-pirate. Instead I found an untidy city on the banks of a dried-up river, facing a modern commercial harbour, the streets full of cafés and slummy bars, and its finest building the post office.

I stayed at an inn by the dried-up river, where I shared a courtyard with about a dozen families. Cooking went on all day at their separate fires, in pots mounted on little stones. The reek of fat and charcoal was always in the nostrils, giving one a pungent sense of well-being – though the presence of the fires was more comforting than the food, which was usually a gruel of unmentionable scraps.

But the posada was home, and I bedded down in my place with the mules and wives and children. Honour, not modesty, was what we lived by here, together with a watchful sense of protection. Food and drink might be shared at any time, but each man's goods were sacred – these could be left all day, piled in a heap by the wall, and no one, not even a dog, would touch them.

The courtyard was mostly occupied by mountain people who had come down to the city to sell baskets and cloth – the beautiful hand-woven blankets of the Alpujarras, half Arab, half Mexican in style, decorated with bold abstractions in scarlet and black or sprinkled with geometrical peacocks.

The men of the Alpujarras were wiry as Bulgars, but with hazed out-of-focus eyes, as though being cooped up in the city and temporarily robbed of their distances had also robbed them of their power of sight. The women dressed in stiff garments of black and tan, which gave them the look of Homeric Greeks, while the young girls were the most graceful I'd ever seen, light-footed and nimble as deer, with long floating arms and articulate bodies which turned every movement into a ritual dance. When at rest they would stand, narrow hips thrust sideways, instinctively forming a saddle for child or water-jar, half-shading their eyes with a leaf-brown hand as though still dazzled by the Sierra snows.

Squatting together in the courtyard, on the dung-coated cobbles, we were like a wandering tribe at rest. There would be shouts, cries, snarls, and laughter, mixed with the formal obscenities and blessings. 'Carmencita! Come! – I pollute your mother . . .' 'A pinch of salt? – what grace and sympathy.' 'May my testicles wither, but I agree with you, man . . .' 'God's codpiece, you're very kind.'

Old women, as shrivelled as carob beans, joined in the shouting with tongues like razors; or sat watchfully chewing with that timeless rhythm of the aged, folding their faces like old felt hats. The children ran free, squirming under the horses, half-naked in their grimy vests. The men sat apart, smoking and drinking, mending a sandal or piece of harness, talking ceaselessly together with the dry throaty rattle of pebbles being rolled down a gully.

When it rained I would spend the whole day in their company, sitting under the gallery, watching the heavy sky. The mules steamed gently, the balconies dripped. We drew closer, bored but secure. A woman mended my shirt and folded it up at my feet. Another asked questions about my sisters. A child of eight knelt beside me and peered into the holes of my ears. 'Maria, cuño, do not molest the Frenchman!' Sometimes a half-mad girl stood weeping in the rain while the men teased and taunted her. The huge eyes puckered, melting with slow slack tears. She made no attempt to escape.

When night came, the light-bulbs were dim and ghostly. People sank back into their shadows. Eyes only were visible, touched by the red of the fires, sleepily slatted like the eyes of bats. Blankets were spread on the stones, families stretched out together – the girls in the centre with the younger children. Everyone sighed and settled, curling up on their sides, talk dying with the dying fires. Then nothing would be heard but the occasional shudder of a mule, the sudden wrestling of man and wife.

*

The rains stopped, and I went out again with the fiddle and began playing under the dripping palm trees. Málaga was full of foreigners – effeminate Dutch, sandy Germans, mackintoshed Frenchmen, and English debs. I lazily wandered among them playing tunes of all nations and being rewarded with drinks and money. Most of the visitors, it was clear, were not strangers to each other, but formed a snug expatriate colony, moving from table to table, bar to bar, in constantly changing liaisons.

All, that is, save the English debs, who sat separately, wearing little hats, keeping one eye on the Consul and talking musically of Mummy while sipping glasses of pallid tea. Seeing them under the palms in the warm autumn haze, cool as doves in their tennis white, what hungers they started for their cream-of-wheat textures, tang of toothpaste around the lips, and that particular rainswept grey of their English eyes, only noticeable when abroad.

But it was the young Germans, a complex and mysterious crowd, who outnumbered the rest of the colony. Most seemed to be engaged in inexplicable errands and few were as poor as they looked. But they were friendly enough, and I began to see quite a lot of them in their hideouts behind the cathedral. There was Karl, from Hamburg, for whom I wrote love-letters. (He loved Mrs Lucas, an English widow.) And Heinz, a teacher (said to be a stool-pigeon and agent, though I never gathered for what). There were also three Bavarians who paraded the streets in sackcloth and sandals as though on their way to the scaffold. And Walter and Shulamith, two Jewish refugees, who had walked from Berlin carrying their one-year-old child. I see them today as part of the shadow of the times, and most of them obviously led double lives. They suspected me too, and were always trying to catch me out, hinting at roles I was supposed to be playing. But for all their apparent gaiety and solidarity as a group, they were more suspicious of one another.

The moist hot days began to fill up the city with a kind of amiable lethargy. Gypsies from the river started to rob the markets, and nobody tried to stop them. Children swarmed in the belfries, madly ringing the bells, and nobody interfered. Even the mules stopped working and wandered aimlessly round the streets like sightseers in from the country.

One stifling midday I decided to climb to the Castle to get some air and perhaps a view of the sea. Hovels scattered the hillside, stacked one above the other, and women sat on the doorsteps fanning themselves with cardboard. They flashed bright gold teeth when they saw me coming, and called out friendly invitations. Then one of them beckoned me indoors and offered me her giant daughter, who lay sprawled on a huge brass bed. The sight of the girl and the bed, packed into that tiny room, was like some familiar 'Alice' nightmare. I could only smile and stutter, clutching the doorpost and pretending not to understand. 'Love!' cried the mother, shaking the bed till it rattled, while the girl bounced slowly like a basking whale. I complimented the woman and made some excuse, saying that it was too early in the day. 'Light of heaven!' she cried, 'what else is there to do?' Fortunately, it was impossible even to get into the room.

Much of destitute Málaga, like this hillside slum, lived directly off the dockyard. By day the poor went to the ships for food; at night the sailors came into the town. I met a group of them one evening, straight off a British tanker, four short little battered men, who I saw straggling down a street in single file calling to each other like ships in a fog. 'Where we goin' then, Geordie?' 'Dunno, Jock – bash on.' They were carrying bars of carbolic soap.

I took them to a tavern at the back of the market, where we swapped the soap for bottles of brandy. The local soap, at that time, was like millstone grit, and ships' carbolic was better than money. With the drink in their hands, the sailors relaxed, opened their shirts, and began to beam and sweat. Their talk built up quickly in spurts of dialect; vigorous, clipped, and funny; composed of that fusillade of fantasy, filth, and insult which marked them together as British mates.

Jock, Geordie, Lenny, and Bill; two were from Liverpool, two from Glasgow. They were all older than I was, yet they addressed me with careful courtesy, tempering their oaths as they did so. But their main concern, having come safely ashore, was that they should get enough to drink. So they drank like maniacs, their faces shining with purpose, grabbing bottles, knocking over glasses, mixing brandy, anis, wine, and beer in one frantic obliterating rout.

Semi-paralysis was the target, and there were no middle stages, no songs or tears or fights. Geordie, the stoker, was the first to go, sliding slowly down from his chair. 'Y'know, I loved that woman,' he said from the floor. 'I loved that woman, y'know. Know what I mean? . . .' He clutched the leg of a passing fisherman. 'It's the truth – I loved that woman . . .' Jock and Bill soon joined him, blank-eyed and speechless, falling crumpled across each other. Then it was Lenny's turn. 'I'm on duty,' he said, got up, and walked into the wall.

It was long after midnight when I got them back to their ship and stowed them away in their bunks. I was far gone too, and the watchman let me sleep on board – that is, if he noticed the difference. The next morning the sailors were bright as larks, plunging their heads into buckets of water. 'Up the spout we was, the lot of us.' They gave me a breakfast of mutton chops.

The rain returned, with great black thunderstorms rolling daily in from the sea. So I exchanged the exposure of the open courtyard at the inn for a six-bedded room upstairs, where for a peseta a night one could sleep in damp grey sheets under a bent and dripping roof. My companions were artists from a travelling circus, temporarily stranded by the weather, including an asthmatic ventriloquist who talked in his sleep (and ours), four dwarfs who shared one bed, and a white-whiskered bird-tamer who slept by himself, fully clothed, in top hat and boots.

Another inmate was Avelino, a student from Ronda, who occupied a dark little room down the passage. He was a tense young man, with the soft eyes of a lemur and a tormented blue-furred face. He used to creep nervously about on the tips of his toes, fingering a rosary made of plumstones.

Perhaps he saw in me someone lost to heaven, a sorry exile without god or country; anyway, I soon became the object of his inexhaustible attention, a chosen burden for charity.

Tirelessly, speechless, and self-effacing, for a week he was my day-long shadow. If I was eating in a café, I'd see him watching me from the doorway, and when I left I'd find that he'd paid the bill. If I was fiddling in the street, he'd march silently up and down, dropping pennies into my hat as he passed. If I was writing in my room he'd suddenly steal up behind me and place a lighted cigarette between my lips.

There were also the discreet little gifts I'd find laid on my bed: a bunch of flowers, some tobacco, a shirt; and then one morning, a poem, neatly pinned to the pillow, freshly written in a copper-plate hand: 'He sleeps, the young man, far from his home and people, forgetting his doleful life, not knowing that tomorrow his music will be torn by the winds and scattered above the rooftops.'

At the end of the week, Avelino broke his silence, saying that he'd worked out a plan for our future. He would start a school, and I would join him. He'd teach Ethics and Philosophy; and I, English and Art – and so take my proper place in the world. 'You would wear a suit and cravat, and walk proudly in the streets, and bow to your friends and call "Adios". And they would reply "Adios", and give you respects. It would be cultured and very gracious . . .'

His voice suddenly faded. He tore a crucifix from his shirt, covered it with kisses, and fled from the room. They told me next morning that he'd gone back to Ronda, having given his money and clothes to the porter.

During my last days in Málaga I was faced by a near disaster – my violin suddenly broke in my hands. Over-exposure to the sun seemed to have weakened the joints, and the instrument simply fell to pieces.

Friends at the posada did what they could to help, melting glue in their cooking pots. The violin, which by now looked like a mess of chicken bones, was reassembled and the joints reset. For several days it lay strapped-up under my bed, rolled in sacking and weighted with stones. But the joints wouldn't hold, and as soon as the strings were tightened, the whole thing fell apart again.

I was anxious. Without the violin I knew of no other way to live, and I would soon be out of money. It had all been too easy, wherever I happened to be, scraping out a few odd tunes for a meal; now I wandered round Málaga in a kind of daze, as though I'd lost the use of my hands. There seemed only one thing to be done – join the crew of some ship, leave Spain, and perhaps go back home.

Fortunately, this wasn't necessary. A liner arrived in the bay carrying five hundred British tourists, and I set up as a guide, arranging for cut-rate taxis, English teas, and excursions to the hills. I was doing quite well, and thought this might see me through the winter, when the local guides ganged up on me. If I didn't go back to my fiddle-playing, they said, they would throw me into the harbour.

So I was stuck again. But another stroke of luck saved me. I met a young German from the School of Languages. Did I know anyone, by chance, who wanted a violin? He had one he didn't need. It belonged to his girl-friend and she'd run off with a Swede. He gave it to me for nothing.

10

Almuñécar

As December closed in I decided to hole-up for the winter at Almuñécar, sixty miles east of Málaga. It was a tumbling little village built on an outcrop of rock in the midst of a pebbly delta, backed by a bandsaw of mountains and fronted by a grey strip of sand which some hoped would be an attraction for tourists.

There were two hotels, one of them run by a Swiss, who offered me hospitality in return for certain odd-job duties, which included helping in the kitchen, mending doors and windows, and playing the violin in the saloon at night. The hotel was new, but had been built on the beach, so that the waves broke over the windows, and already the fine concrete walls were beginning to crumble and the proprietor was drawn with worry.

Herr Brandt must have been something of a pioneer on the coast, but he'd arrived twenty years too soon, and I found him on the verge of a nervous breakdown, convinced that his investment was at the mercy of anarchists. He was always washing his hands, then washing the soap, and changing all the locks on the doors. But he was resourceful, almost desperate, at running his business, and while the neighbouring hotel shut down for the winter he was determined to keep his going, turning its booming rooms into a centre for the local gentry, for musical teas, buffet suppers, and dancing.

So I was enrolled on the staff and encouraged to get some new clothes. Then I was given a room in the attic with a Jewish boy from Cologne – 'Don Jacobo', as the housemaids called him.

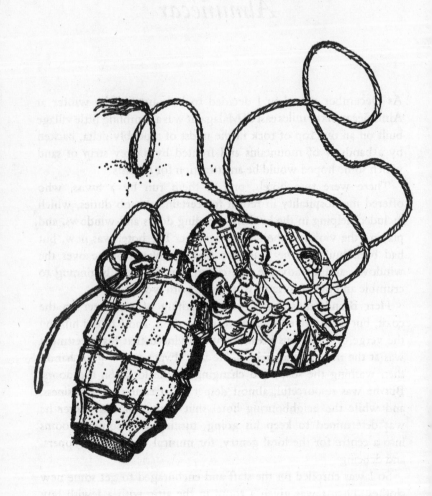

Jacobo was in his twenties, short and tubby, with a Hitler moustache and a rubbery bounce. Already bald at the crown, he had a tuft of hair on his forehead which rose and fell with emotion, and had to be plastered in place with heavy slicks of oil and sometimes even with lard. He was a boon to Herr Brandt, acting as interpreter, tout, hotel secretary, boot-boy, and gigolo. He also played the accordion which, together with my fiddle, made up the hotel band.

Jacobo spoke English with slapdash gusto, worrying the words like a terrier. The first time I met him he was on his hands and knees, pawing frantically through a pile of laundry.

'This morning,' he said, 'I am having many disgusts with the washwife – she has forlorn me my new chemise. And tonight, you see, I was having a girl from the village – she was coming from suppertime.'

He knew everyone in Almuñécar and everyone liked him. He could be convincing in several languages. He had a kind of liquorice charm, both yielding and elastic, and in spite of his looks was considered a dandy.

I remember being woken late one night, soon after I arrived, to find him powdering his head in the mirror. He was dressed in a long blue gown, like a Chinaman, and smelt richly of exotic oils. Seeing he'd disturbed me, he gave a fat little giggle and laid a finger along his lips.

'Say nothing, my friend. I am expecting downstairs. Anybody is waiting for me in this hotel.'

Anybody, it seemed, was a widow from Paris, who'd come for the day and stayed three weeks, during which we spent a succession of broken nights, with Jacobo on call like a doctor.

Each morning we practised together on the roof, working up a selection of musical tit-bits. Jacobo was a nimble accordionist and played the instrument with windy pleasure; it seemed well suited to his pneumatic passions. Quite soon we'd developed a reasonable repertoire, enough to satisfy Herr Brandt's demands – operatic arias for the tea-rooms, serenades for the evening, pasodobles and tangos for dancing.

The Sunday before Christmas we gave our first Grand Concert, but this was ruined by exploding wine-bottles, a series of reverberating incidents due to faulty supplies which put our audience in disarray We had somewhat more success with our weekend dances, which were held in a kind of white-tiled washhouse downstairs. These were formal affairs, full of suppressed sexuality, but controlled by rigid Andalusian manners. The chaperoned girls sat on display round the walls, pretty as coloured paper, quivering to the music with butterfly vibrations which soon brought the young men in from the night. Approaches could only be made through a watchful third party – mother, brother, or aunt – but the dances, though stilted, concealed much emotional grappling, and for a while were the height of fashion.

Almuñécar itself, built of stone steps from the delta, was grey, almost gloomily Welsh. The streets were steep, roughly paved, and crossed by crude little arches, while the square was like a cobbled farmyard. Part of the castle was a cemetery, part of the Town Hall a jail, but past glories were eroding fast.

In the days of the Moors, Almuñécar had been a front-line fortress standing high in the mouth of the delta, guarding the rich river valley which wound up through the Sierra towards the Islamic paradise of Granada. Several centuries later, it was also the point of farewell for the defeated caliphs when they were driven from Spain, and a wave-battered cross standing on an offshore rock celebrated the spot where they sailed away.

Apart from a few merchants, landowners, and officials from Granada, everybody now in the village was poor, and the ruined castle on the hill seemed to serve as a perpetual reminder that not they, but someone else, had conquered. The peasants had only two ways of living, and both were loaded against them – the sugar canes and the offshore fishing.

The strip of dirty grey sand dividing the land from the sea was a frontier between two kinds of poverty. The sugar canes in the delta, rustling dryly in the wind, were a deception even at harvest time, for the best they could offer was a few weeks' work and in the meantime the men stood idle.

But the land was rich compared with the sea, which nourished only a scattering of poor sardines. There were no boats or equipment for deep-sea fishing, the village was chained to the offshore wastes, shallow, denuded, too desperately fished to provide anything but constant reproaches.

I remember the cold red mornings, just before sunrise, when the fishermen came down to the beach, padding softly through the mist in their rope-soled shoes, or bare-footed, with feet like ink. Two boats would put out into the sullen sea, indigo shadows against the dawn, while the men rowed madly, dipping their long oars deep and calling hoarsely to one another.

At least thirty more men would remain waiting ashore, watching the rowers with screwed-up eyes. The boats were racing the fish, paying the net out fast in an attempt to encircle what few there were. Painfully they spread it across the sea in a long and bobbing line, then turned and rowed back, dragging the two loose ends – which was when the men on the beach went to work.

In two teams, trousers rolled, they splashed into the waves and seized each end of the sagging net. Then for an hour they hauled in, panting their way up the beach, bent double, clawing the sand with their toes, the leaders running back to join the end of the line, each man silent, his face to the ground. The two long files of fishermen trudging out of the water might have been coolies or Egyptian slaves, slowly drawing behind them the weight of a net which encircled almost a quarter of a mile of sea.

It was labour without mercy, dignity, or reward, and the men hauled at the net without hope, each one grunting and straining in the horizontal position of a beast, his face to the buttocks of the man in front. It was a grinding hour of expended strength, too mindless even for comradeship. When the cod-end at last had been dragged ashore, the men gathered round it in silence, while the few kilos of sardines, a heap of dirty silver, died flickering in the sand.

The auctioneer arrived, unshaven, in his pyjamas, and a dismal price was set. Perhaps fifty pesetas – half to the owner of the boats and the rest between forty men. Sometimes the price was so low that no sale was made, and the men divided the fish between them, slowly counting them out into forty little heaps, a sandy fistful for each man's family.

Set against this background, the hotel on the beach was a tawdry interjection, out of scale and taste. I continued to work and sleep there, and eat my meals, but spent as much time as I could in the village.

It had little to offer, except for the people, who had all the time in the world. The little cave-like shops had almost nothing to sell save sandals and sunflower seeds; strangely enough there was a bookshop, though it only had four books – Milton, Homer, Andreyev, and Machado.

Physically, the villagers showed the strong Arab blood which the Catholic conquest had been unable to dispel – the old women stark and black as desert matriarchs, their bodies loaded with unhealthy fat; the men small and bony, like dried-up birds, perched moodily round the edge of the sea. The men spent much of the day just staring at their hands and sucking cigarettes made of beech leaves – a tongue-blistering smoke flavoured with the juice of sugar cane and some hot harsh root from the hills. The only people with jobs seemed to be the village girls, most of them in service to the richer families, where for a bed in a cupboard and a couple of pounds a year they were expected to run the whole house and keep the men from the brothels.

As elsewhere on the coast, the villagers were infected with fatalism, a kind of subdued and deliberate apathy. Only sometimes in the eyes of the younger men did one see the violent hopes they lived for. The children, on the other hand, were a different race, inhabiting a brief but confident gaiety – beautiful verminous creatures with strong white teeth and diseased red-lidded eyes. Prancing about in their rags, snatching what food they could get, they never whined but lived on charm, were pampered, indulged, and smothered with easy love, and punished only for rude manners to strangers.

The bad weather came, the hills disappeared in mist, and the village began to look more like Wales than ever. Gutters splashed and gurgled, people crept about in sacking, and the rain fell solidly, like cold wet lead.

There were no clients in the hotel, no boats on the sea, so I went like everybody else to the bars. Here I'd find Manolo the waiter, Felipe the chef, and 'Gambas' the crippled porter, and always a group of young fishermen with wet sand on their feet, and a few labourers down from the farms. We drank crude brandy mixed with boiling water, often a cheaper drink than wine, and ate morunos – little dishes of hot pig flesh, cut from the fat and stewed in sauce.

Mostly we talked, with the rain drumming the windows and the drinks steaming along the bar. Conversations were oblique, full of hints and proverbs, well guarded by careful custom. Figures in authority were never exactly named but referred to in cipher, usually by their sexual parts. Opinions and judgements were also cloaked in metaphor, phrases of folklore dipped from a common well.

'He who sleeps with a dog gets up with fleas.'

'Horns are visible to every man but the wearer.'

Or when the barmaid, carrying washing, stumbled on to an old man's lap: 'God always sends nuts to the toothless.'

During those cold soggy days, ducking from bar to bar, one met the usual town eccentrics. There was Manolo's brother, who always carried a pebble in his mouth because it prolonged the taste of the brandy And Jorge, who'd trained a sparrow to sip other men's drinks and then carry them to his mouth by the beakful. When the bird died, said Jorge, he would weep weep, weep. Every man in the bar agreed. There was also Pau, a young fisherman who was teaching himself to write by using the tavern wall

as a copybook, but who sometimes exploded with frustration and
beat the wall with his fist till his knuckles ran with blood.

Occasionally a day turned unhealthy, when idleness and ennui
led to an outburst of mirthless riot. Then the village idiot would
be seized, and strapped to a chair, and tormented until he screamed.
Wine would be poured on his head, or a man would hold him by
the ears while another spread his face with mustard. After a session
of this everyone looked flushed and relaxed. Even the Civil Guard
would come in to watch.

At other times the men would grow quiet and gentle, standing
with arms round each other's shoulders, someone singing in a
voice that seemed to come from far away, a muted falsetto cry. In
spite of our long hours in the bars there was almost no drunkenness,
perhaps due to the spacious rhythm of our drinking. But being
less used to the brandy, it would sometimes hit me hard, till
I found myself staring at the room in wonder. I'd see a gypsy
come in wearing a great red mouth as though he'd bitten into a
harvest moon. Such were moments of that pure, almost virginal
intoxication, to which all subsequent drinking tries in vain to
return.

Manolo the waiter protected me when I was drunk and
humoured me like a grandfather. One night, I remember, during
a particularly flashy thunderstorm, the sky spitting with electric
sparks, he telephoned the lighthouse and asked them to stop fool-
ing about, saying the Englishman didn't like it . . .

Manolo was about thirty years old, handsome as a playboy, but
moody and idealistic. He was the leader of a group of fishermen
and labourers into which I was gradually admitted. We met in a
pink-washed room at the back of the bar and talked about the
world to come – a world without church or government or
army, where each man alone would be his private government.

It was a simple, one-syllable view of life, as black and white as
childhood, and as Manolo talked, the fishermen listened, bobbing
their heads up and down like corks. Their fathers had never heard
or known such promises. Centuries of darkness stood behind them.

Now it was January 1936, and these things were suddenly think-able, possible, even within their reach.

But first, said Manolo, there must be death and dissolution; much had to be destroyed and cleared away. Felipe, the chef, who liked food and girls, was the pacifier, preaching love and reason. No guns, he said; they dishonoured the flesh; and no destruction, which dishonoured the mind. Everyone knew, all the same, that there were now guns in the village which hadn't been there before.

Life must start clean, Manolo said, if only for the children's sake. Not till the tyrants had been destroyed, and their infection burned from the ground, could love and freedom etcetera . . . His apocalyptic phrases fell like hammer strokes – but every so often the spirit went out of him. Then he would double up at the table as if in sudden pain, beating his fists together. 'They'll stop us,' he'd groan. 'They'll bring in the army. We haven't got a chance.'

Behind the radiant plans and surges of optimism hovered this sick and desperate disquiet. All of them seemed to feel it at some time or other, and it made their meetings even more tragic. In spite of the naïve abstractions, these were councils of war, aimed at the local enemy they knew. Sometimes Manolo would come in with his pockets bulging with pamphlets, which he'd spread care-fully around the table. They were crudely printed, on ash-grey paper, but might have been tablets handed down from the Prophets. Each man would pore over them, stroking the letters or slowly spelling out the words. The fraternal greetings in scarlet, the drawings of heroic workers with banners, were strange new myths in their lives. So was the spirited advice on the reorganizing of farms and fisheries once victory was won. Yet they knew, as they read, that this was no easy paradise. The village would burn for it first.

'Lorenzo,' said Manolo, with a touch of shame in his voice. 'We are going to need the help of all the world.'

Winter went out with the 'kissing of Christ's feet', preceded by a

sombre procession with torches. The black-edged notices had gone
up around the village, jostling the grafitti for revolution – 'Besapies
al Santissimo Cristo de la Buena Muerte en su Capilla de la
Patrona.' Sacred Christ of the Good Death, in the chapel on the
hill, in a cleft of rock just below the castle.

The women and girls came wailing through the streets,
stumbling barefooted over the slaty cobbles, bearing the terrible
image upon their shoulders like a drowned man brought from the
sea. The Christ was carved from old wood the colour of
moonlight, transfixed in a rigor of ugly death, his wounds wetly
shining with fresh red paint, his face cavernous and decomposed.

The women took it in turns, bent double like crones and gasping
under their load, jerking the awkward figure round the narrow
corners while its nailed arms scraped along the walls. Most of the
men, it seemed, had stayed away that night; this was an occasion
for female mourning. The pitch-pine torches dripped, and bubbled, and fires of brushwood dotted the hill. A high-pitched wailing possessed the village, threading moodily among the houses,
while the flames of the torches threw up primitive shadows, giant
flickerings of garish light, covering the women's faces with
convulsive masks, half sorrow, half grinning gargoyle.

I followed the procession till it reached the chapel, where a stern
young priest was waiting. The Crucifix was propped among stones
and surrounded by flares. The women went down on their knees.
Then the priest addressed us, saying how unique were the faithful
and how damned the materialists of today. There were cries of
'Piedad!' 'Señor!', and 'Salvame!', and lilies were tied to the feet of
the Christ. He towered woodenly above us in the light of the
torches, his toes already shining from the lips of the women.

In February came the Election, with a victory for the socialists.
This was not deliverance, merely a letting up of confusion. An
end to years of listening and waiting· for something to happen.
Suddenly everything was out in the open.

A Popular Front, they said: a People's Government at last.

Manolo went about with his face lit up. The peasants and fisher-men stood all day in the plaza, talking more openly now, but tense. The result of the election had given them power, but it was still too hot to grasp. The news, in fact, was not victory for anyone but a declaration of war.

Almuñécar, like Spain, was split down the middle, and the two sides drew apart, on guard. Little happened at first – the fishermen took over a boat, the peasants commandeered some land. Meanwhile the owners lay low and sat whispering in the casino, peering through the curtained windows, and waiting.

Spring came in with a rush of snow-water from the Sierras which carried a long red stain out to sea. A young girl died and was taken round in an open coffin on a last visit from house to house. I remember her smooth quiet face, as green as moss, and the cotton wool in her nostrils like puffs of frozen breath.

A kind of brilliant green film suddenly broke over the fields, sheets of wild flowers covering the dried-up hills – orchids spiking the dust, rocks crowned with anemones, almond blossom exploding like popcorn. The uneasiness in the village was part of this spring, like a rush of blood to the head, bringing with it a curious relax-ation of behaviour and manners, a new freedom among the sexes.

Jacobo and I still organized the hotel dances, but their flavour was different now. Gone were the stiff and sweltering little marriage markets, with their chaperones and wax-haired suitors; now the floor was commanded by young fishermen and labourers, casual in sky-blue shirts, who swung their cotton-dressed girls through the stamping fox-trots in an embrace of assured possession.

Herr Brandt, more jumpy and nervous than ever, read the signs and admitted them free. They drank the cheap fizzy beer rather than the high-toned sherry, and Manolo served them with comradely pride. Together with the chef and the porter he more or less ran the hotel now, and treated Herr Brandt with scrupulous insolence, too proud to rob him, but making it clear all the same that these new clients were the only ones that mattered.

So the boys and girls of Almuñécar used our rackety dances to explore their new-found liberties. During the warm spring evenings they clung earnestly together, as though intimacy was a new invention, dancing, holding hands, or walking in couples along the shore, arms entwined, watching each other's faces.

There were also other freedoms. Books and films appeared, unmutilated by Church or State, bringing to the peasants of the coast, for the first time in generations, a keen breath of the outside world. For a while there was a complete lifting of censorship, even in newspapers and magazines. But most of all it was the air of carnality, the brief clearing away of taboos, which seemed to possess the village – a sudden frank, even frantic, pursuit of lust, bred from a sense of impending peril.

Early one morning I got word from Manolo asking me to meet him in a bar. I found him head down in a corner with two comrades from Málaga, diminutive and clerk-like men.

'Lorenzo,' said Manolo. 'We want you to do something for us.'

The strangers looked at me doubtfully.

'If he can do it, that is.'

'Of course he can do it,' said Manolo. 'He has legs like a bull. Mountains are nothing to him.'

It was simple enough; they wanted me to take an innocent-sounding message to a farmer up in the hills, telling him when to expect a delivery of seed-potatoes – in other words, hand-grenades.

'You're always walking about,' Manolo said dryly. 'Of course you'll be seen, but no one will wonder.'

I said I'd go, so they drew me a Red Indian map, dotted with rocks and streams and haystacks, with a series of arrows leading through fishbone forests to the lonely farm on the hill. It was about eight miles inland, at the foot of the Sierra; somewhere I'd always wanted to go. Manolo gave me a half-bottle of coñac, and I set out through the fresh spring landscape, which was full of the sound of gushing water.

The journey took about three hours and I saw no one on the way, only congregations of dishevelled storks, who kept dropping out of the sky like wind-blown umbrellas and stumbling about in disorder. The map was all right as far as it went, but suddenly the path petered out in a bog. I could see the farm just ahead, but found there was a flooded river between us which Manolo hadn't bothered to mention.

At that moment a young man crept out of breast-high reeds as though he'd been expecting me. He gave me a quick sharp look, then shouted across the river:

'From Almuñécar! Send Ignacio!'

I saw the farm door open and a woman run out. Then a horseman appeared and galloped down the hill. Without drawing rein, he reached the bank of the river, plunged in, and swam across towards me.

Horse and rider for a moment seemed to sink from sight, but the horse swam low and fast, his wet mouth gaping with enormous teeth, his nostrils snorting for breath. When he reached our side he rose magnificently from the water and came floundering among the reeds, while the rider slid slowly out of the saddle and stood grinning in the mud.

'Ignacio,' he said. 'At your service. Do what I say and you won't get wet.'

He turned the horse round, helped me on to its back, and told me to kneel on the wooden saddle. Then he leapt up in front of me, straddling the horse's neck, and advised me to hang on to his belt.

The horse bucked and staggered among the rushes, then appeared to step into a bottomless hole. We sank deep in the river, which seemed as wide as the Congo, and headed back for the other side. The flood raced around us, tossing up pale green scum, and little waves whipped over the saddle. My boots filled with water and I felt my knees grow cold – it was like floating on top of a cupboard.

The farmer's wife was standing on the opposite bank, and she gave me her apron to dry myself. Then we walked up to the house where the farmer himself was waiting, a stiff old man in a high-crowned hat. 'Blasco Vallegas,' he said, removing his hat for a moment and holding it across his stomach. I gave him Manolo's message, at which he nodded briefly and asked me to stay to lunch.

First he showed me the farm – a structure of uncut boulders packed with clay and thatched with bulrushes.

'I built it myself,' said the farmer, 'with these very hands – when I married, forty years ago. My wife brought the stones from the Sierra on her head. Apart from herself, it was all she brought.'

He led me into the kitchen, where we sat on little chairs and drank wine out of leather cups. The room was a mazy violence of light and shade which dazzled the eyes at first, but slowly the jigsaw began to fit together and the details reveal themselves, The floor was of trodden earth, the furniture shaped by axes, and chickens perched blinking on the backs of the chairs. A pig slept in one corner, and a girl knelt in another burning her head with a lighted candle.

'My daughter,' said Blasco. 'She molests herself.'

The girl moaned 'Ay!' as though in agreement.

'She is curing a headache or some such trouble. She weighs heavily upon us all.'

He shrugged her away and poured me another cup of wine, then went to a wooden chest by the wall. He rummaged inside for a moment and returned with a pig-skin bag which he emptied upon the table.

'Look!' he said, sorting out the objects with his fingers and separating two of them. One was a small bronze figure of a naked goddess, and the other a rusty iron bracelet. He said he'd turned them up ploughing, together with other things now lost, including the jewelled tooth of a 'Moroccan Princess'.

'Do you know how long we have lived in these hills?' he asked. 'Since the very sun was made. Since before kings and altars, or the Virgin herself was a mother. Since there were leopards in the caves . . .'

Vallegas didn't look like a patriarch, he was too thin and dried, but he managed to talk like one.

'Everything you see around you has come from these,' he said, holding up his hands, then striking his loins. There was the farm, and his five grown sons out working – whom I would see when it was time to eat – Ignacio with the horses, Curron down by the river, and three others up on the hill. His daughters were gracious, too – 'Except that one with the headache.' He referred to his wife as his breastbone.

But although he'd made everything, he owned nothing here – forty years working the land for others. Tomorrow might be different, he said, squinting out of the window. Tomorrow, when the 'potatoes' came.

Rocking quietly in his chair, the old man seemed to be talking to himself, recalling riots that had stirred the past – ploughing up derelict land in times of famine, soldiers coming to destroy the crops, Civil Guards on horses the size of elephants riding down the women and children. Starvation, martyrdom, jail, massacre, the slaughter of animals, homesteads burning ... The soldiers, he thought, would be on their side now; and the Civil Guard with the Devil, as usual.

As he talked, he sat stroking a piece of painted glass, a miniature portrait of the Holy Family, which he said had been tied round his neck the day he was born and which he'd carried with him ever since.

When the sons returned, we sat down to eat, and the little kitchen was crammed like a horsebox. The mother served up a pot of migas stew – a thick porridge of maize sprinkled with dried sardines, filling, but tasting of sack-cloth. Blasco ate in silence, with toothless attention, his face working like a tent in the wind, while the sons lowered their heads and ravenously gobbled, plugging their mouths with bread. It was a serious meal without conversation, the jug of wine passing formally among us. Meanwhile the women waited in the background; the mother squatting by the stove and tossing scraps of food to the pig: the girl standing behind her father, patiently watching his plate, her forehead blackened by candlesmoke.

As soon as the meal was over the men relaxed, grunting and stretching their legs. Ignacio spat on his hands and cleaned his sister's face. Another took a gun and went out to shoot partridges.

'There are many partridges here,' the youngest boy told me. 'Also rabbits, wild pig, and deer. But we may not touch the deer. They belong to the Duke.'

'To who?' barked the father.

The boy paused, open-mouthed, swallowed, and began again.

'We may touch the deer – if we can find them,' he said. 'They belong to anybody now, I think.'

The weeks leading towards summer were hot and steely, and except for the radios in the bars, crackling with political speeches, the village seemed entirely cut off from the world. The coast road to Málaga lay empty in the sun. Few people went anywhere, the air of listening returned, and the mountains moved closer like a ring of bayonets. A slow brew of expectation simmered over the houses, raising poisonous bubbles that exploded every so often in little outbreaks of irrelevant violence.

First the ice plant was sabotaged and the power station blown up – both of which belonged to a marquis. In spite of the inconvenience, everyone seemed to enjoy these gestures, and the whiff of dynamite was considered a tonic. A number of shops were looted, their windows broken, and the word BOICOT painted across the doors; a few stray priests were insulted in the streets, and a store of wine barrels rolled into the sea. Next, a group of old women went to the house of the tax collector and tossed his furniture into the street, after which they piled him and his wife on top of a cart and drove them out of town.

Then one morning the church was set on fire. 'They've done it at last!' cried Manolo. We hurried through the streets, which were full of the sweet scent of woodsmoke, and joined the villagers crowding the square. The church tower was blazing like a cardboard box, and most of the watchers seemed in a state of rapture.

I remember the faces of the fishermen, awed but beaming, and their satisfied grunts at each burst of flame. Sensing the mood of their fathers, the children ran wild, bombarding the church with showers of stones. Only the women stayed silent, squinting sideways at their men, waiting for some stroke of doom to fall.

A week later came Feast Day, and a quick change of heart. The smoke-blackened church was filled with lilies. The images of Christ and the Virgin were brought out into the sunlight and loaded as usual on to the fishermen's backs. Anonymous, invisible, hidden beneath the embroidered drapes, they shuffled once more up and down the streets, sweating, bent double beneath their canopied burdens, the Church's traditional porters.

As the procession moved by, a peasant tore off his cap and threw himself on his knees with outspread arms.

'Holy Mother, Maria, intercede with your Son! Queen of Heaven, strike me dead! Blessed be the Virgin of Almuñécar, mother of the seas. Do not forsake us. Live for ever.'

It was a day of tears and breast-beating, a day of contrition. The invincible Christ had risen again – the private Christ of Almuñécar, scorched and defiled, yet returning to forgive his sons. Rocking, swaying, borne on rafts of wild iris, the holy images passed in triumph, preceded by the plump, red-bonneted, skirted priests, and the young girls with their trays of petals.

All was normal again. A brass band played. Rich and poor mixed their cries together. The peasants knelt with bowed heads or raised their contorted faces. 'Maria, salvame!'

Profanity, sacrilege, had been a passing madness. This was the Faith as it had always been. Then, a few days later, the church was fired again, and this time burned to a shell.

It was now the middle of May, and tension increased in the village as the news from Madrid grew more threatening and vague. To the peasants of Almuñécar, the visionary promises of February seemed to have dried up in the heat. There were strikes, parades, shows of proletarian force, boys and girls marching in coloured shirts, arms raised in salute, clenched fists and slogans, painted banners and challenging speeches.

When there was a strike it was total, enforced by the police, and the fishermen picketed the sea. One saw rich old women dragging their laundry to the river, or queueing up at the village wells. At the hotel, the chambermaids sat gossiping in the sun while the chef stayed home with his wife; Herr Brandt did the cooking, wrapped in Manolo's apron, and the guests slept in unmade beds.

Each day more peasants came in from the country, massing in the square to be on hand for trouble. Many of them brought guns slung over their shoulder, sticking out of their waistbands, or tied to the saddles of donkeys – flintlocks, pistols, and old rusty muskets which might have been saved from the Peninsular War.

The split village now emerged in clearer focus and its two factions declared themselves, confronting each other at last in black and white – labelled for convenience, 'Fascist' or 'Communist'. The 'Fascists' seemed ready to accept the name, this being frankly what they aspired to, with the Falange already organized as a fighting group, a swaggering spearhead of upperclass vengeance, whose crude fascist symbols, Italian-inspired, were now appearing on walls and doorways.

The 'Communist' label, on the other hand, was too rough and ready, a clumsy reach-me-down which properly fitted no one. The farm labourers, fishermen, and handful of industrial workers all had local but separate interests. Each considered his struggle to be far older than communism, to be something exclusively Spanish, part of a social perversion which he alone could put right by reason of his roots in this particular landscape.

In fact, I don't remember meeting an official Communist in Almuñécar – though 'communism' was a word in the bars. Manolo, who was a leader, had no political status at all, but was a romantic anarchist of his own invention. The local flag of revolution was the Republican flag, the flag of the elected government. The peasants strung it like a banner across the Town Hall balcony and painted their allegiance beneath it in red: 'We swear to defend this bandera with the last drop of our blood.' Sombre and ominous words.

Yet the government they supported must have seemed remote to many, being composed entirely of middle-class politicians – without a Communist, Anarchist, or even a Socialist anywhere in its cabinet. The peasants looked to this government because their hopes lay with it, hopes they thought to realize for the first time in centuries, an opportunity to shift some of the balances which had so long weighed against them, more than against anyone else in Europe.

Spain was a wasted country of neglected land – much of it held by a handful of men, some of whose vast estates had scarcely been reduced or reshuffled since the days of the Roman Empire. Peasants could work this land for a shilling a day, perhaps for a third of the year, then go hungry. It was this simple incongruity that they hoped to correct; this, and a clearing of the air, perhaps some return of dignity, some razing of the barriers of ignorance which still stood as high as the Pyrenees.

A Spanish schoolmaster at this time knew less of the outside world than many a shepherd in the days of Columbus. Now it was hoped that there might be some lifting of this intolerable darkness, some freedom to read and write and talk. Men hoped that their wives might be freed of the triple trivialities of the Church – credulity, guilt, and confession; that their sons might be craftsmen rather than serfs, their daughters citizens rather than domestic whores, and that they might hear the children in the evening coming home from fresh-built schools to astonish them with new facts of learning.

All this could be brought about now by an act of their government and the peaceful process of law. There was nothing to stop it. Except for that powerful minority who would rather the country first bled to death.

★

June came in full blast, with the heat bouncing off the sea as from a buckled sheet of tin. All day in the bars the radios spat and crackled – violence in Madrid, demonstrations in Valencia, strikes and riots in Barcelona.

I met Manolo in the street on his way back from a meeting, and he laid a shaking hand on my shoulder.

'Are you going?'

'Where?'

'Home to your country.'

'No.'

'The roads are still open if you want to go.'

That morning a group of Falangists in the neighbouring village walked into a bar and shot five fishermen. The murderers, wearing arm-bands, escaped in a car to Granada. Almuñécar lay silent, like a shuttered camp.

In the afternoon I walked out into the country with Jacobo. Daylight nightingales were singing by the river. The air was brassy, thunderous, and only a thread of brown water ran trickling down the river bed. Some girls we knew had been gathering poppies in the field, and now they came down the path towards us, walking slowly in the heat, the red flowers wilting at their breasts, looking as though their bodies had been raked by knives.

An hour or so later we returned by another path and found two children standing under the bridge. They stood stiffly, holding hands, staring at the figure of a man who lay sprawled on the river bank. We recognized him as a local Falangist, a boy of about twenty, whose father had once been mayor. He had been shot through the head, and lay staring back at the children, flies gathering around his mouth.

11

War

It started in the middle of July. There were no announcements, no newspapers, just a whispering in the street and the sound of a woman weeping.

I was now living near the church, in the house of an expatriate English writer, who'd lent me a room overlooking the bay, and as I went out that morning I saw a woman lying face-down on the pavement, beating the ground with her hands. A group of neighbours stood by, making no attempt to move her – her attendants rather than comforters. They said she was weeping for her son – a young conscript in Morocco, who to her was already dead.

Down at Manolo's bar he told me what he knew; a see-saw of fact and fantasy. There had been anti-government uprisings in the garrisons of Spanish Morocco – at Melilla, Tetuan, and Larache. On the other hand, said Manolo, there was nothing to worry about, the situation was under control . . . General Francisco Franco, 'the butcher of the Asturian miners', had flown from the Canaries to lead the rebels. There were reports of other risings in Saragossa, Madrid, and Seville . . . But, no, the government had put them down. Franco himself was dead, had been brought down in the sea, had been arrested, assassinated, shot . . . Even so, Moorish troops were pouring into the south of Spain . . . But they would be slaughtered before they could advance an inch . . .

Indeed, there was no firm news. The café radios were silent, or jammed, or stridently at odds with each other. People gathered in the streets, staring up at the sky as though expecting to see some great

proclamation written across it. And as always – impelled by the oldest instinct of the countryside – the fields emptied and peasants poured into the village, bringing their wives and children, their sheep and goats, and settling them down under the castle walls. Some of the men brought guns, but most were unarmed. They crowded the plaza, simply waiting to be used, standing with their backs to the Town Hall, shoulder to shoulder with the fishermen, as though ready to defend it with their bodies. There was no authority yet; theirs was just a defensive laager drawn up spontaneously in the face of the unknown. Meanwhile Manolo, and El Gato (the leader of one of the new-formed unions) started to organize some kind of militia.

The police had suddenly disappeared and the village was on its own: government supporters facing the enemy within. A round of searches began among the houses of suspected 'fascists'. Manolo took men to barricade the coastal road. Then in the afternoon there arrived the first car from Málaga, driving fast and smothered with dust. It was stopped at the road-block and Manolo's bayonets surrounded it, pricking open the doors and windows. A couple of white-faced young men were hurried off to jail, while rifles and grenades were dug out of the boot. Later, a Frenchman drove up in a battered Fiat with a white flag tied on the roof. He said half Málaga was in flames and that there was fighting in the streets. He didn't know which side was winning, or even where he was going, but he showed us a score of bullet holes in the back of his car.

Night brought more rumours, smuggled in with the dark, along the coast road and down from the hills. Granada was held by the rebels, and so was our neighbour, Altofaro. The fate of Málaga was still unknown. Meanwhile, our confused little fortress seemed to be caught between the mountains and the sea, with fires spreading on either side.

The militia were busy that night, determined that there should be no rising in Almuñécar. The house-to-house searching of suspects began to reveal the little caches of arms so carefully hidden for months – packed in wine barrels in cellars, hung in baskets down wells, in cupboards, in clocks, up chimneys. The loot was piled in the plaza and guarded by El Gato's militia – the best arms they were to get in the war.

A wave of summary arrests also began that evening. Elegant and resigned in their lacy white shirts, the young 'señoritos' sat waiting in the paseo. When the patrols approached them, they rose casually to their feet, crushed out their cigarettes and strolled away under guard. The priest was rounded up too, and I saw him brought flustered from his house and led off to jail with the others. Few of the local 'fascists' attempted either to escape or hide. The hour was too late for that.

'There was a plot,' said Manolo in the bar that night. 'Now we have them tied like mules.' He looked drained, pallid, and his face seemed to have burned down to the wick. He knew that bloodshed was imminent. El Gato poured him some brandy, saying he would need it for the executions, but Manolo only shook his head. El Gato was a large, noisy, rather teasing man, and tonight he was drinking heavily. 'You need fire,' he said. 'You are vengeance like a trickle of ice-water.' Manolo turned away with a ghastly smile.

These two ill-assorted men were now in control of the village, and the bar was their headquarters – with men coming and going, raising arms in salute, bringing reports, and carrying messages. Málaga would hold, said El Gato, and if Granada attacked from the north they would find Almuñécar a nest of swords. Their chief concern was Altofaro, only ten miles down the coast and near enough to Africa to be used as a beach-head. If the rebels made a landing there they could out-flank Málaga from the east, and then Almuñécar might become the key to the war. Manolo and El Gato, having no facts to confine them, began to expand before each other's eyes, grew vast as generals, became emperors of armies, possible liberators of the entire peninsula.

Walking home after midnight, I saw a heavy guard round the prison and another round the captured arsenal. The militia were bivouacked in the street, crouching over flickering woodfires, their faces outlined in red – high cheekbones, pitted eyes, hungry sunken cheeks, soldiers of Goya come alive again.

*

Early next morning, four truckloads of militia drove off to Altofaro to attack the rebels. They swung singing through the streets in their bright blue shirts, waving their caps as though going to a fair. El Gato was in charge, dynamite strapped to his body; the others shared a musket between three. Once they were over the hill, we expected to hear the sounds of war break out, but the morning passed in silence.

About noon, a white aircraft swung in low from the sea, circled the village, and flew away again – leaving the clear blue sky scarred with a new foreboding above a mass of upturned faces. Many felt, till that moment, their village to be secure and forgotten; now the eye of war had spied them out.

Throughout the afternoon nothing happened. Families ate their meals in the street, seeking the assurance of one another's company. Once again the fierce sunlight obliterated everything it fell on, burning all colours to an ashen glare. When people stepped out of their houses they seemed to evaporate for a moment, as if the light had turned them to vapour; and when they passed into shadow they disappeared again, like stepping into a hole in the ground. That afternoon of waiting was the hottest I've known. Fear lay panting in the street like a dog. It was as though El Gato and his men had been swallowed up in silence, or had followed the war to another country.

But war was not far away, and after nightfall, unexpectedly, it paid its first mad call on Almuñécar. A destroyer crept into the bay, unseen by anyone, and suddenly began probing the shore with its searchlight. The beam swept over the hills, up and down the coast, and finally picked out the village and pinned it against the darkness. Held by the blazing eye, opening so ominously from the sea, the people experienced a moment of naked panic. There seemed nowhere to run to, nowhere to hide, so they hurried down to the beach, and stood motionless in the glare, facing the invisible warship and raising their arms in a kind of massed entreaty. As the searchlight played over them they remained stiffly at attention, just letting themselves be seen. In the face of the unknown, all they could do was to offer themselves in this posture of speechless acquiescence. Such pitiless brightness had never lit up their night before: friend or foe, it was a light of terror.

For a while nothing happened. The warship just sat in the darkness stroking its searchlight up and down the shore. To get a better view, I joined a group of boys who'd already climbed on to the castle wall. We could see the whole of Almuñécar below us – the crowds on the beach and the spoke of light turning on its invisible hub. As we watched, it began to play over the nearby hills and move again along the coastal road. Suddenly it picked out a lorry heading towards the village, then three more, all packed with men. The beam lazily followed them, as though escorting them home, lighting up their rifles like little thorns. One could hear distant shouting above the sound of the engines – it was El Gato's militia coming back at last.

The trucks roared into the village, horns stridently blowing, and pulled up in the warship's pool of light. The beam was abruptly switched off, followed by a moment of absolute darkness. Then there came a blinding flash from the sea.

Silence. It was as though a great fuse had blown. Then the mountains behind us thundered, a thunder that boomed and cannoned from peak to peak and tumbled in the valleys like showers of stones. There was another flash, another explosion, another hot blast of air. For a moment we imagined it might be some kind of salute to the militia. Then we heard the tearing scream of a shell.

The searchlight came on again. We could see the crowds on the beaches surging inland like a muddy wave. The destroyer fired once more, misting its searchlight with smoke, and we were no longer in doubt about its intentions. A house on our right suddenly shuddered, rose a foot in the air, and slowly collapsed like a puffball. A bundle of stones and trees leapt up by the river. A pall of dust drifted over the village.

After half a dozen more salvoes, the firing broke off; inexplicably, since we seemed to be at their mercy. Then the shocked silence in the village began to fill with a curious whispering and rustling, the sound of a multitude on the move. In the naked beam of the searchlight we saw them come stumbling up the streets, bent double, crying and moaning, mothers and fathers dragging their children behind them, old folk tottering and falling down.

As the village ran for the hills, looking for patches of darkness, we saw a small boat put out from the shore, with two squat figures inside it sitting hunched at their oars and rowing frantically towards the ship.

And that was the end of the bombardment. The destroyer was found to be friendly. It had all been an unfortunate error of war. A case of mistaken identity; the captain sent his apologies, slipped anchor, and sailed quietly away – leaving a few gaps in the houses, a few dead in the streets, and most of the population scattered across the hillsides.

When the sun rose next morning Almuñécar had transformed itself, with flags fluttering from every rooftop. Every scrap of old cloth within the spectrum of red, from orange, vermilion to purple, had been hastily cut into squares and run up on poles to make it clear on which side we stood. Even the houses of the 'fascists' wore scarlet that morning, as did the casino, the bank, and the church. In the face of any more trigger-happy assaults made by passing friends, it was thought as well to take no chances.

But the village seemed purged, curiously enough, by its night of fire. One heard no blame laid against the warship. In spite of the ruins and the dead, the capricious savagery of the bombardment was accepted as one of the traditional blows of fate. Almuñécar, if anything, felt enlarged by the ordeal; it now had wounds to boast of, had smelt the hot reek of powder, stared down the muzzle of guns, and known itself to survive. There was satisfaction, too, in the fact that the destroyer was theirs, and had splendidly shown its powers.

We learned that it was El Gato and the mayor who had stopped the shelling last night, the only ones to keep their heads. They had rowed out alone along the path of the searchlight and asked what in the hell was going on. The captain explained that he'd simply mixed up his villages and mistaken us for the rebel-held Altofaro. Moreover, he'd thought the militia were attacking, rather than returning home, and he'd only meant to help. (In fact, El Gato's expedition itself was also revealed to have been a fiasco: the men had forgotten their ammunition.)

Now that Almuñécar had come out under the scarlet banner, the morning was one of mounting action. This was the day when the peasants and fishermen openly took over the village, commandeering the houses of suspects and the empty villas of the rich and painting across them their plans for a new millennium. 'Here will be the Nursery School.' 'Here will be the House of Culture.' 'Here will be a Sanatorium for Women.' 'Workers, Respect this House for Agricultural Science.' 'Here will be a Training College for Girls'. Each of the large bold words was painstakingly written in red, a memoranda of a brief and innocent euphoria. For who among the crowds could guess, as they gathered in the streets to read them, that these naïve hopes would later be treated as outrage?

Meanwhile the militia were massing for a new attack on Altofaro, undeterred by yesterday's failure. They formed up raggedly in the square, polishing their guns on their trousers and watched by a scattering of wide-eyed dogs and boys. Manolo and El Gato, in long blue overalls, marched up and down the ranks; Manolo pale and stern, El Gato loud and jovial, teasing the men with macabre jokes. The militia were mixed, some old and grizzled, others young, bright-faced, and swaggering. There was also a platoon of teenage girls armed with hand-grenades. Nobody joked with them.

About noon the militia climbed into their open lorries and rattled off up the coastal road, standing stiff and straight, arms raised in salute, calm, but not singing now. We watched the swirl of white dust climb the side of the hill and hang over the ridge in the hot still air. After they'd gone, the village was left in a kind of limbo, not knowing what to do.

I went and sat in a bar, feeling bereft and impotent, as though robbed of some great occasion. I'd seen those silent men and muscular stiff-lipped girls riding to a war just down the road, to a blaze of battle under a burning sky offering all the trappings of heroic carnage. That special adrenalin in the young which makes war easy, and welcomes it, drew me voluptuously towards Altofaro.

Then why hadn't I gone? It would not have been difficult. Manolo would have arranged the thing in a moment. Even so, I hung back, as from some family affair in which I still doubted I had a part.

On the way back to the house I found Emilia, one of our neighbours, raging up and down the street. Her brother had just been arrested as a spy, and she was indulging in a public ecstasy of fury – against him, not against the authorities. She didn't doubt his guilt; he had done it for money; he was always a *bestia*, a *sinverguenza*. Here was someone at last on whom she could blame the war, someone palpable, close to home. 'Give me my brother!' she cried, opening her hands like claws, clutching and strangling the air. 'Give him to me for just a little moment, let me squeeze out his tiny life!'

Crazed and dishevelled, she ran down to the jail and beat on the bars with her fists. 'Suckler of snakes!' she shouted. 'Polluter of our mother! Give me a gun, and I'll shoot him myself!' The guards laughed at her antics but didn't turn her away; instead they quietly opened the gates. Emilia disappeared inside, and when we saw her again, an hour later, she was calmly smoking a pipe on her doorstep.

Later that afternoon we heard the sound of distant gunfire, snapping like pods in the hills. The day was dead calm and the firing came to the ears with dry little displacements of air. Then about four o'clock, two more warships appeared, steaming slowly towards the east. El Gato had boasted they'd come; he'd arranged it by radio, he said, but nobody had believed him. Now the ships moved quietly along the coast and anchored about six miles away, standing in line astern and facing the rebel port which lay just hidden behind the headland.

Once again the village crowded on to the beach to watch. The evening was hazy and peacock-coloured; delicate hues ran slowly over the sea and sky and melted together like oil. The destroyers lay low on the horizon, slender as floating leaves, insubstantial as the air around them. Lights winked, there was a glitter of sun on metal, then little flashes ran along the ships, twinkling eruptions of fire that suddenly starred the air then vanished without a sound ... The shelling of Altofaro had begun; curiously muted at first, its force softened by heat and distance. Then the sound of the explosions reached us, round and hollow, bouncing dully across the water.

The villagers watched in silence, showing no sign of excitement, but rather with a mixture of morbid compassion. Dim, muffled shudders came from behind the headland as the shells began to strike home. The bombardment continued for about an hour, then the ships steamed away, leaving a column of smoke in the air, a black greasy pall that slowly mounted the sky and spread grubbily over the twilit hills.

Long after the firing had died, and darkness fallen, the villagers still lingered along the shore, standing trance-like, rigid, strangely dumb, just staring towards the east. Once again they seemed to be tasting the fumes and the sulphur, and sensing the heat of the guns they knew, but this time the salvoes had been turned elsewhere, and the terror was in their name.

It was not victory, however; there was no victory on the coast that night. Altofaro had not been destroyed, nor had it even surrendered. When the militia returned, round about midnight, there was no singing or cheering welcome. The wounded, the shocked, the dying, and the dead were unloaded in bitter silence. Manolo was missing, and El Gato walked speechlessly away trailing his rifle like a broken limb. Something had gone wrong, something which had not been thought possible when the militia first took up arms.

Under the pale street lamps, amid the weeping and curses, the simple truth was being uncovered. After the day's massacre at Altofaro, and the clumsy impotence of the warships – whose shells appeared to have fallen harmlessly in open country – it was being learned again that men needed more than courage, anger, slogans, convictions, or even a just cause when they went to war. The village became aware that night, not for the first time in its history, that a people's army could be defeated.

The next morning they blew up the bridges on the coastal roads and so far as one could tell we were now cut off. In Almuñécar it was a day of nervousness and shame which led to further outbreaks of mindless violence. As I walked down to the café to get news of Manolo, I saw that the casino had been sacked and burned.

It had been a cheap, florid building, pseudo-Moorish in style, but nevertheless a symbol of civic pride. Now the villagers had set upon it and savagely torn it to pieces, in spite of their love of its gaudy grandeur. By the time I arrived, it was already a littered ruin, a black and degraded mess. Men and women stood around it, sniffing the curling smoke and kicking at broken pieces of furniture: out in the street a grand piano lay with its legs in the air, smouldering gently like a roasted ox; and an air of orgiastic gloom pervaded the scene, a sour and desolate sadness.

The militia were utterly demoralized. There was no more talk of returning to the offensive or of making another attack on Altofaro. The lorries baked in the sun, and throughout the long afternoon the men squabbled or simply slept.

Later that night Manolo returned, having made his way back along the coast on foot. He walked quietly into the bar like an apparition, his face drawn, his clothes dripping with sea-water.

El Gato, who had been drinking and dozing all evening, rose to his feet with a grunt and embraced him.

They stood, the two leaders, the big and the small, holding on to each other stiffly.

'Where were you?' asked El Gato. 'We didn't mean to leave you, man. We had to get out, you understand.'

Manolo nodded.

'I saw you go,' he said. 'I buried myself. Isidro was lying just across the alley. He was still alive when they found him and they cut his throat. When it got quiet, I went into the sea.'

'Is the bridge down?'

'Yes. I swam to the Faro – then I came on over the cliff.'

'What about the ships?'

'You saw them. You saw what they did.'

'Can we get back?'

'Not with this gang, never.'

El Gato gave Manolo some brandy, then stripped off his cartridge belt and tossed it into a corner. An air of absolute exhaustion settled down on the bar. 'We're finished before we started,' said Manolo. His companions sat round in silence staring at the blank bare walls. El Gato went to sleep again.

About midnight, we got through to Radio Sevilla, and heard Queipo de Llano exulting in the fall of the city. The rebel general was drunk, and each slurred, belching phrase was a slap in the face of the militia. Christ had triumphed, he ranted, through God's army in Spain, of which Generalissimo Franco was the sainted leader. The criminal forces of socialism, which had drawn their slime across the country, were being routed by the soldiers of righteousness. He ordered the workers to submit and to return to work, otherwise they and their families would be shot. God's army was merciful, but Spain would be emptied if necessary. 'Viva España! Viva la Virgen!'

'It's true,' said Manolo, shivering with fever and struggling to keep awake. The rebels were steadily building up their forces from Africa, he said; flying in thousands of Moorish troops each day. 'The Catholic kings were the first to drive the Moors from Spain. Now the Catholic generals are bringing them back. What can we do? There's nothing to stop them. The war is over, I think.'

Walking home that night, I was not to know that Manolo was wrong, and that the long war was only just beginning. Nor did I know, as I went to bed, that I had only a few hours left in Spain.

When I awoke next morning there was yet another warship in the bay, swinging gently at anchor in the sunshine. It rode sleepily on the water, deck-awnings in place and with its guns reassuringly covered. Taking breakfast on the terrace with my English friend, we watched it idly over the tops of the palm trees. There seemed to be no movement on board, and the village itself lay hazed in a silence which promised another hot and hooded day.

Then we heard a rush of footsteps in the street, a loud hammering on the door, and the house was invaded by women and children, who came stumbling up the stairs, excitedly calling our names and led by a flushed and dishevelled Emilia.

'Hurry!' she cried. 'Leave everything – you are saved! Your king has sent you a ship. They are waiting for you on the beach and have come to take you home. Before God, who more fortunate than you?'

They dragged me out of the house and hurried me down to the shore, urging me on with impatient shouts. 'Run, run, Lorenzo! Your friend the admiral is waiting!' The women were skipping around me like frogs.

Sure enough, a ship's cutter was drawn up on the sand, guarded by pink-cheeked British sailors. A smart officer in white, who had been making inquiries at the hotel, strolled down the steps and introduced himself.

No panic, he said, but the Navy had sent out a destroyer from Gibraltar to pick up any British subjects who might be marooned on the coast. Could we be ready in an hour? The situation was edgy. Alas, personal baggage only . . .

So it had come – the sudden end to my year's adventure, with the long arm reaching from home, the destroyer bobbing in the bay like an aproned nanny, the officer like a patient elder brother. Responsible, tolerant, but slightly bored, he was here to snatch us from alien perils, to honour the birthright inscribed in our passports, and to stop us making fools of ourselves.

Naturally, he said, it was up to us. We could stay and sweat it out if we wished. But he couldn't guarantee they'd be back, and the Civil War was spreading. His captain advised us to get out now.

I knew I would have to go. I couldn't resist the flattery of the occasion – all the paraphernalia of official rescue, so lavishly gathered and waiting, and the villagers' expectations as they crowded around us. As much as anything else it was their faces which decided me, faces already set for a huge farewell. The king of England had sent a ship for the hotel fiddler and his friend, and our departure was a dramatic necessity.

Almuñécar was a trap in any case, and I'd been looking for other ways out, plotting to join a fishing boat to Málaga or Africa. But fantasies of private action were now swamped by the benevolent presence of the Navy. I went back to the house and began to collect my things.

The novelist was already packed, with a crate of books and papers, some roots of asphodel and a barrel of coñac. Emilia and her neighbours were engaged in fighting their way through the house, helping themselves to the sheets and furniture, weeping as they did so and occasionally throwing their arms around us and saying what a hole we should leave in their lives.

Finally a large happy crowd, loudly bewailing our departure, escorted the pair of us down to the beach, dumped our goods in the water, begged us not to leave them, and lifted us bodily into the boat. The sailors jumped in after us, not a moment too soon, and we were off, launched by a hundred hands. A young friend of the novelist, with a desperate cry, flung himself into the sea behind us, swam a few wild strokes in sobbing pursuit, and then allowed his companions to drag him back to shore.

It was over, finished – the hoarse echoes of Spain slowly dying away in the distance. We headed for the destroyer, which loomed gradually larger, a new and dominating presence; but looking back at Almuñécar receding in the hard blue sunlight we saw its outlines transformed. The white houses, grey sands, silver and orange rocks were blackened with a multitude of watchers. The whole village had turned out to witness our departure and stood in a long dark frieze round the bay, waving and calling across the water, some of them running up and down the sands. There was also something desperate, almost sinister, in the way they packed the edge of the sea, as though in dread of the land behind them.

We reached the waiting destroyer, and were piped briskly aboard to a line-up of saluting officers – an engaging, solemn, and unexpected little ritual which gracefully ignored our down-at-heel appearance. I saw my small bits of baggage passed hand-to-hand up the gangway and piled politely on the quarter deck. The captain welcomed us with a handshake like a squire at a picnic. Room was made for us in the junior officers' cabins.

Once we were safely aboard, the ship leapt into life and sliced in a fast sharp curve out to sea – a multi-million pound vessel, throbbing with power, manned by a hundred and thirty crew, its engines burning up fuel at £X a minute, and all for a couple of English tramps. It was midday now, with the deck-awnings flapping and the starch-blue sea racing by, the officers wandering below for their pre-lunch drinks, and the novelist already typing . . .

But I stayed on deck, watching Almuñécar grow small and Spain folding itself away – all its clamour gone, wrenched so abruptly from me, a year's life in a few hours ended. I saw the long hard coast, which I'd trodden inch by inch, become a clinker of bronze on the skyline. Behind it the peaks of the Sierras crawling jaggedly into view, hung there suspended, then fell away – and in that instant of leaving them I felt them as never before, clutching at my senses like hands of bone. From that seaborne distance, cut off and secure, I seemed only then to begin to know that country; could smell its runnels of dust, the dead ash of its fields, whiffs of sour wine, rotting offal, and incense, the rank hide of its animals, the peppery skin of its men, the sickly tang of its fevered children.

I saw again, as I lost them, the great gold plains, the arid and mystical distances, where the sun rose up like a butcher each morning and left curtains of blood each night. I could hear the talk, the cries, the Spanish-Arabic voices pitched to carry from Sierra to Sierra; the trickling sound of guitars dropping like water on water, eroding the long boredom of afternoons; and the songs, metallic, hatcheting the ear, honed with forlorn and unattainable lusts; the strangled poetry of the boys, the choked chastity of the girls, and the orgasmic outbursts of tethered beasts.

All I'd known in that country – or had felt without knowing it – seemed to come upon me then; lost now, and too late to have any meaning, my twelve months' journey gone. Spain drifted away from me, thunder-bright on the horizon, and I left it there beneath its copper clouds.

An officer came up on deck and handed me a drink. 'Shame to break up your holiday like this,' he said. Later, a German airship passed above us, nosing inquisitively along the coast, the swastika black on its gleaming hull. To Spain, so backward and so long ignored, the nations of Europe were quietly gathering.

12

Epilogue

Back in England it was August, bank holiday time, with the country deep in the grip of a characteristic mid-Thirties withdrawal, snoozing under old newspapers and knotted handkerchiefs.

I returned to my Gloucestershire village, amazed to see once more the depth of the grass and the weight of the leaves on the trees. But the pleasure of being home again, and receiving the traditional cosseting of the prodigal, was quickly replaced by misgivings. I'd been away two years, but was little the wiser for it. I was twenty-two, woolly-minded, and still naïve in everything, but I began to realize I'd come home too soon.

The Spanish War, seen close to within the local limits of an Andalusian village, was not what it had seemed to me at the time. As I learnt more about it from the newspapers – its scale and implications – I couldn't help feeling a private sense of betrayal.

Unlike so many of my age, for whom Spain in the Thirties represented one of the last theatres of political romanticism, I hadn't consciously chosen it as a Cause but had stumbled on it by accident, simply by happening to be there. Now I began to feel shameful doubts at having turned my back on events so easily, just when they were about to affect us all. I thought the least I could do was to give myself a second chance by returning to Spain as soon as I could.

It was a restless summer. I was penniless, without contacts, and totally ignorant of ways and means. Spain was over a thousand miles away and already sealed off by the hypocrisies of non-intervention. I might have given up the idea if I hadn't suddenly fallen in love, but the result of that experience, which went deeper than anything I'd known before, only made my situation all the more intolerable.

For me it was an hallucination of honour, no doubt a self-indulgence, irrelevant to events and certainly irrelevant to the girl. I told her my plans one evening as she sat twisting her hair with her fingers and gazing into my eyes with her long cat look. She wasn't impressed. Others may need a war, she said; but you don't, you've got one here. She bared her beautiful small teeth and unsheathed her claws. Heroics like mine didn't mean a thing. If I wished to command her admiration by sacrificing myself to a cause she herself was ready to provide one.

Of course, I tried to persuade her that I would be doing it for her, but this wasn't true, and she knew it. All the same, it was partly our entanglement that drove me, the feeling of over-indulgence and satiety brought on by too much easy and unearned pleasure. Guilt, too: she was married and had two young children, she was rich and demandingly beautiful, extravagantly generous with her emotions but fanatically jealous, and one who gave more than she got in love. For several days and nights our arguments swung back and forth, interspersed with desperate embraces, ending with threats of blackmail and bitter tears, with cries of 'Go, and you'll see me no more . . .'

With the help of another friend, I left London in the autumn and worked my way down through France, heading in the direction of the Pyrenees, planning, when the chances were right, simply to walk into the mountains and slip across the frontier alone. The Pyrenees, when I got there, were already touched with snow and looked grey and impregnable. Even so, I never doubted that I could get across. Winter was closing in like a cloak.

While I was waiting near the coast and making some rather slip-shod preparations, the girl suddenly turned up again, having driven out from England not in an attempt to dissuade me further but to present me instead with a week of passionate farewell. A week of hysteria, too – embracing in ruined huts, on the salt-grass at the edge of the sea, gazing out at the windswept ocean while gigantic thunderstorms wheeled slowly round the distant mountains.

There were no more questions or arguments; the mountains were always in sight, and the girl made it clear she thought I was going to my death. Our love was more violent than ever, as though we accepted this as its end and wished to leave each other destroyed.

After we parted, I moved on to the little town of Perpignan, only about twelve miles from the Pyrenees. Perpignan, I'd been told, was swarming with Spanish Government agents eager to recruit volunteers and smuggle them over the mountains. Certainly the agents were there, but they must have thought me a doubtful proposition for my approaches were either blocked or met by evasions. When I mentioned the International Brigade, the Spanish Consul was polite and said he had no knowledge of such a body. He appreciated my goodwill but assured me that he ran no excursions across the frontier: such junketings would be unthinkable and lawless. The war was a domestic matter, he said, and everything was going well; but if I really wished to help I should go back home.

I spent a couple of weeks in the town without breaking through this wall of equivocation, and finally I realized I would have to go it alone. The Pyrenees to the south, seen in the sharp winter air, began to look smaller and less non-committal. So early in December I took a bus to Ceret in the foothills, where I spent my last snug night in an inn. Then next morning, at first light, I left the still sleeping village and started off up the mountain track.

Behind me, as I climbed, the gentle slopes of the foothills fell away to Perpignan and the sea, while before me the steep bulk of the Pyrenees Orientales filled the sky with their sunlit peaks. I had about eight hours of daylight but was not too sure of my route, except that it must go up, over, and south. The fact that it was winter seemed to be the only thing in my favour, though I was still glad of the bright clear weather.

The track rose steeply among rocks that were diamond-crusted with ice, and I soon found the going tough. I was idiotically equipped for such a journey, having brought nothing that would help me, though plenty of stuff that wouldn't – no maps, no compass, no tent or ground-sheet, instead a rucksack loaded down with an assortment of books and papers, together with my violin, a folding camera, and a saucepan. I don't really know why I was carrying all this, except that it was all I had in the world.

Throughout the long clear morning I struggled up the mountain path, buffeted by icy winds from the north. The great peak of Canigou stood away on my right, floating in the brilliant sky like an iceberg, and for much of the time, not having a compass, I was able to use it as a sighting post. By noon I'd climbed to about 3,000 feet, but the goat track grew more and more tortuous, so I decided to abandon it altogether and go straight up the mountain, still keeping Canigou on my right.

The way was tricky and hard, and I found myself stumbling on my knees and clawing at rock and tufts of frozen grass. By the middle of the afternoon I was sweating in the cold, slipping and scrambling over the broken slopes. But I was high up now, with a prickling across the back of my neck as I felt the whole of France plunging away behind me. Having been born and brought up at two hundred and fifty feet above sea-level, I was not used to such dizzying elevations.

Suddenly there was an ominous change in the atmosphere, an extra keenness of cold, and a curious glare and whitening of the sunlight. Looking down, I saw that the foothills had disappeared and had been replaced by a blanket of swirling vapour. The shining peak of Canigou began to switch on and off like a lighthouse, intermittently shuttered by racing clouds. Then the wind rose abruptly to a thin-edged wail, and I felt the first stinging bite of snow.

One moment I'd been climbing a mountain in a sparkle of

sunshine; the next, the whole visible world had gone, and I was slapped to my knees and pinioned to a shelf of rock, head down in a driving gale. Gusts of snow swept round me, needling into my eyelids and piercing my clothes like powdered glass. The storm closed in and began scouring the mountain with an insane and relentless frenzy.

For a while I curled myself up and became just a ball of survival, mindlessly hugging the lee of a rock. I lay knee to chin, letting the storm ride over me; then I began to wonder what I was doing here. After all the boasting I'd done in summer fields back home, and in her Chanel-scented bed, what was I doing in France stuck to the face of a mountain alone in a winter blizzard? To lie freezing to death on the wrong side of the frontier was no way to go to a war. There was no point in staying where I was, so I started to move forward, crawling slowly on hands and knees. Distance, direction, movement, and balance were all fused by the driving snow; I may have advanced half a mile, or just a few yards, there was no longer any way of knowing. All I remember is the brightness of the ground, and being swept by waves of almost infantile pleasure, the delirious warmth of impending frostbite.

Then, by one of those long-shot chances, taken for granted at the time, I came upon a rough little stone-built shelter. It was half in ruins, and there was nothing inside it but straw, but I suppose it may have saved my life. Once I'd bedded myself down, I heard the blizzard change gear, rising to an almost supersonic shriek, and for a couple of hours I lay motionless, curled deep in the straw, slowly and painfully thawing out.

Later it grew dark, and the anguish gradually eased as I built up a drowsy fug for myself. The sound of the wind settled down to a steady whine, soporific, like an electric motor. A pleasant comfort crept over me; I seemed to sense the feathersoft snow gathering in deep weightless drifts outside; a bosomy presence, invisible and reassuring, cushioning the naked rocks of the mountain. By now I was exhausted anyway, too drugged by the cold to move, even to attempt to build a fire; so I just lay, sniffing the damp warm smell of the straw, and presently I fell asleep.

Next morning the storm was over and the sun shone brilliantly again. I came out of the dark little hut to find the mountain transformed – trees, rocks, and bushes thickly bolstered with snow and giving off a clean crispy smell, like starch. The French village below me was no longer in sight, but the slope above curved gradually away, smooth and bright, rising a few hundred yards then ending in a sharp blue line of sky.

Abandoning the cosy gully where I'd spent the night, I climbed unsteadily for an hour or so, ploughing through snowdrifts, stumbling over hidden rocks, and slithering about in my sodden shoes. It was a long cold struggle, and I'd had nothing to eat, but at least I was lucky to be on the move at all. Then suddenly there was no more climbing: the slope levelled and stopped, the sky plunged, and I was on top of the ridge.

The icy crests of the Pyrenees stretched east and west, flashing in the sun like broken glass on a wall, while before me, to the south, was what I had come to see – range after range of little step-like hills falling away to the immensities of Spain . . .

But I was not over the mountains yet; there was still another ridge to cross, with a deep valley lying between. I could see a black frozen stream winding a thousand feet below me. I would simply have to go down and up again.

Crossing this mile-wide chasm took me the rest of the day – a vertical, trackless journey. Whipped by flurries of snow and bruising winds I slithered, slipped, and scrambled, seeing no living thing except a boy and a sheepdog who both fled when they saw me coming. Towards evening, very cold, and with a rime of frost on my eyelashes, I was about half-way up the second slope, when I came to a small mountain road, the first I'd seen for two days, winding bleakly among the trees. I sat and stared at it for a while, but it told me nothing; it could have been anywhere on earth – just an inscrutable little cart-track, half mud, half stones, as nameless as a peasant's face.

But darkness was coming now, and I was limp with hunger. I didn't fancy another night on the mountain. So I thought I'd better follow the road and see where it led me, even if it meant a clash with the frontier guards. The track wound upwards for half a mile through a thicket of pine trees and presently emerged in a little clearing. I saw roof-tops, a church, and a cluster of village lights. Then I smelt hot butter, and knew I was still in France.

Except for a hobbled horse and a couple of snarling dogs, the village street was empty. The low wooden houses, crudely thatched with bracken, had a look of dark Siberian squalor; but half-way up the street I saw the lights of a café shining warmly through steamed-up windows. I pushed open the door and entered a noisy room full of little men in sheep's-wool coats. But when they saw me they froze as though I'd let in a blast of snow, and their conversation switched off abruptly.

What rough beast was this slouching towards the bar, dressed in a blanket and crumpled hat, coming out of the night like some ghost of winter, his hair and eyebrows white with frost? Nobody moved or spoke, except the old woman behind the bar who bobbed quickly out of sight as I approached her, and whose place was immediately taken by a huge-bellied man who began setting up bottles like a defensive wall.

I asked if I could have something to eat, and he repeated the question to the room, then, after a pause, nodded to an empty table. I slumped down in the chair, and presently he brought me some soup, which seemed to be a mixture of tar and onions. As I ate, the men watched me – rows of bright little faces wrapped to the ears in their fleece-lined collars. Some quietly shuffled their dominoes, others winked cryptically at one other, all seemed to be waiting for something to happen.

At last a committee of three detached themselves from the rest and came over and sat at my table. They were low-voiced and confidential, and one of them offered me a cigarette. I didn't have to answer, but they'd rather like to know: what exactly was I doing here? I'd come from Perpignan, hadn't I? I'd been seen there several times recently; also down in Ceret, a couple of days ago. It was hard on the mountain at this time of the year. I mustn't mind their curiosity.

They were a strange little trio but seemed harmless enough. One of them wore the look of a sleepy clown; the other had a Karl Marx beard, extravagantly bushy and white; the third was thin, like a weathered pole. But the warmth of the room, the soup, and their polite concern encouraged me to take a chance. I told them I was on my way to the 'south'. I had friends there, I said – I wanted to join them, that was all. They asked a few more questions, then the fat clown smiled. 'Well, since you've got this far . . .' he said. He called for some brandy and poured me a glass 'Drink it up, man. You're going to need it.'

I was lucky. It might just as easily have gone the other way, with an ignominious return to Perpignan. But it seemed I'd fallen on my feet among the very men who could help me: a cosy community of frontier anarchists. I don't know why they decided to trust me, or why they thought me worth the trouble, but clearly they'd made up their minds. The men put their heads together and held a brief discussion, then the thin one looked at his watch and nodded. 'It'll take us an hour,' he said, 'so as soon as you're ready. Better go before the moon comes up.'

He rose to his feet and wrapped a scarf round his long thin neck as though he was lagging a water pipe. The others helped me on with my bags and I was given some more brandy for the journey. The proprietor refused to be paid for the soup. Then the thin man said 'Come', and pushed open the door to admit a flurry of powdered snow, and we left the café to a murmur of benevolent farewells and a flourish of political salutes.

Once in the street, my companion glanced quickly at the sky, put out his cigarette, and rolled up his collar. 'Stay close, and say nothing,' he muttered briefly, then shot off up a narrow lane. I hurried after him, and we were out of the village immediately, climbing a steep and brutish path. The man raced on ahead of me, taking little goat-like leaps and dodging nimbly from rock to rock. I could see his tall gaunt figure bouncing against the hazy stars. He never bothered to check that I was still behind him.

Easy enough for him, I thought: he was built for these mountains while I'd been raised on very low hills. His legs were long and mine were short – I was also carrying a twenty-pound load. I did my best to keep with him but he soon outstripped me and I started to fall farther and farther back. I wanted to shout, 'Wait a minute!' but it didn't seem to be the thing to do. Instead, I began to indulge in a bit of carefree whistling.

That stopped him in the end. I found him perched on a rock waiting impatiently for me to catch up. 'Stop whistling,' he growled. 'Save it for the other side. This is no time for trivialities.' At least I was grateful for the halt, and the conversation. I asked him if he did this often. I must be mad, he said; it was the very first time, and by God he was sorry already.

He started climbing again while I went panting behind him, sweat trickling down my arms and legs. Brittle gusts of dry snow swept by on the wind, striking the face like handfuls of rice. I felt engulfed by a contest that was growing too large for me; something I'd asked for but doubted that I could carry through. My companion ignored this, pushing ahead more relentlessly than ever, as though wishing to put me to the final test. That last half-hour was perhaps the worst I've known, casually unprepared as I was; ill-shod, badly clothed, and lumbered with junk, clawing my way up these icy slopes.

The point of collapse must have been near, but luckily I escaped it, for at last we reached the top of the rise. We were in a narrow pass flanked by slabs of rock which stood metallic and blue in the starlight. I seemed to sense a change in the air, a curious lifting of pressure before me as though some great obstacle had been rolled away. There was also a faint smell of charcoal, woodsmoke, and mules, and an indefinable whiff of pepper. My guide drew me into the shadows and gestured me to silence, sticking out his neck and sniffing the sky. We crouched in the darkness listening. We heard the wind, falling water, and what sounded like a distant gunshot.

'This is where I leave you,' said the Frenchman. He appeared a little more cheerful now. 'The frontier is between those rocks. Follow the path for half a kilometre and you'll come to a little farm. Knock on the door and you'll be among your friends.'

Suddenly it seemed too simple – after weeks of speculation and doubt, and these last two exhausting days – just a gap in the rocks a few hundred yards ahead of me, the tiny frontier between peace and war.

'Move slow and easy. There may be a few guards about but they shouldn't be too lively on a night like this. If you're challenged, drop everything and run like hell. Good luck, then; I can do no more.'

But there was no opposition. I just walked towards the rocks and slipped between them as though on an evening stroll. A narrow path led downwards among the boulders. Then, after about half a kilometre, just as the Frenchman had said, I saw a little farmhouse and knocked on the door. It was opened by a young man with a rifle who held up a lantern to my face. I noticed he was wearing the Republican armband.

'I've come to join you,' I said.

'*Pase usted,*' he answered.

I was back in Spain, with a winter of war before me.

A Moment of War

Illustrated by Keith Bowen

To the defeated

Contents

Contents

1

Return and Welcome

In December 1937 I crossed the Pyrenees from France – two days on foot through the snow. I don't know why I chose December; it was just one of a number of idiocies I committed at the time. But on the second night, near the frontier, I was guided over the last peak by a shepherd and directed down a path to a small mountain farmhouse.

It was dark when I reached it – a boulder among boulders – and I knocked on the door, which was presently opened by a young man with a rifle. He held up a lantern to my face and studied me closely, and I saw that he was wearing the Republican armband.

'I've come to join you,' I said.

'*Pase usted*,' he answered.

I was back in Spain, with a winter of war before me.

The young man slung his rifle over his shoulder and motioned me to enter the hut. A dark passage led to a smoky room. Inside, in a group, stood an old man and woman, another youth with a gun, and a gaunt little girl about eleven years old. They were huddled together like a family photograph fixing me with glassy teeth-set smiles.

There was a motionless silence while they took me in – seeing a young tattered stranger, coatless and soaked to the knees, carrying a kit-bag from which a violin bow protruded. Suddenly the old woman said 'Ay!' and beckoned me to the fire, which was piled high with glowing pine cones.

I crouched, thawing out by the choking fumes, sensing deeply this moment of arrival. I felt it first when threading through the high rocks of the frontier, when, almost by pressures in the atmosphere, and the changes of sound and scent, a great door seemed to close behind me, shutting off entirely the country I'd left; and then, as the southern Pyrenees fell away at my feet, this new one opened, with a rush of raw air, admitting all the scarred differences and immensities of Spain. At my back was the tang of Gauloises and slumberous sauces, scented flesh and opulent farmlands; before me, still ghostly, was all I remembered – the whiff of rags and woodsmoke, the salt of dried fish, sour wine and sickness, stone and thorn, old horses and rotting leather.

'Will you eat?' asked the woman.

'Don't be mad,' said her husband.

He cleared part of the table, and the old woman gave me a spoon and a plate. At the other end the little girl was cleaning a gun, frowning, tongue out, as though doing her homework. An old black cooking-pot hung over the smouldering pine cones, from which the woman ladled me out some soup. It was hot, though thin, a watery mystery that might have been the tenth boiling of the bones of a hare. As I ate, my clothes steaming, shivering and warming up, the boys knelt by the doorway, hugging their rifles and watching me. Everybody watched me except for the gun-cleaning girl who was intent on more urgent matters. But I could not, from my appearance, offer much of a threat, save for the mysterious bundle I carried. Even so, the first suspicious silence ended; a light joky whispering seemed to fill the room.

'What are you?'

'I'm English.'

'Ah, yes – he's English.'

They nodded to each other with grave politeness.

'And how did you come here perhaps?'

'I came over the mountain.'

'Yes, he walked over the mountain . . . on foot.'

They were all round me at the table now as I ate my soup, all

pulling at their eyes and winking, nodding delightedly and repeating everything I said, as though humouring a child just learning to
speak.

'He's come to join us,' said one of the youths; and that set them
off again, and even the girl lifted her gaunt head and simpered.
But I was pleased too, pleased that I managed to get here so easily
after two days' wandering among peaks and blizzards. I was here
now with friends. Behind me was peace-engorged France. The
people in the kitchen were a people stripped for war – the men
smoking beech leaves, the soup reduced to near water; around us
hand-grenades hanging on the walls like strings of onions, muskets
and cartridge-belts piled in the corner, and open orange-boxes
packed with silver bullets like fish. War was still so local then, it
was like stepping into another room. And this was what I had
come to re-visit. But I was now awash with sleep, hearing the
blurred murmuring of voices and feeling the rocks of Spain under
my feet. The men's eyes grew narrower, watching the unexpected
stranger, and his lumpy belongings drying by the fire. Then the
old woman came and took me by the elbow and led me upstairs
and one of the boys followed close behind. I was shown into a
small windowless room of bare white-washed stone containing a
large iron bed smothered with goatskins. I lay down exhausted,
and the old woman put an oil lamp on the floor, placed a cold
hand on my brow, and left me with a gruff good-night. The
room had no door, just an opening in the wall, and the boy
stretched himself languidly across the threshold. He lay on his side,
his chin resting on the stock of his gun, watching me with large
black unblinking eyes. As I slipped into sleep I remembered I had
left all my baggage downstairs; but it didn't seem to matter now.

I was awoken early next morning by the two armed brothers who
were dressed for outdoors in ponchos of rabbit skin. They gave
me a bucket of snow to wash in, then led me gingerly downstairs
and sat me on a stool where the old lady poured me some coffee.
The little girl, her hair brushed and shining already, was fitting

ammunition into cartridge-belts. As I drank my coffee – which tasted of rusty buttons – she looked at me with radiant slyness.

'He came over the mountains,' she said perkily, nodding to herself.

The boys giggled, and the old man coughed.

They brought me my baggage and helped me sling it over my shoulders, and told me that a horse and cart were waiting for me outside.

'They sent it up from the town specially. They didn't want to keep you hanging about . . . Well, not after you came all that way to join us.'

The boys half-marched me into the lane and the rest of the family followed and stood watching, blowing on their purple fingers. The old woman and child had bright shawls on their heads, while, for some reason, the old man wore a tall top hat.

The cart waiting in the lane resembled a rough-looking tumbril, and the driver had a cavernous, nervous face. 'Vamanos, vamanos, vamanos,' he kept muttering plaintively, giving me glances of sharp distaste.

The boys helped me into the back of the cart and climbed up after me.

'Here he is. The English one,' they said with ponderous jocularity.

The driver sniffed, and uncoiled his whip.

'Horse and cart,' said one of the brothers, nudging me smartly. 'We've got to save your legs. They must be half destroyed with all this walking over mountains. And what have we got if we haven't got your legs? You wouldn't be much use to us, would you?'

I was beginning to get a bit bored with all this levity, and sat there silent and shivering. The boys perched close beside me, one on each side, holding their guns at the ready, like sentries. Every so often they pointed them at me and nodded brightly. They appeared to be in a state of nervous high spirits. 'Vamanos!' snarled the driver, and shook up the reins crossly. The old man and his wife raised their hands solemnly and told me to go with God. The little girl threw a stone at the horse, or it may have been at me, but it hit the horse and caused it to start with a jerk. So we began to lumber and creak down the steep rocky lane, the brothers now holding me by either elbow. The Pyrenees stood high behind us, white and hard, their peaks colouring to the rising sun. The boys nodded towards them, grinning, nudging me sharply again, and baring their chestnut-tinted teeth.

Through the iced winter morning, slipping over glassy rocks, we made our stumbling way down the valley, passing snow-covered villages, empty and bare, from which all life and sound seemed withdrawn. This chilling silence was surely not one of nature, which could be broken by a goat-bell or the chirp of a bird. It was as if a paralysing pestilence had visited the place, and I was to notice it on a number of occasions in the weeks to come. It was simply the stupefying numbness of war.

After an hour or so we came to a small hill town still shuttered by the shadow of rocks. A bent woman crept by, bearing a great load of firewood. A cat shot through a hole in a wall. I noticed that the brothers had suddenly grown tense and anxious, sitting straight as pillars, thin-lipped, beside me. Two militiamen, in khaki ponchos, came out of a doorway and marched ahead of us down the street. Even our driver perked up and began to look around him with what appeared to be an air of importance. The militiamen led us into the square, to the dilapidated Town Hall, from which the Republican flag was hanging. The brothers called out to a couple of sentries who were sitting on the steps, and one of them got up and went inside. Now for a proper welcome, I thought. I got down from the cart, and the brothers followed. Then four soldiers came out with fixed bayonets.

'We've brought you the spy,' said the brothers, and pushed me forward. The soldiers closed round me and handcuffed my wrists.

They put me in a cellar and left me for two days. I got a kind of soup the first day, and they forgot me the next – waiting and forgetting being just another part of the war. It was damp and very cold, the walls of the cellar limed with ice like spidery veins of lace. But luckily I'd been toughened up by the cottage bedrooms of home where the water in wash-basins froze solid in winter. The cell had a curious, narrow, coffin-like shape, and even had iron rings round the walls as though to lift it up from inside. There was one dim, yellow-coloured light-bulb hanging from the ceiling, but no furniture; I slept on the rocky floor.

Lying there, shivering, unvisited, well on into the third day, I was wondering idly what now might happen. This was not, after all, quite what I had expected. I had walked into a country at war uninvited and unannounced, and had found no comradely welcome, only suspicion and silence. I am surprised now how little surprised I was then, but I was soon to learn how natural this was.

Captain Perez was again not what I'd expected. He came for me in the late afternoon of the third day, opening my cellar door with a light whispering key. No whiskered revolutionary he, but a slim tailored dandy, a smart gleaming figure in elegantly belted uniform, and with riding boots so glazed and polished his legs appeared to be chocolate-coated. He smiled at me from the doorway, and held out a tin mug of coffee.

'Are you rested?' he asked, in a soft furry voice.

I took the coffee and drank it, hunched up on the floor, while he fetched in two chairs and placed them facing each other.

'Please sit down,' he said gently. 'Or, rather, stand up and sit down.' And he gave a sharp little affected laugh.

The officer seemed to have sleepy eyes and a lazy manner, but once seated in front of me his attitude became abrupt and clinical. How, where and why had I come to Spain? When I told him, he shook his head sadly.

'No, señor! Not over the Pyrenees. Not with all that circus equipment you were carrying. Books, cameras – and a violin, dear Jesus.' He laid a delicate warm hand on my knee. 'You know what we think, young friend? Not over the mountains – no. You came from the sea. You were landed by boat or submarine. From Bremen, was it? You mustn't be surprised that we know all this. We even know what you've come to do.'

He smiled with cream-faced satisfaction, shaking his head against my denials and explanations, and giving my knee another squeeze.

'But, comrade,' I said.

'Captain Perez,' he corrected.

'If you don't believe me, you've got my passport.'

'We've got dozens, dear boy. All of them phonies. And we've got an office that turns out twenty a day.' He looked at me solemnly. 'It was the violin that did it. And the German accent. You would never fool anyone, you know.'

He rose and went to the door, and clapped his hands. There was a heavy marching of feet. The four guards I'd seen earlier came tumbling into the cellar, so wrapped up there was scarcely space for the lot of us. But they circled me close in a friendly manner, trying to keep their bayonets out of each other's eyes.

'Go with them,' said the officer. 'They'll look after you.' And he stepped back into the passage to make room. As we went past him, he snapped a salute in farewell – shining, oiled and immaculate, the last of his kind I was to see in that war.

The guards marched me out into the courtyard and it was night already, with a freezing moon in the sky. The town was empty and silent, dark and shuttered, not even a child or dog could be heard. My guards clumped beside me, jogging me along by the elbows, relaxed now, puffing and whistling. They were all rather short, like Tartars; vapour billowed from their nostrils. The shortest one spun his rifle and grinned up in my face. 'Well,' he said. 'You come a long way to see us. Over the mountains? That's what we hear.' 'That's right,' I said. 'Well, we're nearly there,' he said. 'You won't have to march around much longer.'

Truly we didn't go far – down a short alley and into a rough moonlit scrapyard – till we came to a hole in the ground. The men cleared the snow round the edge, and raised a metal cover, and into the dark cavity they dropped me. It was not very deep – about six to eight feet, narrow, and walled with rock. 'Goodnight, Rubio,' they called. 'Warmer down there than on the mountain tops. In this weather, you understand?' They lowered the iron cover over my head and secured it with heavy bolts. Then I heard them stamping away in the snow, and I was alone again.

The hole was wider at the bottom than at the top, and I curled up on some damp, mouldy straw. The darkness was absolute; I couldn't even see the stars through the grille. Drawing up my knees to my chin, and blowing on my fingers, I now began to consider my position. I was still not altogether surprised at what was happening to me. Indeed, I was letting it happen without question or protest. But since my arrival in Spain something quite unexpected had taken over, and I don't think I realized at that stage how sinister it might be, or what grave peril I had got myself into.

I knew I was not the only one to have wandered over the frontier to join the Republicans. There must have been other volunteers who arrived alone – but were they then always dropped into dark little holes like this? Could it be some sort of discipline to test us out, to prove our loyalty of mind?

I was cold and hungry now, and in this black icy silence I began to get a sharpening taste of danger. No, thought I, this was clearly not a normal reception. The first two shivering days in the Town Hall cell may simply have been a matter of form. But then to have been cast headlong into this medieval pit seemed to suggest that I'd been picked out for something special.

But still my situation didn't disturb me too much, but rather injected me with a sharp sting of adventure. I was at that flush of youth which never doubts self-survival, that idiot belief in luck and a uniquely charmed life, without which illusion few wars would be possible. I felt the seal of fate on me, and a certain grim intoxication, alone in this buried silence. But macabre as things were, I had no idea then how very near to death I was . . .

It may have been a couple of days, or but a few hours, later that I heard the shuffle of returning feet overhead. The iron cover was removed; I saw a brief flash of stars, and another prisoner was dropped into the hole beside me. 'Now you've got a committee!' a voice called down, and the cover was lowered and bolted and the shuffling feet went away.

We stood close together in the darkness, each other's prisoner now, and twin gaolers, in this tomb of rock. 'They sent this for you,' he said, and his hands found me blindly, and I took the hard piece of broken bread. There was just room for both of us if we lay down together; I couldn't see him but at least the air grew warmer. For about a week we shared this black cave together, visited only at night by the guards overhead, who unbolted the manhole and briefly raised it while they lowered us bread, watered wine, and a bucket.

Strange being huddled so close and for so long to another human being whose face one was unable to see. I knew him to be young by his voice and breath and the chance touch of his hand when sharing food or wine. He also had a fresh wild smell about him, an outdoor smell, a mixture of pine and olives. I remember we slept a good deal, prey to an extraordinary lassitude, and, in the intervals, we talked. He was a deserter, he said; and seemed quite cheerful about it, laughing at the looking-glass differences between us. I was trying to get into the war, and he was trying to get out of it, and here we were, stuffed into the same black hole. I'd come over the mountains from France, and he'd been caught going the other way, and most certainly now, he said, we'd both be shot.

And why not, indeed? The deserter appeared quite fatalistic about it. Patiently, drowsily, with no complaint or self-pity, my companion explained the situation to me. The Civil War was eighteen months old, and entering a bitter winter. The Republican forces were in retreat and could afford to take no chances. Franco's rebels were better armed, and had powerful allies abroad, while our side had few weapons, few friends, almost no food, and had learned to trust no one but the dead. What could you expect them to do with a couple of doubtful characters like us? They couldn't afford to keep us, feed us, or even turn us loose. Even less could they afford the luxury of a trial. So it was thought safer, and quicker, that anyone under suspicion be shot, and this was being done regretfully as a matter of course.

My companion was called Dino, he said, and he was twenty-two years old, and he came from a little village in the Guadarramas. When his village had been burned by the Moors, in the early days, he'd run with his younger brother through the lines and become a dynamiter. They'd worked alone, and he'd seen his brother blown up when some of the fuses went wrong. He'd fought at Guadalajara, but didn't like that kind of warfare – mostly hanging about in ditches, then massacre and panic – so he'd taken off again and headed north for France. He'd been picked up twice, and had twice got away, but he reckoned they'd collared him now for good. He knew what to expect, yes sir. He'd seen quite a number of prisoners and deserters shot, and spoke of the Republicans' methods of execution – casual, informal, often good-humoured. Locked in the dark with Dino, and listening to him describe these scenes in his soft, joky voice, I drew steadily, as I thought, towards my hour, and wondered which of the two of us would be called out first.

When it came, it came suddenly, with us both half-asleep, the iron trap-door above raised with a swift muted action, and a low voice calling the young deserter's name, giving us just time enough for a quick fumbling handshake.

As they raised Dino towards the opening he lifted his arms, and I saw his face in a brief glimmer of moonlight. It was thin and hollow, his eyes huge and glowing, his long pointed countenance like an El Greco saint ascending. Finally two dark shapes pulled him through the narrow entrance, and the manhole was lowered again. I heard the clink of glasses, some moments of casual chatter, Dino's short laugh, then a pistol shot . . .

I'd been standing propped against the wall and listening, and now that it was over I slumped back on the straw. My hand touched the deserter's forage-cap, which he'd left behind. It was damp with sweat and still warm from his head.

A few days later, in the red light of dawn, the grille was dragged open and a voice called, 'Hey, Rubio! . . .' Arms reached down to help me, hands caught my wrists, and I was lifted bodily out of the sepulchre.

My legs were shaking, but I put this down to two weeks without exercise; and the dawn light stung my eyes. Was it my turn now? The courtyard glittered with snow; and the hurried preparations which I'd expected – the chair, the hand-cart, the plain wooden box, the sleepy officer with the bottle of coñac, the ragged soldiers lined up and looking at their feet – all were present. But not for me. Another young man sat bound to the chair, smoking furiously and chattering like a parrot.

But I was guided quickly across the yard and out into the lane, where two armed guards stood waiting beside a black battered car. They pushed me into the back seat and sat one on each side of me. A broad man in a hat sat up in front by the driver.

We drove fast and silently through the hunched unhappy town and out into the empty country. We climbed a poor bumpy road on to a desolate plateau across which the wind swept pink ruffles of snow. A plateau of scattered rock and thorn, and a few bent bushes, and the wide winter sky closing in.

It became hot and airless in the car, and the guards, in their heavy brown overcoats, began to steam like sweating horses. Their nostrils steamed too, and their noses shone, and dripped on the bayonets held between their knees.

They were an odd-looking couple, the guards – one small and clownlike, with bright blue chin, the other pink and chubby, a mother's boy. I tried to talk to them, but they wouldn't answer; though one whistled knowingly between his teeth. We drove fast, swaying together on the curves, along a road that was both empty and drear.

Where were we going, and what was in store for me? In spite of the guards' silence, I felt I knew this already. Something irrevocable had taken charge which could neither be reversed nor halted, some mad scrambling of language and understanding which had already misjudged my naïve reasons for being here. I didn't realize then how normal it was for anyone, if put through the right preliminaries, to be swamped by guilt.

Since my sudden arrest and imprisonment, which at first I'd been ready to accept as some light charade touched with military confusion, I felt myself sinking, more and more, into the hands of some obscure accusation against which I ceased to look for an answer.

As the sun rose higher and whitened the rocks, the landscape turned blank, as though over-exposed. And with the whistling guards on each side of me, and the bully-shouldered officer up front, I was sure I was on the road to my doom. As my eyes grew used to the light – after all, I'd been two weeks in darkness – I saw the landscape shudder into shape, grow even more desolate and brutal. Yet never more precious as it floated past me, the worn-out skin of this irreplaceable world, marked here and there by the scribbled signs of man, a broken thatched cabin, or a terraced slope. Every breath I took now seemed rich and stolen, in spite of the oil-fumed heat in the car. Even the two armed guards, grotesque and scruffy as they were, began to take on the power and beauty of fates, protectors or destroyers, who held one's thread of life in their hands.

We'd been driving, I guessed, for about an hour, when the officer suddenly straightened up and snapped his fingers, and we pulled off the road and stopped. The dead icy tableland crept with yellow mist, and seemed quite empty save for a clump of trees in the distance. I was ordered out of the car, one of the guards stuck a gun in my back, pointed to the trees and said, 'March!'

Why had they brought me all this way, I wondered. They could have done the job more snugly back in the jail. Yet the place seemed apt and fitting enough; no doubt they'd used it before. The officer was out of the car now, coughing and spitting, and he came and gave my shoulder a light little shove. 'Come on, Rubio,' he said, 'Come on, march – let's go.' So I put up my head and marched . . .

I saw the vast cold sky and the stony plain and I began to walk towards the distant trees. I heard the soldiers behind me slip the bolts on their rifles. This then, of course, could be the chosen place – the plateau ringed by rock, the late dawn on our breath, the empty silence around us, the little wood ahead, all set for quiet execution or murder. I felt the sharp edges of the stones under my thin-soled shoes. The guards behind me shuttled the bolts of their guns.

If my moment was coming – and I now felt certain it was – I told myself not to look back. My intentions were simple. If they gave me enough time, and I was able to reach the little wood ahead of them, that would be my last chance – and I'd make a break for it. The nearest wind-bent tree looked a thousand years old, its roots pouring over the rocks like wax. The guards were snuffling behind me. Would I reach it before they fired? Would I hear the blast before the thumping bullets hit me? Would I hear anything before the dark? I walked slowly, almost mincingly, trying not to appear to hurry. I reached the trees and prepared to run . . .

One of the guards came up behind me and took my arm. 'OK, Rubio,' he said. 'Sit down.' His comrade was already squatting under a tree and opening a tin of sardines with his bayonet. The officer and driver joined us, yawning and scratching, and we sat down in a circle together. They gave me sardines and some bread, and passed round a bottle of coñac, and as I looked at the food in my hand, and at the raw, safe landscape around me, I was seized by a brief spasm of uncontrollable happiness.

The soldiers stretched out their legs and began talking about football. The officer brushed down his clothes and rolled me a cigarette. He waved his hand at the scenery, the old trees and the rocks, and said it was his favourite spot for a picnic. They came

here, he said, about twice a week. I asked him where we were
going now.

'To Figueras, of course,' he said. They were going to drop me
off at the barracks. 'We thought you'd rather ride than walk.'

But he was still responsible for me, he said, if I liked to think
of it that way. But only till they'd delivered me to Brigade
Headquarters, then he'd be clear of me. He looked at me oddly
with his hazed, blue eyes, slightly mad, amused yet cold.

Why hadn't he explained all this before? The car, the armed
guards, the remote stop in the hills. Had this been another test, or
some daft Spanish trick? Was he really as harmless as he appeared
to be? Would he have been equally amused if I'd made that dash
through the trees? There's no doubt what would have happened if
I had.

2

Figueras Castle

On a bleak naked hill above the town, Figueras Castle stood like a white acropolis – a picturesque assemblage of towers and turrets, walled in by great slabs of stone. The approach road was suitably stark and forbidding, but once I'd passed inside the huge nail-studded doors, I got an impression of almost monastic calm. Indeed the Castle, clamped down on these rocks many centuries ago as a show of force commanding Spain's northern frontiers, appeared now as something a touch over-theatrical, and rather lacking any original ferocity.

But this was the 'barracks', the place to which I had been delivered, the collecting point for volunteers entering Spain from the north. My escort, warmer and more cheerful now after several more stops on the road for anis and coñac, seemed in a natural hurry to get rid of me, and pushed me into a glass-fronted box-office just inside the gate.

'We brought you another one!' he shouted to anyone who might be listening. 'He's English, I think – or Dutch.' With that, he threw my bags across the floor, slapped me on the back, gave me a heavy-lidded wink and left.

An official, bowed at his tiny desk, looked at me with a kind of puff-eyed indifference. Then he sniffed, asked me my name and my next of kin, and wrote down my answers in a child's exercise book. As he wrote he followed the motions of the pen with his tongue, breathing hard and sniffing rhythmically as he did so. Finally, he asked for my passport and threw it into a drawer, in which I saw a number of others of different colours.

'We'll take care of that for you,' he said. 'Would you like some prophylactics?'

Not knowing what these were, I nevertheless said yes, and he handed me a bagful which I stowed away in my pocket. Next he gave me a new hundred peseta note, a forage-cap with a tassel, and said, 'You are now in the Republican Army.' He considered me dimly for a moment, then suddenly shot to his feet, raised his fist and saluted.

'Welcome, comrade!' he cried. 'You won't be here long. As soon as we collect a convoy together we pass you away. In the meantime you have training, political education, fraternal discussion, much to do. Study victory. See a doctor. Dismiss!'

He spoke with a curious accent. It could have been Catalan or French. He kicked my bags back towards me and turned away. I picked them up and went out into the courtyard.

It was now about noon, with the sun at its low winter strength, and across the northern horizon the mountains caught it like broken glass, each peak flashing with blue and white light. Away to the south the land sank in frozen waves, while to the east lay the violet sea. After my two weeks underground the light burned my eyes, and it took some while to get used to the view, focus on its range and open distances, which were immense and exhilarating. The Castle and its courtyard seemed lifted in pure blue air and pressed close to a cold clear sky. I ceased to wonder how I had got here at last. It was simply a moment of magical arrival.

The Castle courtyard was bounded by a bare white-washed wall along the top of which stood pots of crumpled geraniums. Some thirty or forty men lounged round the base of the wall, talking and smoking or eating lumps of bread. A ragged lot, dressed in an odd medley of clothes – some in civvies (as I was), others in long capes like Berbers, or in flashy jackets like white African hunters, while some had their heads thrust through jagged holes cut from the middle of military blankets.

I sat down on the edge of a little group, and was addressed in English by a chap who called himself Danny. Danny was a bone-thin

Londoner, all nose and chin, with a small bent body and red wrinkled hands. He was twenty-two, an unemployed docker from Bermondsey, undernourished and frail; when he moved, his limbs seemed to flap and flutter like wallpaper on an abandoned house.

"'Ere we are then, eh?' he kept saying with a kind of sneezing giggle. Over and over again. Peering at me, then at the great mountain landscape, and clasping his bony knees with his hands. 'Said I'd never make it – the lads. The old woman too. What they call this then? I got 'ere, didn't I?'

He'd clench up his tiny hands and look round him with a trembling squint. A shaking hiss came out of his thin sad mouth. 'We're 'ere then, ain't we? ... Eh, Doug? Eh?' He turned to a man squatting beside him. 'An' 'ere's another one, eh?' he said, pointing a finger at me. 'They're coming over in bleedin' droves.'

The Scot looked at me bleakly, as though he doubted I'd be much of a reinforcement. They'd been at the barracks a week, they said, and both showed a mixture of bravado and bewilderment, though the Scot also seemed to have a profane contempt for most of the others around him.

'Look at this bugga',' he said, jerking a finger at Danny. "E dunno a gun fra' a stick a' rock. If we canna' do better'n tha', Guid 'elp us.'

Danny stiffened and gave him a shrivelled look.

'But we're 'ere then, ennit?' he said.

It was true – and we were. Danny pointed out the others gathered in the courtyard, sitting and standing in their little groups, some playing cards, or just whistling, or staring into the distance, some fast asleep with the daylight exhaustion of waiting. Everybody was here, said Danny: Dutch, Germans and Poles. Exiles from Paris, a sprinkling of thugs on the run from Marseilles, a few Welshmen from the valleys, some Durham miners, Catalans, Canadians, Americans, Czechs, and half a dozen pale and speechless Russians.

The Welsh, in their huddles, were talking Welsh. The Durham miners were protesting about the food. The Scot, who seemed to have found some brandy from somewhere, was rising on the peak of spluttering Olympian disdain.

'We gotta anni-hi-late the lot of 'em,' he growled. 'Teach 'em political authority. Or wipe 'em all out. Thas what we gotta do.'

''E's so drunk,' said Danny, ''e don't know which side 'e's on yet – do ya, you 'eathen bastard?'

Two young men, in dark suits, were playing chess on the ground, using stones in scratched squares in the sand. They were solemn, concerned, and cast disapproving glances at Doug. They talked together formally, in the accents of clerks.

This, again, was not quite what I'd expected. In this special army I'd imagined a shoulder-to-shoulder brotherhood, a brave camaraderie joined in one purpose, not this fragmentation of national groups scattered around the courtyard talking wanly only to each other. Indeed, they seemed to share a mutual air of unease and watchfulness, of distrust and even dislike.

I left Danny and Doug and wandered casually around, pretending I'd been here for weeks. But the pattern of that first morning was to be repeated during the whole length of my stay. The French crooks crouched in corners, shrugging and scowling; the Poles sat in princely silence sunning their beautiful cheekbones. The Czechs scribbled pamphlets and passed them to each other for correction; while the Russians seemed to come and go mysteriously as by tricks of the light. The British played cards and swore.

But we were a young and unclassifiable bunch on the whole, with mixed motives and humours, waiting to test our nerves in new fields of belief. The Castle and its courtyard was our starting-point – a square of pale sunlight surrounded by snow.

How had we all got here? Some by boat, some by illegal train-shuttles from France, but most smuggled from Perpignan by lorry. I hadn't known, in my solitary ignorance, that there was this well-organized traffic for volunteers running from London through Paris into Spain. Which was why I'd done the daft thing and come on my own, and even chosen winter to do it. None the less, I heard later that my progress had not gone altogether unnoticed.

I must have been watched through France, and all the way from Perpignan. Of that I was never entirely certain, but if it was true it probably saved my life.

About one o'clock that first day somebody hit a barrel with a stick and we filed into a long shed for a meal. A couple of old women handed us tin plates and spoons, then ladled out bean soup from a vat. Bean soup hot and chunky, with an interesting admixture of tar, but to me a gluttonous reward after almost two weeks of near famine in the cave.

I remembered again the concentration of the senses, of smell and flavour, that hunger brings to appetite, and with each steaming spoonful I was also aware of the grime of the unscrubbed table, the rusting metal of the soup plate, the sharp frozen landscape outside, almost the fatness of each bean.

The meal was a holiday hour, like at a refugee camp, although there were overtones of an open prison. The men sat huddled, heads down, rapidly spooning their soup, or hobbling around looking for bread; reasonably good-humoured in their ragged, unshaven selves, but showing none of the fire and spirit I thought they should have. It seemed we mixed at these meals – except for the French and the Russians, who sat down, got up, and moved about in a taciturn, self-watchful cadre.

When we'd finished eating I joined a small group outside, sitting cross-legged in the weak afternoon sunlight – Doug, Danny, Ulli, a Dutchman, and Ben Shapiro, a bouncing Brooklyn Jew. We propped ourselves stiffly against a row of white-painted oil-drums, and those with capes wrapped them around themselves.

First we sat in silence, inert. There seemed to be no discipline or programme. No one of any seeming authority came near us.

Doug said, 'I've been here ten days, and I've still not handled a gun.'

'I've not seen one,' said Ulli.

'Too dangerous to leave lying around for the likes of you,' said Doug.

'I have five at home,' said Ulli. 'For ducks on the water. If I'm knowing here they're needing, I am bringing all of them with me.'

We sat idly a little longer, then we were called in to a lecture given by a pink-faced Belgian in a long black mackintosh. With a series of maps and slogans he was proving that Franco had lost the war, when the lecture seemed to peter out through a sudden lack of interest.

'Tomorrow is political education,' he said. 'Now is free time to go down to the town. Class dismissed.' And he picked up his maps and left.

About six of us sauntered through the Castle gates. The sentry had propped up his rifle against the wall. We found him playing with some children in the road outside and he raised a clenched fist as we passed.

Figueras had once been a fine hill town, with ordered streets and pretty houses, and open spaces for walking in the evening. War had shrivelled and emptied it, covered it with a sort of grey hapless grime so that even the windows seemed to have no reflections. The gathering twilight also seemed to bring an unnatural silence, as if all life had gone into hiding.

Down near the station, however, were a couple of low-roofed taverns, bare and cold, with streaming wet floors. Doug and Ulli led me first into one, and then into the other, where they were clearly already well known and where the stooping old women behind the bar threw up their hands at the sight of them.

They were not the taverns I remembered – those with great sweating wine-casks and glistening bottles labelled with posturing bullfighters. Indeed, I could see no drink at all, so in the second bar I asked for some coffee, and was given a glass of hot brown silt tasting of leather and rust.

'Leave all tha',' said Doug, 'an' come along wi' us.' We went down some steps into a dim-lit cellar whose walls were covered with anarchist posters – vivid stark images of fists and faces, mouths crying defiance, shouting blasts for freedom, guns and flags held high, banners billowing with slogans, all in bright, hard, primary colours.

A thin old man in a corner quickly turned his back on us as we entered, bent low, and tried to hide something under his cloak. There was a brief flapping and squawking from between his legs as he furtively pushed a chicken into a sack.

'All right, Josepe,' said Ulli, poking round the littered cellar. 'Where is it? Out with it, man.'

'Ay – ay,' wheezed the ancient. 'Again the Frenchman, by God! Why don't you go away to your country?'

Ulli, in Spanish, and Doug, with black Scots oaths, began to bully and tease the old man till he folded and scrabbled across the room. Mumbling of foreign evils and the curses of war, he searched through some sacking and turned up a stained goatskin flask.

We sat on the floor and passed it round between us. It was a country coñac, vitriolic and burning.

Josepe kept the struggling chicken huddled under his cloak and watched us peevishly while we drank. The black hairy flask smelt richly of goat and resin, the coñac of bitter oils. But it stung, and warmed us deep inside, just right for three men sitting on a cellar floor.

'Bless this place,' Doug grunted, wiping his mouth. 'I never wanna leave it – never.'

Danny came suddenly down the steps on his little web-like feet, noiseless, nose-poking, apologetic.

'Well, 'oo'd a' believed it?' he giggled. ''Ere we are again then, eh? Got a drop left for me? No offence, a' course.'

Doug looked at him with distaste, but passed him the coñac. Danny nodded jerkily to each of us, and drank.

Only a few days in Spain, ripe for Freedom and the Cause, and here we were, squatting in the cellar of a northern tavern, bullying a crazed old man and getting drunk.

When we'd emptied a third leather flask, Josepe begged plaintively for payment, and Doug gave him a new hundred peseta note.

'No, no!' whimpered Josepe, waving it away.

'Guid government money,' said Doug, screwing it into his hand. 'Take it mon – it's a soldier's wages.'

The old man bunched up his knees and hissed and grizzled, pushing at Doug with his tiny fists.

'No, no!' he wailed. 'It is not to be borne! Carmelita! Eulalia! Come!'

A slim gliding figure, as light as a greyhound, moved softly down the cellar steps. The man reached out a shaking hand and gripped the girl by the shoulder while the chicken broke from his cloak and flew into the wall.

'Where've you been, whore?' he growled, pinching the girl viciously. 'Why did you leave me again to the Frenchmen?'

She turned her head towards us.

'Give him something,' she whispered. 'Belt, scarf, cigarettes – anything. But quickly; he's going mad.'

The girl wore the tight black dress of the villages, and had long Spanish-Indian eyes. She pushed the old man up the stairs and told him to go to bed. Doug, Ulli and Danny followed behind him, singing brokenly and urging him on.

A winter sunset glow shone through a high grille in the wall, and I was aware, behind the sharp smell of coñac, of something softer and muskier. The young girl, crouching low in the shadows, had loosened her dress and was pouring brandy over her bare bruised shoulder.

She rubbed the liquor into her flesh with long brown fingers and watched me warily as she did so. Her eyes were like slivers of painted glass, glinting in the setting sun. I heard the boys upstairs stamping and singing to the breathy music of an old accordion. But I couldn't join them. I was trapped down here, in this place, this cellar, to the smell of coñac and this sleek animal girl.

She was stroking, almost licking, her upper arms, like a cat, her neck arched, her dark head bowed. She raised her eyes again, and we just stared at each other before I sat down beside her. Without

a word, she handed me the flask of coñac, turned her bare shoulder towards me, and waited. Her skin was mottled by small purple bruises that ran backwards under her dress. I poured some drops of coñac into the palm of my hand and began to rub it awkwardly over her damp hot flesh. The girl sighed and stiffened, then swayed against me, leading me into a rhythm of her own.

The frayed black dress was now loose at the edges and gave way jerkily to my clumsy fingers. The girl's eyes were fixed on mine with a kind of rapt impatience. With a slight swerve of her shoulders she offered more flesh for healing. I rubbed more coñac into the palms of my hands. Slowly, as my touch followed her, she lay back on the sacking. The boys upstairs were singing 'Home on the Range'.

Apart from the quick stopping and starting of her breath, the girl was silent. The red blanket of sunset moved over her. Her thin dancer's body was now almost bare to the waist and revealed all the wispy fineness of a Persian print. It seemed that in some perverse way she wished to show both her beauty and its blemishes. Or perhaps she didn't care. She held my hands still for a moment.

'Frenchman,' she said thickly.

'English,' I said woodenly.

She shrugged, and whispered a light bubbling profanity – not Catalan but pure Andaluz. Her finger and thumb closed on my wrist like a manacle. Her body met mine with the quick twist of a snake.

When the square of sunset had at last moved away and died, we lay panting gently, and desert dry. I took a swig from the goatskin and offered it to her. She shook her head, but lay close as though to keep me warm. A short while ago she had been a thing of panicky gasps and whimpers. Now she looked into my eyes like a mother.

'My little blond man,' she said tenderly. 'Young, so young.'

'How old are you, then?' I asked.

'Fifteen . . . sixteen – who knows?' She sat up suddenly, still only half-dressed, her delicate bruised shoulders arched proudly.

'I kill him.'

'Who?'

'The old one. The grandfather. He maltreats . . . Thank God for the war.'

The chicken, huddled fluffily against the wall in the corner, seemed now to be asleep. The girl turned and tidied me briskly, then tidied herself, settling her clothes around her sweet small limbs. Then she lifted her long loose hair and fastened it into a shining bun. The stamping and singing upstairs had stopped.

I was astonished that this hour had been so simple yet secret, the opening and closing of velvet doors. Eulalia was not the sort of Spanish girl I'd known in the past – the noisy steel-edged virgins flirting from the safety of upstairs windows, or loud arm-in-arm with other girls in the paseo, sensual, cheeky, confident of their powers, but scared to be alone with a man.

Eulalia, with her beautiful neck and shoulders, also had a quiet dignity and grace. A wantonness, too, so sudden and unexpected, I felt it was a wantonness given against her will. Or at least, if not given willingly, it was now part of her nature, the result of imposed habit and tutoring.

As she pulled on her tattered slippers, she told me she would not stay long in Figueras. She'd come from the south, she said – she didn't know where – and had been working here as a house-drudge since she was ten. Once she would have stayed on till body and mind were used up; the sexually abused slattern of some aged employer, sleeping under the stairs between calls to his room. Not any more, she was now free to do as she wished. Spain had changed, and the new country had braver uses for girls such as she. She need stay no longer with this brutal pig of an innkeeper. She would go to Madrid and be a soldier.

It had grown dark and cold in the cellar. Suddenly she turned and embraced me, wrapping me urgently in her hot thin arms.

'Frenchman!' she whispered. 'At last I have found my brother.'

'Englishman,' I said, as she slipped away.

*

The next morning there was an outbreak of discipline in the barracks. Soon after daylight, scattered committees, in groups, began to gather in the courtyard. The Commandant – who was he? – strode about in mottled riding-boots and a cape, greeting us with uneasy bonhomie.

By majority vote it was agreed we should have some exercise and drill. Somebody blew on a bugle. Men sauntered out on to the parade-ground and arranged themselves in rows. Others ran away, thinking the bugle meant retreat or an air-raid.

Those who were left then marched up and down, shouting orders at each other, forming threes and fours, running at the double, falling over, falling out, standing still, arguing, and finally parading past the Commandant from several directions, while he stood on a chair saluting.

We were an uneven lot; large and small, mostly young, hollow-cheeked, ragged, pale, the sons of depressed and uneasy Europe. But confused as we were as we marched about, there seemed to be a growing urgency in our eyes. We were fumbling to find some order of courage; and there was that moment when we almost came together in line and step, and as we swept past the Commandant once again, our clenched fists raised, we felt that bursting of the chest and tightening of the throat which made heroes and warriors of us all. Even the Czechs and Russians seemed to be briefly affected and smiled faintly at one another.

That afternoon, having declared our brotherhood of purpose, we held a mass meeting in the mess shed to study the tactics of war. Several groups sat round tables shuffling dominoes into lines of battle. A military exercise was proposed, seconded and forgotten. A Russian drew arrows in charcoal on a white-washed wall – all centred on Figueras and pointing eastward, and home.

Doug swept in and out of the shed wearing a new leather jacket and leading a small Frenchman in a Verdun helmet. I sensed an air of busy intention and high resolve around me, and for the first time since I arrived heard strength in men's voices.

"Aven't they told ye?' barked Doug, briskly halting at my

table, his thick Scots overlaid with Military Academy cadences. 'They're putting on a show this afternoon. Parade at 14.00 hours sharp. And get into some decent uniform, you soft English lemon.'

We gathered in the square, blowing in the ice-sharp wind, and were given long sticks for guns. We were going to attack a 'strong point' up the hill, an enemy machine-gun position; a frontal and flanking assault on bare rising ground. 'The attack will be pushed home with surprise and determination,' said the Commandant. 'It happens all the time.'

We jogged up and down, playing football with stones, changing our platoons at will. Then, after rival shouts of command, of which we obeyed the loudest, we were over the wall and up the rocky hill. We could hear the machine-guns stuttering away at the top of the rise – rusty oil-drums being beaten with sticks.

Half-way up, we halted. 'Well, attack!' said someone. We stood undecided, not knowing what to do. Then a fellow ahead of us threw himself face down on the ground, and began to wriggle forward and upward on his belly. So we all did the same, and it was fun for a moment – but we very soon changed our minds. As a method of progress it was slow, uncomfortable, dirty and boring. Some of us swore; I heard a man say, 'Sod this for a lark.' So a few of us got to our feet and started walking again. The oil-drums were still rattling away up ahead, and we were sauntering up the hill in front. Almost invisible among the rocks, his bottom high in the air, Doug was shouting, 'Get yer 'eads down, you stoopid buggers!' Away in the distance, to the left and right of us, straggling lines of other chaps wriggled up the hill. It looked almost realistic, so I dropped into position again, crawling and following another man's boots.

Near the top of the hill, with the banging of the oil-drums much closer, our leaders cried, 'Forward! Adelante! Charge!' We leapt to our feet and galloped the last few yards, shouting as horribly as we could, and cast ourselves on the men who had been beating the oil-drums, who then threw up their arms and surrendered, sniggering.

Twenty minutes' crawling and sauntering up that bare open hill, and we had captured a machine-gun post, without loss. Our shouting died; it had been a famous victory. Real guns would have done for the lot of us.

We finished the day's training with an elaborate anti-tank exercise. A man covered a pram with an oil-cloth and pushed it round and round the square, while we stood in doorways and threw bottles and bricks at it. The man pushing the pram was Danny, from London. He was cross when a bottle hit him.

The next day, in the evening, a child brought me a message, and as soon as I was free I slipped down to the town. This time I went alone, but not immediately to Josepe's, but first to an old wine bar up near the Plaza. The first man I saw was the giraffe-necked Frenchman from the Pyrenees who had guided me over the last peak of the mountains. He'd been taciturn, gruff. 'Don't do this for everyone,' he'd said. 'Don't think we run conducted tours.' Which was exactly what he was doing, as I could see now. Beret and leather jacket, long neck still lagged with a scarf, he stood in the centre of the bar talking to a group of hatless young men, each looking slightly bewildered and carrying little packages. Smoking with rapid puffs, eyes shifting and watchful, marshalling his charges with special care, he handed each one a French cigarette, then pushed them towards the door. His coat was new, and his shoes well polished, and clearly he had walked no mountain paths lately. Perhaps he'd brought this little group across the frontier by truck. As he left the room, he brushed against me, caught my eye for a moment and winked . . .

I went down the street in the freezing rain and found Felipe's bar closed and dark. Through a crack in the shutters I could see a glimmer of candles and some old women sitting by a black wooden box. Bunches of crape hung over the mirror behind the bar which was littered with broken bottles. I was wondering why, and from whom, the message had been sent up to the barracks. It had certainly been laconic enough. The boy had simply sidled in and asked me if I was 'Lorenzo the Frenchman', and then muttered, 'You've got to go down to Felipe's.'

I knocked on the door and presently one of the old women let me in. She asked who I was and I told her. 'Where's Don Felipe?' I said, and she showed her gums briefly, then said, 'Bang! He's gone to the angels.' She stabbed a finger at the open box, and there he was, his face black and shining like a piece of coal. 'Bang!' said the old woman again, with a titter, then crossed herself. 'God forgive him.'

Where was Eulalia? I asked. 'She went in a camion,' she said. 'An hour ago. Away over there . . .' I could get no more from her, except that the old man had been shot and that, in her opinion, he was without shame and deserved it.

Looking into the crone's bright death-excited eyes, and smelling the hot pork-fat of the candles, I knew that this was not a wake, or even a mourning, but a celebration of something cleared from their lives. I also knew that Eulalia, my murderous little dancer, had called me to show me what she'd done, but called me too late, and had gone.

3

To Albacete and the Clearing
House

Ten days after my arrival at Figueras Castle enough volunteers had gathered to make up a convoy. By that time we were sleeping all over the place – in tents in the courtyard, under the mess-hall tables, or the lucky ones in the straw-filled dungeons. Day after day, more groups of newcomers appeared – ill-clad, crop-haired and sunken-cheeked, they were (as I was) part of the skimmed-milk of the middle-Thirties. You could pick out the British by their nervous jerking heads, native air of suspicion, and constant stream of self-effacing jokes. These, again could be divided up into the ex-convicts, the alcoholics, the wizened miners, dockers, noisy politicos and dreamy undergraduates busy scribbling manifestos and notes to their boyfriends.

We were collected now to be taken to where the war was, or, at least, another step nearer. But what had brought us here, anyway? My reasons seemed simple enough, in spite of certain confusions. But so then were those of most of the others – failure, poverty, debt, the law, betrayal by wives or lovers – most of the usual things that sent one to foreign wars. But in our case, I believe, we shared something else, unique to us at that time – the chance to make one grand, uncomplicated gesture of personal sacrifice and faith which might never occur again. Certainly, it was the last time this century that a generation had such an opportunity before the fog of nationalism and mass-slaughter closed in.

Few of us yet knew that we had come to a war of antique muskets and jamming machine-guns, to be led by brave but bewildered amateurs. But for the moment there were no half-truths or hesitations, we had found a new freedom, almost a new morality, and discovered a new Satan – Fascism.

Not that much of this was openly discussed among us, in spite of our long hours of idle chatter. Apart from the occasional pronunciamentos of the middle-Europeans, and the undergraduates' stumbling dialectics, I remember only one outright declaration of direct concern – scribbled in charcoal on a latrine wall:

> The Fashish Bastids murdered my buddy at Huesca.
> Don't worry, pal. I've come to get them.
> (Signed) HARRY.

The morning came for us to leave. But it wouldn't be by camiones after all. The snow was too heavy. We would go by train. After a brief, ragged parade, and when we had formed into lines of three, the Commandant suddenly appeared with my baggage. 'It's all there,' he said, strapping it on to my shoulders, 'all except the camera, that is.' He gave me a sour, tired look. 'We don't ever expect much from you, comrade. But don't ever forget – we'll be keeping our eye on you.'

The Castle gates were thrown open, sagging loose on their hinges, and in two broken columns we shuffled down to the station. A keen, gritty snow blew over the town, through the streets, and into our faces. We passed Josepe's, whose windows were now boarded up and outside which an armed militiaman huddled. On the station platform a group of old women, young girls, and a few small boys had gathered to see us off. A sombre, Doré-like scene with which I was to become familiar – the old women in black, watching with watery eyes, speechless, like guardians of the dead; the girls holding out small shrunken oranges as their most precious offerings; the boys stiff and serious, with their clenched fists raised. The station was a heavy monochrome of black clothes and old iron, lightened here and there by clouds of wintry steam. An early Victorian train stood waiting, each carriage about the size of a stage-coach, with tiny windows and wooden seats. Every man had a hunk of grey bread and a screwed-paper of olives, and with these rations we scrambled aboard.

As we readied to leave, with clanking of buffers and couplings, and sudden jerks backward and forward, the girls ran up and handed us their little oranges, with large lustrous looks in their eyes. The small boys formed a line, shouting, 'Salud, compañeros!' The old women waved and wept.

I shared a compartment with a half-dozen muffled-up soldiers who had only arrived the day before, including an ill-favoured young Catalan whose pox-pitted cheeks sprouted stubble like a grave in May. Garrulous – as we all were – he declared himself to be an anarchist, but one with a pivotal sense of nationalism, which made him boast, quite properly, that having been born in Barcelona, he was no more Spanish than the rest of us.

For this reason he'd joined the Brigade. He kept slapping his chest. 'Pau Guasch,' he said. 'International Catalan, me! International damn Chinese-Russian-Catalan-Polish. No damn father, damn mother, damn God.' He'd helped burn down three churches in Gerona, he said. He'd scattered petrol, thrown a match, and said, 'Woosh!'

In the end we told him to shut up, his spluttering English was too much for us. He seemed in no way put down. He took a potato from his pocket, crossed himself before eating it, and muttered, 'Damn Trotsky, King of the Jews.'

The train jerked and clattered at an unsteady eight miles an hour, often stopping, like a tired animal, for gasping periods of rest. We moved through a grey and desolate country crossed by deserted roads and scattered with empty villages that seemed to have had their eyes put out.

It was then that I began to sense for the first time something of the gaseous squalor of a country at war, an infection so deep it seemed to rot the earth, drain it of colour, life and sound. This was not the battlefield; but acts of war had been committed here, little murders, small excesses of vengeance. The landscape was plagued, stained and mottled, and all humanity seemed to have been banished from it. The normal drive of life had come to a halt, nobody stirred, even the trees looked blighted; one saw no dogs or children, horses or girls, no smoking fires or washing on lines, no one talking in doorways or walking by the river, leaning out of windows or watching the train go by – only a lifeless smear over roof and field, like something cancelled or in a coma; and here and there, at the windswept crossroads, a few soldiers huddled in dripping capes. Worse than a country at war, this one was at war with itself – an ultimate, more permanent wastage.

Night came, and darkness, outside and inside the train. Only the winter stars moved. We were still smoking the last of our Gauloises Bleus, stripping them down and re-rolling them into finer and even finer spills. Our faces, lit by the dim glow of our fags, hung like hazy rose masks in the shadows. Then one by one, heads nodded, fags dropped from sagging mouths, and faces faded from sight.

It was a long broken night, the windows tight shut, our bodies drawing warmth from each other. But there were too many of us packed into this tiny old carriage, and those who chose to lie on the floor soon regretted it. Long murmuring confidences, snores, sudden whimpers of nightmare, a girl's name muttered again and again, Pau Guasch howling blasphemies when a boot trod on his face, oaths in three languages when someone opened a window.

It may have been twenty hours later – waking and sleeping, arguing, telling stories, nibbling bread and olives, or just sitting in silence and gazing dully at each other – that the train slowed down to less than a walking pace and finally halted in a gasp of exhausted steam under the cheese-green lights of Valencia station.

We were to change trains here, and were promised hot food. The time was about midnight, and the great city around us showed no light as though trying to deny its existence, its miles of dark buildings giving off an air of prostration, pressed tight to the ground like turtles.

We had pulled up in a siding. A late moon was rising. Some women arrived with buckets of stew. They moved in a quick, jerky silence, not even talking to each other, ladling out the thin broth in little frightened jabs. Suddenly one of them stopped, lifted her head, gave a panicky yelp like a puppy, dropped her food bucket and scampered away. She had heard something we had not, her ears better tuned already to the signals of what was to come.

Following her cry and departure, the others fled too. Then the station lights were switched off. An inert kind of stillness smothered the city, a stretched and expectant waiting. Then from the blank eastern sky, far out over the sea, came a fine point of sound, growing to a deep throbbing roar, advancing steadily overhead towards us. Such a sound that the women on the platform had learned to beware of, but which to us was only an aircraft at night. And which, as we listened, changed from the familiar, casual passage of peace to one of malignant purpose. The fatal sound which Spain was the first country in Europe to know, but with which most of the world would soon be visited.

Franco's airfields in Majorca, armed by Italian and German warplanes, were only a few minutes' flight from the mainland. Barcelona and Valencia lay as open cities, their defences but a few noisy and ineffectual guns.

As the bombers closed in, spreading their steady roar above us, I felt a quick surge of unnatural excitement. I left the train, and the roofed platform, and wandered off alone to the marshalling yards some distance away. This was my first air-raid, and I wanted to meet it by myself, to taste the full brunt of it without fuss or panic. We'd already seen posters and photographs of what bombs could do to a city, slicing down through apartment blocks, leaving all their intimacies exposed – the wedding portrait on the wall, the cheap little crucifix, the broken bed hanging bare to the street – the feeling of whole families huddled together in their private caves being suddenly blasted to death in one breath. New images of outrage which Spain was the first to show us, and which in some idiot way I was impatient to share.

The bombers seemed now overhead, moving slowly, heavily, ploughing deep furrows of sound. A single searchlight switched on, then off again quickly, as though trying to cancel itself out. Then the whole silent city woke to an almost hysterical clamour, guns crackling and chattering in all directions, while long arcs of tracer-bullets looped across the sky in a brilliant skein of stars. This frantic outburst of fire lasted only a minute or two, then petered out, its panic exhausted.

The airplanes swung casually over the city, left now to their own intentions. Just a couple of dozen young men, in their rocking dim-lit cabins, and the million below them waiting their chance in the dark. A plane accelerated and went into a dive, followed by the others in a roaring procession. They swooped low and fast, guided perhaps by the late moon on the water, on the rooftops and railway tracks. Then the bombs were released – not from any great height, for the tearing shriek of their fall was short. There followed a series of thumping explosions and blasts of light as parcels of flame straddled the edge of the station. I felt the ground jump at my feet and smelt the reek of burnt dust. A bomb hit the track near the loading sheds, and two trucks sailed sideways against a halo of fire, while torn lines circled around them like ribbons. Further off an old house lit from inside like a turnip lamp, then crumpled and disappeared. A warehouse slowly expanded in the gory bloom of a direct hit, and several other fires were rooted in the distance. But it was over quickly – a little more of the city destroyed, more people burned or buried, then the bombers turned back out to sea.

I found I'd stood out in the open and watched this air-raid on Valencia with curiosity but otherwise no emotion. I was surprised at my detachment and lack of fear. I may even have felt some queer satisfaction. It was something I learned about myself that night which I have never quite understood.

Once the planes had gone, there was little to be heard but the crackling of flames and the distant bells of a fire-engine. I was joined by two of my companions from the train, both silent, both fresh to this, as I was. A railwayman crossed the lines, groping about, bent double. We asked him if he was all right, and he said yes, but he needed help. He shone a torch on his left hand, which was smashed and bleeding, then jerked his head in the direction of the nearby street. We ran round the edge of the burning warehouse and found two little houses, also well alight. They were small working-class shops, blazing tents of tiles and beams from beneath which came an old man's cry.

'My uncle,' said the railwayman, tearing away at the smoking rubble with his one undamaged hand. 'I told him to sleep in the cinema.' The roofs collapsed suddenly, sending a skirt of sparks riffling across the road. The old man's cries ceased, and we staggered back while great curling flames took over. 'The fault is his,' said the railwayman. 'He would have been safe in the cine. He used to go there every afternoon.' He stood doubled up, staring furiously at the blazing ruin, his clothes smoking, his hands hanging black and helpless.

Walking back towards the station, we stumbled over a figure on the pavement, lying powdered white, like a dying crusader. His face and body were covered in plaster dust, and he shook violently from head to toe. We rolled him on to a couple of boards and carried him to the main platform, where several other bodies were already spread out in rows. A moaning woman held a broken child in her arms; two others lay clasped together in silence, while a bearded doctor, in a dingy white coat, just wandered up and down the platform blaspheming.

It was a small, brief horror imposed on the sleeping citizens of Valencia, and one so slight and routine, compared with what was happening elsewhere in Spain, as to be scarcely worth recording. Those few minutes' bombing I'd witnessed were simply an early essay in a new kind of warfare, soon to be known – and accepted – throughout the world.

Few acknowledged at the time that it was General Franco, the Supreme Patriot and Defender of the Christian Faith, who allowed these first trial-runs to be inflicted on the bodies of his countrymen, and who delivered up vast areas of Spain to be the living testing-grounds for Hitler's new bomber-squadrons, culminating in the annihilation of the ancient city of Guernica.

About four in the morning, with fires still burning in the distance, we were rounded up by our 'transport officer', who was rather drunk and wearing a Mongolian jacket. Round his neck, somewhat oddly, he'd slung binoculars and a tape-measure, and he scurried about, shooing us back to the train, as though our departure was part of some major logistic.

Some of the men had loud, over-excited voices, shining eyes, and brave tales of survival. Some were quiet and staring, others appeared to have slept unaware through everything.

Our new train was drawn up in another part of the station, where we found Pau Guasch carrying a basket of bread. Once crammed into our compartment he handed chunks of it round, saying we were not fit to eat such victuals. He was half-right there; the bread must have been several weeks old, and was coated with soot and plaster. He looked smug and benign as we tried to gnaw away at his bounty; in the end we swallowed it down.

The night was long and cramped as the train lumbered inland, slowly circling and climbing the escarpment of Chiclana to reach the freezing tableland of Mancha. I had known part of this plateau in the heat of high summer when it seemed to blaze and buckle like a copper sheet. Now it was as dead as the Russian steppes, an immensity of ashen snow reflecting the hard light of the winter moon. No gold path of glory, this, for youth to go to war, but a grey path of intense disquiet.

Apart from Pau Guasch, all the men in my compartment were volunteers from outside – British, Canadian, Dutch. And poor Guasch, the only true native son of the Peninsula, found himself squashed between his own natural assumption of leadership and our teasing contempt for him – the 'foreigner'. So we used him as the butt of our mindless exhaustion, pushed him around, tripped him up, trod him under our feet, and stuffed his shirt with crumbs and crusts of bread.

Fear, exasperation and cruelty gripped us, and we continued to taunt the furious little Catalan till we tired, at last, of our mirthless game and slumped one by one to sleep. We slept stiffly, uneasily, propping each other bolt upright, or toppling sideways like bottles in a basket. We were not warriors any more, but lumps of merchandise being carried to a dumping-ground.

In a bitter dawn we approached Albacete on the plain, clanking through tiny stations where groups of snow-swept women watched us dumbly as we passed them by. A lad at a level crossing, with a thin head-down horse, lifted a clenched fist for a moment, then dejectedly dropped it again. Silent old men and barefooted children, like Irish peasants of the Great Hunger, lined the sides of the tracks without gesture or greeting. We were received, as we trundled towards our military camp, not as heroic deliverers, or reinforcements for victory, but rather as another train-load of faceless prisoners seen through a squint-eyed blankness of spirit.

But as we steamed at last into Albacete station, we found that someone, at least, had dredged up some sense of occasion. We fell stiffly from the train and lined up raggedly on the platform, and were faced by a small brass band like a firing-squad. In the dead morning light they pointed their instruments at our heads and blew out a succession of tubercular blasts. Then a squat mackintoshed Commander climbed on to a box and addressed us in rasping tones. Until that moment, perhaps, cold and hungry though we were, we may still have retained some small remnants of courage. The Commander took them away from us, one by one, and left us with nothing but numb dismay.

He welcomed us briefly, mentioned our next of kin (which we were doing our best to forget), said we were the flower of Europe, thanked us for presenting our lives, reminded us of the blood and sacrifice we were about to bestow on the Cause, and drew our attention to the sinister might and awesome power of International Fascism now arrayed against us. Many valiant young comrades had preceded us, he said, had willingly laid down their lives in the Struggle, and now rested in the honoured graves of heroes in the

battlefields of Guadalajara, Jarama and Brunete. He knew we
would be proud to follow them, he said – then shook himself like
a dog, scowled up at the sky, saluted, and turned and left us. We
shuffled our feet in the slush and looked at each other; we were an
unwashed and tattered lot. We were young and had expected a
welcome of girls and kisses, even the prospect of bloodless glory;
not till the Commander had pointed it out to us, I believe, had we
seriously considered that we might die.

Our group leader came striding along the platform leading a
squealing Pau Guasch by the ear. He wanted to go home, he
cried; he'd got arthritis and the gripe. The group leader kicked
him back into line. We formed up in threes and, led by the
coughing and consumptive band, marched with sad ceremony
through the streets of the town. We saw dark walls, a few posters,
wet flags, sodden snow. Sleet blew from a heavy sky. I had known
Spain in the bright, healing light of the sun, when even its poverty
seemed coloured with pride. Albacete, this morning, was like a
whipped northern slum. The women, as we passed, covered their
faces with shawls.

4

Death Cell: Albacete

Albacete was all wind and knives, surrounded by the white pine-scarred immensities of La Mancha. As we marched to the barracks, other military figures on the pavements, of all shapes and adornment, greeted us with only a few hoots of derision.

At the barrack gates, our little brass band deserted us, and went trundling off down the street shaking out their crumpled instruments. Our brief moment of honour and welcome it seemed was ended; another trainload of scruffs had been duly delivered. We were formed up on the parade-ground, our soaking bags on our backs, snowflakes settling upon our beards. Two officers walked out and looked us over; a clerk with a clipboard stood by taking notes. Nothing was said to us; we were viewed as remote curiosities, while the mounting snow swirled and cut around us. Anonymous, unacknowledged, we stood shuffling and muttering; after all we had not yet been fed. But still they held us there in a kind of suspended detachment while the clerk counted and recounted our numbers.

There was tension, and suddenly I felt specially separate from the others. Even before it happened, I knew it would happen. A soldier hurried from the main building and handed a note to one of the officers, who read it and called out my name. I raised my hand, my companions were dismissed, and I was once more taken away under guard.

Had I been marked down from the very beginning, I wondered? If so, why had I got this far? I was led away to a small room deep in one of the basements which was a jumble of filing cabinets, maps and papers. A young fair-haired officer sat at a littered desk, and he rose to his feet when I entered. He was smartly dressed, deferential, American and charming. He introduced himself as Sam.

'I'm sorry,' he said, and gave me a chair. 'I guess you've been through all this before – but something fresh has turned up . . .'

He produced my passport, which had been taken from me at Figueras, and slowly riffled through the pages. Two of them had been marked with paperclips, and he spread the book open and showed it to me. On his face was an expression of amused resignation – an unspoken 'how could you have been such a fool?'

In the spring of 1936 I'd spent a few days in Spanish Morocco, which General Franco was using as the base for his rebellion at that time, and from where, in July, he started the Civil War. But of course I didn't know this till he started flying his Moors across the Straits from there. I'd been in the very nest of intrigue, but knew nothing about it.

Sam fingered the pages of my passport with almost strained disbelief, then held it up to my eyes: Ceuta, Tetuan, Entrada, Salida – he pointed out the fatal names and dates.

'Just what were you doing there at that time – for Gawd's sake?' he asked. 'That's all we're wanting to know.'

Sam had now been joined by two short, square little Russians, both slightly bald and wearing civilian suits. Plumping themselves down, one on each side of the American, they waited in silence for me to speak.

I could now see the trouble I was in – first suspected as a spy, and now as a Fascist agent. No doubt about it either, Sam had the proof in his hand. I felt that sudden thump in the heart which I remember as a child when I'd been accused of some major though innocent blunder.

Yes, I said, in early 1936 I'd been working in a hotel near Málaga, and I'd made a quick trip to Morocco with a French student from Arles. Yes, it had been spring, but we hadn't seen

A Moment of War

much of the country, we'd spent most of our time in the rooms of small hotels, behind shutters, smoking hash. Sam sighed and passed his hand over his brow. He told me to empty my pockets.

Everything I had was laid out on the desk and the two square little men went to work. Cigarettes stripped, paper held to the light, fountain-pen unscrewed, then probed and smashed. Matches shaken out on to a blotter, then each one split down the middle. The matchbox itself also cut into sections and each piece pressed against a special lamp, as were the odd papers and my notebook and pocketbook, including a few pesetas and family photographs.

While the two squat civilians were at their meticulous inspections, searching for who knows what? – secret messages, war maps, codes, plans – Sam was reading through the papers they had discarded, and keeping up a quiet, continuous stream of questions. What was the name of the student? And where was he now? What hotels had we stayed in? And how much was I paid, and who paid me, huh? Well, it was only a short trip, I said, and the boy paid for most of it. He was the son of a rich businessman from Marseilles. Sam knew I was lying, but he didn't know why I was lying. My journey to Morocco had been solitary, innocent, but damning.

I was told to undress to my pants, and my clothes were searched carefully, including the linings and soles of my boots. Then something desperately unwished-for happened, but now too late to avoid; Sam found a packet of letters in my trouser hip-pocket. They were letters from the English girl who had followed me to the edge of France and tried to dissuade me from crossing the frontier – letters recalling the wildly passionate celebration of our last week together, a rapturous, explicit and tormenting farewell. I knew every word by heart, which were not for any other eyes. But now this neat young Bostonian, who might not have read such letters before, was scanning them earnestly line by line. He read them quite slowly, and looked up once or twice, as I stared blindly at the opposite wall. Sitting on the chair before him, I felt in every way naked, and no man before him had entered my

459

private world. When he'd finished reading, he passed the letters back to me in silence. His face, though flushed, was as blank as mine.

Sam never referred to the letters again, but he was clearly an intense young professional, with a job to do; yet as he began to question me further – about dates, movements, intentions, motives – I was also aware of a look of dazed perplexity in his eyes, as that of a doctor who, while inquiring into one major disease, had unexpectedly stumbled on to another one altogether.

Sam's two gnome-like assistants, having taken their turn with my clothes and boots, now came and sat down, one on each side of me. They picked things up off the desk, and put them down, shook my violin and twanged the strings, and held a little photograph of my mother up to a mirror. They muttered together, asked each other questions, nodded, then just stared at me balefully. I had a feeling they wanted to take me out and hang me up by the heels, that the use of a thumbscrew might not altogether have wasted their day. Sam, on the other hand – warm-voiced, apologetic – addressed me with concerned good-nature.

'Well, I shall have to make a report,' he said. 'And it's not going to be easy. How did you manage to get into such a mess, anyway? You may seem harmless enough, but we can't take chances. You know that, for God's sake, don't you?'

'What's that mean, anyway?'

'I don't have to tell you, do I? I can't help it – none of us can. I'm sorry, but just look at yourself.'

So once again I was taken away under guard and put in a small underground room and left to my own confusions. But Sam didn't neglect me; he made sure I was warm, and brought me blankets, brandy and coffee. He sent an old woman to tidy the place and sweep and delouse it. He even sent in a girl – short and dumpy, with a tousled new look of political liberation, but she huffed and puffed and giggled so much I couldn't see across the cell for vapour.

The old woman, however, was comfort and entertainment. Doña Tomasina, from Cuenca, was a widow of fifty, whose husband, a leper, had been crushed by a rockfall in the cave where they lived. At the start of the Civil War she was starving and walked to Albacete, where she now scrubbed the barracks for two meals a day.

Tomasina was sad about me and kept pulling my shoulders back with her thumbs and doing her best to keep my spirits up. But it wasn't that easy. I'd been in this kind of trouble before and felt I'd been lucky to get out of the last lot. This time the situation was simpler, starker; my interrogators better trained, more implacable.

'But they just young men, like yourself,' said Tomasina. 'They know you don't do bad things. They play a little game with you. You laugh. That's all.'

Not they, I thought. Especially Sam's two Russians with their blue bullet-like faces. And with them around, Sam wouldn't dare.

I wondered how many times Tomasina had gone through all this – teasing and mothering other frightened young lads as they waited their blind and blundering dispatch. Her vivid dark eyes were like split sea-urchins, their jellied pupils flecked with red.

'Your papers upside down. They sort them out tomorrow. Then you walk out and back to your friends.'

But tomorrow came Sam, his cropped head shining and clean, but with a look of embarrassed exasperation on his face.

He held up my old sweat-soaked passport and stabbed his finger at the pages. 'It's these damned Moroccan stamps,' he growled. 'Spring '36. Melilla. Ceuta. Tetuan. That's where it was all cooked up, wasn't it? And what were you doing there at that time? That's what we want to know. Getting special training or something?' He slapped the passport again. 'It's all down here, you know. We can't get round it. Anywhere else, I might have got you clear.'

He'd brought me some writing paper, a pen and a folding table.

'If you want to write some letters, I'll see they get 'em,' he said.

He looked at me helplessly. 'Er . . . if there's anything else you need?'

'Tomasina's getting me a new shirt.'

'New shirt? That's fine.' He was standing awkwardly by the door. 'Well . . . er . . . I guess you don't want me to explain any more?'

'No,' I said.

'Well, if we don't hear from Madrid, that's it, then,' he said.

He hung on for a moment, then raised his doubled fist. 'Jesus Christ,' he growled, and left.

I wrote a few letters that day, but they were brief. I couldn't say I was about to be shot as a spy, a saboteur, a Fascist infiltrator, a capitalist lackey – all of which had been mentioned among my accusers' more polite suggestions. I didn't have to explain the nature of my going at all. Sam and his colleagues, it seemed, had certainly gathered enough evidence against me; but as some small doubts still persisted, Sam promised that there would be no official record of my death.

So my letters were brief. Not even to my Mother did I wish to say farewell. Still less to the girl for whom my heart hungered. To either would have been to admit a clumsy folly, muddled, without point or glory. I had come to support a cause, to give my life to it, I supposed; but not to be rubbed out in a back-yard for having carried a violin over a mountain or for going to Morocco at the wrong time of the year. I sat in my tiny cell, wearing Tomasina's bright new shirt, staring at the table, the walls, and wondering how this could have happened, alternately convinced that I could take anything that came, only to be visited by recurrent moments of piercing terror.

The guards let in Tomasina at midnight, with more brandy and a couple of candles. She was in bustling, chirrupy, rather over-heated spirits. 'You'll not stay here long,' she said brightly, skipping round me to straighten my shoulders. Anxiety, and pity, infected her smile as she lit a new candle from the stub of the old one. 'You've got to keep warm,' she said, dumping the brandy on the table. A bottle of the best, not corriente from a barrel. But it was not only brandy she'd brought me. Standing in the shadows behind her was a boy, about thirteen years old, with the dark curls and eyes of a Moor.

'Warm him,' said Tomasina, pushing the boy towards me, and as she left she touched my hand lightly. 'Lorenzo, may you go with God.'

The boy led me to the bunk and lay down shivering beside me. He seemed to be far colder than I was – or perhaps the reason was something else. 'Hurt me if you want to,' he said, and waited, his hands fluttering about my knees. Was this Sam's or Tomasina's idea? I wondered. Surely, they'd done enough? First the huffing and puffing liberated girl; then this thin little shuddering boy. Well, I could neither accept nor reject him now; God knows I was glad of any comfort that night.

Close to, I could see the long lines of disease running down his beautiful face, and a precocious hardness in his sleepy eyes. He reached me brandy and helped me to drink it; he was cold, but did his wriggling best to warm me. He kept crying my name, and sobbing farewell, and weeping theatrically as the night wore on. I had a feeling he was collecting relationships with the last moments of the condemned. He certainly seemed cheerful enough when he left in the morning. He asked me for my wrist-watch and I gave it to him.

The morning was a muddled embarrassment, without the dramatic clean sweep I'd expected and made myself ready for. Anything that followed now was bound to be fumbled, hurried and probably abominable. Things started at midday. Sam brought me a couple of cigars and a letter addressed to me care of the Socorro Rojo.

'I wasn't sure whether you'd want to have this,' he said, handing me a bulging envelope, already slashed open, and visibly crammed with sheaves of the girl's voluptuous handwriting. 'Then I thought, hell, why not? – shows she's thinking of you, anyway.

Sent you five English pounds, too. Rather a pity about that . . .'

On his smooth face was that expression of guilty exasperation again. But he wasn't looking at me.

'I'll take your letters,' he said, and stuffed them in his pocket. He didn't say goodbye.

That afternoon a doctor visited me and gave me an injection and a couple of pills. Tomasina padded in and out, saying nothing, but giving me shy false smiles as though flicking my face with a handkerchief. I sat at the table drowsing through my girl's extravagant letters and inhaling their heady unforgivable magic.

About four o'clock I was handcuffed and taken under guard to a room where several militiamen were playing dominoes. They got up when I entered, and went away whistling. Through the door they left open I could see a small courtyard, and snow falling from a sunset sky.

One of the guards gave me a cigarette, the other touched my arm. 'Don't worry,' he said. 'It's easy, brother.' Patches of sweat showed through his light blue shirt. Then I heard a murmuring of voices in the next room, subdued salutations and greetings; a sliding panel in the wall was suddenly pushed back. Faces peered at me briskly, one by one – the two Russians, each with a brief nod of the head, an unknown officer in a fur-collared coat, then, framed like some fake Van Gogh freakishly elongated, appeared the unmistakable face of the giraffe-necked Frenchman who had guided me the last few steps across the mountain frontier. One look at me and he covered his eyes in mock horror.

'Oh, no!' he groaned, 'not him again, please. Turn him loose – for the love of heaven.'

He seemed to find the sight of me – manacled and doomed in Albacete's death row – more diverting than anything else. He turned and spoke rapidly to his companions in the other room, and I heard his high-pitched Gallic cackle. A few orders were given, my handcuffs unlocked, and I was told to get back to the barracks. The two Russians, Tomasina, the girl, the boy, the long shivering night and day of preparation were over. Suddenly, inexplicably free again, I realized that a word from the little French guide showed him to have more power than anyone else around.

Crossing the square in the red twilight, on my way to the barracks, I met Sam striding in the opposite direction. Without a word of greeting or even a glance of recognition, he thrust into my hand the packet of farewell letters I'd written.

Restored to the ranks and the semi-liberty of a lax routine, I began meeting with veterans and took on some of their swagger. Albacete, the base camp of the 15th Brigade, was also a rest camp and clearing centre. I had arrived in Spain in a state of blank ignorance, but soon learned the realities of the times. After the atrocious battles of the late summer, particularly on the Aragon front, there was now a slight lull in the fighting. The Republican Army was left holding about a third of the country, backed by the entire east coast running from the Pyrenees to Almeria. Facing Franco, the line was a loose bellying north-south zig-zag containing a vulnerable bulge driven by the General's forces. It was true we had a weak salient reaching towards Portugal in the west, but sweeping in a great curve to the north-east Franco held Teruel in the mountains, only fifty miles from the sea, and threatened to cut the Republican territory in half.

Perilous as the situation may have been, it was a time of crazy optimism, too, and all the talk was of an offensive already mounted to recapture Teruel. Troops were even now moving up the freezing heights to surround the city. It would be an Olympian battle to turn the war.

So far it was an affair of Spanish troops only, some suggesting our leaders wished them to be first with the glory. So the International Brigades 'rested', in and around Albacete – patching their battered weapons, reshuffling their battalions, feeling pretty certain they would be called on soon.

Meanwhile we newcomers and the veterans massed in the town's damp cafés, drinking acorn coffee and rolling cigarettes made from dried oak leaves and mountain herbs. Paying for our drinks with special printed money, little cards stamped with the arms of the city. And eating beech nuts roasted on griddles. For a military base camp there was little formal discipline, though to keep warm we sometimes drilled or paraded through the streets, taking the salute of our Commanders, who stood on upturned wine barrels in the driving sleet, looking exhausted, faintly amused, or bored.

I half-remember the shades and styles of some of these still – Cunningham, Ryan, Paddy O'Daire – black-bereted, black-mackintoshed, tight-belted figures; they were the obscure foreshadowers of coming events, the unofficial outriders of imminent World War, and had already learned more of what its wasting realities would be than any fuzz-brained Field Marshal in the armies of Britain or France.

Fred Copeman was another lion of this breed – veteran of Brunete, and once my strike leader when I was a builder's labourer in Putney. Here in Spain I saw again that hard, hungry face, even more shrunken now by battle and fatigue than by his struggles back home in the early Thirties. When he recognized me his hard eyes glittered with frosty warmth for a moment. 'The poet from the buildings,' he said. 'Never thought you'd make it.' Stoker Copeman was well known for his part in the naval mutiny of Invergordon, Scapa Flow; a rough-cut, hollow-cheeked, working-class revolutionary, and archetype of all the Commanders of the British Battalion, he was to survive the worst slaughter of the war, which was to bury so many like him, and was later to become, after his return to England, Chief Adviser, Civil Defence, to the Metropolitan Borough of Westminster.

Beneath the speculative, often cynical, regard of such as these, we volunteers, our morale mysteriously rising, marched round Albacete shouting new-learned slogans in pigeon Spanish: 'Oo-achaypay! No pasaran! Muera las Fascistas! Salud!'

Bullets were in our mouths if not in our rifles. Indeed, few of us had guns at all. We marched to make a noise, to keep warm, to know that we were still alive, our right arms raised high, punching the freezing air, our clenched fists closing on nothing.

*

I'd been received back into the barracks with some suspicion at first, and I can't say I was that surprised. You didn't get picked off the parade-ground, marched under guard to the 'dispatch house', interrogated for three days, given Tomasina's 'last rites', only to be suddenly turned free, with all your equipment intact – books, diary, violin – without questions or explanations. It was thought, quite naturally, that I'd been planted among them, and was therefore someone to be avoided.

As Danny, my weedy Cockney friend from Figueras, was quick to point out: 'We all bin worryin' abaht you, son. Still are, if you get me.' He pulled his nose with a sleazy giggle. 'When 'telligence blokes get 'old of summick, they don't normly let go of it. We reckon you bin lucky, or sumpen, aincha?'

'Just a small mistake,' I muttered, and Danny nodded: 'That's what I said, then, din' I?' For several days I was watched closely, or treated with loud, false camaraderie. Then the news got round that 'M. Giraffe', whom they all knew, had vouched for me; also that a mysterious high voice of authority in Madrid had sent a favourable word. I understood the one, but not the other. But this seemed good enough for most of them, anyway.

It was cold. We played cards. Meals were of semi-liquid corned beef, or sometimes something worse, with black frozen potatoes and beans. It was an idle time, still a time of waiting: there were arguments, flare-ups, sudden lunging fights, and dreamy liaisons in barrack-room corners. Brooklyn Ben held political classes, which were often crowded, and which painted a world free from betrayal and butchery. Speaking in his quiet, cracked voice, with its soft Jewish accent, he plumped up the dry demands of Communist dialectic into a nourishing picnic of idealism and love.

Sitting cross-legged on his bed, his forage-cap crammed on his ears, his large eyes melting with warm, brown-sugary sweetness, his message could have been a perversion in the middle of a war, but one which both veterans and newcomers – those who had seen death or sniffed the nearness of it – felt somehow the need to hear. Strangely enough, he was the only one I met who had a

good word for the Fascists, calling them 'ice-cream-lolly boys' or 'kindergarten cut-throats'. His classes, advertised on the notice-board and presumably official, were crowded by old lags and new arrivals alike. After about a week, he disappeared. I heard he'd been clubbed in a side-street and carried away. 'Pro-Fascist nark,' said someone.

Many of us were now sleeping on the barrack floor, using muddy pallets of straw as mattresses. It was so cold, we were burning the army beds – breaking them at first accidentally. We fed the wood into a punched oil-drum and sat round it at night, ponchos over our shoulders. There was Doug and Danny, Guasch when we could stand him, a skeletal Swede, and a Yank with crutches – one of those legendary few who could charge a cigarette paper with tobacco, roll it, lick it, seal it and light it, and all with a single flick of one hand.

The Yank and the Swede, sculpted by flames from the fire, were scarred by something we could not know. The eyeballs of each seemed to sit easily in the face, but were almost detached, ringed by deep, luminous hollows. There was a look of exhausted madness in the features of both, backed by a languid bitterness of speech.

They were both veterans of the Aragon offensive. The Yank said he hoped the British were sending out less rubbish. The Swede said he didn't care what they sent so long as he could now go home. While saying this, he rocked gently to and fro, as though riding in a bus on a country road.

'You won't get home,' said the Yank. 'You still got your legs – the Army can use you yet.'

He quickly rolled him a cigarette and held it to his mouth. The Swede licked it, then sucked and gasped.

The Aragon was a cock-up, the Yank said. No artillery, no planes, no timing, no leaders, everybody running around like rabbits. He was a machine-gunner, had a beautiful Dichterer, too – only they gave him the wrong ammunition. That's why he had his ass shot off. Lucky to be alive. None of his pals were left.

They were guarding a hill near Belchite, when the Fascists counter-attacked. They were surrounded; couldn't shoot or run. Some Moors took his pals prisoner, and cut their throats, one by one; then they dropped him off a bridge and broke his legs. He lay for two days, semi-conscious, then dragged himself to the road. The front had shifted, and he was picked up by a battalion bread-van.

He told the story in gritty, throwaway lines – quietly savage, but with no dramatics. 'We were set up, goddam it. Lambs for the slaughter. No pasaran! They pasaranned all over us.' He described with light affectation the Spanish officer who had supervised the throat-cutting, the blood on his shirt and his pansy white hands.

'And d'you know what they gave me when I got back?' he said. 'A kind of welcome home, I guess.' He slowly shifted his crutches, unhooked something from his belt, and passed it to me in silence. It was one of those murderous, deep-bladed Albacete clasp-knives, for centuries a sinister speciality of this town. I prised the blade open from its sheath of horn, and the steel flushed red from the fire. Its glowing length was engraved in antique letters:

No me saques sin razon,
no me entres sin honor . . .

'Don't open without reason or close without honour,' said the Yank solemnly.

5

Tarazona de la Mancha

At last they sorted out a bunch of the greenest among us and put us in open lorries for Tarazona de la Mancha. This was the training camp for the 15th Brigade and lay some thirty miles across the plain to the north. It was the next leisured step in our preparation as fighting-men. Not one of us had fired a rifle, nor even held one as yet, but in Tarazona, they said, this would be seen to.

A half a dozen trucks took us over the frozen stream at La Gineta and humped us across the plateau. Sunlight blazed from the snow like an arctic summer, and blank umbrella pines stood darkly about. For once there was no wind, and although the air was freezing, we sang our way into the waiting town.

When we arrived we stopped singing. Tarazona de la Mancha looked hard and grim, a piece of rusted Castilian iron. The poverty of the snow-daubed hovels, huddled round the slushy square, gave an appearance of almost Siberian dejection. Squat, padded figures crept slowly about, each wrapped in a separate cocoon; and the harsh silence of the place and the people seemed to be sharing one purposeless imprisonment, where nothing soft, warm, tender or charitable could be looked for any more. This was a Spain stretched dead on a slab, a frozen cadaver, where, for all our early enthusiasms, we seemed to have come too late, not as defenders but as midnight scavengers.

Certainly Albacete had been shambles enough, but I remember the glazed astonishment in the eyes of my mates as we jumped off the lorries and gaped round the apparently empty and war-

472

scalloped square. We were, in our forebodings, only half right; it seemed there was still some military life left in the town – up and down side-streets, in and out of the houses, soldiers came and went in ones and twos as though conducting some complicated domestic manoeuvres. Each was dressed in flamboyant rags which seemed to have designed themselves. Others carried baskets of potatoes, or bundles of wood, others broken pieces of furniture.

Some voice of authority we hadn't known we'd brought with us suddenly bawled at us to stand in line. An odd figure appeared, as though from a hole in the ground, said he was the Political Commissar, and addressed us briefly. I remember him well because, in spite of the cold, he was wearing only his pyjamas under a tattered poncho. He said we'd come at the right moment, that victory was just round the corner, in our grasp, awaiting one final effort based on our ideological discipline. As he spoke he kept jumping up and down holding himself, like a little boy bursting to go to the lavatory. The man wore ragged odd slippers, and his toes were bare.

That was our welcome. We were then marched to our barracks, a back-street warehouse with ragged holes in the roof. We were stamped, listed, numbered, named, and each given a mint-new hundred peseta note. I looked at it in wonder, recalling my earlier days in this country, when five pesetas would last me the best part of a week. I stroked this finely engraved and watermarked piece of paper and thought of the princely excesses it might so recently have bought me. Wandering out through the town to see what the shops had to offer, I found only one, and it was selling beech nuts.

The central square in Tarazona must once have had some rough rusting elegance, but it was now badly battered by the fact of war. There'd been no fighting here, but the withdrawal of all normal life, together with a sudden revulsion for the past, had left their sickly marks everywhere. Chief sufferer, of course, was the ancient church, whose high-roofed edifice, hacked from red stone,

now grimly haunted the plaza. The outside looked blind, blank and faceless, but the inside was now bare as a barn – the walls and little chapels cleared of their stars and images, the altar stripped, all the vestments gone. I couldn't help being reminded of our own Civil War, and of Cromwell's followers hatcheting the faces of the old stone saints, and stabling their horses in churches.

Now the inside of Tarazona's own church had an almost medieval mystery and bustle, an absence of holy silences and tinkling rituals, and a robust and profane reoccupation by the people. I found soldiers sleeping by the walls, under slashed and defaced icons, or sitting round flaming wood fires whose smoke drifted in clouds of shafted sunlight up to the smashed stained-glass windows under the roof. Here were arguments, singing, the perpetual boiling of water in cans, curses of men stumbling over sleeping figures, the high jangling of bells rung for sport or mischief, the sudden animal shriek of female laughter.

All over Republican Spain now such churches as this – which had stood for so long as fortresses of faith commanding even the poorest of villages, dominating the black-clad peasants and disciplining their lives and souls with fearsome liturgies, with wax-teared Madonnas and tortured Christs, tinselled saints and gilded visions of heaven – almost all were being taken over, emptied, torn bare, defused of their mysteries and powers, and turned into buildings of quite ordinary use, into places of common gathering.

But in this particular occupation of Tarazona's main church, I noticed something else. The soldiers who made free with these once holy spaces were a little more than normally loud and hearty, whereas the local villagers, who had perhaps regularly heard Mass here and spoken their darkest secrets in confession, now showed half-timid, half-shocked at what they were doing, and broke out at times into short bursts of hysteria like unchecked children amazed at their wantonness.

We spent the first evening mulling wine over a fire, anything to kill the taste. There was Doug, Danny and Brooklyn Ben, who had miraculously reappeared after his back-street mugging, cleansed of both bruising and political suspicion. Also Sasha, a towering White Russian from Paris and a newcomer to our company.

Danny had found some dried sausage which we fried on sticks. Huge shadows moved over the high arched ceilings, and flickered and died along the walls. We were uneasy; we still hadn't got used to the way of the village, to its almost brutal casualness and gloom. We didn't know yet what we were preparing for, or what was being prepared for us. As we drank the hot sour wine Sasha recited some poems of Mayakovsky, and Ben said they sounded better in Yiddish. While they quarrelled, Danny sang some old music-hall songs in a cheerless adenoidal whine, till Doug covered his head with a blanket.

At last we left the Goyescan fires and smoke and half light of the church and went back to the freezing barracks. The guards sat hunched in the gateway, wrapped in balaclavas and ponchos, the late moon glinting on their bayonets. They didn't seem to care whether we were Moors or infidels. They merely burrowed down into the cold like dogs.

The barrack floor seemed to be covered with sleeping men, but we found a free space in the corner.

'By the way,' said Doug, as he settled down in the straw, 'I saw that lassie of yours today. You know, that wee one from Figueras. The one that kilt her father – or was it her grandfather? Aye, I dunno, but I just saw her riding down the street with a Captain.'

Before light next morning, I was awakened by the sound of a bugle – a sound pure and cold, slender as an icicle, coming from the winter dark outside. In spite of our heavy sleep and grunting longing for more, some of us began to love that awakening, the crystal range of the notes stroking the dawn's silence and raising one up like a spirit. There were certainly those who cursed the little bleeder, but the Brigade was proud of its bugler; he was no brash, brassy, spit-or-miss blaster of slumber, but one who pitched his notes carefully to the freezing stars and drew them out like threads of Venetian glass.

I got to know about him later. He was not exactly a soldier but a thirteen-year-old choirboy from Cuenca. Our Commander had heard him, kidnapped him, destroyed his papers of identity, and brought him as a pampered prisoner to Tarazona. One sometimes saw him by day, pretty as a doll, wriggling past in his outsize uniform. I spoke to him once, but he answered me in church Latin, eager to be left alone. Indeed, he seemed always to be alone, squirming quickly down side-streets or hurrying out to hide in the fields. It was only in the dark of dawn or at lights out, when he stood unseen at his post, that he was able to send out his frail and tenuous alarms.

After reveille came the brief luxury of lying awake, while those whose turn it was to do so brought round tin-drums of coffee brewed on fires in the snow outside. Ladled into our mugs, it had two cosy qualities: colour and warmth. Its flavour was boiler grease.

Terry, the company leader, a short, round, forty-year-old ex-NCO from Swansea, began his shouting around 6.30 a.m. He had learned an extraordinary, belligerent parade-ground patter which he kept going in an abstract blood-curdling way even when there was no one left in the room.

The company formed up in threes in the icy lane outside, the big chaps in the front, the midgets hidden in the rear, rather like a display on a greengrocer's stall; then, after much shuffling, we marched off to the plaza.

The morning parade was the only time when our sad little village hardened and seemed to show some purpose and strength. It was then that all the men of the battalion came together from their various nooks and grottoes, and stood under the red-streaked morning sky before our neat and diminutive Commander.

The lines of men were not noticeably impressive, except that we displayed perhaps ,a harmonious gathering of oddities and a shared heroic daftness. Did we know, as we stood there, our clenched fists raised high, our torn coats flapping in the wind, and scarcely a gun between three of us, that we had ranged against us the rising military power of Europe, the soft evasions of our friends, and the deadly cynicism of Russia? No, we didn't. Though we may have looked at that time, in our wantonly tattered uniforms, more like prisoners of war than a crusading army, we were convinced that we possessed an invincible armament of spirit, and that in the eyes of the world, and the angels, we were on the right side of this struggle. We had yet to learn that sheer idealism never stopped a tank.

After parade came training in the snow – little fat figures running and skipping about the fields, everyone padded up with cloaks and scarves like medieval images from Brueghel. This medievalism spread to the streets where off-duty soldiers sat round interminable wood-fires, or scampered about like children, making slides and playing snowball.

Doug, Sasha and I were drawn aside by the company leader and given a Maxim gun. We were told to take it apart, clean it, put it together, fire it, and generally get used to the thing. He thought we would make a team; I don't know why. In an icebox cellar beneath the church, Doug and I took the gun to pieces and Sasha reassembled it. First, second and third time of firing, the Maxim jammed. The giant Sasha cursed. Then Doug put it together, and it fired. 'Sodding Russian,' he said, but Sasha was in no way put out; he embraced Doug and gave him a screw of tobacco.

That night we queued in the snow for food. The day had been a hard one, and the food was late. We sang and chanted in the lane outside the canteen, banging our spoons and forks on our plates. The food, when it came, was the usual heap of gritty beans mixed with knobby pieces of livid meat. But there were no complaints; we were eating donkey, and we were eating better than most.

Then, I remember, a few days after coming to Tarazona, we got an early morning call for a Special Occasion. The bugles started about 5 a.m. There was a lot of shouting from Terry, and a certain excitement was transmitted. It was suggested we smarten ourselves up a bit, even shave for a change. A sack of new forage-caps, with tassels, were handed around, but after trying them on most of us threw them away.

They marched us, not to the parade-ground, but to the dark interior of the church and lined us up facing a platform half-obscuring the altar. We stood in wet, steaming rows, stamping our feet, and coughing. Electric light-bulbs were switched on, and tension mounted, while we glowered at the empty platform and grumbled.

Suddenly a little man jumped on to it, bouncy as a bull-calf, a minotaur in a short hairy coat, with a shiny half-bald head and piercing dark eyes under heavy commanding eyebrows.

'Comrades!' he cried. 'It is a special honour for me to stand before you at last – heroic defenders of democracy, champion fighters against the Fascist hordes . . .' It was Harry Pollitt, leader of the British Communist Party.

Where had he come from, I wondered, and what was he doing here at this hour? Dressed as it were for his King Street office, London, but standing before dawn by a church altar in La Mancha, for half an hour he held us in the grip of his fast, fist-jabbing oratory till he had us all standing with our arms raised, cheering. Pollitt had the true gift of a political leader of being able to rouse a cold and sullen mob, at six-thirty in the morning, by spraying them with short sharp bursts of provoking rhetoric till everyone was howling for victory. Pollitt's was a spare fighting style, calling us to fresh blood sacrifices, mass-solidarity, and other militant jousts of that order; but even his clichés were honed down to projectiles and pebbles for heroic slings.

I think we were astonished that this little man, exhausted from travelling and set down in this strange winter dawn, should pack such fire and fanaticism in him. He was my first experience of a professional working-class leader, who used words like street-calls and bugles. Wilting though we were, he had us convinced that not only would we smash Franco, Hitler and Mussolini, but go on to capture the whole world for the workers. We were all heroes, and he was our leader, and we cheered him as he stood there, larger than life, shining noble and shaking with emotion.

Then it was all over. The spell and magic quite broken. He jumped down from the platform to mix with the men and was immediately surrounded by a jostling crowd. But not to slap him on the back or carry him in triumph through the town. No, they were plucking at his sleeves and pouring out their grievances, asking to be sent back home. 'It ain't good enough, you know. I bin out 'ere over nine months. Applied for leave and didn't get no answer. When they goin' to do something, eh, comrade? . . . eh? . . .' The last I saw of our morning Lucifer, he was backing towards the door, muted, expostulating, eyes groping for escape: 'Sorry, lads – sorry . . . nowt to do with me . . . sorry, I can't do owt about that . . .'

That night a young female voice spoke my name in the dark. I was walking near the church, and I'd thought there were no girls left in Tarazona. But the voice that called me had a familiar, hallucinatory echo. Doug was right; it was the 'wee lassie' from Figueras.

'Lorenzo – little Frenchman.'

'Eulalia!' I said.

She came and leaned against me, threaded her small hand in mine and asked me to take her back to her lodging. She was working for the Socorro Rojo, she said . . . among other things. She knew I was here; a friend had told her. Had I killed any Fascists yet? Ay! what a miracle it was to see me again – 'Lorenzo! – my little French brother . . .' 'English,' I said stolidly. She nibbled at my sleeve. She seemed to bind herself to me like a slim leather thong.

Her 'lodging' was a tiny, windowless room at the top of an old house, empty save for a bed and some posters. And a bottle of wine with two glasses standing near the head of the bed, and a man's great-coat hanging on the back of the door.

Eulalia turned and smiled at me brilliantly, showing her tongue, her face cracking open like a brown snake's egg hatching. Seen again in the pale light-bulb, I'd forgotten how beautiful she was, small and perilous, my murderous little dancer. She was dressed in tight uniform that bit into her tiny waist. She'd cut her hair short. She looked like a ten-year-old boy.

She sat me down on the bed and poured me some wine.

'Socorro Rojo,' she said. 'I heard they tried to shoot you.'

'A mistake.'

'All the time they make mistakes!' She lifted my hand with the glass towards my mouth. 'My poor little brother. They don't shoot you now.'

'Later.'

'Perhaps later. Not now.'

In the pale cold light she quickly unzipped her uniform, peeling off the crumpled green to reveal the strange pulsing fruit within. As soon as I was ready, she ran to fetch the man's great-coat from the door, helped me on with it, then wriggled inside. Burning cold she was, close as a second skin, her mouth running across my chest. In spite of the cold, I smelt her unforgettable smell, something I'd never known in anyone else – a mixture of fresh mushrooms and trampled thyme, woodsmoke and burning orange.

It didn't occur to me to wonder how such things could happen so easily, or to question the long and mysterious coincidence. At my age one was not surprised. Girls seen fleetingly, but memorably, from a train passing through Reading the wrong way, suddenly appeared at one's table in a London café. Or one whose face stopped one's heart as she got off a crowded bus in the City turned up days later sitting beside one in the cinema. Rare and magnetic driving patterns of youth, cutting across the humdrum chaos of multitudes.

So I found myself once more with the lyric-shaped girl, who had first held me without question in that far Figueras cellar, who had cried out her fears and hatreds in the ears of a stranger, and then disappeared in a flurry of kisses. Now, four hundred miles from there, she had casually reappeared in the night, in this beleaguered and sterile village, and here again she lay close against me, and I felt the anguished hunting of her hands, and heard again her familiar but incomprehensible whispers. All I understood her to say, in the last desperate throes of our night, was that she had found her father and brother, Lorenzo, little Frenchman, and would never lose sight of us ever again.

I got back to the barracks before anyone was awake, crawling through a hole in the wall beyond sight of the sentry. As I stretched out beside Doug he roused himself for a moment and said someone had been looking for me. He didn't know who it was, he said. Some boss from Albacete. Then he grunted and went to sleep again.

The next day, after a fumbling morning with the Maxim gun, I was called from my company and moved to 'special duties'. I don't know whether Sam, my old interrogator, had arranged it, or who, or why, but it became a secret and complicated little life. I was based, with a few others, in a small private house near the plaza. Few of our numbers were of the same nationality. Our leader, Kassell, was from Marseilles.

The house had pretty azulejo tiles on the floors and walls, tiny cold rooms, and Romano-Moorish pillars. It had probably belonged recently to a lawyer or doctor, to the son of a local land-owner, even a priest. It was stripped bare now, except for its elegant proportions. We cooked for ourselves on brushfires, and slept on the floor.

There was a fragmented madness about our group, but it seemed to be necessary. Three of us spoke English, another three Spanish; but the lingua franca indeed was French. I won't attempt to detail the extent of our antics; they entailed meetings, reports, the issuing and signing for revolvers, notebooks, walking and stalking in twos. They also included covering-up, overlapping, watching, listening, and long hours wondering just what we were doing. Sometimes there were jovial evenings, fires burning, coñac and music, when we almost began to know each other. There were other times when we might doubt the purpose of our actions, and certainly when the means and the ends seemed squalid.

I can't, at this length of time, recall all the characters in the group; many are shapes in a shadow play only. I remember Kassell, the boss, thin as a peeled birch tree, with a starved face and feverish eyes. We had Emile, a Dutch professor, hunched and bearded; peachy-cheeked Rafael, a horse-breaker from Jaen; two tiny Belgians – Jean and Pip – agile and feminine as lemurs; and a dark, silent Catalan we nicknamed Compadre, who may once have been a monk.

I had arrived late in Tarazona, and found it in turmoil, no longer simply a base for the International Brigades. Politically and physically its battalions were dispersing or dead, and a deliberate new nationalism was taking over. Those ragged ranks, once packed with the innocents and scatterings of Britain and Europe, were now being officially stiffened by troops from the Republican Army – Basques, Catalans, Gallegos, Castillanas, Valencianas, even Mallorquins. In such a pivotless mêlée our group found its natural home, and could operate without guide or comment.

I recall one little job, just before Christmas, but still can't swear to its reality or purpose. Kassell called us together in one of the inner rooms of the house and passed round a photograph telling us to memorize it carefully. It was of a slight, round-shouldered youth, with dark fruity lips and the wide dream-wet eyes of a student priest or poet. His brow was smooth and babyish, his long chin delicately pointed.

Kassell told us his story – improbable for such a face. A rich Mallorquin, it seemed, son of a Count, he was also a hero of the Barcelona risings. A gunman, dynamiter, he'd executed three leading Trotskyists, been kidnapped, tortured and sentenced to death. He'd escaped and come south, had been seen in Albacete, and it was believed he was on his way here.

'Why here?' asked Emile.

'He knows he'll be safe with us,' said Kassell.

The two little Belgians looked at each other.

'What's his name?' asked the Dutchman.

'Who knows?' said Kassell. 'Could be anything.' He turned over the photograph. 'But it says "Forteza" here.'

So Forteza we called him, and we went out to start our search – first to watch the morning camiones coming in. I paired up with Rafael, and together we scrutinized each newly arrived face while pretending to be listing numbers and counting heads. The trucks lurched to a halt in the square, their bonnets steaming, the men dropping off them like clods of mud. A mix of spiritless faces passed before us in the bleared light: white, hungry, blank – Anglo-Saxon, Slav, Latin-French, Iberian. But no sign or shade of Forteza.

For two days we met all the camiones, checked the church and barracks and outlying billets. Then the second night Kassell called us together. 'He's here,' he said, his face soft with concern, 'but not wishing to show himself.' Our job was still to find him, quickly before someone else did, and so give him our protection. Forteza was young, valuable, dangerous and hunted – but he'd also lost his nerve. If he falls into the wrong hands, Kassell was saying . . .

I remember staring bemused at the pretty tiles on the walls, half-drowsing in the warmth of the wood-fire. Kassell's voice went smoothly on; Rafael sat on the floor, sorting and soaking beans; Emile, hunched and cross-legged, scribbled in the margin of a book; Jean and Pip played at pocket chess. All of us seemed to be waiting for something, but at the same time were relaxed and cosy.

Suddenly there was a muffled knock at the door, and Kassell went to answer it. When he returned his face had a curious tight radiance about it. He took Rafael aside, and they looked at me, then Rafael beckoned, and threw me a heavy coat. Before we left, he led me through the kitchen where we drank a couple of glasses of coñac each.

It was after midnight when we set out together in a fine and freezing darkness. Rafael began muttering obscenities that seemed more pointed and personal than the usual flow of Spanish rhetorical oaths. Tarazona was without lights, but the stars were big and fierce. This wasn't a patrol; Rafael knew exactly where he was going; and so, with a chill certainty, did I.

We came quite soon to an alleyway which even in the starlight I recognized by the peculiar winding of its walls. I knew the darkened house we entered, and the flapping wood on the stairs. I knew the sagging door on which we knocked.

Eulalia was not surprised to see us. She had obviously been waiting some while. She held a candle to our faces and turned and nodded towards the bed. She was in her tight, trim overalls, and wore a scarf round her head. 'Venga, Rubio,' she said to me.

On her rumpled bed, shaking with fear or fever, was the youth we instantly recognized from the photograph, except that the once smooth face of the priestlike dreamer was now savagely and bitterly scarred. When he saw Rafael and me, he shrank back on the bed, doubled up, and drew his knees to his chin. He broke into a paroxysm of coughing, while Eulalia soothed him, and wrapped a ragged blanket round him.

We sat down on the bed and waited for him to stop coughing. He coughed like a little dog. Eulalia stood by the door, her long eyes shining with candle-light, but they were no longer the whispering eyes I knew.

'Frenchman,' she said, and jerked her head sharply. Rafael cursed and laid his hand on my knee. 'We could carry him,' he said. 'He's only a baby. Anyway, he's got to come.'

Forteza grew quiet, then pulled himself into a sitting position. He asked if we had any coñac. Rafael was carrying a flask, and gave him some, which he drank in little birdlike sips. Then he smiled and let us draw him to his feet. Rafael grew hearty and wrapped his arm round Forteza's shoulders. 'We were worried about you, man,' he said, guiding him towards the door. 'For God, why d'you take such risks?'

I saw the panic slowly fade from Forteza's eyes as he struggled to find his balance. Eulalia lightly touched the back of his neck, then put her cold hand to my cheek. 'He could be you, little brother,' she said. We helped the lad down the stairs and supported him through the streets. Forteza's skeletal frame between us was as light as a bundle of sticks.

When we got him back to the house, Kassell was drinking coffee by the fire. Jean and Pip left their chess game, the Dutchman stopped writing, and all joined Rafael and me by the door. Then Kassell got up and strode forward, crinkling in his black leather mackintosh, threw his arms round Forteza and kissed him.

Forteza stood quiet, neither shivering nor coughing now. 'Welcome, comrade,' said Kassell, with his watery smile. 'We thought something bad had happened to you.' He ran his hands quickly over the boy's thin body and led him into the inner room. Jean and Pip returned to their chess game, and the Dutchman to his writing. A little later we heard the sound of a shot.

6

The Tarazona Trap

We spent most days now just watching and waiting; watching each other and waiting for the war to move. It was a festering time, drenched in doubt and suspicion. The Republic was in peril, and one took no risks with its enemies. But of the several dark little games in which Kassell involved us, few of them seemed to bear the stamp of reason, and the authority behind them, if any, was a mystery. One hoped, yet doubted, that they had a purpose, but as in most wars they were bungled and malevolent jokes.

One day Rafael and I were told to go and track down an old farmer who lived out in the wasteland towards Madrigueras. There'd been some small acts of sabotage – a couple of lorries blown up, part of a bridge destroyed – and the old man was thought responsible. He'd been seen by a neighbour packing long sticks of dynamite into a box, so we were told simply to go out and get him.

It was a cold walk through the snow, and for once Rafael had no coñac. He smoked instead, using the dry edge of a newspaper wrapped round a small bundle of herbs. Rafael would smoke anything: old beech leaves, sugared-moss, corn-husks, even crushed pine bark with tar – at least that was the smell of it. For cigarette papers he preferred foreign journals – *Paris Soir* or *L'Humanité* – or the thin pages of antique prayer-books.

'These amateur dynamiters are the worst,' said Rafael. 'And where did he get the stuff? Not by parachute, that's for sure. We need it, anyway. And him.'

We came to the farm in the late afternoon. There was a thicket of thorn bushes round it, and a leashed demented dog. The brushwood roofs of the buildings were held down by heavy stones and the light on the walls was a sort of dimpled pewter. We saw no horses, mules or donkeys – we'd probably eaten the lot in Tarazona.

We dodged the dog and approached the buildings. A short thin woman came to the door and saw our guns. She smothered the fierce flash in her eyes and told us the house was ours. 'Come in. There is only the old one,' she said. The howling wolf-dog leapt to the full extent of his chain, clawing the air, his wet teeth shining like ice.

We went into the small bare room and found the dynamiter standing ready, black hat in hand, dressed in his best corduroy suit.

'Mario Nuñez, at your service,' he said.

'It's lies,' cried the woman, walking angrily up and down, bobbing jerkily as though riding a miniature bicycle.

The farmer stood with bowed head, resigned and waiting.

'It's a lie – a lie!' the woman cried again.

Rafael shouldered his rifle and said it was time to go. The farmer raised a long brown hand and brushed the woman lightly across the forehead, and for a moment they stood motionless together in the bare luminous room, like two age-worn wooden carvings.

Outside, a car blew its horn, and we led the farmer through the door. Emile and Jean were waiting to take him to Albacete. There was much, it was thought, that the dynamiter could tell us. Meanwhile, Rafael and I had to search the place.

The woman followed us as we returned to the house.

'What do you want, you pollutions?' she asked.

'Only the dynamite, grandmother,' said Rafael.

'You're as likely to find the Holy Virgin as dynamite here,' said the woman.

'That I believe,' said Rafael.

We searched, but found very little in the house. Only a picture of Saint Teresa and the political icon Largo Caballero on the walls and some rolled-up mats and a wooden bowl on the floor. How could this man have been a saboteur, or even dangerous at all? Yet he'd been seen packing dynamite in a box.

We went into the yard and examined the outhouse. The woman followed us like a strutting hawk. The building was of crumbling mud-brick, the thatch breaking away in the wind. Bits of harness lay around, and the remains of a cart, and some olive stones in a broken barrel. Rafael began stamping the floor and eventually he found it – a mouldering trap-door fitted with an iron ring.

'Ojala!' said Rafael, and lifted it open. We climbed down the ladder into the small dark cellar below, lit a match, and saw a padlocked chest. Then the old hawk struck, flew down the ladder behind us and began clawing at us with her long black nails.

While she fought, she cursed us and all our families. Then she turned and threw herself across the chest. I remember her tattered black clothes splayed from her arms and legs, reminding me of a shot crow hung up on a fence. So that's where it was. Rafael lifted the now exhausted woman and set her down in the corner, where she remained bolt upright, weeping.

We kicked the padlock from the chest and opened the lid. In the dim light we saw the long white sticks stacked neatly together. Dozens and dozens of them. Rafael crowed. 'Mother of God! The cunning old devil. Enough here to blow up an army.' Breathing heavily, and with great care, he lifted a stick in his hands. It fell in two parts, each joined by a thread. The sticks of dynamite were long altar candles which the old farmer was holding in trust for the church. Together with some items of priests' regalia hidden away at the bottom of the trunk. Pandering to the priesthood was thought by many of us at that time to be as bad as blowing up our bridges.

Quite soon, and without explanation, I was dropped from Kassell's little outfit and switched to another company. I don't know whether I'd passed a test or simply been discarded, but it was back to the ranks for me. No longer the feminine little house with its tiny balconies, the shadowy evenings by the wood-fire, the privileged suppers with Kassell rehearsing his macabre and amorphous exercises.

He shook my hand when I left.

'None of us are specialists,' he said vaguely. 'We can't afford specialists in this war. We must follow the struggle wherever it leads us.'

My new Company Commander was Polish-American and wore a Siberian hat. He had a beautiful absent face and a drowsy manner that quite swallowed up his authority, so that one frequently lost sight of him for hours together, only to find him perhaps marching in the rear of the ranks carrying somebody else's kit. Comrade Caplin believed in equality to the point of personal self-effacement.

I'd been in the company for several days, packed at night in a warehouse with some hundred others, when the word came that we'd been found new billets. We paraded leaderless in the plaza, stamping our feet while the search began for Caplin. He was found in the cinema, writing poetry, and he came and led us out of the town.

He took us to a gaunt little chapel on the edge of a hill; an old, beautifully proportioned, but crumbling building which was, it seemed, to be our new headquarters. The heavy main door had been ripped from its hinges and now leaned half-burnt against the wall.

The interior of the chapel was wrecked and gutted. Nothing remained but some small empty niches and the bare, naked altar. As we stamped in from the slushy street, our clothes and ponchos soaking, each man bagged his personal patch of ground by throwing down his kit. The chapel filled rapidly, the territories staked out; but I hesitated as under a spell. The altar, beneath its tinted east window, was a stripped pedestal of stone and plaster lightly washed in flaking blue paint. Quickly I went up to it, threw down my bags, stretched myself along it, and lit a cigarette. With this gesture, this idiot impulse of brash bravado, I believe I stained the rest of my life . . .

Half the members of my new company were Spanish now – stocky, grinning, round-headed types from the villages north of Madrid. Although young, their faces had that wizened, russet-apple texture that came from exposure to fierce winters and roasting summers. When they saw me claim the altar for my bed, some of them looked at me with blank, frozen stares, while others flashed their teeth and chanted crude parodies of the litany.

But for most, even the most ribald, profane and godless, there seemed to be an invisible area here which it was still impossible to cross without the blessing of a priest. Even in this bare and mutilated chapel a holy charm seemed to lie on the ground surrounding the sacred stone. An unseen line ran from wall to wall and everyone appeared content to remain behind it. Except for me, the petty violator.

The chapel soon took on a humid male cosiness, while the ghostly aura of incense which had impregnated the walls was quickly obliterated by our musky presence. We plugged the doors and broken windows against the heavy cold. We built up a thick atmosphere of smoke and coffee; we talked, played cards and quarrelled. There was nothing to do. A great pause, a great silence had settled on Tarazona. In the snows of the Sierras the battle for Teruel had begun, a last desperate attempt to cut off Franco's north-eastern salient which threatened to slice our territory in two. For the sake of pride, politics and the people's morale, only Spanish Republican troops were being used in this attack. The International Brigade was temporarily set aside; indeed, it was hoped officially it would not be needed at all.

So at this time, when the frozen peaks were aflame and the slow bloody encirclement of Teruel city began, we just lay around in our smoky chapel, waiting as Christmas came.

We had one true veteran among us, the only one with battle

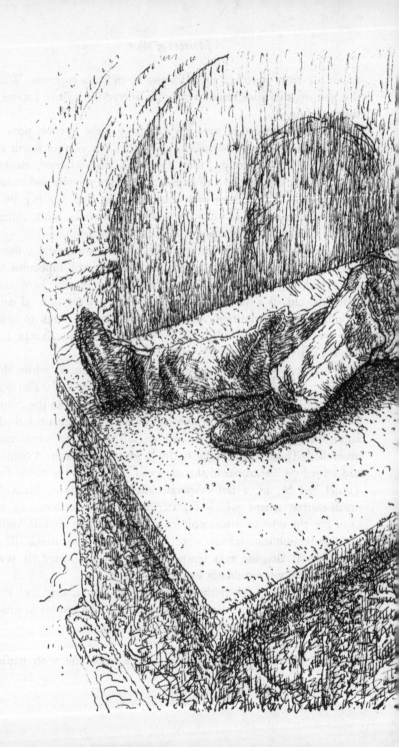

experience, and he showed it with a moody lassitude and a quiet indifference to discipline. Arturo, from Bilbao, was the company machine-gunner, weedy and strangely tall for a Basque. His was the long recumbent figure I saw every morning stretched out near the altar steps. After the breakfast bucket of coffee had gone round, he would remain for hours lying spread on the floor, rigid, motionless, like a medieval stone relic, while his cadaverous face flickered with fever. Someone found a priest's robes in the chapel cellars and these Arturo wrapped round himself. He'd then lie stiffly cocooned in scarlet and black, cursing and shivering.

Our company leader by this time had lost himself. There were no parades or drill; we ruled ourselves. Sometimes Arturo would rise up, throw off his robes, assemble his machine-gun, and blow great holes in the walls. This raised our spirits, and under Arturo's instructions we formed teams and did it ourselves. The din in the long narrow chapel was ear-blasting, but we were pleased with our training; it was all we got.

At night especially, under the string of light-bulbs, I think there was a simplicity about us. Some new Americans and British had joined our company. Wine was brought in, and we began to use the altar as a kind of bar. We were young and, as I remember, direct and trusting, even in our fights and excesses. Among us the young Spanish peasant, American student, Welsh miner, Liverpool dock-worker had met on a common shore.

We didn't talk about it much, during those days of waiting. I played chess with Paul, a scholarly mechanic from Ohio, whose dark trembling earnestness concealed a sharp Jewish wit. We were restless, moody, charged for action. Girls came whispering at the door and the chapel windows. Stubby little virgins, with wide liberated eyes. They stood waiting outside, in solemn groups of two. They would go with us anywhere, into farm huts and hovels. But none would cross the threshold of our sacred building.

An almost wolf-like hunger, too, was now part of our lives, sharpened by the winter cold and idleness. At last, wearying of our acorn coffee and thin donkey soup, a half a dozen of us pooled our pay – over a thousand pesetas in fresh-printed notes – and persuaded an old farmer to part with three chickens, each of which looked as hungry as we were. These bony birds we took to two widowed sisters who lived with their old father on the other side of the town. They had one of those bare stone kitchens which were still almost medieval – a paved floor, high roof, brick and tiled stove by the wall, a few chairs, a table, a twist of olive wood in the corner, and hanging from the rafters an old ham-bone and some harness.

The sisters were wispy, watchful, bright-eyed, sunken-cheeked, their bodies almost mummified in their widow-black. The father sat on a high-backed chair near the stove, his limbs as lean as a whippet's. He slipped to his tiny feet as we came crowding in and raised a wrinkled fist.

'Your house,' he said. 'José, at your service. And my daughters – Doña Anselm – Doña Luisa . . .'

The sisters bridled at this, but lost none of their watchfulness. They took the birds we had brought with us with little clucks of the tongue. 'Come back in two hours,' they said.

So we walked around in the snow, and when we returned Doña Anselm swept our boots with a broom. The old stove blazed with a mixture of wood and refuse, and a great iron pot stood bubbling upon it. The entire kitchen simmered and was awash with steam, a steam banked on the long-forgotten juices of real home-cooked food, swimming aromas of tomatoes, dried beans, and garlic sausage, and boiled chicken peeling on the bone. How the widows had done it seemed a miracle. We stood there in a swoon of hunger. A hunger more blest in that it was about to be appeased. The widows could have asked us another thousand pesetas.

I'd been hungry before, and had also known the simple, voluptuous appetite of youth when taste was never jaded. I remember as a boy being so in love with bread and butter and the cloudy meat of a new-boiled egg that I could hardly wait to go to sleep at night so that morning breakfast should come again. So it seemed now, that long moment of delayed consummation, as we sat round the table while the sisters fussed and quarrelled by the stove and carried us at last the stew in a great earthen dish. We had brought our slabs of grey bread, our metal knives and spoons, and the plates we had were of curved polished wood. The farmer's three birds, who must have been survivors of at least two long winters, now swam brokenly in a thick soup of beans and sausage, splendidly recharged with succulence. Doña Anselm guarded the dish while her sister spooned out our portions, one squashed steamy limb to each plate.

A jar of thin reedy wine was passed around, a brew strangely flavoured with sage and cinnamon – a lacy, fastidious old woman's drink which hinted at secluded and secret comforts.

'Eat!' snapped Doña Anselm, and we broke our grey bread with solemn ritual under her scaring eyes. Six young strangers at their private table, for whom they had cooked three old and irreplaceable hens; we were guests, visitors, but also the enemy in possession. The sisters clearly took no sides in this war, which had occupied their land and must be endured. They served but did not join us as we plunged into our food, while the old man by the stove stared at the floor and waited.

Lopez, a late arrival, and the only Spaniard among the six of us, set himself up as a surrogate host.

'Three in one pot,' he said, beaming round at us proudly. 'Few of you could have eaten better.'

Carried away by the majesty of the moment, he began to pick out pieces from the dish with his stubby fingers and hand them to us with a bow. Doña Anselm hit him with a spoon.

'What are you doing?' she cried. 'Have some culture, man.'

'At my brother's wedding,' said Lopez, 'we had two birds and a rabbit – stewed in wine. I have never forgotten.'

Doña Luisa sniggered. 'Yes. The bride, the bride's mother and the groom.'

Lopez lowered his face to his plate. We others were now deep in our meal, skewering, spooning, using our fingers, awash with flavours and greed. Few of us, I think, had been long from home; none of us, except perhaps Lopez, were married. Instead of great chunks of swede and donkey thrown into a rusty bucket and boiled by some lout in the barrack bath-house, we were now eating food prepared by the hands of women, especially and particularly for us.

In reality, it must have been a poor and scratch-me-down meal. But it was a memorable banquet in that winter of war. In the end it cost each of us several weeks' pay. We were bullied, cursed, perhaps even despised by the sisters, but we were not cheated. There was enough on the stove for all of us. Sprawled at the table, feet up, near repletion, chasing the pimply chicken skins through the thinning soup, digging out the last bits of sausage with our bread, we wallowed now, wheedled more wine, sipped it slowly and grew sentimental. As the afternoon passed, even the sisters softened a little, and found us some beech nuts and raisins.

We gave them the rest of our money, and the old man in the corner said, 'Now you'll be able to buy that clock.'

When we'd finished all there was, we sang, sleepy-eyed, while the sisters cleared the table and put all the chicken bones on a plate and set them down on the old man's lap. Slowly, one by one, he picked them up and passed them between his naked gums, dwelling on each with a delicate bliss as though he was sucking asparagus. He had waited five hours for this moment and now his time had come. He tasted his portion of bones with the absorbed grace of a prince.

Christmas was on us, and the wind blew from the north with a cutting edge of pain. The gritty snow was pretty and pitiless. We fetched cartloads of wood from out of the countryside, chopping down century-old olives to build up our fires. In our state of mind, I don't think there was one among us who wouldn't have burned a rare church carving, relic of a thousand years' piety, to have gained himself five minutes' warmth.

Gradually news from the front was ferried down from the Sierras, news we could scarcely believe. Launched in one of the worst winters in Spanish memory, in one of Spain's coldest, remotest mountains, our army, without artillery and at the height of a blizzard, had attacked and surrounded the city of Teruel, and was even said to be fighting in the streets. After the remorseless decline and atrocious defeats of the summer, we had at last a hope to believe in. Slowly, bloodily, month after month, Franco's forces had been sopping up Spain, pushing our lines back towards the eastern coast. Now we were aimed at a forward city, at a point of greatest threat and danger. People talked now of tides turning, and paths to victory reopening at last.

Yet in Tarazona, in the silence, the cold idleness of our lives, crouched around in our ponchos, cleaning and re-cleaning our guns, we thought of the hundred thousand fighting our war in those mountains, and wondered what this training camp was for.

In this silence, Christmas came, muted, inglorious, and small Red Cross parcels were passed among us, some from Britain and some from France. On Christmas Day I tasted, with almost erotic excitement, a twopenny bar of Cadbury's Milk Chocolate, and smoked a shilling packet of Players. I was as affected as much by the piercing familiarity of their flavours as by the homely reassurance of their wrappings.

Then I remember the see-saw of news, reports and rumours. A van-driver arrived seeking a supply of blankets. It had taken him three days to cover the hundred miles from the front. Here was no hero or victorious eagle but a shivering and ragged man. He told us of pain and snow-blindness, panic and exposure on the road, while his eyes jumped like beans in his head. Oh, yes, we were winning in Teruel. He'd seen the dead stacked like faggots of wood round the walls. Frozen barricades of flesh you could shelter behind, protecte. from the wind and bullets. He'd seen mules drop dead in the cold, then set stiff and rigid in the road so that they held up the traffic and had to be sawn up in solid blocks and removed. His tales were of a reversal of hell, and he seemed as astonished by them as were his hearers; that he, a Spaniard, had seen such weather in his own country, such acts of slaughter in death's own climate, and the young soldiers, even alive, dressed in sheeted white.

As we listened to this pop-eyed, half-demented man, something of our secure camp Christmas went away. It was as if he'd opened a door and admitted a blast of arctic and charnel house, wiped the frost from our cabin window and shown us the wolves.

A few days later, a quite different messenger turned up: Bill Rust, the editor of the *Daily Worker* – a dapper, soft-spoken, rather chummy man, wearing a dark London overcoat and a warm felt hat. I remember having seen him a few weeks earlier, on his way through Albacete, his face tense with anxiety and exhaustion. Now he had a pink glowing look of half-suppressed triumph, like a football manager whose team had just won the cup.

Teruel had fallen, he told us; the mountain fortress was ours, and he'd walked in the liberated streets of the city. To prove it, he showed us the inside of his hat. On the sweat-band it said: Sombreros de Teruel.

It was, it seemed, his only loot. Modest as ever, he'd picked it out of a broken shop window. There was some rejoicing that night. Rust's tale of that victory was perhaps our most hopeful moment of the winter – for most even the best in the war.

Then, in the beginning of the new year, all news of victory ceased. In fact, there was suddenly no news at all. Our soldiers, first one or two, and then in companies, began silently to disappear from the town. One morning I woke to find that more than half my friends had gone. I never saw them again.

7

Radio Madrid

Early in January I was ordered to go to Madrid, which rather surprised me as I'd been expecting to be sent elsewhere. The order was passed on from the Political Commissar, and came from Captain Sam of Albacete, who apparently had not forgotten me.

He wanted me to go, together with himself and some others, to make a few broadcasts from Madrid Radio to America. This was the capital's second winter of front-line war, beleaguered, half-besieged, and stuck like a fist in Franco's mouth and crammed fast against his teeth.

A dozen of us took off just after dawn, packed in an open truck. We were a mixed lot, and I couldn't believe all of us were going to make short-wave broadcasts; some, by the look of them, were on more solemn errands. We sat on wooden boxes at the back of the truck, and waited for the dawn landscape to lighten. It was flat, frosty, with umbrella pines on the horizon, like dirty paper fastened down with pins.

We had a hundred and fifty miles of this vacant country to cross, a straight melancholy road scoring the sterile La Mancha, with no mark of man save a few broken windmills. As we bumped slowly along, I thought again of the huge emptiness of this country, where, apart from cramped slums of the still medieval cities, raised on crusts of imperial and religious splendour, there remained little more than the untenable plains and vertical deserts of the Sierras, yielding to and supporting no one.

The road was bare save for a few sleepy road-blocks; though one was less sleepy than the others and was manned by a heavily armed anarchist who stopped our truck and objected to Captain Sam's cap, saying it wasn't sufficiently democratic. But Sam, with a few key phrases and his cold clear smile, sent the vigilante scurrying off with apologies.

Passing through Mola de Cuervo we had a burst tyre, but this caused us no difficulty either. Our driver simply went up to another truck, parked unattended by the church, walked round it slowly, removed the wheel he wanted, and left a receipt, signed by Sam, on the windscreen.

For the rest of the journey Harry and Bill, two Glaswegian veterans of the Aragon front, played cards on a board and quarrelled dramatically in a slurred incomprehensible accent. A couple of Spanish comrades, with long Cordobese faces, dozed sitting upright like Easter Island gods. Another soldier, I think he was Dutch, played for several hours a series of monotonous airs on the harmonica – that tinned exhalation of all the boredom of war.

Captain Sam had been busy scribbling notes on his knee. We went over them together, suspicious and watchful. I added a few bits of my own, and smiling Sam cut them out. This was to be the script for our broadcast tonight.

As the afternoon darkened we entered the suburbs of the city, threading close to the enemy lines. There was little to be seen: rotting sandbags, broken roads, barricades of brick and bedsteads, shuttered windows, closed shops and bars.

I'd known Madrid briefly in the summer before the war, when it had a light air of penurious, unassuming fiesta. Now with siege and winter, the skies had come down, and as we neared the centre of the city, passing through the cloaked guards of the road-blocks, the streets seemed empty save for bent hurrying figures, wrapped in blankets, making their way home.

We found, however, a quite cushy spot for the night. We were billeted in a small gypsy hotel just off the Calle Echegarry, near to the Puerta del Sol. Ramon, our Asturian driver, camped out on the cobbles under his truck – just to keep it in the family, he said.

The hotel was run by a committee, who welcomed us at a table in the hall, and gave out meal tickets accompanied by clenched raised salutes. We sat round the dining-room, at first cowed and prim, like orphan children awaiting our institutional soup. But the meal, when it came, though poor, was ribald, and served by rollicking militia-girls. They had the dark physical power that Spanish girls are conscious of early, with small jungly bodies, split olive eyes, and voices like laser beams. They wore blue baggy overalls, but so tightly belted at the waist, and deeply slashed at the throat, they appeared to have arisen half-naked from tumbled beds.

Only Captain Sam seemed unaware of the erotic atmosphere of the place, as he sat head down, dashing off manifestos on the table-top, a bent cheroot in his mouth. He, and a couple of black-smocked old men, probably delegates from some distant village commune, who remained in stiff formal silence, skin tightly wrapping their cheekbones, rough hands gripping their knees.

Otherwise I remember the noise, the near frenzy, in that base-ment dining-room, that winter night, in the heart of besieged Madrid; the war posters on the walls with their flat, cut-out heroes and their slogans of arousal, defiance, hope; the plates of ordinary steamed potatoes, many of them black with frost; the cheeky militia-girls twisting nimbly among the groping hands of the soldiers; and the soldiers, foul-mouthed, grabbing at girls and food, and grinning around them with vacuous pleasure.

Here were young veterans and half-trained newcomers, combat-ants but a short bus-ride from the front, those who had slipped past death and returned, and those who must very soon die; a few officers, agents, spies, touts and journalists – all who found in this cellar in this huge dark city an incongruous moment of temporary comfort.

After supper Captain Sam called me up to his room, where I found two dramatically dissimilar persons crouched over a table nodding and chanting in broken English. One was bald and round as a Michelin tyre man, the other slim and pretty as a schoolgirl.

Spread before them on the table were two half-eaten tomatoes, some crumbling dried fish, and an English translation of Machado, which both were intoning.

Sam introduced us: the round man, Esterhazy, an Austrian writer; the pretty youth, Ignacio, ex-student of English and Arabic at the University of Salamanca.

'Tell us the accent!' cried Esterhazy, waving to me. 'Come along, comrade, instruct us, please!'

Sam said my accent was terrible, even he couldn't understand it. Nevertheless, we rehearsed the poem, which they were going to broadcast together that night, in chorus, and taking alternate verses.

Ignacio was most rousing, even feminine, speaking as it were below the waist, his voice slender, flesh-warm and caressing, his eyes changing shadow with every line. Billowing Esterhazy, meanwhile, provided the windy brass-section, grunting and blaring beneath the other's treble.

In the end, they built up a fine duet between them, swaying together at the littered table, while Sam and I worked out the rest of the programme which was made up of chatty interviews, propaganda and 'culture'.

Our first short-wave broadcast was timed for midnight, and theoretically beamed to East Coast America. It was planned as a beleaguered, backs-to-the-wall, defiant call for help; and some of those things it certainly turned out to be.

A couple of armed militiamen picked us up about eleven, their job to guide us through the streets to the radio station. We'd drunk several bottles of wine by then and considered ourselves well rehearsed, and we swaggered out through the dim-lit hall. The streets were almost deserted – no traffic, a distant cry, a few late footfalls of the night, the wind from the Sierras lightly ruffling the shutters.

Sam told us to stick close to the militiamen and, if challenged, to freeze. We moved by the faint glimmer of oil-lamps shining under the curtains of doorways, by the thin glow of starlight on the edge of the rooftops. The air was as cold as mile-high Madrid could be. Sam shivered and swore. Esterhazy blew self-comforting bubbles in his cheeks. The militiamen coughed and spat. From the next street came a shout and the sound of running feet. Young Ignacio gripped my arm.

'I am a poet,' I remember him saying. 'I don't wish to be here. I belong to music and song, not war.'

We had left the city centre and were stumbling down side-streets, when one of the militiamen tripped up and cursed. A shadowy bundle lay on the pavement, a bundle that gave a weak, old cry. The soldier lit a match. 'You can't sleep here, grandmother. If you try to sleep here, you'll die.'

We knocked at a nearby door, and roused a trembling couple, who lit a candle while we carried the old soul inside.

The wife recognized her with a cry, and said she used to run a kiosk in the square; it was her home, but it had just recently been destroyed by a shell.

'They fall at all times, as you know. Both night and day. We are none of us safe, before God.' Distraught and whining, she clutched at her throat and threw a helpless glance at her husband.

'Dead by our door. The shame of it! How shall we face the world?'

The husband told her not to be stupid, and said he would fetch a hand-cart in the morning and wheel the old woman to hospital. He peered at us nervously, then raised his hand. 'Go with God,' he said. 'And long live the Republic!'

Now it was late, and we hurried on to the next road-block, which was under a railway bridge. It was heavily armed, but no one knew the password, not even our guides, or Sam. We saw the gleam of teeth, the glitter of bayonets, and heard the jaunty cocking of rifles. Then suddenly one of the sentries cried, 'Aren't you Rocio?' and one of our soldiers said, 'Yes.' They were fishermen from the same village, were brought up together, but, judging from their conversation, didn't like each other much. But they let us through, stumbling over tins and stones, accompanied by jolly in-bred insults.

The broadcasting studio was in a dank dark basement in a Victorian-style tenement. As we stumbled down the stairs, stepping over heaps of refuse, the building throbbed and snored with sleepers of all ages, most of the rooms having been set aside for soldiers' families.

Sam led us to a cramped little room stuffed with coils and valves, where a young blond announcer, sweating in his shirt-sleeves, read a war communiqué in Teutonic English. He winked at Sam as we entered and nodded towards a table, around which we grouped ourselves. Finally, from this tiny cell in Madrid, fumed by wine and tobacco smoke, we went into our broadcast – three thousand miles across the winter seas. Who could be listening, I wondered – truck-drivers sealed in their cabs, young radio hams skimming the air-waves, bored barmen and husbands seeking the evening sports news, widows in Long Island mansions awaiting their lovers?

I doubt that they could, or would, or did. Sam took the mike and read out the manifesto we had stitched up together, ending with a list of names of some Lincoln Brigade heroes. As a climax we had planned to play a few bars of the 'Internationale', but we mixed up the labels and put on 'The Skater's Waltz' instead. But I had a feeling that we could not be heard at all, that the microphones were simply not connected to anything, that this was all a pantomime to placate the gods.

Nevertheless, we kept on with it. Esterhazy and Ignacio took their turn, and droned and fluted into their prepared Machado. I don't know what the effect of an obscure Spanish poem, in a bad English translation, delivered in unison by a booming Austrian and a nervous young Madrileño, would have on an uncertain audience thousands of miles away, but one doubted that it would command their single-minded attention or cause them much stirring of the breast.

Not that Sam's and my contribution was any more compelling.

We had worked out an interview in which Sam questioned me about the volunteer routes across the Pyrenees. This had seemed easy and matter of fact enough when we rehearsed it earlier that evening, but once returned to the microphone, in this more casual role, Sam's personality suffered a cardinal breakdown – gone was the urbane propagandist, the donnish debater, the merciless interrogator of spies and traitors, the ice-cold political killer – suddenly I was confronted with an oily and unctuous crawler, and this fawning Sam was an unsettling experience.

The unreality disappeared when the shelling began, somewhere about three in the morning. We heard it first as a distant metallic bark, honed and polished by the freezing air, followed by an indrawn silence, a rapidly approaching whine, then the brief uproar of exploding masonry. Curiously, these sounds then seemed to fall back on themselves, receding in waves of silence, shouts, running feet, and finally in distant cries.

The first shell broke some glass, shook the studio walls, juggled the furniture, and brought down some dust. The engineer signalled to us to go on, and this we did, and at last the broadcast seemed to make some sense. We began to talk together in normal voices, to ask each other why we were here. Captain Sam's face returned to its original protean calm. His back straightened and he reclaimed his authority. With several minute intervals, both near and far, the shells continued to fall. The studio door opened and a group of women came in, carrying bundles of sleeping or whimpering children. Each of the women's faces had that pallor of patience and hunger as though they had been rubbed in damp grey ashes. They bowed to us apologetically, hesitated a moment, then sank in a circle around the walls. If we have to die, let us die where there is light, among each other, and near the power of these men talking a kind of Latin, like priests.

So in this cramped semi-basement in the beleaguered city, surrounded by our cloaked, fugitive audience, and to its background of shuffles, sighs and murmurs, and the occasional spiked thud of explosions outside, we talked on, read poems, swinging the microphone between us, while the large frightened eyes of the women stared up at our mouths as if we were conjuring for them, in our foreign tongues, magic spells, incantations and prayers.

Some time later the German announcer suddenly handed me a battered violin, with an old bow like an unravelled horsewhip. At the sight of the instrument faces softened, eyes brightened, sleeping children were awoken with pinches. 'Musica! ... musica!' the whisper went round. And I saw again those expressions of gentle pleasure and anticipation that I'd known in poor Spanish villages before the war.

I didn't play much, the strings were frayed and greasy, but I scratched away at some old Spanish dances which I'd learned on my previous visit, and I played them as loud and as fast as I could. An intense experience – to the smell of cold and cordite, and with the passing of shells overhead, the veiled women nodding and bowing, and the Madrid night we shared together – intense and not to be forgotten. When I'd finished, Captain Sam announced that a British volunteer had just given a violin recital. We both knew it wasn't that. The women on the floor gazed at me with benign indulgence, as though watching a neighbour's child just beginning to walk.

Around about dawn the shelling stopped and the restless children slept. But the families continued to sit round in clumps, forged like clinkers, black and immobile. I slipped out into the street, stepping over pieces of timber and piles of broken brick. In the building next door a great hole had appeared through which one could see the pale morning stars behind. A shell seemed to have passed right through one of the downstairs apartments and cleared out all the furniture except for the carpets. Nothing was left save for one mumbling old woman who sat stiffly upright in the middle of the room.

The stretcher-bearers arrived as I was passing. They took the woman's arm, but she snatched it away. Her thin grey legs stuck out in front of her, her mouth was twisted with shock. Her family

had suddenly disappeared with the furniture, she said. She kept going through their names like a litany. 'Mi marido, Jacinta, Puelo, Ramon . . .' There must have been a dozen or more of them at least. They had been carried away as by some mighty wind, she said. She shook off her rescuers and would not move.

The streets around were blocked with debris. Carts and wagons were clearing up. Oddly enough, there had been no fire, only destruction. A few bodies lay under blankets along the pavements. Here and there somebody hobbled away. There were no shouts, no raised voices, just subdued, desultory, matter-of-fact exchanges as of neighbours starting another day.

The experience of being in Madrid again, contrasting its present cold desolation with the easy days of my earlier visit, made me want to search out some of the places I'd known.

I found the Puerta del Sol smothered in a pall of greyness, and I remembered the one-time buzz of the cafés, the tram bells, the cries of the lottery-ticket sellers, the high-stepping servant girls with their baskets of fresh-scrubbed vegetables, the parading young men and paunchy police at street corners.

Now there was emptiness and silence – the cafés closed, a few huddled women queuing at a shuttered shop. Poor as it had been when I'd known it, there had always been some sense of holiday in the town, a defiant zest for small treats and pleasures, corner stalls selling popcorn, carobs, sunflower seeds, vile cigarettes, and little paper packets of bitter sweets. Nothing now, of course, no smell of bread, oil, or the reek of burnt fish that used to enliven the alleys round the city centre – just a fusty aroma of horses, straw, broken drains and fevered sickness.

I'd previously stayed at an old inn near the Calle Echegarry, where I'd rented a room for sixpence a night and had been looked after by Concha, a young widow from Aranjuez. Carters from the Sierras slept with their beasts in the stables, and the landlord kept a cow in the cellar.

I found the place transfigured. The great twenty-foot doors, which for some five hundred years had hung or swung on their elaborate tree-sized hinges, had now, after withstanding generations of war and plague, been torn down and burned as fuel. The cobbled courtyard within, once crowded with mules and wagons, was now scattered with dismembered motor lorries. The slow carters, with their coatings of chaff and road dust, had been replaced by oil-faced repairmen and truck-drivers. In little over two years, this unchanged inn of Cervantes had become a repair depot for army vehicles. Indeed, in one corner, surrounded by an ardent group of greasy lads, they were even reassembling a captured Italian tank.

I went to seek out my old landlord and his wife, and found them freezing in the kitchen trying to heat some water over a smouldering brazier of oily rags. Coughing and weeping, they rose to embrace me, bidding the saints witness their surprise and delight. The thick smoky fumes made us grope for each other. There was much calling on the heavens in amazement. Eighteen months had transformed me, the young passing stranger of that summer, into a returned son, a reminder of tranquillity and the riches of peace. They gabbled eccentric endearments, and inquiries as to my health. Had I all my limbs sound? had I good boots? had I the gripe? did I want something to eat?

I insisted I wasn't hungry, but I let the landlord take me to an underground tavern across the road, once a roaring kind of whorehouse, now shuttered and dark and used only by a few neighbours and soldiers. The innkeeper had changed much in the last two years, not an ageing of time but of things happening around him. This was not the towering man I'd known who used to throw the carters about and who once, when I was playing the violin in the courtyard, struck a chiming-clock with a brandy bottle for daring to interrupt. Thin now, and bent, shuffling and shaking, one of his magnificent dark eyes was half-closed and blind.

In the tavern he took me to join some of his friends, all old men dressed in black velvet suits.

'This is Lorenzo,' he said. 'Violinista, muy amigo. English or French – but it is not significant.' The old men showed no surprise, or much interest, in this information; but one of them poured me some wine, thin as the blood of a gnat.

A couple of militiamen came in and sat with their rifles across their knees. One was swearing and the other trying to quieten him. The old men watched them in silence, but sharpened their eyes.

The soldiers were Spanish, about my age, lean-faced and nervy.

'If I see another light in a window, I'll give it a blast with this,' said the younger one.

'But there were children there – you heard them.'

The young one leapt to his feet.

'Yes, and there were children killed last night.'

It had happened before, when night-shelling was heavy and precise – someone, some 'Franco agent', would have been flashing a torch from a rooftop or an upper window, and then, when the bombardment was heaviest, would toss a few grenades down into the street to confuse the fire-trucks and rescue parties.

After two winters of siege, the inside war was still active, and not everyone, even in this poor bare tavern, as he talked and moved his eyes about, could be absolutely sure of the man who sat beside him.

'We caught one of them, anyway,' the younger soldier said fiercely. 'Running across the tiles with a cart lamp.'

'Could have been trying to save his skin,' said someone.

'Did you arrest him?'

'Hell, no. We just threw him off the roof. He'd done enough. His body's outside in a barrow.'

Someone drew back the shutters on the cold grey street. A boy sat on the shafts of a hand-barrow, smoking. Stretched out on sacks between the high wooden wheels lay the crumpled body of a thin, old man. It was smartly dressed, and the head which hung down from the tailboard still wore a whitehaired look of distinction.

'Know him?' asked a soldier.

'Yes,' someone said. 'You threw off the wrong one. That's Dr Cardenas. He has two sons in the Air Force . . .'

The two soldiers left; but there was no awkward silence, nor was the conversation changed too abruptly. First there was praise for the hero-pilots of the Republic – young eagles tackling the German vultures. Then in tones I was to remember – a mixture of death-bed reminiscence, shock, a reassurance of survival – the old men of Madrid drew together round their bare, bitter tables, and began to talk of the air war over the city; the black Junkers and Condors and snapping little German fighters, and the long night raids during the first winter of siege. 'There had never been such a sound before. The Devil's hand tearing holes in the sky. I was crossing the street. I saw a house come down before me. Like a man dropping a dusty cloak. Then there came a hot rushing wind which lifted me up and blew me into a fountain.' 'Soltero, down by the market. His house was cut in two. He woke to find half his bed and his wife had gone.' Then there were the fire-bombs, calculated, dropped on the old town and the poor. The Luftwaffe was clinical.

Franco had said that he was willing to wipe Madrid from the earth rather than let it remain 'in the hands of the Marxists'. So he gave it up to the Luftwaffe, who were interested to see what mass-bombing could do to a major European city. Inhabitants in their thousands were splintered, broken, pulped or incinerated; survivors driven by fire from one district to another, forced to camp in the streets, in cellars, or the country. But the effect on the victims of that bombing – as it was often to prove in other cities later – was never the major cause of a people's defeat.

It was about midday now, and soon I would have to leave the tavern and report back to Captain Sam. Suddenly the street door broke open and a hunched shape crawled in, a huge cripple with withered legs. He'd opened the door with his head and now scampered around the room on all fours, with bits of motor tyre strapped to his hands and knees. I recalled him from earlier days –

that fine, classical face, the powerful shoulders and thick arms of a boxer. 'Ay, Lorenzo!' he said with his deep-throated growl, as though he'd seen me but yesterday.

He'd always been a bit of a cynical wit and joker. Now, listening to the old men's tales of the air war, he added a few of his own – how his survival to date, for instance, depended on his God-given ability to scramble down drains quicker than anyone else. And did the honoured company of comrades remember, he asked us, when that lone Fascist plane flew low over the city and released four little boxes attached to four separate parachutes? Wooden boxes, not bombs. Boxes tied with ribbon. People imagined they might be gifts. But when they were opened they were found to contain the carefully quartered body of a young Republican pilot. Ah, yes – very bad. But there'd been one flash of genuine kindness, added the cripple. When that other bomber flew over the city later one afternoon and dropped a fine, fat serrano ham. It was just before Christmas, and people hadn't seen ham for years. It fell on a man and tore off his arm.

I walked with the landlord back to his smoky kitchen, and we embraced, and his wife gave me some socks. Before leaving I slipped upstairs to see my old room, but found the door nailed up. As I came back down a voice called my name. Concha's rose cheeks had cooled, but her eyes were deeper than ever, though less assured than they had been. She had guided me the first time, now I was older, stronger. 'Man,' she said hesitantly, hanging back in the shadows. Then she put up a trembling hand and gently touched my mouth.

8

The Frozen Terraces of Teruel

Sam didn't return with us from Madrid. He stayed in the capital on other business. We found Tarazona half empty, the billets deserted, with most of the men gone to the Teruel front. The high heady news of Christmas victory had all changed since we'd been away. How had we not known what was happening? In Tarazona they knew well enough . . .

Franco had held Teruel for three years, a vulnerable line towards the coast, and when the Republicans recaptured it that Christmas it was thought that fortune had changed at last, that the days of retreat were over.

The worst was only beginning. The occupation of Teruel had been by Spanish troops only. No International Brigades were called on. Then Franco began his counter-attack with an artillery barrage so heavy, they said, that it clipped off the tops of the hills and completely altered the landscape. Protected by the Condor Legion, and two Generals in a twelve-carriage train, the Army Corps of Castile and Galicia began to advance and the Republicans had to give up their brief-held prize.

As the weather worsened, the International Brigades were at last brought in. Fred Copeman, who commanded the British battalion, fell ill, and Bill Alexander took over. The 'Major Attlee' company received its christening, and thirteen men were killed the first day. Slowly the Republicans retreated outside the city, when the very war itself was halted by a four-day blizzard, the worst in generations, during which men and their weapons froze together.

*

Such was the situation as we heard it when we got back from Madrid. A chill pall of wretchedness hung over the town. The chapel where I'd camped out formerly was being turned into a hospital, so I returned to the small house by the plaza, once quarters for black-coated Kassell and his crew, who it seemed had all departed. Instead, it was now occupied by two mysterious brothers from Cartagena, stern ascetics who scarcely spoke. They'd stripped the villa of its decorations, its posters and maps, and left only bare walls across which they'd painted VITORIA! in large red letters.

It was said that they were ex-priests, and they certainly seemed single-minded enough, and had a zealous, passionate hatred for General Franco and his words – and were not all that fond of us either.

They were men of authority, a new power in Tarazona, and I felt that their taking over of this minor headquarters – so long dominated by Kassell, Political Commissars, British Company Commanders, and instructors – may well have marked, in its small way, the beginning of the break-up of the International Brigades. For these men were not internationalists or politicos, but simply Spanish patriots. They seemed to wish this to be understood.

The brothers – both young, perhaps in their early thirties – had sharp, blue-tempered chins, and the eyes of religious assassins. They were self-mortifiers, too, and slept on the floor without covering, and sometimes walked barefoot in the snow.

One morning, soon after my return, they called me into their back room, together with a Portuguese youth named Serrano, and said they were sending us up to Teruel. I remember the interview in the 'office' – the brothers wearing single blankets like hairshirts, both squatting on the floor, but making us stand. They looked at handsome young Serrano with lechery and contempt; they looked at me as possible fuel for a burning.

'Portuguese and Inglese,' one said to the other. 'Worse than French. No salt in the bone.'

We left the next morning at dawn. Our orders were few and ambiguous. I gathered the brothers wanted us out of the place. We drove out of Tarazona in brutal weather in a lorry rattling with thick chained wheels. The squat olive trees on the hillside rolled in the cutting wind like bundles of black barbed wire. Serrano had a heavy cold now and was no longer pretty; he was also intensely miserable. We had rations for one day, but the journey was likely to take two. We huddled together against a roll of tarpaulins.

We were the only passengers in the truck; the rest, it seemed, was cargo. I'd been told we were carrying ammunition, but we were bouncing too light for that. Under the tarpaulins there was only donkey harness, the gaily tasselled stuff they wore down in Andalucia. Why were we carrying such rubbish to the front, I wondered?

About noon we reached the hills, but the snow was heavy, so we pulled up under a bridge. Our driver climbed out of his cab and stumbled round to join us, followed by a small and muffled figure. In a cloud of breath they climbed into the back of the truck, and the driver asked for a cigarette. From the snow's bright glare one saw a flushed, drunkard's face, darkly sprouting with bristles, a powerful torso, and small bent legs. All that was visible of his crouching companion was a pair of deep slanting eyes peering through a thick wrapping of scarves.

The driver spoke rough bullying Spanish with a Russian accent – the first I had heard for weeks. His small companion crawled towards him and answered with the low voice of a girl, agreeing, placating, wheedling. He dug into his pocket, produced a tin of sardines, and slowly broke it open. Then he scooped out one of the brittle little fish, gave it a shake, and held it in front of the girl. She lifted the scarf from her face, opened her mouth like a bird's, and he popped the oily morsel between her lips. She seemed to swallow it whole, with only the faintest flicker of her throat, then stretched her mouth open for more. So he patiently fed her till the tin was empty, wiping her lips at last with his sleeve.

He'd found her in the mountains, he said; thin and bony as a stork's nest. He was fattening her up to be a proper armful. All she does, he said, is eat and sleep. And when she slept, he ate.

There was something Grand Guignol about these two, their incongruity and their different sizes, he bull-like, a great black minotaur, and she – in spite of her wrapping of scarves – no more than a doll. With her face uncovered she was waxenly beautiful and not more than fourteen, I would have thought. Was he the father-protector he appeared to be, or she as childish as she seemed?

Serrano, who suddenly came awake in a paroxysm of coughing, rolled off the tarpaulin and asked where we were. I explained about the snow, the bridge, the Russian driver and the girl, but he only shook his head and moaned. The driver opened another tin of sardines and shared it with us, pushing back the girl into a corner as he did so. He seemed to be loaded with food, he even had bread, and the pockets of his greatcoat clinked and clattered. Serrano asked him why we were carrying donkey harness instead of guns, and the man laughed and said did we want to be blown up?

The girl gazed long and silently at Serrano, and was about to say something, when the Russian took her back to his cab, pulled the truck on to the road and began the long slow climb up the Sierra. The snow had thinned a bit now, and came only in large flaky gusts as though someone was opening and shutting a gigantic door. Along the roadside, among the rocks and tree stumps, we passed strings of broken-down trucks and wagons. Men, swaddled in blankets, crouched in the cabins or huddled by blowing fires. There seemed to be no traffic at all going towards the front, it all appeared to be coming away towards us – lorries, strings of mules; occasionally a scattered bunch of men, and now and then an ancient high-roofed ambulance.

We drove in silence, in a dumb state of nothing, having no part of what we saw, nor any certain direction. Serrano let his head fall lower and lower between his shoulders, and his shoulders between his knees. Even the shouting Russian in the front had suddenly grown silent. Then as darkness fell, and the snow squalls lessened, quick flashes of fire, like summer lightning, began to dapple along the hill ridges ahead of us.

The road was bad now, cluttered with rocks and holes and the litter of smashed-up vehicles. We stopped by a derelict barn, sheltered in a kind of quarry, and bedded down there for the night. The Russian propped his girl in the corner, helped us build a fire, then handed round more sardines. He was now the big shaggy leader, the guardian, the provider, and we began to wonder what we would have done without him. Shuffling round on his knees, smacking our hands with bread, then hobbling away to feed the girl, his busy bulk seemed to crowd the barn like some amiable restless bear.

With the fire and the food Serrano was on the mend; his fine curls glistened, as did his eyes. And the girl watched him silently, first uncovering her face, then more slyly her shoulders, wriggling inch by inch towards him. In spite of the cold, her expression was one of simple rapture, which I don't think the boy even noticed. But the driver did: he cuffed her ears with his paws and pushed her back whimpering against the wall. Then he came and squatted by the fire and told us the story of his life, which, being Russian, was long and dank.

At intervals, in the distance, we heard the snapping of gunfire, sound sharpened by the edge of frost. So Teruel was not far, and the front still awake, but we were too exhausted to care. To the epic drone of the driver's story Serrano and I fell asleep. The sleep was unhealthy and broken. The gunfire drew nearer. I woke to the blank glimmer of a dying fire. Serrano lay curled and twitching like a dreaming dog, his mouth giving faint little yelps; while sprawled on his back in the corner, the Russian snored heavily, the girl held over his chest like a blanket.

It was one of the coldest nights I could remember. I lay with my hands between my thighs, my clenched teeth chattering, my overcoat crackling with frost. A deadening numbness assailed the toes and fingertips, and the nostrils stung as though split by skewers. Eventually, I got to my feet and stamped about. Snow whipped in gusts through holes in the roof. Indifferent, in his corner, the Russian continued to snore, while the girl on his belly sniffled and wept.

Just before daylight the gunfire stopped, and I woke Serrano — who seemed to be sleeping in a posture too close to death, his mouth hanging open like a poisoned rodent's. I lit a new fire and boiled some snow and we dipped our last crusts of bread in it. Suddenly, as the fire blazed up, we saw that the Russian's corner was empty. Then we heard from outside the mad whirring of a starting handle, a shout, an engine bursting into life and then fade as the truck drove away.

We had been dumped. The driver hadn't even said goodbye, or even left us a single tin of sardines. We were on our own – wherever that might be – without direction, orders or food. What was I doing in these Spanish mountains, anonymous of purpose, with this pretty Portuguese boy of whom I knew nothing?

As the late daylight came, I left Serrano huddled by the fire, and went outside and got my first view of Teruel. It stood some five miles distant and slightly above us, a gleaming city of ice, its cathedral, castle, turrets, towers, all dusted with a silver, shimmering light. A city of silence, without dimension; it could have been a life-size mural, or an intimately carved ivory for some medieval cardinal or pope. A perfect relic, in its brilliant stillness, chaste and bloodless as a martyr's tomb. Yet already, I was to learn, within the last few days, its citizens were walling up and massacring each other.

Its silence, now, could have been the silence of exhaustion after the excesses and bombardments of the night. Its sleep, not the sleep of peace and restoration, but a readying of strength for further outrage. So in this brief moment of armistice Teruel hushed itself, bathed in the mother-of-pearl morning, motionless, save for the tendrils of slender smoke spiralling into the sky.

Presently, as I stood there, my back to the barn, blowing on my fingers and watching the town, I saw three figures approaching in the distance, running doubled up, in little stumbling spurts. They were roly-poly bundles, dressed in fluttering blankets, and they fanned out to encircle the place. As they drew nearer, popping up and down like hares or pheasants, I wondered if they thought they were invisible. I slipped back into the barn and woke up Serrano, and we watched through a hole in the wall. The smoke from our fire must have drawn their attention, but they seemed in no hurry to come to close quarters. Then I heard one call to the others to keep their heads well down, that he'd soon 'flush out the little buggers'. His lilting voice had a South Welsh accent, and he lifted a grenade to his teeth.

I leapt out of the barn, held up my empty hands, and shouted to him not to bother. 'Come on over,' I said. 'We're from Tarazona.' After a silence, they all straightened up and joined us. The Welshman came first, dragging a giant foot wrapped in a bundle of sacking. 'Sod the bugger,' he said, prodding the lump with his musket. 'Well, what's going on here, then, boyo?'

The three stood round me, awkward, dumpy, ageless in their woollen mufflers. Well might they ask, I thought; I didn't know. I took them inside to the last of the fire. They crouched around on their haunches, shuddering with cold, gasping and blowing on the ashes. In their damp balaclavas only their eyes were visible and these darted about like mice in a basket.

'Who's that?' asked the Welshman, jerking his head towards Serrano, who was rocking on his heels and blubbering and sneezing. I tried to explain who he was, and realized I didn't know either.

The Welshman guessed it, then turned to Serrano and addressed him in perfect Spanish. He got no answer but sighs and moans. 'It 'ould pay us to get rid of 'im I reckon.'

His companions got to their feet and began to turn the boy over with their rifles. Serrano went limp like a doll. The Welshman spat.

'Bin on patrol all night,' he growled, 'just to pick up two tarts from Tarazona. Well, no offence, you – but just look at *him.*'

Fear had curled Serrano's hair with a glorious shine. His fragile fingers clasped one of the soldier's boots.

'Might as well,' said the soldier, cocking his rifle. He had a teasing Liverpool accent.

At that moment, with a clapping of giant hands, the bombardment began again.

'Well, come on boys,' said the Welshman, almost cheerful now, 'better get you all back to base.'

Then we were out of the barn and running, bent low, following the limping, shouting Welshman. The bombardment was not so distant as it had been, the ground shook as though being beaten, the air screamed and tore, and we all fell flat, face down.

Under bombardment, the body takes over the mind; it stiffens and melts, the mouth floods and dries, and all one's senses rush to the back of one's neck. The barn disappeared in a woosh of clay and splinters, and I tried to bury myself among the slush-covered rocks.

When a shell hit the ground and exploded near by, the snow rose in the air like a dirty ghost, and hung there spikily billowing, before collapsing into the ground again. Such apparitions increased all around me, lifting, hovering and falling, together with the brutal rending and peeling back of the air, and the knowledge that under bombardment one has no courage.

I learned only later that this great build-up of shelling marked the end of the Teruel battle. Franco's troops, helped by Italian tanks and planes, were hitting back at the fortress city. The Republican forces, together with the International Brigades, began their inevitable withdrawal, clinging briefly to the open heights and little gullies round the walls, before continuing their retreat southwards and towards the sea. The gift of Teruel at Christmas had become for the Republicans no more than a poisoned toy. It was meant to be the victory that would change the war; it was indeed the seal of defeat.

Pinned down throughout much of the morning, with the Welshman's great foot in view, about noon I heard him call out, 'Come on, then, follow me!' and saw his foot bouncing before me like a snowball.

The landscape around showed all the rubbish of failure, the end of charity and hope. The fate of new Spain – that 'arid square' – was decided among the frozen terraces of Teruel. As the gully widened, the Welshman leading, we clambered among more trucks and debris. Three soldiers lay propped against a wall, their bodies half-stripped by the wind, their flesh a bluish-black. Their eyes were open, glazed like ice. Most certainly they had frozen to death.

I don't think the Welshman knew where he eventually brought us – a bunker scraped out of rock and snow and half-covered by a sheet of tin. There was a dog, and a cooking-pot, and a few shivering men eating out of rusty cans. Grey-faced and in rags, their heads moved in quick animal jerks as they ate, up and down, left and right, as though hunted. They were Spanish and the Welshman hurried past them without speaking and scrambled further off down the hill with Serrano.

The Spaniards asked who I was. Ingles, I said. Then why had I come all this way too late? They were the Spanish Army. They didn't need the help of foreigners. Or they needed the help of the world.

But they let me stay with them. 'All your comrades have gone anyway.' They gave me an old Winchester rifle with a couple of clips of cartridges. 'At least you can shoot yourself.'

I stayed with the Spaniards for several days in the frozen vault of their bunker. Never had I seen any men so drained of hope and spirit. Except when the bucket of food came up each morning they seldom stirred from the foetal position in which they hunched themselves. They had no field-telephone, the place seemed to have no purpose; and their leader – an ex-schoolmaster from Talavera – said he had no idea what his men were supposed to be doing.

'Papa Guido' they called him, their voices intoning with bitterness. His eyes were plum-coloured with fear and exhaustion, and somewhere about his person he kept a tasselled cap which every so often he clapped on his head, whereupon everybody saluted him gravely. Stowed away in their almost speechless lethargy a black humour sometimes showed itself.

They'd had ten days' bombardment, said Guido, and been overrun twice, though no one seemed to notice them hidden away under the bunker. But one of them had been bayoneted by chance by a running Moor who had returned to finish him off. The wounded man, middle-aged, rather plump, swung half between coma and delirium. Sometimes he sang in a faint, faraway voice, or lay inert, covered by dead men's coats. His bleeding had stopped, but there seemed not much hope. They'd been trying to get him away, but no help came.

There was a lull, then one night a ghostly fog curled around us, a heavy vapour half-drawn from our breath and half from the circling banks of snow. It brought with it a deadlier cold than ever. With this, Guido seemed to come awake from his torpor. Stuttering madly, he began formally to address his troops, issue commands, and divide the night into watches.

Away to the left of the city we saw lights moving about and heard clear but distant shouts. 'They're coming back,' said Guido, touching his lower lip with his finger in an effort to still his stutter. And sure enough, in the morning, they came.

A long burst of shellfire straddled over us just before daylight, followed by the rattling metal of tanks and their sharp coughing guns, and the swooping buzz of Italian aircraft above. The main attack of the armour was up ahead of us, even so we were briefly overrun; our machine-gun blew up, and we pulled back down the gully, scrambling and falling over the ice. First, I remember a running close-up of the enemy – small, panting little men, red-faced boys, frantically spitting Moors. There was the sudden bungled confrontation, the breathless hand-to-hand, the awkward pushing, jabbing, grunting, swearing, death a moment's weakness or slip of the foot away. Then we broke and raced off, each man going alone, each the gasping centre of his own survival.

I headed for the old barn where I'd spent my first night. I lay in a state of sick paralysis. I had killed a man, and remembered his shocked, angry eyes. There was nothing I could say to him now. Tanks rattled by and cries receded. I began to have hallucinations and breaks in the brain. I lay there knowing neither time nor place. Some of our men found me, I don't know who they were, and they drove me back speechless to Tarazona.

Was this then what I'd come for, and all my journey had meant – to smudge out the life of an unknown young man in a blur of panic which in no way could affect victory or defeat?

9

Way Back

The white daylight was like pain; I could see it and feel it – a plastic stretch of silence pulled over the face. I sat on the chapel steps; half-blind, half-drugged, while melting ice trickled over my feet. The sound of war, several days old and imprinted in the back of my head, seemed ready to return at the touch of a button. The man sitting beside me wore a crumpled white coat. He looked like a doctor or butcher.

'Comrade, we're sending you back to London,' he said.

A tubby young man, with a French moustache: the Political Commissar of Tarazona.

I said I didn't want to go.

'You'd be more use to us there. After all, you're not much use to us here. You could write about us, make speeches, paint posters – or something ...' He gave me his soft butcher's smile, patted me on the arm, stood up and left, taking his white coat with him.

There was no one to say goodbye to in Tarazona; they were all of them gone, dead, deserted, or swept away in the snows. I collected my blanket, and canvas bag, and took a truck down to Albacete. The soldiers there, mostly Spanish now, flapped about in their mud-edged ponchos. There was a moist scummy air of impending spring, but a spring without warmth or profit.

I dropped my bags at the barracks and went round to the tavern where previously we'd sucked sugar and drunk crushed acorns. There were no acorns now, and the victory posters were peeling from the walls like skin. War-cries and slogans, reversed, in-growing, perversely coiled on themselves.

The young Spanish soldiers, squatting around, were not as conventionally foul-mouthed as usual; instead their speech now was almost clerical and precise, using abstract and ritual phrases.

'We were outnumbered. We were betrayed. We were punished. God froze us.'

'God what?'

'He froze us with his mighty breath.'

The talk was still of Teruel; the unforgivable, unimaginable, the snatching away of the cup; the sudden tilt from light into darkness.

I left the tavern and found two men under a bridge, one bandaging the other's knee. The first was about my age, his chin a tar-brush of beard; the other was younger, and beardless.

'My brother,' nodded the youth, gently twisting the bandage.

'He followed me . . . I couldn't get rid of him,' said the younger boy.

'I didn't. I went with the major.'

'How did you find me then?'

'I smelt you out like a rat.'

'Rather some fat-breasted nun had found me!'

His muddy trousers had been split up the seam and a wound ran from knee to groin. His brother had lightly bandaged half of it, and now cleaned the knee with water from a can. The edge of the broken flesh was green and the man was sweating gently.

'No decent nurse would come near you, porco,' said the youth, propping him into a sitting position. 'I got you here, and I'll get you home. So try not to be a burden.'

He rolled him slowly, carefully, on to a little hand-cart standing by, and pushed him off through the melting snow.

It was not going to be easy getting me back to England. I'd entered illegally and must return the same way. But the general opinion was: go I must. I reported to Captain Sam, the intelligence officer, in his little office off the main street. But something had happened to him since last we met; he seemed drowsier, plumper, more evasive. He sat in his German flying-jacket, not quite looking at me, picking at a saucer of olives. I wondered what the winter had done to change that spry little killer into this heavy somnambulist lump.

'All you got to do,' he said, 'is get to Barcelona, then over the border – then it's up to you.'

He seemed amused by this, and opened a drawer.

'They told me to give you this.'

He handed me an envelope which contained my passport and five swoony Chanel-scented pound notes. Still in their envelope inscribed Socorro Rojo in the girl's galloping cumulus handwriting. I could have wished the pound notes less pungent and the girl's letter unresurrected, but I stuffed the lot in my shirt.

'You know, Lorenzo,' said Sam, looking out of the window, 'I've often wondered about you. Just what your game is. What you've been doing here. They say you don't know which side to get on a bus.'

He tore a form from a book, and stamped and signed it. Then he handed it to me gravely.

'Your Safe Conduct,' he said. 'It won't be much use to you, though. As you're not officially here.'

The railway to Barcelona had just been bombed again, so I joined a convoy of trucks. We did the trip in one night, staying close together and keeping an eye on one another's rear-lamps. It was a long cold night, sitting on sacks of sodden straw and sliding about at each curve in the road. The passengers were mostly army (or ex-army, as I was). There was also a middle-aged politico clutching a crocodile brief-case who huddled in a corner and kept up a whispered commentary of bitter reproaches addressed to Largo Caballero. As for me, all I wished was an end to this somehow; a quick sharp bomb, or a lucky escape across Europe, and to get back to her bed and rest.

We drove fast and bumpily through the night, tailboards and mudguards clattering, racing for the most part without lights over the stony plateau, the frightened politico whispering and whining, the driver shouting, the reek of burnt petrol rising from the floor. Stopping under a blue shaded light of a sleeping village, or to the muffled torches of sentries, or for freezing wine in a bar. Then the pleas of women and girls wanting to be taken to the city, the good-natured obscenities of the driver, families sitting round wood-fires under the broken arches of stables, running over to beg for lifts to other villages; sounds of doom, hysteria, shrieks of laughter, cries – everybody wishing to be somewhere else.

We drove for about twelve hours that night, refuelling at road-blocks, and reached the outskirts of Barcelona in a late grey dawn. After the medieval towns and villages of central Spain, Barcelona revealed an alien industrial Europe, long squat suburbs and shabby concrete factories – a language far more cynical, knowing and enervating than the primitive naïveties of Castile.

The small greedy streets crossed each other like lines in a ledger, leading finally to the grand ruled boulevards. Compared with dandy, spendthrift Madrid, Barcelona had been the clever, rich uncle, aloof, scarcely Spanish at all. All its fine calculations, now, seemed blurred, blotted and cancelled. Across banks and offices sagged the war's first banner of defiance and challenge, muted and fading as the grey figures in the streets.

Jaime, the man I had been told to seek out, lived at the top of an old Victorian-style house down a narrow side-street at the harbour end of Las Ramblas. The house bulged with men and meaty women and thumped with squeals and laughter. Girls' faces like pom-poms peeped from half-open doorways. There were such aromas of oils and powders and warm flesh on the stairs that winter and war seemed wiped away.

Jaime, a tough young Catalan with a Prussian moustache, welcomed me into his tiny attic. Packed on shelves round the walls he had books and records and pretty Tanagra figures. There was a wind-up gramophone with a horn in a corner on which he was playing a Beethoven sonata. He turned it off as I entered, and the happy din from downstairs surged up through gaps in the stairs.

I'd met Jaime in Tarazona. Besides Catalan, he spoke Spanish, Basque, French, German, and English with a Dublin accent. He was a Professor of Theology from the University of Seville, and was also a wounded veteran from the Aragon front.

He showed me his new wooden leg, beautifully turned and finished, and knocked up by a local guitar-maker.

'Rosewood, cedar and ebony,' he said, and stamped on the floor. 'When they play music, he dances.'

He gave me some brandy, and told me what I had to do. It was like taking part in some surrealist chess, where pawns became Kings and Queens without warning, and the value of the pieces changed in mid-play. The Police, the Army, the City Militia, the Syndicates, all had power, but its order, they said, altered daily.

'Anyway, it will be no trouble, I promise you. Present yourself to the Secretariat. They'll give you an exit visa. Say nothing – it will be all right.'

He must have seen the look of doubt on my face.

'It happens all the time. Don't worry. They know what we're up to. But if you fall among fools – destroy your papers.'

Jaime, grinning thinly, was giving the impression of the big spider with his fingers on all the webs, controlling the city's sprawling underbrush and all its secret comings and goings.

Well, I believed him, and strolled up Las Ramblas and presented myself straight away at Police Headquarters, where, in some grand inner office, they examined my passport and Chanel-scented pound notes, and promptly arrested me as deserter and spy.

★

I asked at least could I have my scented money back, but the notes were shovelled into a drawer. The Chief gave me a straight, hard look. 'That goes towards the "Effort",' he said. 'After all, you didn't do much for it, did you?'

So once more I was being marched along the streets between two steel-helmeted soldiers armed with fixed bayonets. To the afternoon crowd I was a figure of just casual interest, children and girls gave me only the briefest of glances. A young man under guard, especially a blond young foreigner, was clearly no longer a remarkable spectacle in the city. Though one whiskered old man hobbled out of a doorway, crossed the road, and pinched my thighs.

'Don't shoot him,' he said. 'Just give him to me. I'll take him home to the wife.'

The guards marched me on into a large black building near the docks and pushed me through a side-door, saying, 'We've brought you another one.' My reception was disinterested, no names in a book, no questions; I was merely told to wait. The vast ante-room was like a Dickensian debtors' prison; a dark, shadowy space only dimly lit, and crowded with men, women and children sitting around on the floor. Some cooked, or played games, or slept or fumbled. There was a high chattering and glitter of teeth. I saw men in old tattered uniforms, with bandaged legs, sur-rounded by what seemed to be mothers, wives and cousins. They stroked the men's feet and fed them soup. The place was a chamber of limbo.

After an hour or so, I was taken to an iron grille which spanned the far end of the room. Behind were the cells of the prison proper, and there they installed me without word or ceremony. Each cell had a couple of bunks and a cracked hole in the floor, down which a trickle of water flowed. In my cell I washed away every piece of paper that could identify me – notes, army cards, pencilled instructions, the Salvo Conductos, even the girl's wanton and bubbling letters. Then anonymous, unknown and I hoped forgotten, I settled in my cell with a companion who never spoke.

I hoped it would stay like that. I wanted no sudden keys in the lock, or my name called in the night. I hoped that by now I'd just be a blank in the system.

I stayed in that cell for about three weeks. No guard or authority came near me. There was a heavy damp staleness about the air as though the walls were hung with sour blankets. After a few days I began to understand what it meant to rot in jail. Daylight moved slowly across a distant skylight. No food or drink was provided. We sipped water from the metal cup chained near the spout in the corner, and each day, about noon, a nun would bring us a small flat sandwich and pass it through the bars in silence.

In twenty-four hours it was all we got, and how we longed for noon. But that sandwich, even whiter, smaller than the nun's quiet hand, flavoured on the inside by a thin scraping of mincemeat and on the outside by her ineffable fragrance of touch, what a feast it was to our shackled appetites and hungers. And how voluptuously remembered since.

Meanwhile, apart from these wisplike visits, we were left alone. Nobody came and nothing happened. There were no shouting inspections or calling out for exercise or punishment. We seemed to have been abandoned. This was hard to believe in a huge military jail like this, but to begin with I was glad of it.

Then after the second week, lying in the twilit vacancy of my cell, I gradually grew concerned by the silence. My companion had disappeared. What fate, I wondered, were they storing up for me? And when would they come to declare it? After the third week I began scheming to smuggle out messages for help, to Jaime, or anyone at all. Three weeks, without threat or sentence or even occasional persecution seemed thoughtless indeed.

I was sick now, shivering on the concrete floor, scraping the mould from the walls with my finger-nails. An escalating series of panics broke away from each other and led nowhere except back to my head. Only night, the black skylight, and the noon-whispering nun bearing the half sandwich in her small lace-lined basket, looped the empty silence of the sprawling jail.

Deliverance came, suddenly, unexpectedly, and with a casual lack of drama. A shabby old porter was unlocking my door, and I saw that he had no gun. 'Go away,' he said, 'out!'; and he gave me a daft grandfatherly smile that was a thin red slit in his face. 'What a surprise,' he said, 'eh?' And he thumped me in the ribs, then fumblingly unlocked the outer grille. We walked through a network of passages to the ground floor, through half-light and darkness, through whispers of sound and the smell of unwashed men drawing their body heat from one another.

Back again in the huge open hall of the jail, still crowded with women and barefoot children, I picked my way through the waiting, watchful, ragged groups, and followed where the old trusty led me.

'There's your friend,' he said at last, nodding towards the door. It was a surprise indeed.

Leaning against a pillar near the entrance was a short tubby man wearing a smart overcoat and trilby hat. He gave me a shy warm smile, slightly tinged with embarrassment. It was Bill Rust, editor of the *Daily Worker*.

'You should be in London,' he said. 'How d'you manage to end up here?'

I told him I'd been following instructions.

'Ah, Jaime – yes.' He shifted uncomfortably. 'Well, come on. I've got a car outside.'

And so he had, with all my bags piled in the back of it. I was free, sprung suddenly from my mildewed cell into the clear air of the Barcelona night. Rust had been having a drink that evening with the Chief of Police, who mentioned he'd an unexplained Englishman down in the jail. Rust guessed it was me. Vouch for him, you can have him, said the Chief.

I was glad, but a bit sore at the mess I'd been in.

'So you came as soon as you heard?' I said.

'You were lucky. I don't drink with police every night.'

'But I've been stuck down here for over three weeks.'

'You could have been stuck here for the rest of your life.'

Rust drove me to his flat, high up in one of the boulevards, and said I should stay there till things got untangled. He lit a geyser for a bath, gave me a tumblerful of whisky, then cooked me a piled plateful of corned-beef hash. He was a quiet, gentle man, tough with bureaucrat bullies, but a kindly uncle to such strays as myself. I stayed in his flat for two or three days, not over-eager to return to the streets in case I got picked up again. To keep me occupied he asked me to sort out his filing cards, which were in shoe-boxes and needed putting in alphabetical order. Cards with the names and addresses of British and Irish volunteers; next of kin (if any); dates of enlistment; Brigade postings; brief historics, comments. There must have been five or six hundred of them. Many – more than half – were marked 'killed in action' or 'missing', at such fronts as Brunete, Jarama and Guadalajara. Public schoolboys, undergraduates, men from coal mines and mills, they were the ill-armed advance scouts in the, as yet, unsanctified Second World War. Here were the names of dead heroes, piled into little cardboard boxes, never to be inscribed later in official Halls of Remembrance. Without recognition, often ridiculed, they saw what was coming, jumped the gun, and went into battle too soon.

Rust was in and out of the flat most of the day, and in the evening we drank whisky and talked. He never spoke of his newspaper, or the war or his connection with it, but told mild stories of childhood atrocities. He asked me no questions, except about my health, which seemed to concern him closely. There was, indeed, something almost nannyish about his care of me, even to the extent of giving me his card-index to play with.

On the third day, taking no chances, Rust drove me round to the French Consulate and the city Police Headquarters, and got me my exit visas. The officer, who had already swiped my Chanel-scented pound notes, crisply stamped my passport: salé sin dinero – departed without money. 'Farewell, brother,' he said. 'I think you've not been defrauded.'

Jaime came to the station to give me last-minute instructions, together with coded addresses in Paris and London. Also apologies and excuses which didn't matter now and were unearned anyway. Already in my mind I'd left this doomed city and country, where women queued hopelessly outside shops, hospitals and prisons, waiting in the rain for miracles.

The night train to the frontier was waiting – crowded, murmuring, without lights, unheated, and smelling of unwashed wounds. I found a space in a tiny wood-slatted compartment already dotted with the red stubs of cigarettes. At first we stumbled slowly through the shiny black suburbs of the city while searchlights moved over the sea. Nothing could be heard but half-stifled coughing, heavy breathing, and the faint, frightened moan of a woman. Reaching the open country we picked up speed, in a steady slouching way, and my companions suddenly found their voices with a carefree release of bravado. Two of them were obviously from the same village up the coast. They were reunited and returning home.

'You remember Don Anselmo – the fish-factor?'

'Of course I remember him.'

'A thief and a robber he was.'

'A peseta a day he paid us – before they shot him.'

'Who shot him?'

'Well, the Committee shot him, wasn't it?'

'Yes, the Committee, they shot him. They shot a lot of them.'

'A little peseta a day – God shame him.'

It was a shaking out of justice, hoarse agreement all round, then with prolonged coughing and shuffling everybody settled to sleep. Cigarettes went out, and there was silence, except for the distant moan of the woman.

We arrived at Port Bou in the dirty light of dawn. On the

platform stood a bunch of grey-faced men. Their hands were manacled and they were dressed in rags of uniform and guarded by a couple of old veterans with muskets. Deserters, someone said, trying to scramble out over the mountains. When I came in, I remembered, coming the other way, something like this had also happened to me.

Now I was on my way back, with official papers to help me, salé sin dinero, and little else. The two mountain boulders I'd walked between, on my way into Spain, had seemed almost too simple a way to enter a war. In reverse, it was even simpler; our train took a gulping breath, left the underworld behind it, and screwed through the short tunnel between Port Bou and Cerebere. Curtains were lifted, we saw fresh morning skies, neon-lit cafés, and smelt the hot fat butter of France . . .

At dawn the next day I arrived at Victoria station and saw the cloud of her breath where she waited. She looked at my hands, then my face, and gave her short jackal laugh. I sniffed the cold misty fur of her hair.

As we drove north she watched me as much as she watched the road. 'Well, I hope you're pleased with yourself,' she said. 'Didn't give me a thought, did you? I've been through absolute hell – you know that? I even went to a call-box one night, a public phone-box – can you imagine? – and I got right through to Socorro Rojo, Albacete. Just think – across France, and those frontiers – and all Spain and that war . . . It took me three hours, and I was crying all the time. I just wanted to talk to you, *talk* to you, can you understand? A man was watching me from a car, and kept giving me money for the phone. No wonder you look so smug.'

Then I was back in her flat. In high wealthy Hampstead. She drew me in with her blue steady gaze. I remember the flowers on the piano, the white sheets on her bed, her deep mouth, and love without honour. Without honour, but at least with salvation.

He just wanted a decent book to read ...

Not too much to ask, is it? It was in 1935 when Allen Lane, Managing Director of Bodley Head Publishers, stood on a platform at Exeter railway station looking for something good to read on his journey back to London. His choice was limited to popular magazines and poor-quality paperbacks – the same choice faced every day by the vast majority of readers, few of whom could afford hardbacks. Lane's disappointment and subsequent anger at the range of books generally available led him to found a company – and change the world.

'We believed in the existence in this country of a vast reading public for intelligent books at a low price, and staked everything on it'
Sir Allen Lane, 1902–1970, founder of Penguin Books

The quality paperback had arrived – and not just in bookshops. Lane was adamant that his Penguins should appear in chain stores and tobacconists, and should cost no more than a packet of cigarettes.

Reading habits (and cigarette prices) have changed since 1935, but Penguin still believes in publishing the best books for everybody to enjoy. We still believe that good design costs no more than bad design, and we still believe that quality books published passionately and responsibly make the world a better place.

So wherever you see the little bird – whether it's on a piece of prize-winning literary fiction or a celebrity autobiography, political tour de force or historical masterpiece, a serial-killer thriller, reference book, world classic or a piece of pure escapism – you can bet that it represents the very best that the genre has to offer.

Whatever you like to read – trust Penguin.